Leadership in Organizations

D0060984

Leadership in Organizations outlines new agendas for leadership and its development. It offers innovative ideas about what truly constitutes 'leadership' and the ways in which it can – and cannot – be developed. With contributions from some of the most distinguished experts in their various fields, this book provides a rounded, balanced and sober evaluation of the latest issues and trends in the newly vibrant leadership debate. The book makes a trenchant critique of many of the leadership training and development products and approaches currently available to managers and it offers some constructive alternatives.

Topics covered include:

- An interpretation of post-transformational leadership
- Leadership competences
- The meaning and significance of integrity for leaders
- Methods of 'learning leadership'
- Corporate university solutions
- Leadership development in the public sector
- Leadership and career development
- The fit between leadership and business strategy

Addressing the legitimate uncertainties about the nature of leadership, this is a distinctive and challenging text. It will be essential reading for students and practitioners of organizational leadership.

John Storey is Professor of Human Resource Management at the Open University Business School and a consultant to leading corporations. He has authored and edited 15 books on business, management and organizations.

A fascinating set of papers dealing with many current problematic issues in leadership development. John Storey has assembled a sparkling set of leading edge contributors whose contributions are highly thought-provoking and challenging. A 'must' for any researcher in this area.

Karen Legge, Warwick Business School

Leadership in Organizations goes beyond other mainstream leadership texts by providing both creativity and insight in its approach to leadership development. A focus on key issues and critical themes highlights the importance of the context within which any interpretation of leadership takes place and within which efforts for leadership development must be designed and evaluated.

Jeanie Foray, School of Business, Western New England College,
Massachusetts and Editor-in-chief of the
Organization Management Journal

Leadership in Organizations

Current issues and key trends

Edited by John Storey

LONDON AND NEW YORK

First published 2004
by Routledge
11 New Fetter Lane, London EC4P 4EE

Simultaneously published in the USA and Canada
by Routledge
29 West 35th Street, New York, NY 10001

Routledge is an imprint of the Taylor & Francis Group

Typeset in Baskerville by Taylor & Francis Books Ltd
Printed and bound in Great Britain by MPG Books Ltd, Bodmin

British Library Cataloguing in Publication Data
A catalogue record for this book is available from the British Library

Library of Congress Cataloging in Publication Data
Storey, John, 1947–
Leadership in organizations: currrent issues and key trends / John Storey
Includes bibliographical references and index.
1. Leadership. 2. Executives–Training of. 3. Leadership–Study and
teaching. I. Title.
HD57.7.S765   2004
658.4'092–dc21   2003009701

ISBN 0–415–31032–6 (hbk)
ISBN 0–415–31033–4 (pbk)

Contents

Illustrations

Figures

Tables

Contributors

John Alban-Metcalfe, Director of Research, Leadership Research & Development Ltd.

Beverly Alimo-Metcalfe, Professor of Leadership Studies, University of Leeds and Leadership Research & Development Ltd.

Dr Elena P. Antonacopoulou, Lecturer in Human and Organizational Analysis, Manchester Business School, University of Manchester.

Catherine Bailey, Programme Director, Advanced Development Programme, Cranfield School of Management.

Dr Regina F. Bento, Hatfield-Merrick Distinguished Professor, Merrick School of Business, University of Baltimore.

David Butcher, Director of General Management Programmes, Cranfield School of Management.

Martin Clarke, Programme Director, Cranfield General Management Programme, Cranfield School of Management.

Stewart Clegg, Professor of Management, University of Technology, Sydney, Australia, and Visiting Professor of Management, University of Aston Business School, UK.

Ron Glatter, Professor of Educational Management, Centre for Educational Policy, Leadership and Lifelong Learning, Open University.

Ray Gordon, Senior Lecturer, School of Management, University of Technology, Sydney.

Dr Wendy Hirsh, Associate Fellow, Institute for Employment Studies.

Iain Mangham, Professor Emeritus, University of Bath School of Management, and Visiting Senior Research Fellow, Management Centre, King's College, London.

Dr Graham Mole, Group Training and Development Director, Willis Group Limited.

Rob Paton, Professor of Social Enterprise, Open University Business School.

Tim Ray, Senior Lecturer in Knowledge and Innovation, Open University Business School.

Graeme Salaman, Professor of Organization Studies, Open University Business School.

Peter Scott, Head of the Centre for New Media, Knowledge Media Institute, Open University.

John Storey, Professor of Human Resource Management, Open University Business School.

Jane Sturges, Lecturer in Organizational Behaviour, Kings College, London.

William Tate, Organization strategy consultant and writer, specialising in organization development, change and learning. Head of Prometheus Consulting.

Scott Taylor, Lecturer in Organizational Behaviour, Birmingham Business School, University of Birmingham.

Dr Sheila Tyler, Developmental Psychologist and Lecturer in Management Development, Open University Business School.

Preface

The origins of this book stem from a series of discussions with managers from public and private sector organizations of all kinds. While working with them on training, research and consultancy projects concerning strategy, change management, human resource management, innovation, performance management and other related issues, they would often ask – often in passing – about 'leadership'. They were usually perplexed by the subject and were anxious to discuss it. What finally prompted commencement of the book was a series of enquiries from management development directors, most of whom were uncertain how, or whether, to respond to the expectation that they should be doing 'something more or different on leadership'.

These managers were well aware that there is a vast supply of courses readily available on the subject, but they were looking for some independent guidance on how to negotiate their way through the many issues that faced them as corporate customers and suppliers. It subsequently became apparent that their general manager colleagues also harboured similar concerns. What they were looking for was not simply another course or another book describing the value of leadership or extolling a particular development solution, but a systematic evaluation of the terrain. Further, stemming from and building on this realist assessment they also wanted some pointers to more effective ways forward.

The book aims to equip readers with the analytical perspectives and tools to make up their own minds about the significance of the huge emphasis on leadership in contemporary discussions about business and organizations. Specifically, the book offers new insights into the ways in which understanding about what constitutes leadership have changed over time and it makes a critical assessment of the range of conventional leadership training and development provision.

The book is written primarily with the needs of management development specialists in mind, but it has also wider relevance for general managers and for students of business and management, especially those studying for a Master's of Business Administration (MBA) or specialist master's courses.

I would like to acknowledge the support of colleagues at the Open University Business School, most especially my close working companion Graeme Salaman, with whom I have enjoyed many fruitful discussions and many rewarding collaborative assignments. Thanks are also due to Karen McCafferty, who has continued to display excellent secretarial skills. I am also grateful for discussions with Professor Iain Mangham and Professor Ron Glatter, each of whom has offered wise counsel. Former academic colleagues whom I would also like to acknowledge for their friendship and insight include Professors Keith Sisson, Paul Edwards and Karen Legge at the University of Warwick, David Buchanan at Leicester De Montfort and David Guest at King's College, London University.

I am indebted to numerous managers with whom I have worked on fascinating assignments in recent years. In particular, I am grateful to Maurice Dunster, Management Development Director, and Sir Stuart Hampson, Chairman of the John Lewis Partnership; to Mike Scott, Brigadier Seamus Kerr and General Sir Mike Jackson of Land Command; Geoff Armstrong, Director General of the Chartered Institute of Personnel and Development (CIPD); and senior managers at Abbey National, AstraZeneca, Barclays, British Airways, BT, Deutsche Telekom, Hewlett-Packard, ICI, Lloyds TSB, Marconi, NatWest, Nortel, Philips, Tesco and Unilever.

Finally, I wish to thank all the other contributors to this book. Each, a specialist in his or her own area, has produced a chapter of distinctive value. Taken together, I believe they have helped to fulfil the purpose which drove the production of this book.

John Storey

Part I

Introduction

1 Signs of change

'Damned rascals' and beyond

John Storey

There are few, if any, hotter topics in management, business and organization theory at the present time than 'leadership'. I have been struck over the past few months and years when visiting scores of corporate training centres and hotel 'conference suites' by the sheer number of workshops being held on this subject. Virtually every sector and all levels of staff appear to be represented and engaged. Everyone, it seems, is being invited to join in. 'Are you here for the Leadership Workshop?' receptionists would cheerily and routinely enquire. Leadership in contemporary organizational life has become a pervasive phenomenon. The climate in relation to it certainly seems to have changed significantly when compared with the traditional mode of approach used, for example, by US navy captains with respect to relations with their crews. Standard form, it is reported, was for captains to address their men as 'you damned rascals' (Leiner 2001). Nowadays, public and private sector organizations alike are caught up in a frenzy of activity as they seek to demonstrate that they are taking responsible steps to populate the 'leadership pool' with a set of competences far wider than the navy's formerly no-nonsense approach.

Likewise, the literature on leadership is enormous and expanding apace. A search of the Amazon.com website in the spring of 2003 using the single word 'leadership' netted an overwhelming 11,686 results. This testifies, if nothing else, to the cultural significance of this concept at least in the minds of authors, archivists and editors. Notably, however, a search of 'leadership and development' only secured 4.8 per cent of the total results. This suggests that the *ways* in which leadership qualities might be produced carry considerably less popular appeal than the wider leadership mystique.

But perhaps even more telling than absolute numbers is the apparent increase in attention to the theme over recent time. A search of the Ebsco site, which indexes and abstracts published articles on business and management, reveals a phenomenal trend. During the two-year period from January 1970 to the end of December 1971 there were just 136 published articles, according to a search using the defaults field. During the equivalent period ten years later (1980–1) the number had doubled, to 258. But in the two-year period 1990–1 the number mushroomed to 1,105 articles, and even more remarkable was the result for the equivalent two-year period a decade later (2001–2), which revealed an astounding 10,062 published articles – an average of 419 per month. The growth in interest in leadership during the 30-year period 1970–2000 was apparently exponential.

The incredible focus on leadership is an international phenomenon. In the USA, numerous surveys reveal increased attention paid to, and increased resources allocated to, the topic (Conference Board 1999). There is evidence that investment in leadership development has increased significantly (Vicere and Fulmer 1998; Fulmer 1997). All the usual signs are present – there are conferences galore, dedicated journals, courses, workshops and so on. But, perhaps most indicative of all, there are plentiful indications that large numbers of organizations are actively trying to 'do something' about leadership development. Leadership and management development is very big business indeed. One estimate of annual corporate expenditure on the activity in the US put the total at some $45 billion in 1997 – up from $10 billion a decade before (Fulmer 1997). The growth of the corporate university phenomenon in the US and in Europe is one manifestation of this increased attention to leadership development. Having dispensed with their administrative staff and senior management colleges one or two decades ago, large corporations have spent the past few years launching corporate 'academies' and 'universities' – and one of the critical foci of activity for these new creations has been 'leadership'. One recent assessment of the overall picture in the USA indicates that there are now 900 leadership programmes in colleges and universities in that country (which, notably, represented a doubling of supply over a four-year period), over 100 'majors' (specialist degrees), three dedicated journals churning out regular articles, and many new professorial appointments in this new 'subject' (Sorenson 2002).

In the UK and Europe, meanwhile, there has also been a veritable welter of 'leadership initiatives'. The notion of the central importance of leadership has been accepted and institutionalized insofar as it is embedded as the prime 'enabler' in the influential Business Excellence model sponsored by the European Foundation for Quality Management (EFQM). This central enabler is elaborated in the EFQM framework with a series of sub-criteria such as 'leaders develop the mission, vision and values', and they are 'involved with customers, partners and representatives of society' and so on (EFQM 2000). The construct is also central to, and embedded in, other variants of the quality movement. For example, it is asserted and accepted as central in influential quality schemes such as the Malcolm Baldridge National Quality Award (MBNQA), and various total quality gurus have emphasized it and sought to identify best practice in leadership style (Deming 1986; Oakland 1999; Dale 1994). Leadership is likewise taken as a critical given in modern strategy thinking – especially by figures associated with influential global consultancies (for example Gattorna 1998).

In parallel, activity in the public sector has also been especially intense. For example, the civil service reports that it is undertaking 'extensive work on leadership issues in all departments' (Cabinet Office 2000: 99); there is a new competency framework designed to promote civil service leadership; and there is an overall, concerted, effort in the form of a 'public service leadership development forum'. For good or for ill, central government is signalling that it is getting serious about leadership. Local government too has its own programme of activity designed to develop leaders both for local authority executives and as politicians. In education there has been significant investment in the National College of School Leadership – an institution described as 'the largest leadership development programme in the world'. And, not to be outdone, the university sector launched a new dedicated Master's in Business Administration (MBA) specifically to 'meet the needs of university leaders'. The National Health Service has its own leadership programme and new leadership centre; the police service, not to be left behind, has launched new leadership programmes, and so too has the Ministry of Defence. Indeed, following the emphasis on leadership in the Modernization Government white paper (Cabinet Office 1999: 57), virtually all segments of the public services have felt compelled to respond with renewed efforts and initiatives to promote 'leadership'. The sheer scale of activity and response is at one level impressive. Less clear is the extent to which all these separate and intertwined initiatives are genuinely tackling a new and worthwhile agenda.

The frenzy of activity has been further fuelled by official, and semi-official, policy-led promotion. For example, the Department for Trade and Industry (DTI), the Department for Education and Skills (DfES), the Institute of Management and DEMOS, the think tank, have also weighed in with a major report (Horne and Stedman-Jones 2001). The 'project' was chaired by Sir John Egan and its report was notably entitled 'Leadership: The Challenge for All?' This gathering of the great and the good 'found agreement' that what was required from leadership was 'an ability to inspire' (described as 'absolutely key') along with 'clarity of thinking, clarity of communications and being able to articulate direction'. The report also noted that the quality of leadership was rated more highly in those organizations where there was an explicit and systematic policy statement about leadership development (*ibid.*: iii). Other officially sponsored reports have simultaneously emanated from the Cabinet Office (2000), the Ministry of Defence (Modernizing Defence People Group 2000) and the police service (NPLF 2002).

When these numerous reports are taken together, the problem is not so much that the analysis is wrong, rather that precise meanings and connections are usually under-specified. There is a tendency to treat 'leadership' as a catch-all and a panacea. It is made to stand for all the qualities that are desirable in a top team or responsible post-holder – for example 'clarity of vision', 'a performance focus', 'flexibility' and 'innovation', 'HR capability' and 'winning commitment'. In reality, most reports make little detailed examination of the concept of leadership. Its value is simply asserted and its nature assumed. Attention then typically switches to what are commonly seen as the apparent training and development 'needs' in order to attain these desirable ends.

Further, there is an increasing tendency to assume and assert that leadership is the answer to a whole array of intractable problems. For example, the Home

Office (2001) *Report of the Review of Senior Officer Training and Development*, states in its opening paragraph:

> The Lancaster House seminar on police reform in October 2000 identified the training and development of senior officers as a pressing issue. Improved leadership is critical to the effective modernization and improvement of police services and a core factor in the programme to increase the Police Service's ability to reduce crime and reassure the public.
>
> (Home Office 2001: para. 1.1)

This is an unambiguous declaration of a belief in leadership and leadership development as solutions to the identified problems of contemporary policing.

This kind of analysis is given apparent empirical legitimacy by findings – such as those of the HM Inspectorate of Constabulary (2002) report *Getting Down to Basics: Emerging Findings from BCU Inspections* – suggesting a clear link between performance outcomes and leadership. This report states: 'The first eight months of inspections for real, confirm a finding from the pilot phase in 2000 – that the leadership exercised by the commanding officer and his/her management team is the critical success factor differentiating BCUs' (*ibid.*: 5). Just how this link was demonstrated is not described, but 'consensus' of viewpoints seems to play a key part (*ibid.*: para. 12). But the commonsense tendency to suggest that the leader is the source of unit failure or success seems not to have been properly factored in or taken fully into account.

So, against this backdrop of intense activity two key questions arise. First, what are organizations looking for and seeking to achieve when they elevate the subject of leadership up the corporate agenda? Second, why is this impressive degree of attention being paid to this topic at this time? These questions are very much interrelated.

The argument advanced in this book is that the accumulation of weighty and extensive reports to date tends, in the main, to regurgitate a now familiar thesis – but it is a thesis which remains incomplete, insufficiently tested, inadequately debated and not properly scrutinized. The majority of the reports propound the argument that the environment has changed in such a way that organizations of all kinds are forced to respond to increasing uncertainty, instability, deregulation and competitiveness. In consequence, the argument continues, there is a perceived need to change organizational shape, size, scope and methods of operation. Resources are tight, organizational structures are flatter, power is to this extent more distributed and devolved, staff are in need of motivation, direction and reassurance. This reflects an agenda brought to prominence in the 1980s. 'Change management' became the urgent requirement. 'Leadership' offered a widely appealing response. The case 'for leadership' is thus seemingly easily made. The agenda in the reports quickly turns to how to meet the need.

The questions of 'why leadership and why now' are also intimately related to the idea of what 'leadership' constitutes and to the changing context viewed in a

rather different light. For example, the obsession with leadership could potentially be explained at least in part by the focus on individualism – the media
representation of business and government behaviour as dramas played out
among personalities. For example, the initiatives and policies of the massive
General Electric (GE) corporation became routinely reported as the personal
predilections of Jack Welch, the erstwhile chief executive officer. Thus, the new
focus on leadership in the 1980s and 1990s could, in part at least, be interpreted
as an expression of the 'cult of individualism' (Senge 2000: 64).

In the private sector, the large, orderly corporations with measured steady
career progress through a clear hierarchy gave way to downsized, delayered and
devolved organizational forms. Corporate planning became discredited. People
(leaders) with vision were required. The soft skills associated with leadership –
inspiration, vision and creativity were said to be required in place of 'management', which became regarded as too operational and system-maintenance
focused. The typified contrast between leadership and management invariably
encountered in courses, consultants' presentations and the literature over the
past couple of decades is depicted in summary form in Table 1.1. This is evident
with leadership now in the public sector especially. The extensive analysis made
by the Performance and Innovation Unit of the Cabinet Office envisages 'leadership' as the answer to a host of hugely complex, large-scale and endemic
problems: comparative lower pay than in the private sector, recruitment difficulties, low morale and so on (Cabinet Office 2000).

Despite the accumulated onslaught by leadership campaigners, a number of
evident gaps and problems remain. First, those occupying top positions in organizations have remained largely unmoved by the widely promulgated case. For
example, recent research by the Work Foundation (2003) confirms what many
suspected, namely that chief executives and board directors are still less likely
than more junior colleagues to receive leadership coaching and tutoring. Only
25 per cent of top echelon managers in the sample of 221 organizations had
been tutored in leadership, compared with nearly 50 per cent of junior
managers in the sample. As expected, the vast majority of senior managers (78
per cent) espouse the value of leadership as a core organizational priority, but in
practice they just do not seem to get round to doing much about it at the highest
levels.

Table 1.1 A summary dichotomy: managers versus leaders

Managers	*Leaders*
are transactional	are transformative
seek to operate and maintain current systems	seek to challenge and change systems
accept given objectives and meanings	create new visions and new meanings
control and monitor	empower
trade on exchange relationships	seek to inspire and transcend
have a short-term focus	have a long-term focus
focus on detail and procedure	focus on the strategic big picture

A second area where gaps and loose ends remain is in relation to the serious scrutiny of the issues. As we have indicated in the account so far, the main part of the 'debate' about leadership in recent years has been constituted by a fairly simplistic 'case'. The campaign extolling transformational leadership rests on a series of basic propositions each of which turns out to be contentious. In this volume it is argued that there is a series of critical issues which deserve much closer analysis. The rationale and purpose of the book is to identify and explore these critical issues.

The first of these is the extent of stability in the conventionally dominant model(s). This relative and time-bound issue is explored in Chapter 2. It is argued that the interpretation of what constitutes 'leadership' and thus the associated critical issues in leadership have changed over time. In broad terms, three eras are identified in that chapter. During the first, prior to the 1980s, 'leadership' and 'management' were terms rarely subject to differentiation. They were regarded as either interchangeable or as extensively overlapping activities. When 'leadership' was studied or taught it was usually regarded as a small sub-set of management and the focus was on 'influencing' of small groups. To a large extent leadership was a first-level management or a supervisory concern. Then, in the 1980s, there was a paradigm shift and the mood changed substantially. A new message was propounded in numerous influential books and countless consultants eagerly conveyed it. The message was that 'transformation' was required and that this required a new type of senior leader. These leaders were to a considerable extent definable as 'not managers'. To a large degree some of this thinking is still prevalent. But now there are signs of a new shift. This third era harbours much stronger doubts about the transformational thesis and remedy. This new mood is associated with a new set of issues, and these form the purpose of the remaining chapters in the volume.

Thus in Part II, Chapter 3 the theme of the post-Enron (post-charismatic?) leadership environment is picked up by Iain Mangham. He examines in detail the rapidly emerging theme of 'integrity' in relation to leaders.

In Chapter 4, another central idea associated with the current leadership debate – the required capabilities and competences – is examined critically by Graeme Salaman.

Part III of this book contains a cluster of chapters which assess various aspects of leadership development methods. A radically different paradigm for thinking about leadership and the way it is learned is presented in Chapter 5 by Elena Antonacopoulou and Regina Bento. Then in Chapter 6 the way in which the enormous number of new corporate universities are approaching leadership development is described and assessed (Rob Paton, Scott Taylor and John Storey). This is followed, in Chapter 7, by a trenchant critique of much of the 'training for leadership' currently on offer. Graham Mole, a corporate customer with experience of training consultants extending over many years, argues that much of the conventional training is flawed and he outlines the kinds of criteria which he looks for when seeking an alternative approach. Then, in Chapter 8, Peter Scott, head of the New Media Centre in the Open University's Knowledge

Media Institute, explains and illustrates how innovations in electronic media allow for new enactments of leadership. A final chapter in the leadership development methods section focuses on evaluation and the way in which evaluation methods can shape the process of development (Sheila Tyler).

Part IV has a particular focus on leadership development initiatives in the public sector. We noted above how the public sector had in some respects addressed the leadership development agenda in a particularly high profile and emphatic way. The chapters in this part of the book help to unravel, and critically assess, the nature and impacts of the actual initiatives which have taken place.

In all of the discussions about distributed leadership and development opportunities there tends to be a neglect of career development implications. And yet, as Wendy Hirsh points out in her chapter (Part V, Chapter 12), up to 90 per cent of actual development activity occurs through the sequence of work experiences, the career paths, of leaders and managers. Whether campaigners like it or not, many people still do associate investment of their time in training and development activity as having some connection with their potential career progression. The chapters in Part V of the volume assess this issue.

Another set of critical issues concerns the uncertain link between leadership and that other contemporary business topic, strategy. According to some accounts of the heroic leadership variety, one gains the impression that strategy and planning are no longer possible or even required as the all-capable leader can steer an adaptive path through the seas of uncertainty. Two of the chapters in Part VI of this book examine the link between leadership and business strategy and argue that the two, in practice, work best when aligned.

In summary, the critical issues and trends identified and examined in detail in this volume can be listed as follows:

1   The temporal shifts in the understanding of what constitutes leadership. The signs of disenchantment with the recently orthodox transactional and charismatic models of leadership.
2   The reappraisal of the charismatic and transformational model in the light of a series of corporate collapses and scandals such as Enron, and a subsequent concern with the idea of integrity as a crucial quality of leadership.
3   A critical reassessment of attempts to identify and catalogue a set of 'competences' associated with leadership.
4   An assessment of the raft of ways in which leadership training and development has been attempted. What methods are actually being used to 'teach' leadership and what evidence exists of their impact and outcomes? A number of chapters examine the extent to which, and the ways in which, leadership capabilities can effectively be developed.
5   A critical reappraisal of the more serious and significant leadership development initiatives in the public sector. What have they really entailed, what have been their consequences and what implications do they carry for the future?

6   A reassessment of leadership development initiatives in private sector businesses – most especially in relation to the extent and nature of the alignment or lack of it with business strategy and mission.

7   And, finally, but by no means least, what kind of linkage can be shown between leadership and performance? What evidence is there about whether leadership makes a difference to organizational performance?

These current issues and trends are brought together and assessed in relation to each other in a final chapter. From that point of synthesis, an attempt will be made to assess the real extent of progress beyond the 'damned rascals' school of thought.

References

Cabinet Office (1999) *Modernising Government* (Cm. 4310), London: Stationery Office.
——— (2000) *Strengthening Leadership in the Public Sector: A Research Study by the PIU*, London: Performance and Innovation Unit.
Conference Board (1999) 'Developing Leaders', *HR Executive Review* 7(1): 1–19.
Dale, B.G. (ed.) (1994) *Managing Quality*, New York: Prentice-Hall.
Deming, W.E. (1986) *Out of Crisis: Quality, Productivity and Competitive Position*, Cambridge: Cambridge University Press.
EFQM (2000) *Assessing for Excellence: A Practical Guide for Self Assessment*, Brussels: European Foundation for Quality Management.
Fulmer, R.M. (1997) 'The evolving paradigm of leadership development', *Organizational Dynamics* 25(4): 59–73.
Gattorna, J.L. (ed.) (1998) *Strategic Supply Chain Alignment*, Aldershot: Gower.
HM Inspectorate of Constabulary (2002) *Getting Down to Basics: Emerging Findings from BCU Inspections in 2001*, London: HMSO.
Home Office (2001) *Report of the Review of Senior Officer Training and Development*, London: HMSO.
Horne, M. and D. Stedman-Jones (2001) *Leadership: The Challenge for All?*, London: Institute of Management/DTI/DEMOS.
Leiner, F. (2001) 'Decatur and naval leadership', *Naval History* 15(5): 30–7.
Modernizing Defence People Group (2000) *Sustaining the Leading Edge: A Report on Leadership Training and Development*, London: Ministry of Defence.
NPLF (2002) *Analysis of Needs of the National Police Leadership Faculty*, Bramshill: NPLF.
Oakland, J. (1999) *Total Organizational Excellence: Achieving World Class Performance*, Oxford: Butterworth Heinemann.
Senge, P. (2000) 'A conversation on leadership', *Reflections* 2(1): 57–68.
Sorenson, G. (2002) 'An intellectual history of leadership studies in the US', paper presented at the EIASM Workshop on Leadership Research, Said Business School, Oxford, 16–17 December.
Vicere, A. and R. Fulmer (1998) *Leadership by Design*, Boston, MA: Harvard Business School Press.
Work Foundation (2003) *Developing Leaders*, London: Work Foundation.

2 Changing theories of leadership and leadership development

John Storey

It was suggested at the end of the previous chapter that certain new themes and concerns are emerging in leadership research and practice. These grapple with a number of vital questions, including the kind of leadership behaviours now thought to be required (and, conversely, those which are deemed worthy of discouragement); the allocation of leadership responsibilities across organizational members; and the kind of leadership training and development methods which are deemed to be appropriate in new contexts. In large part these current issues and concerns in leadership and leadership development reflect key changes in the environment within which organizations have to operate; for example shorter product life-cycles, deregulation, increasing uncertainty, globalization of competition, turbulence in markets and technologies, and higher expectations from public services. They also reflect structural and cultural changes within organizations themselves, such as devolved, delayered and downsized corporations alongside more permeable organizational boundaries, if not outright 'boundaryless' enterprises. Indeed, one of the leading writers in the field refers to 'The brave new world of leadership training' (Conger 1993). It has been suggested that it is the increased complexity of society and its faster pace which explain the demand for leadership. Thus, as argued by Fullan, '[t]he more complex society gets, the more sophisticated leadership must become' (Fullan 2001b: ix).

Consequently, as was pointed out in the previous chapter, a number of interconnected issues and key questions are moving to the forefront of current debate about leadership, echoes of which can be found across the world. It was noted that the list of critical issues centres on recent shifts in understanding of what constitutes appropriate modes of leadership. Doubts about the transactional and charismatic model of leadership are growing, and these concerns merit analysis. Closely associated with this issue is the increasing interest in the idea of integrity as a crucial quality of leadership.

In addition, on a wider front, the whole set of 'competences' associated with leadership requires robust critical reassessment. A further identified critical issue was the need to make a dispassionate and frank assessment of the raft of ways in which leadership training and development have been attempted – both in public and private sector organizations – and the outcomes to date of such interventions.

Against that agenda, the purpose of this particular chapter is to locate these emerging elements in the context of the extensive literature on leadership and leadership development. In particular, the chapter will offer a summary guide and, from this, will draw out those elements deserving of the future attention of organizational decision-makers and organizational theorists. This chapter will also seek to make sense of the range of alternative 'theories of leadership' and to point a way forward. A key part of the argument will be that the corpus of writing which is normally understood to constitute evolving or competing theories of leadership is in fact made up of studies, speculations and hypotheses about a variety of different things. In this chapter we are as much interested in the obsession with leadership as a phenomenon as with the subject of 'leadership' as a presumed real social practice or thing. The purpose of the chapter is in fact to theorize the theories of leadership. Why has leadership been defined in different ways at different times? Why have different models of leadership achieved plausibility, acceptance and popularity at different times? To put this point another way, the objective of the chapter is not simply to offer yet another description of the literature to date, but rather to explain its existence and nature.

The chapter is organized into three sections. The first offers an overview of the way in which theories of leadership are conventionally approached and understood. The second presents a conceptual framework in order to help interpret current issues and enduring themes in an organized way. The third section examines the proposition that understandings and attitudes to leadership have entered a new phase – one which is increasingly wary and sceptical of the prescriptions for charismatic and transformational leadership which have dominated the subject for the past couple of decades. This third section therefore, in the main, focuses on current trends.

The multiple and evolving theories of leadership

The mass of literature and experiments on leadership are illustrated rather well by the periodic surveys by Stogdill and his successors in the *Handbook of Leadership* (Stogdill 1974). The 1974 edition was subtitled 'A Survey of Theory and Research' and this is precisely what the volume and its subsequent editions have offered. The *Handbooks* seek to provide a systematic review of the literature on leadership. Over 5,000 abstracts were prepared for the first edition and only those which were judged to be based on competent research were included – the 'inspirational and advisory literature was ignored' (*ibid.*: viii). And it is interesting to note that Stogdill also stated that, for similar reasons, at that time he had purposely excluded 'charismatic leadership'. This was because the literature was largely based on 'numerous biographical studies' which provide 'comparatively little information that adds to the understanding of leadership' (*ibid.*: viii). Even the first volume noted the 'bewildering mass of findings' which had 'not produced an integrated understanding of leadership' (*ibid.*: vii). To a considerable degree, much of this observation remains valid today.

For many years, the focus of leadership studies derived from a concern in organizational psychology to understand the impact of leader style on small group behaviour and outcomes. Moreover, the focus was further directed to just two main dimensions – 'task focus' versus 'people orientation' – and there were various reworkings of this theme (for example Blake and Moulton 1964; Vroom and Yetton 1988).

In the 1980s, attention shifted dramatically to the elaboration and promotion of the concept of transformational, charismatic, visionary and inspirational leadership. This school was labelled the 'New Leadership' theories (Bryman 1992). This has shifted attention to leadership of entire organizations rather than the leadership of small groups. (Though, as the work of Alimo-Metcalf and Alban-Metcalf in Chapter 10 of this volume reveals, there are some important current attempts to pull the agenda back to distributed leadership). While, on the face of things, much of the debate over the past two decades appears to have been about 'styles of leadership', in reality the sub-text was mainly about a propounded dichotomy between 'leadership' versus 'management'. This message was extolled graphically and influentially in a *Harvard Business Review* (*HBR*) article by Abraham Zaleznik (1992) – originally published in *HBR* in 1977. This article argued that 'It takes neither genius nor heroism to be a manager, but rather persistence, tough-mindedness, hard work, intelligence, analytical ability and perhaps most important, tolerance and goodwill' (*ibid.*: 127). Since that time, a huge management consultancy industry has grown around this notion of 'leaders' rather than 'managers'. More recently, the importance of the distinction has been downplayed by the suggestion that organizations need both leaders *and* managers. However, Zaleznik had anticipated that kind of response, and he argued that

> It is easy enough to dismiss the dilemma…by saying that there is a need for people who can be both. But, just as a managerial culture differs from the entrepreneurial culture that develops when leaders appear in organizations, managers and leaders are very different kinds of people. They differ in motivation, personal history and in how they think and act.
>
> (Zaleznik 1992: 127)

Allegedly, leaders 'think about goals, they are active rather than reactive, shaping ideas rather than responding to them'. Managers, on the other hand, aim to 'shift balances of power towards solutions acceptable as compromises, managers act to limit choices, leaders develop fresh approaches' (*ibid.*: 128). Evidently, the controversy about the essential differences between leadership and management will continue for some time. The essence of the debate, however, is switching to the key task requirements and the contribution of leaders/ managers. This more practice-oriented agenda is itself evolving.

For example, one significant development has been the linking of the idea of leadership with that of strategic management (Westley and Mintzberg 1989; Tichy and Devanna 1986; Pettigrew *et al.* 1992). The problematic is clearly very different if one is contemplating the capabilities required to be a 'team leader' in contrast to the capabilities required to lead a large-scale organizational transformation.

In order to gain broad oversight of this and other main trends in leadership theory it will be useful to view the summary of leadership theories shown in Table 2.1. Much of this chronology will be familiar to many readers of this volume, and so there is no intention to work through the details of the 'story' of the journey from trait theory through style theory and contingency theory and so on again here. Readers looking for such coverage can find useful summaries elsewhere (for example Shackleton 1995; Grint 1997; Yukl 2002), and indeed in most textbook coverage of the subject of 'leadership'. Our purpose here, however, is not to describe each 'stage' in this supposedly linear pathway, but rather to note the underlying trends and to identify the echoes and connections with the key current issues discussed throughout this volume.

There are some recognizable trends and patterns in the history of leadership research. A great deal of the early theory took a rather 'essentialist' perspective – that is, viewed 'leadership' as a concrete phenomenon, a thing which could be measured as if it were a natural physical phenomenon. Also, much of the early research focused on the leadership of small groups – the early experiments with styles of leadership in boys' groups exemplify this. There was much less research

Table 2.1 Summary of the main theories of leadership

Theory	Text
Trait theory; innate qualities; 'great man theories'	Bernard (1926)
Behavioural theories: task related and relationship related; style theory (e.g. autocratic vs democratic)	Ohio State University studies; University of Michigan (Katz and Kahn 1978; Likert 1961); Blake and Moulton (1964: 383)
Situational and contingency theory; repertoire of styles; expectancy theory	Fiedler (1967); Vroom and Yetton (1973); Vroom (1964); Yukl (2002); Hersey and Blanchard (1984)
Exchange and path–goal models (relationship between leader and led as a series of trades)	Graen and Uhl-Bien (1995); House (1971, 1996)
'New Leadership'; charismatic and visionary leadership; transformational leadership	Burns (1978); Bryman (1992), Conger and Kanungo (1998); Bass (1985a, 1985b); Tichy and Devanna (1986); Kouzes and Posner (1997)
Constitutive, constructivist theory	Grint (1997, 2000)
Leadership within Learning Organizations: leadership as a creative and collective process; distributed leadership	Senge (1990a, 1990b); Semlet (1989); Brown and Gioia (2002); Tichy (1997)
Post-charismatic and post-transformational leadership theory	Khurana (2002a, 2002b); Maccoby (2000); Fullan (2001a, 2001b)

on the leadership of large organizations, though the small group research was often extrapolated as if it applied more widely.

Recent research and theory have paid much more attention to non-essentialist forms of analysis. Thus leadership is more likely to be seen as a 'meaning-making' activity. There are two variants.

The first focuses on the meaning-making behaviour of leaders. Here, 'leaders' are those who interpret the complexities of the given unit within the environment on behalf of the followers. Leaders thus make sense of the plight of the collective – weighing up threats and opportunities in the environment, and evaluating the strengths and weaknesses of the unit within that environment. The capabilities required are those frequently described in recent transformative literature: clarity of vision; environment scanning and interpretation; ability to condense complex data into simple compelling summations; and ability to communicate clear messages. The training and development implications stem from these required capabilities. They relate therefore to opportunities for plentiful exposure to the 'big picture'. This might mean, for example, attendance at a corporate 'Academy' where global issues are discussed.

The second variant, the 'constitutive' approach, is also concerned with meaning-making, but this time with more attention to the part played by the 'followers' and the wider audience being rather more to the fore. Individuals celebrated as leaders under this interpretation are those who enact the behaviours and articulate the messages which are in tune with the preferred and desired requirements of those who can confer the status of leader. To illustrate the point, one can refer to the case of one of the most famous great leaders – Winston Churchill, the prime minister of Britain during the Second World War. The constitutive approach is able to make better sense of his rise and fall than seems possible from an essentialist perspective. The latter sees leadership as something embodied in individuals which simply awaits 'discovery' through the appropriate psychometric instrument. While Churchill is now one of the most frequently instanced examples of an indisputable great leader, for much of his career this most-cited figure (for example Bennis 1994) was adamantly rejected by his party and his fellow parliamentarians. Far from being accepted as a leader, he was marginalized and even isolated. However, when the previous consensus about the preferred leadership collapsed with the onset of war, the Churchill proposition became acceptable and increasingly pre-eminent. The oratorical skills, decisiveness and other like attributes which have been so frequently cited as quintessentially evident of leadership were exploited to impressive effect. But it needs to be recalled that the 'followers' were rather less impressed by these same skills just a short time previously – and indeed these skills and attributes were nullified once again when the war ended. The case helps to illustrate the constructivist interpretation: leadership was 'recognized' or *constructed* within the confines of a specific set of social circumstances – it was not a phenomenon unambiguously existing independent of the social context.

The lesson from the Churchill story carries across into the corporate and work organization domain. Preferred styles of leadership evidently vary across time and place. On the time dimension, there may even be varying degrees of reaction to previously experienced approaches. Leadership style is thus path-dependent. A style may be more relatively acceptable precisely because it appears to correct for the perceived excesses of a previously experienced style.

Leadership effectiveness therefore depends upon:

1   the extent to which people follow and give legitimacy (this can be termed internal validation);
2   the extent to which the unit or organization succeeds and survives (this may be termed external validation).

There must also be a time dimension to the judgements – it may be short, medium or long term. It further implies that the judgement of the effectiveness of leadership may fluctuate (see Weick 1995).

While a review of leadership theory based on the chronological development of the literature can be useful, it also has a number of limitations. The chief problem is that the evolutionary accounts tend to imply that previous theory has been refuted and superseded. In reality, questions concerning leadership qualities and characteristics, appropriate styles, contingent conditions and transactional, as well as transformational, relations continue to perplex and prompt debate. For our purposes in this volume, therefore, it is more appropriate to focus on emerging and continuous themes and issues. In the next section these are identified and a conceptual framework is developed.

A conceptual framework for current themes

Current debates, as we saw in the Chapter 1, reveal a series of paradoxes and contradictions within the dominant accounts. For example, one strong narrative strand centres on the idea of current environmental 'uncertainty and instability'. This, in turn is seen to require and justify the search for a strong, responsible organizational leader able to handle difficult and ambiguous conditions through the exceptional use of 'envisioning and energizing' capabilities. This strand therefore focuses attention on the vital need for exceptional, decisive and charismatic leadership. Exceptionality is further seen to justify unusual and generous ('internationally competitive') reward packages. And yet another strand of contemporary narrative highlights and emphasizes the need for 'distributed leadership' and empowered co-workers and associates. The tensions created by these competing perspectives reoccur in much contemporary discourse – but the potential contradictions are usually insufficiently examined or even acknowledged.

A clear example of a contemporary attempt to come to terms with the tensions between the idea of the exceptional individual, on the one hand, and changing values and norms, on the other, can be found in the recent work of Warren Bennis, an established authority on leadership. Bennis argues that leadership can be understood as deriving from a mixture of time, place, predisposition and potential (Bennis and Thomas 2002). Taking a long view by studying today's leaders (from the laidback and informal high technology world) and comparing and contrasting them with a cluster of interviewees from the immediate post-war world of half a century ago, there is an explicit acknowledgement of the difference which time (captured here in the concept of 'era') can make in the meaning of leadership. Nonetheless, Bennis is reluctant to let go of the idea of 'leaders' as inherently special people with unique qualities – indeed this is the underlying assumption of his approach. The research method (interviewing individuals *qua* leaders and asking how they explain their biographies) seems highly likely to reinforce this bias.

Bennis's most recent work thus reflects a continuing essentialist interpretation of the nature of leadership – its essence, in other words, is to be 'discovered' within the attributes (one might say the 'traits') of exceptional individuals found to be occupying leader positions. In this particular instance, the methodological device used to identify and catalogue these attributes of the accomplished leader is to 'uncover' the different ways in which people deal with adversity. He claims that one of the most reliable indicators and predictors of 'true leadership' is an individual's ability to find meaning in negative situations and to learn from trying circumstances. Bennis calls these experiences that shape leaders 'crucibles'. He provides a variety of examples to explore the idea of the crucible in detail. From these examples, essential skills are derived which, he believes, great leaders possess. The first three of these are familiar restatements of what leadership is frequently understood to be, as well as its apparent prerequisites. These essential skills are the ability to engage others in shared meaning, a distinctive and compelling voice, a sense of integrity (including a strong set of values). The fourth is identified as 'adaptive capacity'. This turns out to be 'an almost magical ability to transcend adversity, with all its attendant stresses, and to emerge stronger than before' (*ibid.*: 121). It is of course this final aspect which the narratives of informants were most able and willing to illuminate.

The underlying Bennis and Thomas (*ibid.*) 'new model' is that *leadership competences* are *outcomes* of these formative experiences. The key competences are said to be adaptive capacity, an ability to engage others in shared meanings, voice and integrity. Tellingly, 'adaptive capacity' is said to be exemplified through the case of Jack Welch, the famed erstwhile chief executive officer (CEO) of General Electric. This capacity enabled him to 'transform himself from staff-slashing Neutron Jack to Empowerment Jack as the needs of the corporation shifted' (*ibid.*: 122).

This example is illustrative of the partial nature of much current literature and thinking about leadership. In order to progress theory in a more systematic manner it is necessary to stand back and appraise the *range of factors* which influence our understanding of the leadership phenomenon.

In fact, analysis of contemporary organizational discourse, and of recent literature, reveals a large number of critical factors which, on closer examination, reflect a cluster of core, enduring, themes. There are five in particular which are essential in any systematic analysis of organizational leadership. As shown in Figure 2.1, these five factors are: context, perceived leadership need, behavioural requirements, capabilities and development methods. Moreover, as is also illustrated in Figure 2.1, each of these key factors interrelates with all of the others. Together they form the leadership constellation.

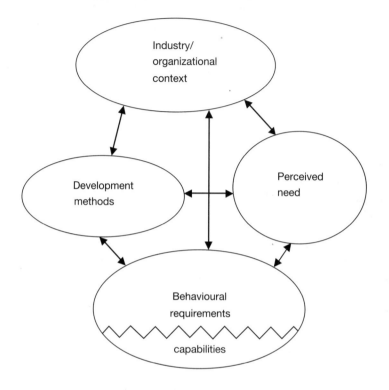

Figure 2.1 The leadership constellation

We will describe and assess each of these in turn, beginning at the top of Figure 2.1 with context, and then proceeding clockwise around the figure.

Context

Despite the seemingly unabated search for the essential attributes of leaders, there is also abundant reference to the importance of context in current leadership research. There are extensive literatures exploring the importance of international cultural differences, industrial sector differences, organizational structural differences and other contextual variables.

For example, various researchers have explored the idea that concepts of leadership may differ between different *national cultures*. Sometimes even regional groupings are contrasted. Thus the differences between the understandings of leadership in Anglo-Saxon, Arab and Asian traditional cultural values have been studied (Mellahl 2000). This and other studies have challenged the idea of the universality of leadership values and themes. The findings carry implications for the content and methods of leadership development and training.

Similar findings emerged from an extensive 22-country study across Europe which revealed cultural variation in notions about leadership (Brodbeck 2000). The study suggests that there are pre-existing leadership 'prototypes' or expectations about leaders in the different cultures; these affect the willingness of followers to go along with certain roles and styles of leaders. Brodbeck identifies a set of dimensions which reveal core differences in leadership prototypes. Cultural differences in the understanding of and attitudes to leadership have also been explored in another study by Brodbeck in the even more widely variant comparative contexts of Europe and Africa. These differences, he notes, carry important implications for leadership development methods (Brodbeck *et al.* 2002).

Yet, despite prevailing and persisting cultural differences between certain countries, the diffusion and increasingly dominant influence of American values in recent years may also help to explain the increased attention given to leadership across much of the world. The American Dream and the focus on individualism and the can-do attitude have permeated international teaching and development in relation to how organizational leadership is viewed.

This individualized interpretation is fuelled by the media. Business magazines such as *Business Week*, *Fortune* and the *Director* are especially prone to focus on the supposed crucial impact of top managers. Even serious financial newspapers such as the *Wall Street Journal* and the *Financial Times* tend also to profile and give huge prominence to individual personalities and attribute to them apparent critical importance. News about corporations tends to be translated all too readily into human dramas in the boardroom. Certain chief executives become lionized and company fortunes are deemed to be closely linked to the actions of these figures. When Kodak's performance came under criticism in the 1990s, Wall Street analysts and the media focused blame and criticism on the chief executive, Kay Whitmore. Eventually the board bowed to pressure and Whitmore was sacked and replaced with a high profile recruit from Motorola. The share price rose by nearly $5 on the receipt of this news (Khurana 2002a: 5). Nonetheless, the lack of competitiveness continued and by the end of the decade the share price had lost two-thirds of its value. There are numerous other examples of this phenomenon (Khurana 2002b). Collectively, these cases illustrate the huge significance of context in shaping the agenda and meaning concerning leadership – and its perceived importance and nature.

In addition to national context differences, other studies have pointed up the importance of industry sector as a factor influencing receptivity to types of leadership. For example, the leading analysts of transformational and charismatic leadership (Bass 1985a, 1985b; Avolio and Bass 1988) have noted how sector plays a part in the way these roles are performed, how effective they are and how they are perceived.

There are numerous other studies which reveal the particularities of leadership in different sectors. These include a growing number of studies of headteachers as leaders – most notably tracking the headteachers leadership programme(s) in the UK (for example Blandford and Squire 2000). There have also been studies drawing comparisons and contrasts between headteachers as leaders in the US and in the UK (Daresh and Male 2000; Brundrett 2001).

In addition, there are many other sector specific studies of leadership and leadership development. Overall, they tend to emphasize the critical importance of sector context when it comes to leadership development interventions – a point made emphatically by Graham Mole in Chapter 7.

Beyond the level of industry sector, other studies have drilled down and focused on variations in *organizational context* as a governing independent variable. Indeed, one major analyst has made the point that 'the theory of leadership is dependent on the theory of organization' (Selznick 1957: 23). In similar vein, Charles Perrow observed that 'leadership style is a dependent variable…the setting or task is the independent variable' (1970: 6). In other words, each of these theorists emphasizes that leadership behaviour is extensively shaped by organizational characteristics.

And yet much leadership discussion and research is conducted as if the organizational context did not matter. One strong attempt to link contextual features with transformational leadership is revealed in the work of Pawar and Eastman (1997). They showed how a combination of four factors – different organizational emphases on efficiency or adaptation, the relative dominance of the technical core versus the boundary spanning units, the type of organizational structure and the mode of governance – impact on organizational receptivity to transformational leadership. Likewise, organizational cultures can limit the potential for leadership: 'adaptive' organizational cultures, Pawar suggests, give more opportunity to charismatic leaders.

Perceived need

Early work on context often tended to adopt a rather mechanistic approach. This was characterized by a simplistic notion of 'fit' – that is, a proposition that different types of context could be matched with appropriate types of leadership. But contemporary approaches to leadership research are more alert to the interpretist perspective, which allows insight into the socially constructed nature of perceived 'need'.

We saw in Chapter 1 that there have been a number of attempts to explain why the topic of 'leadership' is so especially salient at the present time. Usually, the argument is that the nature of the contemporary competitive environment – with high uncertainty, a need for agile and speedy response to customer expectations and client demand – necessitates a shift from the orderly, planned and bureaucratic mode to a more adaptive and entrepreneurial mode. The perceived 'need for leadership' deriving from this kind of analysis thus reflects a perceived shift in the environment–response equation. There are, however, also other accounts which lead to different interpretations.

For example, a very different form of explanation, both in terms of the focus on leadership as a priority and for the kind of leadership solution seen as appropriate, can be found using so-called 'institutional theory' (DiMaggio and Powell 1983). From this perspective, the frenetic activity catalogued in Chapter 1 can be viewed as a record of managerial responses to perceived informed action by their competitor or comparative reference point organizations. There does indeed seem to be more than a little emulation taking place among the impressive array of organizations queuing up to 'do something' about the leadership question. This is seen most clearly in the phenomenal growth in 'corporate universities' and 'academies' (see Paton *et al.* in Chapter 6), but is replicated more generally in relation to leadership 'interventions' and 'programmes' of all kinds. Senior executives themselves are not unaware of this element of 'me-too-ism', as they often term it. The ones I have interviewed in a range of different countries have often been willing to admit that a key driver upon them has been a sense of anxiety among their colleagues that their organization must be seen to be responding in some way to a general trend. A related perspective is found in the theory of organizational symbolism. Organizational action – such as an emphasis on leadership – can be interpreted as a 'representation'. These representations reflect a *symbolic meaning* which organizational actors and their 'audience' of stakeholders read and interpret (Pondy *et al.* 1983).

The perceived 'need for leadership' and hence for leadership development can be interpreted in a different way when viewed from a sociological perspective. One major approach is to explain the phenomenon from the angle of interpreting 'authority'. The classic works of Reinhard Bendix (1956) and of John Child (1969) illuminate the ways in which occupants of elite positions – and their 'spokespersons' – seek to legitimize authority, power and privilege. As Bendix and John Child both point out, virtually all accounts of the contributions and roles of managers and leaders contain dual aspects – that is, they express *ideological* as well as technical dimensions (Child 1969). As Bendix observed:

> Wherever enterprises are set up, a few command and many obey. The few however have seldom been satisfied to command without a higher justification even when they have abjured all interest in ideas, and the many have seldom been docile enough not to provoke such justifications.
>
> (Bendix 1956: 1)

The specific circumstances of commercial and industrial power and authority are addressed in detail by Bendix:

> Industrialization has been defended in terms of the claim that the few will lead, as well as benefit, the many...industrialization has been defended by ideological appeals which justified the exercise of authority in economic enterprises. Qualities of excellence were attributed to employers or managers which made them appear worthy of the positions they occupied. More or less elaborate theories were used in order to explain that excellence.
>
> (Bendix 1956: 2)

This sociological perspective is taken up by Miller and Form, who describe this ideology of top leaders and management:

> A highly self-conscious group whose ethnocentrism leads them to believe that they have special gifts and attributes not generally shared by the population. The greatest of these is the ability to manage and organise people.... Top management is an authority-conscious group. Men at the top of the supervisory structure are consumed with decision making and commanding. Yet they do not like to believe that men obey them because they have power...they want to feel they command because they are gifted to lead.
>
> (Miller and Form 1964: 186)

Bendix echoes this theme: 'Like all others who enjoy advantages over their fellows, men in power want to see their position as "legitimate" and their advantages as deserved.... All rulers therefore develop some myth of their natural superiority' (Bendix 1956: 294).

Drawing on this sociological insight, one can readily explain the tremendous appeal to, and the receptiveness of, the burgeoning population of leaders and managers in subsequent decades to the idea of charismatic leadership. Consultants and authors elaborating the charismatic paradigm could be regarded as fulfilling the ideological function as spokespersons for power holders. Likewise, it is hardly surprising that occupants of top roles have been so willing to collaborate with researchers in 'uncovering' and cataloguing the array of special attributes, traits, qualities and competences which they uniquely possess – and which help 'explain', and thus legitimize, their privileged position.

Turning now to a strategic management perspective, another interpretation of the recent emphasis on leadership can be found, though it is one not necessarily in conflict with, but arguably complementary to, the sociological view just described above. From a strategic management perspective, the need for leadership is currently often addressed in terms of the *'reputational capital'* which a celebrated leader can bring to an organization. This is a very interesting and revealing concept because it highlights the importance of *stakeholder perception*. In the case of a company, the stakeholder perceptions which would matter most would be those of City analysts, brokers and investment fund managers. As we noted earlier, loss of faith by these actors in a chairman or chief executive can have disastrous consequences for a company's share price and ability to raise funds. To this extent at least, therefore, the critical importance of 'leadership' is hard to overstate.

In the case of a voluntary sector organization or non-governmental organization (NGO) such as Oxfam, the significant stakeholders whose perceptions would matter will include the donors and the commentators whose opinions will influence the donors, such as the press. In public sector organizations such as a local authority, a school or a health trust, important stakeholder perceptions will be those held by central government fund allocators and by clients and other sponsors. Each of these can influence the fortunes – for good or ill – of these institutions. Under such circumstances, the importance of leadership again becomes a truism.

What is of further interest is that the significance of leadership can spiral depending on the prevailing political, social and economic circumstances. During those periods when government, for example, determines that leadership in the public services is to be treated as of crucial importance, as a self-fulfilling prophecy it indeed becomes so. Funds and reputation will flow in accord with the contours of this initial determination. Other actors in the system, even those of a more sceptical disposition, are prevailed upon to play by the new rules of the game. Thus, when the Cabinet Office (1999, 2000) discussed the crucial importance of leadership in the context of its 'modernizing agenda', it was not merely reflecting a state of affairs but constructing them.

Reputational capital is thus found to have an important bearing on the understanding of leadership. By extension, 'leadership', under certain cultural and economic conditions, becomes a vital *intangible asset* to an organization. It becomes virtually a component of the brand and is potentially just as valuable. It is, accordingly, easy to appreciate why organizational chiefs feel compelled to play along with the leadership mystique. Being seen to have a competent leader, and indeed *being seen to be attending to* the task of building a constantly replenishing 'leadership pool' is virtually *de rigueur* for any self-respecting organization. The symbolic presence of these attributes is arguably of even more importance than whether there is any evidence of their impact on organizational outcomes. It is the accomplished performance of leadership and the accomplished performance of leadership building which matter.

So far, we have looked at the context of leadership and the different perceived needs for leadership which emerge at different times and in different places. But the ultimate heartland of leadership comprises a set of behaviours and capabilities. It is to an analysis of these that we now turn.

Behavioural requirements and competences

Research has continued unabated on the subject of the behaviours and capabilities required of leaders. To be adjudged a competent leader, an individual would usually be expected to possess a range of capabilities. In addition, leaders are also expected to make a series of 'accomplished performances' – that is, to display requisite behaviours. These latter usually depend on the former. Thus, capability and behavioural requirements are intimately intertwined. Hence, competency frameworks normally express both required skills and required behavioural accomplishments.

The capabilities or 'attributes' of leaders have proved to be a source of endless fascination. We noted earlier Warren Bennis's recent description of what he believes are the central hallmarks – the ability to find meaning in negative situations, a compelling voice, integrity and adaptive capacity. But other researchers, practitioners, trainers and consultants have emphasized different attributes. The continuing variation in the competency frameworks thus echoes the problems of the early work on leader traits, which also suffered from multiple and non-congruent profiles of leaders. However, some have argued that beneath the variety there are a number of more or less commonly agreed core capabilities. For example, numerous surveys reveal that large numbers of respondents identify leaders as having and displaying vision, strategic sense, an ability to communicate that vision and strategy, and an ability to inspire and motivate (Council for Excellence in Management & Leadership 2001).

To what extent respondents to such surveys are truly capturing respondents' own interpretations of their direct experience of leaders or simply reflecting conventional wisdom about accomplished leadership is very hard to determine. But there does seem to be evidence that the stylized preferred account of the nature of leadership does change over time – and, as we saw earlier, varies also by culture. Of course, leadership may still be important, even though, as the literature reveals, it derives from, and varies with, social context.

Current work on behavioural requirements and capabilities is very varied, but it can be organized within three main categories – or what might be termed meta-capabilities. These are shown in Figure 2.2.

The first meta-capability shown in Figure 2.2 emphasizes *big picture sensemaking*. This includes the ability to scan and interpret the environment; to differentiate threats to, and opportunities for, the organization; to assess the organizations' strengths and weaknesses; and to construct a sensible vision, mission and strategy. As has constantly been emphasized in the literature and in the dominant mode of thinking over the past couple of decades, the result of this big picture work may entail a transformative agenda for the focal organization. Indeed, the distinct impression is easily gained that in modern perception leadership work is of this nature almost by definition. Steady-state maintenance, it often appears, is not so much one variant of leadership as one might logically

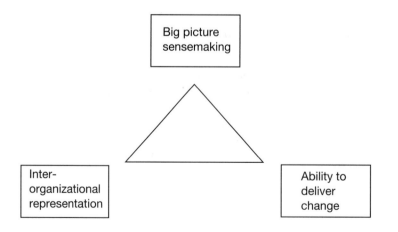

Figure 2.2 Meta-capabilities of leaders

suppose, but rather a function of that 'other' subordinate position, namely management. What this expresses, of course, is that leadership is closely identified with change-making. The crucial capability here, then, is correctly to discern the direction of change.

This inevitably points next to the second meta-capability – *the ability to deliver change*. This capability hinges on a cluster of constitutive skills such as mobilizing support, communicating, energizing and inspiring followers, active listening, adopting a supportive stance, enabling others by investing in their training and development, and empowering them to take decisions. An element within this meta-capability which has received a great deal of attention in recent years is that of 'emotional intelligence' (Goleman *et al.* 2002; Humphrey 2002; Vitello-Cicciu 2002; Wolff *et al.* 2002). This is a catch-all construct designed to capture a number of interpersonal skills such as self-awareness, self-management and social awareness (such as empathy).

There are two levels to this behavioural attribute and therefore to this capability. The first level includes team or group leadership – or, as it is sometimes termed, 'near leadership'. At this level interpersonal skills are at a premium. The second level is termed 'distant leadership' and it refers to those situations where the leader is not in direct personal contact with the followers – perhaps because of their large number – and so has to lead through the multiple tiers using means other than interpersonal skills. Different kinds of leadership capabilities are needed for the accomplishment of these different roles. It is also worth noting that there may be misalignment of the perceptions between distant and near group followers (Waldman 1999).

These two levels of distant and near refer, of course, to the conventional idea of the hierarchical leader – that is, a leader who occupies some position of authority. Other skills will be required of those exercising lateral leadership. The necessary skills in such circumstances have been identified by Fisher and Sharp (1998), who explain 'how to lead when you are not in charge'.

The third meta-capability concerns inter-organizational representation and the ambassadorial role. While this is a vital capability for a chief executive in a private sector company it is one which has reached special prominence in the public sector as a result of the increasing requirement for inter-agency working. Indeed, the cluster of capabilities required to 'lead' in a network context is one of the key current themes in the leadership debate. Skills such as coalition building, understanding others' perspectives, persuasion and assessing client needs in a holistic rather than a single agency manner become the premium requirements.

Leadership development methods

As will be very evident from the review above, much of the literature on leadership is about the nature, the types, the qualities and the need for leadership. However, a certain segment of the literature also attends to the methods for *developing* leaders. This agenda, the expressed desire to improve and expand leadership development, lies behind the kind of campaign exemplified recently by the Council for Excellence in Management & Leadership (CEML). The general case is as expressed by Robert Fulmer: 'Leaders who keep learning may be the ultimate source of sustainable competitive advantage' (Fulmer *et al.* 2000: 49). But, as the periodic worries and campaigns suggest, there is a concern that there is an insufficient supply of high quality development opportunities. From time to time, this concern becomes wrapped up in the even wider agenda, held by some, that the business schools are not fully delivering what businesses 'need'. This criticism is variously expressed: university business schools are 'too academic'; they do not make enough efforts to tailor their products to the needs of their clients; and/or they pay too little attention to the 'real-world' skills of managers.

There is often a hidden agenda to such critique and, not infrequently, also an anti-academic stance. The truth is that outside the business schools there is already huge provision for 'training for leadership'. The important question here, therefore, is not so much the alleged 'neglect' of leadership, but rather how to evaluate the quality and relevance of the overall provision already available. Graham Mole (in Chapter 7) questions the value of much of the training and development currently offered for leadership development. But his main argument is not that training and development are not worthwhile; rather, his criticism relates to the generic training which pays insufficient regard to context. An equally trenchant critique of conventional leadership training methods is made by Elena Antonacopoulou and Regina Bento (Chapter 5). They propound the case for an entirely different approach to 'learning leadership' – an approach which emphasizes continual learning and adaptability by leaders and followers alike.

Most of the training and development interventions which are available both in-house and as offered by external providers can be classified in terms of four main types:

1   Learning 'about leadership' and understanding organizations. This includes study of the work of Maslow (1954), McGregor (1960), Hersey and Blanchard (1984), and Kouzes and Posner (1997). This kind of traditional education is made available to a wide range of audiences. It comprises the basic fare for many leadership workshops.
2   Self-analysis, team analysis and exploration of different leadership styles. These interventions are usually based on psychometric questionnaires and instruments. These 'getting to know yourself' sessions usually also involve feedback, coaching and sensitivity training.
3   Experiential learning and simulation. This mode of provision is very popular. It usually takes place in mountainous locales or in close proximity to the sea and small boats. Courses of this type operate on the basis of action learning or learning by doing. The work of John Adair (1983) often provides the basic underlying framework. The residential courses offering this approach are built around a series of outdoor tasks and challenges. The trainers act as facilitators and feed back information about behaviour patterns; from these, participants embark on a journey of self-discovery.

4   Top level strategy courses. For the highest level managers it is more commonly the practice to send them either individually or in groups to prestige business schools for short 'executive courses'. These are invariably very expensive, exclusive and much valued by the participants. American business schools such as Harvard and Wharton are especially favoured, but certain European schools such as INSEAD are also part of the perceived magic circle.

In addition to the above four types of courses, there is a whole array of leadership development activities within companies. These include executive coaching, 360 degree feedback, accelerated development programmes, special project assignments, seminars and career planning for so-called 'high potentials' (or Hi-Pos), courses to align with critical transition moments (such as first and subsequent leadership tier promotions), secondments, and special conferences for leaders (London 2002; Vicere 2000; Avolio and Bass 2002; Dotlich and Noel 1998; McCauley *et al.* 1998; Conger and Benjamin 1999; Hollenbeck and McCall 1999; Giber *et al.* 2000).

There is a fundamental dilemma that haunts many leadership development events. Because leadership is perceived as fundamentally about 'doing' rather than 'knowing', there is an inherent bias towards activity-focused and indeed briskly paced encounters. The hours are long and the programme is normally packed. Participants, clients and providers often collude in fulfilling the prior expectation that events must be exciting and fast moving. In consequence, there is little time for reflection or strategic thinking. These characteristics of leadership development events are self-evidently in tension with the kind of clear thinking supposedly required of top leaders.

So far in this chapter, we have taken an overview of the different ways in which leadership has been approached and understood, and we have introduced a basic conceptual framework which helps to locate the relevant key variables. In the following section we turn to an examination of the proposition that there is an overall trend towards a new theory of leadership.

Post-charismatic and post-transformational leadership?

To what extent is there evidence that the enthusiasm for heroic, charismatic and transformational leadership is waning? In this final section of the chapter this is the issue which will be assessed.

The terms 'charismatic' and 'transformational' are used more or less interchangeably in much of the literature. However, it is of course possible to make a distinction between the two. Distilling here a large literature on the 'charismatic leader' (Bass 1985a, 1985b, 1990; Bryman 1992; Conger and Kanungo 1998, 1987; Sankowsky 1995), the notion can be broadly captured by reference to six elements:

- an heroic figure (usually with attributed past success stories);
- a mystic in touch with higher truths;
- a value-driven individual rather than one who is apparently purely self-serving;
- someone who is perceived to 'know the way';
- an individual who has a vision of a more desirable and achievable future;
- and finally someone thought to be capable of caring for and developing followers.

It is evident from all six points that they reflect attributes of personality and behaviour. The construct of the 'transformational leader', on the other hand, although closely related in many ways, is distinct in that it refers to an approach to leading which aspires to significant organizational change through engaged and committed followers. It was John McGregor Burns (1978) who emphasized the meaning and significance of transformational leadership by contrasting it with transactional leadership. This theme was picked up and elaborated by Bass (1985a, 1985b, 1990). According to Bass, *transformational* leadership has four components:

- individualized consideration (the leader is alert to the needs of followers and also takes care to develop them);
- intellectual stimulation (the leader encourages followers to think in creative ways and to propose innovative ideas);
- inspirational motivation (energizing followers to achieve extraordinary things);
- idealized influence (offers followers a role model).

The component which most centrally captures the idea of transformational leadership is that of 'inspirational motivation'. This notion is decidedly change-focused. It holds forth the idea of ordinary people achieving extraordinary things through the influence of the leader. This kind of leader reduces complexity, doubt, cynicism and ambiguity by cutting through to the 'essential' elements, and these are expressed in simple, readily understandable language. Moreover, these simple truths are expressed with conviction. The goal – or better still the vision – is rendered clear and it is made to seem both desirable and achievable. Organizational members are asked to forsake mediocrity and routine and aspire instead to reach a future state of such high achievement that it deserves the willing expenditure of extra discretionary effort and commitment (Bass 1985a, 1985b, 1990).

Thus, there are evident overlaps between the notions of the charismatic leaders and the transformational leader. In brief, transformational leaders usually require many of the attributes of charisma; but, conversely, charisma alone is not enough to enable transformational leadership.

However, for the purposes of the present analysis we are rather less interested in the distinction or the differences than in the way in which the general notion of charismatic and transformational leadership captured the imagination of analysts, observers, consultants, trainers and organizational decision-makers at the end of the 20th century. In general, these and other players were mobilized behind the prescribed shift from the old and supposedly discredited transactional approach, to the new supposedly transformational approach. The campaign – urged along by management consultants and trainers – sought to explain and persuade a wide audience of the advantages and the elements of the 'new' approach. Especially influential – mainly because they were widely used by consultants – were the works of Tichy and Devanna (1986) and of Kouzes and Posner (1997). These, and similar works, emphasize the work and skills of transformational leaders in recognizing the need for change – even when an organization appeared to everyone else to be enjoying continued success; the creation of a new vision, developed and refined most probably with others in the organization; and the embedding or institutionalizing of changes within the organization.

Much of this message is amplified in the influential general works on leadership, management, marketing and business by management figures such as Tom Peters, one of the most successful management gurus of all time. For example, a key part of his constantly reiterated message was:

> You have got to know where you are going, to be able to state it clearly and concisely – and you have to care about it passionately. That all adds up to vision, the concise statement/picture of where the company and its people are heading, and why they should be proud of it.
>
> (Peters and Austin 1985: 284)

Given the extraordinary reach which the Tom Peters message achieved among the management populations of the Western world, it is hardly a matter of surprise that surveys of managers find these attributes readily reflected back when questions are asked about the nature and 'meaning' of leadership. Similar powerful messages were diffused by management consultants using the works of Bradford and Cohen (1984), Kouzes and Posner (1997) and Kotter (1988, 1990). Transformational leadership was part of the wider message of 'excellence' and 'high performance' which has been – and to a large extent still is – so pervasive since the 1980s.

For example, it has been argued recently that the inspirational leadership style of Steve Jobs at Apple Computer in the 1980s created

> a corporate culture that has become widespread. In this new organisation, employees were supposed to work ceaselessly, uncomplainingly, and even for relatively low pay not just to produce and sell a product but to realise the vision of the messianic leader.
>
> (Khurana 2002a: 4)

Hence, our argument here is that the profile of 'transformational leadership' mirrored and reinforced other wider themes of the late 20th century. 'Change management' was also very much to the fore for a whole array of reasons – not least because of concern about fierce competition from fast-growing economies in various parts of the world. Large proportions of public and private sector organizations were persuaded that they had to embark on significant restructuring and revitalization. Increased global competition and deregulation of markets led senior executives to feel less secure. Traditional formulas such as large scale, market dominance and mass production seemed to offer far less reliable answers. New technologies and new forms of consumer behaviour made the large industrial and commercial bureaucracies seem slow, out of touch and vulnerable. Many of them embarked on extensive downsizing, delayering and outsourcing. Employees were less likely to be offered long-term careers or jobs for life. Employment contracts became looser, as part-time, short-term and fixed-term contracts appeared to proliferate. The challenges were huge and numerous. Who could divine which of the radical paths should be chosen? How were the new and far-reaching uncertainties to be confronted? Who could explain to organizational members the imperative to change and at the same time convince them of the need for new behaviours and the need for a 'new deal' in their relations with their employing organization?

Under these sorts of conditions, it is no surprise that the idea of the transformational leader became so appealing. The introduction of a *deus ex machina* figure became almost formulaic. Health trusts were prevailed upon to bring in larger-than-life chair figures from the private sector and to parachute in 'interim managers' as chief executives. The government and the health trust non-executives wanted 'leader' figures – people who would exude confidence, energy and enthusiasm. These were in effect 'interim managers' whose role was seen as temporary 'experts' parachuted in at the top with a mission to bring about significant change before they went native and became embroiled in local culture and assumptions. The same concept was extended to 'failing schools', where 'superheads' from successful schools were parachuted in to effect dramatic transformations. (But now the educational world seems to have move beyond this model. The superheads initiative has encountered a number of harsh realities and the concept appears to have been quietly de-emphasized in favour of a new accent on communities of learning.)

The overall thrust of the transformational leader proposition was prefigured in the hugely influential management bestseller *In Search of Excellence* (Peters and Waterman 1982). It is worth recalling that much of the Peters and Waterman case was, in effect, a treatise on the need for transformational and charismatic leadership. As was the case 20 years later in the expressed concerns leading up to the launch of the Council for Excellence in Management & Leadership, there is an incipient critique of the 'rational model of management' associated with, though not confined to, the business schools. Peters and Waterman were critical of the overemphasis on central strategic planning, central control systems and complex formal organization structures. Drawing on their assessment of the success factors in a number of 'excellent companies', they made a case for correcting all of this with a new formula.

It is worth reprising this new formula and the 'recipe for excellence' as espoused by Peters and Waterman. They comprised a series of eight attributes. These were

- a 'bias for action' rather than excessive analysis and committee work;
- 'close to the customer' rather than concern with internal processes;
- autonomy and entrepreneurship – innovative units rather than bureaucratic procedural hierarchy;
- 'values-driven' and 'strong corporate culture' rather than rules and procedures;
- 'stick to the knitting' (focus on core business where passion can count and avoid the dissipation of energy implied by conglomerates);
- loose–tight properties (strong values but mistakes are tolerated and experimentation rewarded);
- hands-on, values-driven (senior executives engage directly in the core business);
- success through involved people.

Looked at afresh, it is easy to see that *In Search of Excellence*, and the subsequent numerous management workshops and presentations which made Tom Peters a multimillionaire, could quite easily have been sold as a treatise on 'leadership'. Notably, in the sequel, *A Passion for Excellence* (Peters and Austin 1985), a new explicit emphasis was indeed placed on leadership, but Peters claimed that it was implicit in the original work. In my view this is true. It reinforces the interpretation that the original work could have been recast as an analysis of the importance and impact of leadership.

In a trenchant critique of *In Search of Excellence*, David Guest assesses the work as 'Right enough to be dangerously wrong' (Guest 1992). The Guest critique is also pertinent, I suggest, to much of the wider literature on leadership. There are methodological criticisms – it is relevant to note that a great deal of the transformational leadership literature is similarly superficial in its evidence base – see, for example, Tichy and Devanna's (1986) influential work which was in fact based on a study of only 12 chief executives in the US. There are also conceptual and theoretical shortcomings. For example, it is not clear which of the attributes have the greater importance; there is a neglect of environmental factors such as changes in market conditions (the subsequent failures and difficulties of the original 'excellent' case were indicative of this partial attention to relevant variables). In other words, just as Peters and Waterman were *partially* right to emphasize the range of skills and issues which had been arguably neglected, so too were the transformational leadership enthusiasts partially right to point up the limits of the transactional mode. What was dangerously wrong was the naïve and singular attention to this new solution.

There are now increasing signs of disenchantment with the concept of the assertive, no-nonsense leader, whether of the charismatic or transformative variety. Some of this discontent and doubt we have already noted. But there is more, and it is increasing.

The 'shadow side of charisma' has been noted by a number of writers (Conger and Kanungo 1998; Howell and Avolio 1992; Sankowsky 1995). The dangers of narcissism and the associated misuse, and even abuse, of power were thus known about even at the height of the period when charismatic and transformational leadership were being celebrated. There were even specific case analyses where malign effects had been experienced in corporations such as Peoples Express, Polaroid-Kodak and Disney (Garrett 1986; Berg 1976; Sankowsky 1995). But overall, against the cacophony of general applause, they were inconspicuous spectres and ones very much in the background at this time.

Sankowsky (1995) explored the problems of exploitation of dependency among the followers of charismatic, narcissistic leaders. And the highly regarded Manfred Kets de Vries (1989, 1994, 2000) has been especially notable for his clinical reflections on some of the dysfunctional aspects of leadership.

But these isolated warning signs have been brought together in a far more developed way in recent times, to such a degree that the charismatic-transformational model itself is now being questioned. The research has also become more systematic and critical. For example, following a study of CEO successions in the US, Khurana (2002a) found that the widespread faith in the power of charismatic leaders had resulted in a number of problems. There was an exaggerated belief in the impact of CEOs on companies because recruiters were pursuing the chimera of a special 'type' of individual. There was a further tendency for companies to neglect suitable candidates while entertaining unsuitable ones. Finally, appointed charismatic leaders were problematic because it was found they 'can destabilise organisations in dangerous ways' (*ibid.*: 4).

A common trait in the charismatic leaders studied was their willingness to deliberately fracture their organizations as a means to effect change. The destructive impact of a charismatic leader is exemplified by the case of Enron. Its CEO Jeff Skilling 'induced blind obedience in his followers', and, while his abilities as a 'new economy strategist were overrated' (he instigated the shift to an asset-light position for the company), what he excelled at was 'motivating subordinates to take risks to think outside the box – in short to do whatever pleased him' (*ibid.*: 7). The case illustrates the dangerous downside of charismatic leadership – the dismissal of normal checks and balances and the impatience with, if not complete disregard for, convention and rule. These are, of course, the qualities which prompted the appointment of charismatic leaders and which helped shape their remit in the first place. As Khurana observes, the recent display of 'extraordinary trust in the power of the charismatic CEO resembles less a mature faith than it does a belief in magic' (*ibid.*: 8).

A similar critique, albeit from a different perspective, is mounted by Michael Maccoby (2000). Writing prior to the burst of the dot.com boom and the corporate scandals which burst on to the scene in 2001, Maccoby warns presciently of the risks and downsides of the eager search for, and celebration of, corporate leaders with charismatic qualities. He argues that the 1980s and 1990s provided fertile ground for the rise to prominence of the type of personality which Freud termed 'narcissistic'. Narcissists were one of Freud's three main personality types. Unlike the popular stereotype, the term as used in clinical psychology denotes a set of orientations which have positive as well as negative attributes.

Among the important positive aspects, such people help disturb the status quo and stimulate change.

However, Freud also noted the negative side to narcissism. Narcissists are distrustful, suspicious and even paranoiac. Their achievements feed tendencies to arrogance and 'feelings of grandiosity' (Maccoby 2000: 70). They are poor listeners and tend to have an overblown sense of their own good judgement even in the face of opposition. They thrive on risk and are prepared to destroy current practices and strategies. They seek power, glory and admiration. They present a persona of supreme self-confidence and hubris. They suggest to themselves and others that they can do no wrong.

Maccoby's case is that the last two decades of the 20th century provided the environment which allowed an unprecedented number of narcissistic personalities to occupy prominent leadership positions.

> With the dramatic discontinuities going on in the world today, more and more organizations are getting into bed with narcissists. They are finding that there is no substitute for narcissistic leaders in an age of innovation. Companies need leaders who do not try to anticipate the future so much as create it. But narcissistic leaders – even the most productive of them – can self destruct and lead their organizations terribly astray. For companies whose narcissistic leaders recognize their limitations, these will be the best of times. For other companies, these could turn out to be the worst.
>
> (Maccoby 2000: 77)

For Enron, WorldCom, Andersen, Marconi and many other companies these proved to be prophetic words. But have the dramatic events of the past few years been enough to signal the end of the love affair with charismatic and transformational leaders?

People are beginning to look for alternatives to the charismatic transformational leader. There is a growing realization that there are no easy answers and that an alternative mode of leadership must be one which promotes learning and is more capable of being sustained than the Quixotic heroic concept normally allows. One excellent example of the new mood is to be found in the work of Michael Fullan (2001a, 2001b). Fullan presents an implicit model of post-charismatic or new leadership based around embedded learning, devolved leadership in teams and learning as a product of conflict, experimentation and false starts. The incipient leadership model here is one which shapes a context in which practice is made public in a collaborative culture and one which is open to challenge, testing and refinement.

Looking to the future

The campaign for a shift from transactional to transformational leaders which dominated the leadership and management agenda for at least two decades from the late 1970s or early 1980s has evidently run into some choppy waters of late.

But has the model of the charismatic and transformational leader truly been abandoned? There is certainly much more caution, suspicion and scepticism of the kind of overblown claims which were relatively unquestioned at the height of the charisma boom. This caution and scepticism carry consequences for modes of leadership development.

However, even now in the period of aftershock following corporate collapse and salutary lessons in stock market fluctuations, it seems unlikely that all of the ideas surrounding the idea of the transformational leader will be abandoned. There will be more caution certainly, and the apparently unbridled optimism and enthusiasm of the kind of management consultancy works exemplified by Kouzes and Posner (1997) may not find such easy favour. Moreover, there may, for a while, be some greater attraction for the less bombastic style of charismatic leader. This is the thesis of Birkenshaw and Crainer's *Leadership: The Sven-Goran Eriksson Way* (2002). The more modest, thoughtful, quieter approach will always be attractive in some quarters, but it seems highly unlikely that it represents an entirely new dominant model. A more balanced approach is now in evidence. It is increasingly being argued that effective leaders are *both* transactional and transformational in their leadership styles (Avolio and Bass 2002). They describe their leadership development approach as encouraging 'the full range of leadership styles'.

While stakeholders will probably approach staffing decisions in a more judicious way in future, the allure of a leader who promises to point to new appealing directions and also mobilize and energize followers will continue to be irresistibly appealing. Indeed, as long as organizations require innovation this kind of leader will be sought. There may, however, be less naïvety about what a leader can achieve among all the other variables which influence organizational outcomes and success.

In the chapters which follow, the broad themes, issues and trends overviewed in these first two chapters are explored in greater detail. In the final chapter, we bring all the threads back together and assess the prospects for the future of leadership and management – and of their methods of development.

References

Adair, J. (1983) *Effective Leadership*, London: Pan.

Avolio, B. and B. Bass (1988) 'Transformational leadership, charisma and beyond', in J. Hunt, H. Baliga and C. Dachler (eds) *Emerging Leadership Vistas*, Lexington, MA: Lexington Books.

—— (eds) (2002) *Developing Potential across a Full Range of Leadership Styles: Cases on Transactional and Transformational Leadership*, Mahwah, NJ: Lawrence Erlbaum Associates.

Bass, B. (1985a) *Leadership and Performance Beyond Expectations*, Cambridge, MA: Harvard University Press.

—— (1985b) 'Leadership: good, better, best', *Organizational Dynamics* 13: 26–40.

—— (1990) 'From transactional to transformational leadership: learning to share the vision', *Organizational Dynamics* 19(3): 19–31.

Bendix, R. (1956) *Work and Authority in Industry*, Berkeley, CA: University of California Press.

Bennis, W. (1994) *On Becoming a Leader*, Reading, MA: Addison-Wesley.

Bennis, W.G. and R.J. Thomas (2002) *Geeks and Geezers; How Era, Values, and Defining Moments Shape Leaders*, Boston, MA: Harvard University Press.

Berg, N. (1976) *Polaroid-Kodak*, Boston, MA: Harvard Business School Press.

Bernard, L. (1926) *An Introduction to Social Psychology*, New York: Holt.

Birkinshaw, J. and S. Crainer (2002) *Leadership: The Sven-Goran Eriksson Way*, London: Capstone Publishing.

Blake, R.R. and J.S. Moulton (1964) *The Managerial Grid*, Houston: Gulf Publishing.

Blandford, S. and L. Squire (2000) 'An evaluation of the Teacher Training Agency head-teacher leadership and management programme (HEADLAMP)', *Educational Management & Administration* 28(1): 21–32.

Bradford, D.L. and A.R. Cohen (1984) *Managing for Excellence: The Guide to Developing High Performance in Contemporary Organizations*, New York: Wiley.

Brodbeck, F.C. (2000) 'Cultural variation of leadership prototypes across 22 European countries', *Journal of Occupational amd Organizational Psychology* 73(1): 1–29.

Brodbeck, F.C., M. Frese and M. Javidan (2002) 'Leadership made in Germany: low on compassion, high on performance', *Academy of Management Executive* 16(1): 16–29.

Brown, M.E. and D.A. Gioia (2002) 'Making things click – distributive leadership in an online division of an offline organization', *Leadership Quarterly* 13(4): 397–419.

Brundrett, M. (2001) 'The development of school leadership preparation programmes in England and the USA', *Educational Management & Administration* 29(2): 229.

Bryman, A. (1992) *Charisma and Leadership in Organisations*, London: Sage.

Burns, J. M. (1978) *Leadership*, New York: Harper & Row.

Cabinet Office (1999) *Modernising Government*, London: Stationery Office.

—— (2000) *Strengthening Leadership in the Public Sector: A Research Study by the PIU*, London: Performance and Innovation Unit.

Child, J. (1969) *British Management Thought*, London: Allen & Unwin.

Conger, J. (1993) 'The brave new world of leadership training', *Organizational Dynamics* 21(3): 46–58.

Conger, J.A. and B. Benjamin (1999) *Building Leaders: How Successful Companies Develop the Next Generation*, San Francisco: Jossey Bass.

Conger, J. and R. Kanungo (1987) 'Towards a behavioural theory of charismatic leadership in organizational settings', *Academy of Management Review* 12: 635–47.

—— (1998) *Charismatic Leadership in Organizations*, Thousand Oaks, CA: Sage.

Council for Excellence in Management & Leadership (2001) *Leadership Development: Best Practice Guide for Organisations*, London: CEML.

Daresh, J. and T. Male (2000) 'Crossing the border into leadership: experiences of newly appointed British headteachers and American principals', *Educational Management & Administration* 28(1): 89–101.

de Vries, M.K. (1989) 'The leader as mirror: clinical reflections', *Human Relations* 42(7): 607–23.

—— (1994) 'The leadership mystique', *Academy of Management Executive* 8(3): 73–92.

—— (2000) 'When leaders have character: need for leadership, performance, and the attribution of leadership', *Journal of Social Behavior and Personality* 15(3): 413–30.

DiMaggio, P.W. and W. Powell (1983) 'The iron cage revisited: institutional isomorphism and collective rationality in organizational fields', *American Sociological Review* 48: 147–60.

Dotlich, D. and J. Noel (1998) *Action Learning: How the World's Top Companies Are Recreating their Leaders and Themselves*, San Francisco: Jossey Bass.

Fiedler, F. (1967) *A Theory of Leadership Effectiveness*, New York: McGraw-Hill.

Fisher, R. and A. Sharp (1998) *Getting it Done: How to Lead When You Are Not in Charge*, New York: HarperCollins.

Fullan, M. (2001a) *Leading in a Culture of Change*, San Francisco: Jossey Bass.

—— (2001b) *The New Meaning of Educational Change*, London: RoutledgeFalmer.

Fulmer, R.M., P.A. Gibbs and M. Goldsmith (2000) 'Developing leaders: how winning companies keep on winning', *Sloan Management Review* 42(1): 49–59.

Garrett, E. (1986) 'The troops are restless at People Express', *Venture* 8: 102–4.

Giber, D., L. Carter and M. Goldsmith (2000) *Leadership Development Handbook: Case Studies, Instruments and Training*, Lexington, MA: Linkage Press.

Goleman, D., R. Boyatzis and A. McKee (2002) *Primal Leadership: Realizing the Power of Emotional Intelligence*, Boston, MA: Harvard Business School Press.

Graen, G.B. and M. Uhl-Bien (1995) 'Relationship-based approach to leadership: development of leader-exchange theory', *Leadership Quarterly* 6: 219–47.

Grint, K. (ed.) (1997) *Leadership: Classic, Contemporary and Critical Approaches*, Oxford: Oxford University Press.

—— (2000) *The Arts of Leadership*, Oxford: Oxford University Press.

Guest, D. (1992) 'Right enough to be dangerously wrong: an analysis of the "In Search of Excellence" phenomenon', in G. Salaman (ed.) *Human Resource Strategies*, London: Sage.

Hersey, P. and K. Blanchard (1984) *The Management of Organizational Behavior*, Englewood Cliffs, NJ: Prentice-Hall.

Hollenbeck, G. and M. McCall (1999) 'Leadership development', in A. Kraut and A. Korman (eds) *Evolving Practices in Human Resource Management*, San Francisco: Jossey Bass.

House, R.J. (1971) 'A path–goal theory of leadership', *Administrative Science Quarterly* 16: 321–38.

—— (1996) 'Path–goal theory of leadership: lessons, legacy and a reformulated theory', *Leadership Quarterly* 7: 323–52.

Howell, J. and B. Avolio (1992) 'The ethics of charismatic leadership: submission or liberation?', *Academy of Management Executive* 6(2): 43–54.

Humphrey, R.H. (2002) 'The many faces of emotional leadership', *Leadership Quarterly* 13(5): 493–504.

Katz, D. and R.L. Kahn (1978) *The Social Psychology of Organizations*, New York: John Wiley.

Khurana, R. (2002a) 'The curse of the superstar CEO', *Harvard Business Review*, September: 3–8.

—— (2002b) *Searching for the Corporate Savior*, Princeton, NJ: Princeton University Press.

Kotter, J. (1988) *The Leadership Factor*, New York: Free Press.

—— (1990) *A Force for Change: How Leadership Differs from Management*, New York: Free Press.

Kouzes, J.M. and B.Z. Posner (1997) *The Leadership Challenge: How to Get Extraordinary Things Done in Organizations*, San Francisco: Jossey Bass.

Lawler, E.E. (1988) 'Substitutes for hierarchy', *Organizational Dynamics* 17 (summer): 5–15.

Likert, R. (1961) *New Patterns of Management*, New York: McGraw-Hill.

London, M. (2002) *Leadership Development: Paths to Self-Insight and Professional Growth*, Mahwah, NJ: Lawrence Erlbaum Associates.

McCauley, C.D., R. Moxley and E.V. Velsor (eds) (1998) *The Center for Creative Leadership Handbook of Leadership Development*, San Francisco: Jossey Bass.

McGregor, D. (1960) *The Human Side of Enterprise*, New York: McGraw-Hill.

Maccoby, M. (2000) 'Narcissistic leaders: the incredible pros, the inevitable cons', *Harvard Business Review*, January–February: 69–77.

Maslow, A. (1954) *Motivation and Personality*, New York: Harper & Row.

Mellahl, K. (2000) 'The teaching of leadership in UK MBA programmes', *Journal of Management Development* 19(3/4): 297–309.

Miller, D. and W. Form (1964) *Industrial Sociology*, New York: Harper & Row.

Pawar, B.S. and K.K. Eastman (1997) 'The nature and implications of contextual influences on transformational leadership', *Academy of Management Review* 22(1): 80–110.

Perrow, C. (1970) *Organizational Analysis*, Belmont, CA: Wadsworth.

Peters, T. and N. Austin (1985) *A Passion for Excellence*, New York: Random House.

Peters, T. and R. Waterman (1982) *In Search of Excellence*, New York: Harper & Row.

Pettigrew, A., E. Ferlie and L. McKee (1992) *Shaping Strategic Change*, London: Sage.

Pondy, L., P. Frost and G. Morgan (eds) (1983) *Organizational Symbolism*, Greenwich, CT: JAI Press.

Sankowsky, D. (1995) 'The charismatic leader as narcissist: understanding the abuse of power', *Organizational Dynamics* 23(4): 57–71.

Selznick, P. (1957) *Leadership in Administration*, Evanston, IL: Row Peterson.

Semler, R. (1989) 'Managing without managers', *Harvard Business Review*, September–October: 76–84.

Senge, P. M. (1990a) *The Fifth Discipline: The Art and Practice of the Learning Organization*, New York: Doubleday.

—— (1990b) 'The leader's new work: building learning organizations', *Sloan Management Review*, fall: 7–23.

Shackleton, V. (1995) *Business Leadership*, London: Routledge.

Stogdill, R. (1974) *Handbook of Leadership: A Survey of Theory and Research*, New York: Free Press.

Tichy, N. (1997) *The Leadership Engine: How Winning Companies Build Leaders at Every Level*, New York: Harper Business.

Tichy, N. and M. Devanna (1986) *The Transformational Leader*, New York: Wiley.

Vicere, A.A. (2000) 'Ten observations on e-learning and leadership development', *Human Resource Planning* 23(4): 34–47.

Vitello-Cicciu, J.M. (2002) 'Exploring emotional intelligence: implications for nursing leaders', *Journal of Nursing Administration* 32(4): 203–10.

Vroom, V.H. (1964) *Work and Motivation*, New York: John Wiley.

Vroom, V.H. and P.W. Yetton (1973) *Leadership and Decision Making*, Pittsburgh: University of Pittsburgh Press.

—— (1988) *The New Leadership: Managing Participation in Organizations*, Englewood Cliffs, NJ: Prentice Hall.

Waldman, D.A. (1999) 'CEO charismatic leadership: levels of management and levels of analysis effects', *Academy of Management Review* 24(2): 266–86.

Weick, K.W. (1995) *Sensemaking in Organizations*, Newbury Park, CA: Sage.

Westley, F. and H. Mintzberg (1989) 'Visionary leadership and strategic management', *Strategic Management Journal* 10: 17–32.

Wolff, S.B., A.T. Pescosolido and V.U. Druskat (2002) 'Emotional intelligence as the basis of leadership emergence in self-managing teams', *Leadership Quarterly* 13(5): 505–22.

Yukl, G. (2002) *Leadership in Organizations*, Englewood Cliffs, NJ: Prentice Hall.

Zaleznik, A. (1992) 'Managers and leaders: are they different?', *Harvard Business Review*, March–April: 126–35.

Part II

The elements of leadership

3 Leadership and integrity

Iain Mangham

Every year some of the most senior politicians and business leaders attend the World Economic Forum in Davos. It is a gathering of the great and the good, the movers and the shakers, to debate matters of common concern. The main theme of the World Economic Forum held in Davos in January 2003 was trust. According to the commentator Hamish McRae, many of the 'more thoughtful people' who run large companies have been shaken by the decline in the reputation of the business community and 'of course the lapses in the ethical behaviour of both commercial and the investment banks that have led to this decline'. It was widely expected that the participants would determine 'that they behave more honourably in the future' (McCrae 2003).

The anxious discussion at the Davos conclave was a response to the near hysteria generated by the spectacular collapse of some of America's largest companies, notably Enron and WorldCom. The demise of the former in particular has been called 'cataclysmic' and 'the most egregious example of executive piracy in American corporate history' (Lambert 2002). Many other companies have been tarred with the same brush. Richard Lambert, for example, in an article in *The Times*, noted that 'The grandest companies on Wall Street stand accused of behaviour that would embarrass a Coney Island card sharp' (*ibid.*).

This chapter is about leadership and integrity and takes the form of a response to the responses. It is neither a review of theories of leadership, nor of the equally vast literature on ethics in business. My concern here is to consider issues of leadership and integrity in contemporary rapidly growing businesses. In this chapter I propose to take Enron as an example. In many respects it can serve to illustrate the issues facing many of the other companies that have been accused of behaving in a morally reprehensible manner. As my starting point I will outline how its collapse has been seen by some commentators, and I will overlay these descriptions with the model of leadership developed by Badaracco and Ellsworth (1989), which promotes integrity as central to high achieving managing. I will go on to comment upon both Enron and the model, and will offer some thoughts on character, ethos, leadership and integrity.

The rise and fall of 'the world's leading company'

The description of Enron that follows is based upon a limited number of sources: partly on articles that appeared in the press in the months after the company went into administration and more substantially upon three books that were published within a year or so of its demise. The first to appear was *Pipe Dreams: Greed, Ego and the Death of Enron* (2002), written by Robert Bryce, a business journalist; the second was *Anatomy of Greed: The Unshredded Truth* (2002), by Brian Cruver, a sometime senior manager at Enron; and the third was *Enron: The Rise and Fall* (2003), by Loren Fox, another business journalist. Their descriptions offer differing versions of Enron's history, but to a greater or lesser extent they are all concerned with attributing blame for the company's catastrophic fall.

Robert Bryce is probably the most direct: 'Fish rot at the head. Enron failed because its leadership was morally, ethically, and financially corrupt' (Bryce 2002: 12). The 'key miscreants', from Bryce's perspective, are the most senior managers in Enron – Kenneth Lay, chairman and founding CEO; Jeffrey Skilling, sometime president and CEO; and Andrew Fastow, chief financial officer – and 'the Enron board members, the hapless, hoodwinked Greek chorus of fat cats – many of whom had special "consulting" deals with Enron – who stood idly by while Enron was ruined' (*ibid.*: 12).

Professor Steve Salbu, who offers a foreword to the second book – Cruver's *Anatomy of Greed* – provides us with a taste of what is to come. He compares the demise of Enron with the attacks on the World Trade Center and argues that each has had a cataclysmic effect: 'Bad people can obliterate the world's most massive skyscrapers; bad people can destroy the world's most powerful corporations' (Cruver 2002: xi). As elsewhere, the usual suspects – Lay, Skilling and Fastow – are paraded as having some responsibility for the company's failings, but Cruver argues that the true villains are those who should be the company's real leaders: the so-called independent members of the board, who – as he sees it – were required to have an agenda strictly in line with shareholders. He claims that these are the people who ought to have been challenging, arguing with the management and closely monitoring their plans, reports and results instead of 'just sitting on their hands (sometimes in a blacked out room), agreeing to whatever recommendations were put before them' (*ibid.*: 22).

Loren Fox is more circumspect in attributing blame than the other two authors. In his introduction he asserts that Enron cooked its books, but argues that the system allowed – possibly even encouraged – rule breaking. He concludes that '[n]early everyone is to blame, from Republicans to Democrats, from accountants to lawyers, and from Wall Street to Main Street' (Fox 2003: vi). However – like the other writers – he considers that the board is particularly culpable. He asserts that the role of its members is to ask probing questions. He notes that in Enron they routinely 'rubber-stamped' the practices of the three most senior managers in the company. In 2001 Enron's board included one accounting professor, two former energy regulators, and four executives of financial and investment firms. 'Couldn't one of these directors', Fox asks, 'have had the expertise to spot problems in Enron's accounting practices?' He cites the

Powers Report – by a committee set up to investigate Enron – apparently agreeing with its conclusion that there was 'a systematic and pervasive attempt by Enron's Management to misrepresent the Company's financial condition…. There was a fundamental default of leadership and management' (*ibid.*: 300). He does, however, single out one named person for particular attention and blame. The sometime CEO Jeff Skilling is seen to be at the centre of the company and of its problems:

> As Skilling's stock was rising in the company, Enron took on more of the entrepreneurial and extremely competitive personality that he had hoped to fashion. Unfortunately, it could also be a greedy, self-involved, overconfident personality – and those characteristics sowed the seeds of hubris.
>
> (Fox 2003: 97)

Although the books and articles vary in the extent to which they attribute blame to specific actors within Enron, they appear to agree that – in the final analysis – it is not the culture or the systems but individuals that are responsible for the perceived wrongdoing.

Beyond all of the comment and outrage there is a feeling that given better leadership many of the problems in Enron and other companies would have not have occurred. In many respects this is a difficult argument to sustain in the case of Enron. Until shortly before its problems became public Enron was seen to be a very well-managed company. In February 2000, for example, *Fortune* magazine's survey of America's most admired companies named Enron the most innovative US firm for the fifth straight year. In the same survey, Enron also topped 'the quality of management' list, coming in ahead of Jack Welch's General Electric. Later that year the magazine included Enron in its list of '10 stocks to last the decade'. *Fortune* was not alone in its assessments – many newspapers, articles and analysts hailed its management and its stock. Business schools – notably Harvard – fell over themselves to write case studies demonstrating the strength of the company and the skilled leadership of Enron (*ibid.*: 189). However, to the best of my knowledge none of those cheering Enron on in its good years questioned its integrity or the moral leadership of the company.

A model of leadership

So how might a theory of leadership re-describe the spectacular demise of companies such as Enron? Perhaps what is required is a theory that can accommodate the perception that the company was managed well in what we may call the technical aspects of management and leadership, a framework that also focuses on the moral aspects of managing that so many perceive to be a major reason for Enron's fall from grace. Joseph L. Badaracco and Richard Ellsworth (1989) offer such a tool. It rests on their experience of working in companies, consulting for them and writing and teaching hundreds of cases at Harvard Business School. It is informed by the literature on leadership and tested and refined through extensive discussions with high achieving senior executives. The authors hold that integrity is 'at the very heart of understanding what leadership is'. For them, integrity suggests wholeness and coherence. It also suggests 'rightness, a sense of moral soundness' (*ibid*.: 98).

The authors hold that the key to high achievement lies in consistency and coherence among three elements: a leader's personal values, a leader's aspirations for his organization and a leader's actions. They describe the personal values that lead to outstanding managerial performance under three headings: strong personal ethics, positive belief in others and a compelling vision for their company. The second, central, element of their model of leadership is that high achieving leaders have visionary, perhaps even idealistic, aims for their companies. Overlapping somewhat with their description of personal values, Badaracco and Ellsworth maintain that there are five aspects to a leader's aims for his company: recruiting, developing and promoting people with high intellectual ability and the desire to excel; ensuring that members of the organization have a deeply shared sense of community and of the company's goals and purpose; seeing that communication is open and candid even to the point of heated, emotional debate; structuring the company in such a way that subordinates have substantial autonomy; and determining that a desire for high ethical standards pervades the company (*ibid*.: 103–5). The third element of the model – action – consists of the link that a leader makes between his/her personal beliefs and the aims he/she has for her/his organization. It is through action that a leader will 'move a company toward the ideal organization, one that is consistent with the leader's personal values' in a world beset with choices and dilemmas (*ibid*.: 109). Consistency is the essence of leadership:

> commitment to high ethical standards and to a vision for a company must remain firm, regardless of situational pressures. Respect for others, demanding standards, and expectations of candor must all remain constant. Preoccupation with substance should not give way to the shifting tides of varying situations.
>
> (Badaracco and Ellsworth 1989: 206)

Applying these ideas to Ken Lay at Enron, it is possible to argue that he espoused a strong personal ethic. He was instrumental in setting up the company's code of ethics and he was a 'prominent speaker on business ethics before his company bit the dust' (McCrae 2003). Badaracco and Ellsworth argue that the principal standards against which personal ethics should be adjudged are honesty and fairness. These were attributes that Lay was proud to hold dear to himself and his company. They were the attributes that he stressed in his introduction to the company's code of ethics, which everyone was required to sign: 'We want to be proud of Enron and to know that it enjoys a reputation for fairness and honesty and that it is respected' (Cruver 2002: 333). They were the 'core values' that were drummed into new starts and were printed at the bottom of every sheet of Enron stationery – RICE: respect ('We treat others as we would like to be treated ourselves'), integrity ('We work with others openly, honestly, and sincerely'), communication ('We have an obligation to communicate') and excellence ('We are satisfied with nothing less than the best in everything we do') (Cruver 2002: 42; Fox 2003: 79).

The second personal value is a strong belief in the ability of other people. Badaracco and Ellsworth believe that good leaders can attract high calibre individuals to their organizations and can shape and motivate them to act for reasons beyond personal economic self-interest. Lay clearly attracted very high calibre people to Enron, who – in turn – recruited and trained the brightest and the best. By the year 2000 over half of Enron's 17,000 employees had college or advanced degrees (Fox 2003: 87). Lay delegated responsibility, and gave many people the opportunity to show what they could do. Many employees appeared to be proud to work for the company. Throughout the 1990s, the company increasingly developed a name as a centre for smart, ambitious young professionals. They saw Enron was the ultimate launching pad for a business career: 'Highly respected, bitterly admired – if you were craving the fast track, you dreamed of working at Enron' (Cruver 2002: 1). It is also possible to argue that – together with Jeff Skilling – he was largely responsible for shaping the motivation and behaviour of those he recruited. Although the desire for personal gain appeared to be strong amongst Enron employees, to the point of greed in some of them, there is strong evidence that many were enthusiastic about building a strong and respectable business. To this extent they reflected the fact that Lay and Skilling in particular appeared to have a compelling vision for the company. Badaracco and Ellsworth claim that this vision has its source in 'personal and imaginative creativity' that extends beyond analysis and is embodied in actions that reflect 'initiative, risk taking, and an unswerving commitment to its achievement' (1989: 101). Few would dispute that Enron was such a company – it aspired to become the world's leading company and it nearly made it.

Furthermore, there appears to be evidence of open communication and of plans being tested through vigorous debate. All three of the authors cited above provide instances where the various levels and divisions of the company challenge and debate ideas, plans and procedures. Fox, for example, speaks of the circumstance where business groups were set to compete against each other as though they were different companies (Fox 2003: 86). Skilling boasted that 'the whole organization is like a free market of people and ideas' (*ibid*.: 89). However – as we have seen – these writers also provide strong evidence that this challenge and testing was not a feature of the board; or, it would seem, of the accountants, bankers and analysts who so faithfully followed Enron into the abyss. As an instance, Andersen clearly knew of Enron's practices and even described aspects of them as 'intelligent gambling', but, after having decided to make some suggestions to Enron in order to mitigate their concerns, when asked they said nothing (*ibid*.: 229).

It is clear that the aspect of leadership that Badaracco and Ellsworth hold dear – a desire that high ethical standards pervade the company – is the one that is found wanting in Lay, Skilling, Fastow and the members of the board. For

Badaracco and Ellsworth ethical standards are the crucial links between leaders' aims for their organizations, on the one hand, and their own personal beliefs and actions, on the other. The values that Badaracco and Ellsworth hold to be important to the promotion of high ethical standards are 'honesty, fairness, mutual respect and trust, and compassion and sensitivity in the exercise of power' (Badaracco and Ellsworth 1989: 104). Lay claimed that fairness and honesty were the watchwords of Enron, but, as others have claimed since Enron's fall, unfairness and dishonesty may well have been the order of the day within the company (Cruver 2002: 333). Rupert Cornwell writes about an investigation into Enron's tax avoidance that it apparently included the bribing of tax officials. He reports the words of a Republican Senator who claimed that the tax avoidance schemes read like the plot 'of a conspiracy novel' (Cornwell 2003: 21). Enron's treatment of its own employees when bankruptcy loomed – reneging on its pledge to meet the terms of their individual employment contracts and restricting their rights to cash in the value of their Enron stock until it was worthless – is seen to indicate the senior management's lack of fairness (Bryce 2002: 2–10). More than one commentator has noted that the senior managers realized much of the value of their own share options shortly before the steep decline in the share price set in.

I could go on citing instances, but the story is by now becoming well known. Clearly the leadership of Enron is seen to fall well short of the characteristics that Badaracco and Ellsworth deem to be necessary for a high achieving company. Were they to take a look at Enron I feel that they would probably concur with Bryce's judgement that 'Enron failed because its leadership was morally and ethically corrupt' (2002: 12).

Comment

But are the criteria and the standards promulgated by Badaracco and Ellsworth the ones that should be adopted in considering the behaviour of employees of Enron? Here I will argue that morality and ethical behaviour are usually situated socially within distinct communities and culturally within particular structures of moral reasoning and practice. Badaracco and Ellsworth derived their theories from and tested them with managers and leaders whose heyday – by and large – was in the twenty or thirty years after the Second World War. Enron's brief time was – effectively – that of the last six years of the century. I will argue that the ethos of these two periods was different; that what was required of Badaracco's generation of leaders was different from what was required of the generation to which Enron's leaders belonged and that the ethical foundations of the two periods differ. I will begin with some examples that illustrate the moral reasoning and practice of Enron.

All three of writers with whom I began this chapter make some reference to the circumstances in which Enron employees found themselves. Cruver (or his editor), writing on his book jacket, notes 'the insidious group-think that made Enron employees unquestioningly accept propaganda' and attributes it to having been 'spoon-fed [to the employees] by Ken Lay and Jeffrey Skilling' (Cruver 2002: jacket blurb). Elsewhere Cruver makes a direct reference to the power of the immediate situation that he and the other writers speak of as corporate culture: 'For those who argue that companies are "controlled" by people, I refer them to Exhibit X: Enron. The people were "controlled" by the company' (*ibid.*: 343). In an interesting insider's view of the company he offers many insights into the culture. It is Fox, however, who writes in more systematic way about the culture of the company. He notes that by the mid-1990s the trading floors physically dominated the entire organization. He describes a 'football-field-sized' office in which, 'yelling and gesturing with the cockiness most associated with traders of stocks and bonds, the employees were constantly working their phones' (Fox 2003: 77). He claims that there was a culture of risk-taking and greed, and depicts it as a highly competitive environment in which success was richly rewarded and failure meant a quick exit from the company. There was a heavy emphasis upon short-term results. Deal originators and traders looked to maximize their profits on a deal before they moved on to another business unit within the company. He describes the twice-yearly performance reviews in which colleagues as well as superiors rated each other as having a 'harsh Darwinian twist' – those ranked in the top 5 per cent move onwards and upwards, those in the bottom 20 per cent were marked for dismissal (*ibid.*: 83). He goes on to quote Skilling's proud boast that '[o]ur culture is a tough culture. It is a very aggressive, very urgent organization' (*ibid.*: 86). Enron, it seemed, was always in the throes of fundamental reorganization. Fox sums up the culture as one of putting profit first, a circumstance in which Enron hired smart people, gave them responsibility, set them to work in a highly competitive environment and rigorously ranked their performance. Those who did not make the numbers were shown the door, a procedure which created a highly stressful workplace where some simply 'wanted to make their mark' and move on. This, Fox concludes, simply 'accentuated Enron's tendency to focus on the short-term' (*ibid.*: 88).

Not surprisingly, this 'trading culture' often appeared to conflict with RICE – the company's statement of values – and with its code of ethics. Bryce and Cruver are by turns scathing and cynical about the failure of the company to live up to its espoused ideals, but it is Fox who cites chapter and verse. He notes that Enron employees occasionally sabotaged each other's work and – more frequently – that competition for bonuses resulted in 'the compartmentalization of the company into competing fiefdoms' (*ibid.*: 85). Elsewhere he asserts that, although Enron managers talked up the core values, in fact these same people often displayed 'arrogance and ruthlessness' that went against the 'respect' value, and that the way that individuals and units were rewarded led to the 'communication' value coming under severe pressure (*ibid.*: 79). As I have indicated above, integrity, honesty and fairness appear to have been similarly traduced. No one spoke publicly about these departures from the published code until the company came on hard times. I will spell this out with reference to a specific instance of behaviour that – *after* the demise of the company – was held to be deceitful.

All the world's a stage

Both Cruver and Davies offer a description of what happened at an analysts' conference to launch Enron Energy Services (EES) in 1998 (Cruver 2002: 273; Davies 2002: 43). The problem for Enron was that the EES was not up and running in time for the conference. The response was to create and show the analysts around a 'fake dealing room where Enron employees were choreographed to simulate trading months before the room went operational'. An entire floor of the headquarters building was gutted and fitted out with 'over £350,000 worth of screens and computing equipment to make a "war room" to wow Wall Street' (Davies 2002: 43). With Skilling, Lay and other members of senior management leading the way, 'the analysts were brought through the trading floor', where the people at the machines and manning the phones were 'urged to look like they were putting deals together' (Cruver 2002: 273). It is claimed that the performance, which had been rehearsed with the staff by Lay and Skilling the day before the analysts were due, lasted barely ten minutes. It worked. The analysts were impressed and went away happy.

The fake conference took place in 1998. Those outside Enron only became aware of it in late 2001/early 2002. Cruver was not part of the company in 1998, but he heard about it from others when he joined Enron and *later* wrote about it as an example of deceitful behaviour. As I have indicated, Davies considers it a 'scam' although he also is writing long after the event. Somewhere between a couple of dozen and a couple of hundred people could well have been involved in the activity. It is not known if any one of those involved in the performance regarded it as deceitful or as a scam when they did what their leaders required of them. However, at the time it occurred, no one appeared to tip off the analysts, no one blew the whistle, and no one – as far as has been made known – refused to take part.

Extrapolating from this incident, thousands of employees were party to other aspects of Enron's behaviour that have now been declared to be 'deceitful' and 'corrupt', and again – as far as is known – no more than a handful appear to have questioned it, not one of them blew the whistle publicly and only a few walked away from the company

There could be a number of explanations for this: personal ambition, fear of the management, cynicism, etc. I want to suggest that perhaps the reason that no one did speak out was because they saw no reason to do so. That there was in fact little or no conflict between the thoughts and practices of Enron leaders *and* employees and the values and ways of interacting approved of by the wider community. It is possible that the trading culture of Enron, with its emphasis upon behaving ruthlessly, upon risk, aggression, individualism, competitiveness and short-term results overwhelmed the publicly declared values of the company because it was fully in accord with the ethos which dominated (and continues to dominate) the moral reasoning and practice of a large number of companies and a growing number of governments in the last decade of the twentieth century – an ethos given impetus by Margaret Thatcher's infamous declaration that 'there is no such thing as society'. I derive the notion of ethos from the work of Adam Morton, who argues that crucial aspects of our understanding of one another work because they are shared (Morton 2003: 175–8). Morton argues persuasively that in order to interact successfully with one another we must have a shared conception of how to understand, and how to act so as to be understood. These factors he sees as closely linked to a shared conception of cooperation. This echoes some of the arguments of the symbolic interactionists, who would use terms such as the 'definition of the situation' and 'presentation of self' (Mangham 1986). In order to work successfully together we need to have a handle on one another's motives, character and action. A particular ethos will be recognized by a stable combination of explanatory devices, a set of values both acknowledged and implicit, and norms of action. And we should expect these combinations to vary from one time to another, from one place to another and from one social group to another. Thus the Athenians had a particular ethos – a perspective on the world and a consequent set of values and specific ways of behaving towards one another – and the Spartans had quite a different ethos. The managers from whom Badaracco and Ellsworth drew their framework had a way of perceiving, valuing and interacting, and Enron's generation of managers have quite another way.

The next few paragraphs draw extensively upon Khurana's excellent book on corporate leadership and upon my own work that looks at the financial institutions in the City of London before and after deregulation (Khurana 2002: Mangham 2003). The time in which Badaracco and Ellsworth's managers achieved their success was the time when the market was regulated, when foreign trade was relatively slight and international competition was in its infancy. A time when, as Khurana puts it: 'the steady visible hand of the professional trained manager directing the company towards long-term growth was seen to be the natural way to do things' (Khurana 2002: 53). The actions of these managers were constrained by the government, through regulatory authorities, by the unions and by the employees, with whom they were enmeshed – *inter alia* – by notions of trust and loyalty (Sennett 1998: 122). During the era of managerial capitalism, business may be seen to have been conducted within a set of generally accepted rules that maintained a relatively ordered, stable business environment, a circumstance in which managers did what was expected of them and were respected for it (Fligstein 1990). In short, an institutional structure obtained which – in theory at least – protected and represented the community, acted on its behalf and promoted public and social interests.

As I indicated earlier, for Badaracco and Ellsworth (1989) consistency was the essence of leadership. An effective leader was someone with the *character* to deny the shifting tides of varying situations. They use the term 'personality' interchangeably with 'character', but whenever they do so they are referring to persistent traits that are deeply ingrained in the individual. We speak of personality when our concern is how a person presents himself or herself to others (Quinton 1982: 21). Personality in most of its uses has to do with how one establishes oneself as different from other people. One can have a distinctive personality, but we do not speak of having a bad personality as we speak of people being of good or bad character. Character has moral overtones that the word personality lacks

(Kupperman 1991: 5). This is not to argue that morality is all there is to character, but it is to argue that in any account of character thoughts and actions that are related to moral choice would loom large (*ibid.:* 7). To have character is to act in such a way 'that the person one is plays a major role in any explanation of one's behaviour'. To lack character is 'to act in such a way that one's behaviour might be viewed as (at least approximately) the product of forces acting on one' (*ibid.:* 7). Character is a notion deriving from another millennium that argues for a bundle of enduring traits which are, generally, dispositions to have thoughts and feelings of a certain sort, and thus to act in certain ways (Aristotle 2000). As relatively perma-nent features of the individual's make-up, these dispositions will explain not merely why he/she acted in the way that they did, but why he/she can be counted on to act in a similar way in the future. The forces which inculcate character are primarily friends, the family and the community (Sherman 1989). And for Badaracco and Ellsworth's generation of leaders character clearly matters. Hunter (2000) outlines the importance of character to generations of Americans from the early revolutionaries through to the mid-twentieth century. Character was always related to an explicitly moral standard of conduct 'oriented toward work, building, expanding, achieving and sacrifice on behalf of a larger good' (*ibid.:* 7). By the mid-twentieth century the ethical requirements placed upon individuals began to change, with more emphasis being placed upon the cultivation of personal prefer-ences. The notion of personality began to replace that of character. Structural changes in the economy led to a greater emphasis upon self-expression, self-fulfilment and personal gratification (*ibid.:* 7).

This emphasis was dramatically reinforced in the last couple of decades of the twentieth century. Shareholder capitalism appears to have taken its toll on the moral life of society. Richard Sennett argues persuasively that what he terms 'flexible' or 'impatient capitalism' has corroded character. The aspects of char-acter that he sees as under attack are those that 'bind human beings together and furnish each with a sustainable self' (Sennett 1998: 17). He argues that the hall-marks of impatient capitalism are instability and uncertainty. Behaviour that earns success in the company offers little to the employee at home or in the community. Frequent job changes and consequent relocation mean that friends and communities no longer serve as witness to one's character. Families too cease to be reliable inculcators of morality. My own contribution to this debate has been to note that the threads of character may well have been further shredded by the wholesale embrace of the cult of individualism derived – directly or indi-rectly – from the writings of Nietzsche (Mangham 2003). The followers of Nietzsche welcome upheaval and the upsetting of social relations as 'harbingers of individualism' (Thiele 1990). The resultant ripping apart of the social strait-jacket liberates the individual from the morality of custom and renders him or her sovereign. He or she no longer has to follow the script written by others, but feels free to improvise.

Others have gone further and argued that character is dead (Himmelfarb 1995, 1999; Hunter 2000). Like Sennett, Himmelfarb regrets the loss of families, neighbourhoods and communities as moralizing forces. Citing Schumpeter's argument that the very entrepreneurial spirit that would ensure the triumph of capitalism would undermine the institutions that sustained it, she declares that the creative destruction of rampant capitalism has taken its toll on the moral life of society (Himmelfarb 1995, 1999). Hunter (2000), in his emphatic declaration of the death of character, regrets the loss of stable communities and blames the market economy and the demands of multinational capitalism for the changes that have arisen in the ethical standards of individuals. We are all now subject to an extraordinary diversity of information and communication and are influenced by lifestyles and ideas from well beyond our own communities, and some of us clearly identify with ethnic, religious, commercial and political groupings well beyond local and national borders. Globalization is 'hollowing out' states, eroding their sovereignty and autonomy. As Beck (1999) remarks, state institutions are increasingly like 'zombies' following the dictates of the global economy whilst failing to determine any substantive basis for enhancing public good. Enron's leaders and Enron's employees, like the rest of us, lack character. In effect, the terms of behaviour are now increasingly set by global markets and corporate enterprise. For Enron's generation of leaders and managers the world is not one of 'closed communities with mutually impenetrable ways of thought, self-sufficient economies and ideally sovereign states' (O'Neill 1991: 282). Ethical discourse – such as it is – has become separated from deliberations in families, communities and nations, but is developing at the intersection of relatively new institutions such as the World Trade Organization and the International Monetary Fund (Soros 2002; Singer 2002).

The ethos of managerial or gentlemanly capitalism has been replaced by an emerging individualistic, less community-centred set of explanations and values, and a brasher, harsher, more exploitative variety of interaction. Its essence is perhaps most clearly stated in a treatise published in America in 1994 by James Taggart and others, in which they argue that 'shareholders are not interested in what the company *per se* will look like in ten years'. They are only interested in one thing: 'How much wealth will the company create in the future? And that very simple unadorned question must be the chief executive's focus as well' (Taggart *et al.*, quoted in Roberts and Kynaston 2002: 146). These words are echoed in Samuel Brittain's assertion that, '[m]otivation apart, businessmen do not have the *knowledge* to advance the public interest directly and will serve their fellows best if they concentrate on maximising their shareholders' equity' (Brittain, quoted in Roberts and Kynaston 2002: 150). In pursuit of shareholder value, restrictions and laws have been torn up and deregulation – seen as the key to releasing the financial systems and the companies so that they could pursue wealth creation unfettered – has become the order of the day (Kynaston 2001). Quoting the words of Lord Desai – an eminent British economist – to the effect that there was really no choice, Richard Roberts and David Kynaston assert that an infinitely mobile, profit seeking international capitalism is the only game in town: 'It is whether to work with the grain of the system based on profitability…and follow policies which enhance rather than impede profitability, or go under' (Roberts and Kynaston 2002: 151).

The ethos of shareholder value marked by a determination to see and control what the organization is doing on almost a daily basis theoretically shifts some of the power from the managers and the board of directors to the investors, particularly the institutional investors. According to Roberts and Kynaston, by 2001 the major British companies were under 'far more intensive day-to-day shareholder scrutiny – scrutiny that was liable to turn to intervention – than had been the case even as recently as ten years earlier' (*ibid*.: 158). In turn, the senior management of the companies had to learn to deal with the analysts and the banks in a manner which they were not called upon to do in the era of managerial capitalism. What is more, they are to operate in an international arena that is focused upon wealth creation, where the fortunes of large companies are intimately connected with the prosperity of particular nations. Not surprisingly, politicians and the media show much greater interest in the fluctuations of their respective stock exchanges than they did several years ago.

This ethos demands a new type of leadership. In the brave new Darwinian world of shareholder capitalism there is a greater focus on the individual *leader*. He or she is no longer a *professional manager*. His/her role is to set the direction for the company, to motivate and energize the employees, but primarily to deal with the analysts, the accountants, the banks, the government authorities, the media, the public and – above all – to deliver ever richer dividends to the shareholders. Becoming a leader in this day and age is seen to be a matter of 'communicating an essential optimism, confidence and can-do attitude' (Khurana 2002: 71). Leaders have become much more visible, subject to much more comment from analysts, the business media and the gossip sheets; some, for example Richard Branson in the UK and Bill Gates in the US, have become celebrities. Some have become important players whose advice is sought by governments, and some pontificate at international economic forums.

A specialized market has arisen for such people. They are induced to take on the responsibilities by very large salaries, substantial bonuses and extensive stock options, as well as guaranteed redundancy/pension rights. Personality, image, dynamism and charisma are now the attributes that are seen to be the key criteria in selecting a leader. Khurana notes that as the emphasis on image-projection has become so prevalent in the selection of leaders, that head-hunters and search committees have tended to place less emphasis on factors such as industry experience or technical knowledge in evaluating candidates for the role of CEO (Khurana 2002: 79). The newer form of capitalism demands very different attributes from those sought in the days of managerial capitalism; those who appear truly at home in the new capitalism are 'those that signal a capacity to let go [their] past, a confidence to accept fragmentation and to dwell in disorder' (Sennett 1998: 23).

Conclusion

The picture of a late twentieth century business leader that emerges from the foregoing is that of a personality; someone who is paid a great deal of money to advance the interests of a limited number of large shareholders, which includes him/herself. He or she operates in a multinational structure and a cultural nexus that emphasizes individualism, aggression, ruthless behaviour, risk-taking, competitiveness and the importance of short-term results, whilst paying lip service to the moral dimension of business. Like Enron, many companies publish codes of ethics and offer high-flown descriptions of their purposes in their mission statements. Philip Morris, the cigarette manufacturer, for example, claims to be guided by the values of 'Integrity, trust, passion, creativity, quality and sharing'. Dupont does not just produce chemicals; instead, it is dedicated to 'the work of improving life on our planet' (Khurana 2002: 70). High-flown rhetoric perhaps, leaving some of us in no doubt that passion and creativity will be deployed to ensure that – come what may – the shareholders' interests will come before those of the planet. Leaders are not measured by vision, mission statements or codes of ethics, but like the wrapping on Christmas presents these serve as appropriate decoration. They are measured by the growth in shareholder value: 'everything in Enron is driven…by earnings per share' (Cruver 2002: 79). Not surprisingly, leaders give their full attention to that, proving the power of the adage: show me how someone is measured and I will show you how he/she will behave.

None of this is to suggest that leaders of companies such as Enron do not behave with integrity. Badaracco and Ellsworth's use of the term is one of approbation. Saying that the leaders from whom they took their cue show integrity is – for them – equivalent to saying that they are admirable people. That is certainly one meaning of the word, now well on the way to becoming redundant. Another meaning is 'the state of being whole and undivided' (*OED*). It is possible to argue that the leaders who are now somewhat hypocritically vilified for their actions in Enron and elsewhere were behaving in line with the ethos of the society in which they live; their actions could be seen to be fully in accord with the values which hitherto they were enthusiastically encouraged to embrace. It is important to remember that many of their actions were applauded by the accountants, the bankers, the analysts, the business academics, the media, the general public and – above all – the shareholders, large and small. Much of their behaviour was a matter of 'bending the rules', rather than of them acting illegally. Some of their behaviours were illegal and some of those who looked on approvingly were complicit with them in these actions. And Enron is not a case of one rotten apple in a barrel of good ones. Other scandals have come to light in the United States and in Europe in which similar characteristics have been observed. By February 2003 as many as 1,200 companies had been forced to restate their accounts. In late February 2003 Ahold – a Dutch company and the third biggest food retailer in the world – announced the resignation of its chief executive and finance director after finding that it had overstated its profits by the equivalent of $500 million. The *Economist* notes that,

> rather like Kenneth Lay at Enron, Ahold's departing boss was until the end lauded for turning a dull company into a growth machine. As with Enron

accounting rules were bent to give the impression that double-digit growth was continuing long after the company was actually in financial trouble. Accountants failed to pick up the deception and investors applauded long after they should have been asking hard questions.

(Economist 2003: 63)

As long as the current ethos prevails, leaders will continue to bend the rules and will be richly rewarded for it. They owe their appointments, their continued employment and their opportunity to make a great deal of personal wealth to their ability to hear and act upon the call for higher and higher returns for the shareholders. In obedience to this strident call it is hardly surprising that some have lied, cheated and manipulated information whilst others have looked on in barely suppressed admiration. There is little point in demanding that they behave more honourably in the future. Honour has little value in today's market place. Some commentators demand more regulation of the behaviour of all concerned: companies, banks, accountants, analysts, the media and the institutional shareholders. The United States has begun this process by rushing through the Sarbanes–Oxley Act, which provides rules for managers and boards, and they suggest that it be implemented throughout Europe, a proposal from the new world that is being actively resisted by the old one. The United Kingdom is notably dragging its business feet, wanting nothing to do with Sarbanes–Oxley and arguing about the recommendations put forward by the Higgs Report to regulate British boardrooms, with many leaders resisting these reforms in the same manner as they successfully resisted those put forward by the Cadbury Report in 1992 and those offered by the Hampel Report in 1998. On the other hand, statutory independent regulation of auditors is seen to make sense everywhere. There is also growing support for rules promoting the mandatory rotating of auditors and to prevent accounting firms from doing consulting work for audit clients (Economist 2003: 12).

The cynic within me argues that there are two problems with more rules and regulations: the first is that they simply offer more opportunities to bend or subvert them; the second is best summed up in the Latin tag *quis custodiet ipsos custodies?* – who is to control the authorities? Accountants are supposed to oversee company accounts, but driven by the same desire to maximize their own returns as their clients they may choose to sit upon their hands, turn a blind eye and keep their mouths shut. Although it is Andersen that shredded documents and that has gone to the wall with Enron, and it is Andersen that has been cited in a number of other scandals, most of the other large accounting firms have also been tarnished in the past year or so (Economist 2003: 12). Regulations spawn regulators and regulators spawn yet more regulations.

Regulators seek to control behaviour; educators seek to change it. In the wake of the Enron scandal some business schools have acknowledged culpability. They have recognized that they may have had some part in promoting the ruthless, aggressive turn that management and leadership took over the last decade of the twentieth century. Dennis Gioia notes that business schools do turn out a very skilled group of people, but acknowledges that some may leave the schools bereft of social responsibility (2002: 2). He believes that the business schools' contribution to making a change is to make corporate social responsibility and ethical practice a more significant part of the curriculum (*ibid.*: 5). It is perhaps somewhat ironic that one of the reasons he puts forward for it not being taken seriously is that ethics teaching is not one of the criteria that go into the rankings of business schools. As you are measured, so shall you behave? Others doubt that even well-taught courses will have an effect on the behaviour of would-be managers and leaders. Writing in the *Washington Post*, Etzioni pointed out that a recent Aspen Institute study covering 2,000 graduates of the top thirteen business schools in the US found that business school education 'not only fails to improve the moral character of the students, it actually weakens it'. Those believing that the prime responsibility of business is to maximize shareholder value went up from 62 per cent upon entrance to the schools to 82 per cent at the end of their first year (Etzioni 2002: BO4).

I will not conclude this chapter on a wholly negative note. Change may come – if change there is to be – from the institutional shareholders. Given the events that have been detailed here and the recent dramatic falls in share values around the world, it is possible that boards of directors will dispense with their high profile leaders. Two things may contribute to this seemingly unlikely outcome. First, it is a strong possibility that slower growth over the next few years will mean that everyone will have to get used to lower returns. Interest in the long-term growth of companies may become fashionable once more. This will promote very different measurements and hence different behaviours to those that were current until very recently. The market may well push boards of directors and executive-search firms into showing much less interest in high profile charismatic and highly costly *leaders* and into showing much more interest in less expensive or turbulent *managers* who have industry track records of quiet achievement (Mintzberg *et al.* 2002). In short, industry may well fall out of love with the whole notion of leadership, particularly when it comes to realize that what little research there is points to a relatively minor cause-and-effect relationship between leaders and company performance (Khurana 2002: 23). Secondly – and perhaps consequently – there may well be a growing realization of the damage Enron-type failures have done not just to the companies themselves, to their former employees, their shareholders and their bankers, but also to society as a whole. The future of all companies depends upon those who are prepared to join them, and the young may well turn out to be very careful about whom they choose to work for. Hamish McCrae sums it up well: 'Just as the 1930s unemployment encouraged young people to seek "safe" jobs, the end of 1990s excess will encourage them to seek "honourable" ones' (McCrae 2003).

Change may also be brought about by the growing demand to regulate the global economy. I do not think that more rules and greater regulation will produce integrity in the terms that Badaracco and Ellsworth would recognize. Like character, it may well be a notion whose time has passed. Both require anchoring in a particular community at a particular time. When leaders are stripped of moral anchoring there is nothing to which they are bound to submit, nothing engraved within them to keep them in check. What is needed is the development of global ethics for a global community in parallel with and informing global regulation of the market (Soros 2002; Singer 2002). There is already a demand for closer scrutiny and closer regulation of the relations between companies and their stakeholders: employees, shareholders, suppliers, customers, communities, societies and those representing the environment (Stiglitz 2002). The purpose of such scrutiny and regulation should be to ensure that companies meet their obligations to all concerned. Profit seeking in the interests of shareholders alone need not be the only game in town.

At the moment, however, perhaps the best hope lies with the people at Davos, both those inside the compound and those outside it. Post-Enron there may be a surprising consensus emerging. Commentators and regulators, consultants and shareholders, thoughtful business people and academics appear to be united in the view that all those concerned in commerce and business should indeed behave differently in the future. Beyond the wire fences, the demonstrators against capitalism and globalization have been growing in number and sophistication. Who knows, in the next couple of years they may be all inside the wire involved in a more productive dialogue. We may be on the cusp of a new ethos. Only time will tell.

References

Aristotle (2000) *Nicomachean Ethics*, Cambridge: Cambridge University Press

Augur, P. (2000) *The Death of Gentlemanly Capitalism*, London: Penguin Books.

Badaracco, J.L.E. and Richard R. Ellsworth (1989) *Leadership and the Quest for Integrity*, Boston, MA: Harvard Business School Press.

Beck, U. (1999) *What is Globalization*, Cambridge: Polity.

Bryce, R. (2002) *Pipe Dreams: Greed, Ego and the Death of Enron*, Oxford: Public Affairs Ltd.

Cornwell, R. (2003) 'US threatens post-Enron corporate tax clampdown', *Independent*, 14 February.

Cruver, B. (2002) *The Anatomy of Greed: The Unshredded Truth*, London: Hutchinson.

Davies, R. (2002) 'How Enron wowed Wall Street with a fake dealing room', *Evening Standard*, 21 February.

Economist (2003) 'Ahold: Europe's Enron', *Economist*, 1 March.

Etzioni, A. (2002) 'A few lessons in right thinking', *Washington Post*, 4 August.

Fligstein, N. (1990) *The Transformations of Corporate Control*, Cambridge, MA: Harvard University Press.

Fox, Loren (2003) *Enron: The Rise and Fall*, Hoboken, NJ: John Wiley & Sons.

Gioia, D. (2002) 'Business education's role in the crisis of corporate confidence,' comments, National Academy of Management Meeting, Denver, CO, 11 August.

Himmelfarb, G. (1995) *The De-moralization of Society*, London: IEA Health and Welfare Unit.

—— (1999) *One Nation, Two Cultures*, New York: Alfred A. Knopf.

Hunter, J. Davison (2000) *The Death of Character: Moral Education in an Age without Good or Evil*, New York: Basic Books.

Khurana, R. (2002) *Searching for the Corporate Savior*, Princeton, NJ: Princeton University Press.

Kupperman, J. (1991) *Character*, New York: Oxford University Press.

Kynaston, D. (2001) *The City of London: A Club No More 1945–2000*, London: Chatto & Windus.

Lambert, R. (2002) 'Are Wall Street's ethics dead?', *The Times*, 8 October.

McCrae, H. (2003) 'Trust is a vital part of good business', *Independent*, 18 January.

Mangham, I.L. (1986) *Power and Performance in Organisations*, Oxford: Blackwell.

—— (2003) 'Character and virtue in an era of turbulent capitalism', in H. Tsoukas and C. Knudsen (eds) *The Oxford Handbook of Organization Theory: Meta-Theoretical Perspectives*, Oxford: Oxford University Press.

Mintzberg, H., R. Simons and K. Basu (2002) 'Beyond selfishness', *Sloan Management Review* 44(1): 67–74.

Morton, A. (2003) *The Importance of Being Understood: Folk Psychology as Ethics*, London: Routledge.

O'Neill, B. (1991) 'Transnational justice', in D. Held (ed.) *Political Theory Today*, Cambridge: Polity.

Quinton, A. (1982) *Thoughts and Thinkers*, Oxford: Oxford University Press.

Roberts, R. and D. Kynaston (2002) *City State: A Contemporary History of the City of London and How Money Triumphed*, London: Profile Books.

Sennett, R. (1998) *The Corrosion of Character: The Personal Consequences of Work in the New Capitalism*, New York: W.W. Norton & Company.

Sherman, N. (1989) *The Fabric of Character: Aristotle's Theory of Virtue*, Oxford: Clarendon Press.

Singer, P. (2002) *One World: The Ethics of Globalization*, New Haven, CT: Yale University Press.

Soros, G. (2002) *George Soros on Globalization*, Oxford: Public Affairs Ltd.

Stiglitz, J. (2002) *Globalization and Its Discontents*, London: Allen Lane.

Thiele, L.P. (1990) *Friedrich Nietzsche and the Politics of the Soul*, Princeton, NJ: Princeton University Press.

Usborne, D. (2002) 'Truth or consequences time for the chiefs of corporate America', *Independent*, 8 October.

4 Competences of managers, competences of leaders

Graeme Salaman

The nature of management and managers and of leaders and leadership is highly problematic: there is no agreed view on what managers or leaders should do and what they need to do it. And there never can be, since such definitions arise not from organizational or technical requirements (which are themselves the product of managers' theories of organization), but from the shifting ways in which over time these functions are variously conceptualized. The manager, as much as the worker, is a product of history.

Yet although in any particular epoch of management thinking the necessary morality, competence and character of these critical organizational roles and types may seem obvious and overwhelming – supported by all the weight of airport bookstall analysis, media insistence and business school courses – the obviousness and dominance of such definitions should warn us of their precariousness. The character and technical requirements of those who direct and manage businesses are the subject of intense and purposeful ideological – and ultimately managerial and expert – activity as different philosophies of or approaches to management define the nature and tasks of management and the attributes necessary for successful managers. And such philosophies or discourses of management do not stop merely at definition. They are real, being supported by processes and frameworks of recruitment, measurement, promotion, development: selection, assessment frameworks, psychometrics and expert advisers (recruitment consultants, occupational psychologists).

This chapter is not concerned to advocate or advance the achievement of such persons. These concerns are for others. Clearly there is a large literature devoted to the advocacy of these approaches, supported by considerable training and consultancy activity from business schools and commercial organizations. The concerns of this chapter are to understand the ways in which conceptions of the desired character of the manager have varied with changing regimes of organization and with wider discourses of power and government.

Much recent work on these issues has addressed changes in conceptions of government, organization and employee arising from the dominance of an apparent anti-bureaucracy project advocating the new morality and value of enterprise. And if the contemporary organization is no longer conceptualized as a pyramid or bureaucracy but as a 'web of enterprise', then the new manager must demonstrate the appropriate qualities of entrepreneurial character.[1] But how is this new manager to be achieved? And what purposes and benefits support such efforts? Little is known of these matters.

Bendix's classic study (Bendix 1956) sets the scene for such analyses, which is the starting point for the analysis of this chapter: 'the role of ideas in the management of economic enterprises' (*ibid.*: 1). More recently writers such as Jacques (1996), Rose and Miller (1988), Du Gay (1991), Rose (1990), Guest (1990), Miller and Rose (1993), du Gay and Salaman (1992) have analysed the nature and pervasive impact on both organization and employees of wider societal discourses of enterprise and the market. As well as plotting the impact of the content and logic of such discourses – especially the discourse of enterprise – for organization and employee subjectivity, these studies also focus on their role in achieving and legitimating power within the organization – governmentality – and on the links between these themes (Rose 1990).

This chapter will add detail to these analyses of the linkages and alignments between these three levels through an analysis of the recent ways in which the nature, tasks, concerns and required skills and attributes of management have been defined and constructed through management competences, with particular attention to the implications and functions of such regimes of management.[2]

This analysis must address a number of key factors.

First, an historical perspective is important. If distinctive, discrete and coherent approaches to the definition of management and managers (regimes of management) can be seen to vary over time, then the possibility arises that successive regimes of management must be seen not only in terms of their connections with and dependence on contemporary societal overarching structures of meaning (which supply crucial legitimacy), but also in terms of the ways in which they address the deficiencies of, or in other ways relate dynamically to, the previous regime of management or the demands of new, emerging and changing organizational forms.

Second, as noted above, recent approaches to changing conceptions of the moral character and technical proficiencies of those who direct and manage organizations have largely focused on the links between such definitions of managers and wider societal regimes of truth; the latter supplying critical underpinning and legitimacy for the former. Such analysis is necessary and valuable. Recent work by the author and Paul du Gay, for example, seeks to show affinities between recent widely prevalent discourses of management which stress at the management level the critical role of enterprise, strategic thinking, concern for improvement, customer focus and commerciality, and prevailing overarching discourses of organization and government which define market structures, relationships and principles as moral standards essential for the achievement of organizational effectiveness and efficiency (du Gay *et al.* 1996). Work by David Guest (1992) and Brad Jackson (1996), among others, charts the ways in which the appeal of various forms of management thought derives from the way these ideas claim connections with prevailing core values, logics and assumptions.

Thinking on organization and on the nature of managers within models of organization is unquestionably influenced by such discourses. Current difficulties in imagining – far less creating – effective and efficient organizations within the public sector in the UK, for example, arise from the unwillingness to identify and confront contradictory ideological assumptions which exist simultaneously within current approaches to organizational thinking.

Analysis of higher order resonances and alignment (by virtue of which a particular conception of management and managers gains legitimacy and purchase by its affinities with wider discourses) needs to be complemented by discussion of the ways in which these particular conceptions of organization and management are employed in practical circumstances by senior members of organizations in pursuit of their objectives. This involves an attempt to identify and locate the ways in which particular (i.e. current) conceptions of managers and management are realized and translated in practical organizational contexts by senior managers seeking to use these in the achievement of wider organizational purposes.

But there is more to it than this: the function of a regime of management may mean more than simply the purposes senior managers pursue. It means identifying the regime's purposes and affinities at a broader level by focusing on the ways in which its underlying logic and assumptions – the core argument – of a regime of management as a whole has attractions and benefits; for example because of their perceived potential role for solving or reducing identified organizational weaknesses.

These issues will be explored through analyses of two recent developments in the definition of the tasks, character and attributes of those who direct and manage organizations: an analysis of the nature, application and implication of a definition of managers in terms of management competences, and an analysis of current views of the transformational organizational leader.

Redefining the competent manager

Management competences are distinguished by their advocates from previous attempts to define the nature and requirements of management through a focus on what managers have to do and be in order to do their jobs well, rather than on the qualities or qualifications necessary to enter a managerial role: that is, on behaviour rather than qualities.. The original, widely used competence modelling methodology proposed by Boyatzis (1982) derives from a psychological model of the individual developed by McClelland (1961). Consultancy companies, including Boyatzis' and McClelland's own, have conducted research programmes to define the behaviours and actions that distinguish and differentiate high performing managers in the view of their peers (see, especially, Boyatzis 1982; Lucia and Lepringer 1999). Competences are presented as enabling senior managers to recruit and promote on a more 'scientific' basis, and so, it is suggested, provide an externally validated, internally legitimate system to identify and assess individuals. Competences represent a comprehensive and expert way in which management and managers are rendered knowable and therefore open to new forms of intervention, analysis and modification.

The competence approach has proved enormously appealing. Its claimed scientificity is an attraction. So is its claim to focus on behaviour ('outputs') rather than on characteristics which are claimed to determine – and thus be used to predict – behaviour ('inputs'), for this in theory allows all managers the opportunity to become what is required of them. There are other attractions which this chapter explores below. But, like all such schemes, the essence of competences is that they supply a means for systematic comparison and measurement – between people, between people and jobs, and between the same person at different points in time – and thus constitute a basis for understanding and assessing people and for necessary action on them.

Competence research project

In a recent research project Paul du Gay and I explored the nature of management competences in four case study organizations, investigating the purpose behind their installation and use and the implications of their use.[3]

The main cases consisted of a health trust (HealthCo), a cosmetics retailer (CosmeticsCo), a university (EducationCo) and a publicly owned communications organization (CommunicationsCo).

How competences are used

Competences and competence frameworks were used to establish job descriptions, performance standards and route maps for career planning, to establish the requirements and standards of jobs by providing generic standards by which jobs could be defined and compared, performance could be assessed, personal development organized, training designed, promotion decided.

This integrative possibility was explicitly seen to supply a 'common language'[4] that enables discussion with a common set of performance and normative standards:

> One of the great things is that it is a language that you can use to talk about things, in a way that has some commonality. We have been doing a kind of ongoing review of the whole management development architecture and we have been using competencies as one of the binding pieces of that, as a language and framework to put things into context. Clearly it is the attitude of the people, and I think competencies are very powerful in that way, in describing what you want people to do, and also to get the right individuals in the right positions.
>
> (Senior Manager, CommunicationsCo)

Organizational government – like other forms – requires that a means of representation is developed within which the issues in question (strategic purpose, legitimacy, the role and nature of managers, performance problems) are described, known and constructed in a form which makes intervention logical and legitimate. Competences supply such a language.

Senior managers in this company acknowledged that the competences would be used to assist each individual's self-assessment, initially alone, then with the manager. This process would lead towards the generation of the 'Holy Grail – a way of achieving organizational capabilities through the definition of individual capabilities', as one senior manager put it – a mechanism to shape the conduct and attitudes of individual managers while preserving their apparent autonomy and discretion – an achievement that Miller and Rose (1993) describe as 'action at a distance' – which promote the purposes of the powerful through mechanisms which ensure the appropriate yet autonomous behaviour of subordinates.

At HealthCo all management roles were profiled in terms of the necessary level of competence required in defined fields. This framework then provided the basis for integration of all aspects of the organization's human resource (HR) activities: recruitment, selection, appraisal, training and development, career planning and job evaluation. Each competence had an associated development strategy, and this process was thought to provide a 'tool' for people to identify their job requirements and development needs. All managers were assessed against the competence profile of their jobs, and each had a competence-based development plan.

The chief executive's intentions were clear: 'The whole process is to make the organization move forward to meet the business objectives of the Trust...the (competences) will be used to ensure that people meet those objectives.'

Furthermore, it was intended that as the needs of the organization continue to change, the actual content of the competences would be changed to meet these new needs.

The chief executive officer (CEO) made it clear that the competences were developed to integrate what the organization was trying to achieve through the development of a basic structure which would allow all key aspects of organizational functioning to be in line with organizational objectives. They were seen as fundamental to the achievement of a basic change of focus (or change of culture) – from a 'professionally driven service' to a 'customer driven service' – this change was seen as necessary in order to succeed competitively and to achieve the business plan. Specifically, the competences were developed in order to force the organization to focus on the new strategy – to focus on customers' needs, to satisfy these needs, to develop new ways of working (more flexible, integrated, more teamwork), and to do this within reduced budgets. All these priorities were seen as sharply different from traditional, professional values, which had dominated the NHS previously.

> [HealthCo] was totally resistant to change – dinosaurs, left wing and elitist – but demarcations are slowly blurring and we are challenging their [clinicians'] practices so that people are beginning to think differently. The type of manager that the competences encourage is someone who understands the vision of the business, and the strategies of the business and who

achieves these through the people s/he manages. This isn't how managers behave at the moment. [The competences] are a major element in the attempt to control and shift power from the professionals, and to place emphasis on new organizational values.

(CEO, HealthCo)

At HealthCo competences were seen as a way to redefine and clarify management roles, enabling managers to assess their development within the new framework. The benefits for the organization were presented primarily in terms of senior roles being more 'aligned' with the new business objectives, standards and values. Managerial performance could be tracked against these new and explicit requirements through the shared language of the competences. Competences were thus intended to provide a link between business objectives, role requirements and individual development.

The competencies are about the behaviour that we believe will enable us to succeed – the commercial behaviours, the marketing behaviours, the team building behaviours.

(CEO, HealthCo)

The actual competences developed within HealthCo are typical. A total of 34 competences were 'identified' and organized under four families or headings: marketing, team effectiveness, personal effectiveness and service implementation. These were subdivided into sets of specific constituent competences. For example, marketing consists of nine specifics, including 'living the aims and values', 'building credibility' and 'meeting agreed service requirements'. Each competence is presented at six gradated levels, all of which are specified in concrete, behavioural terms. For example 'living the aims and values' level one is: 'shows sincerity, demonstrates loyalty to others, gets involved, behaves consistently, engenders trust.'

At EducationCo the competences were identified in four clusters, each subdivided into constituent competences in the usual way:

- interpersonal: leadership, communication skills, team membership;
- visionary: strategic vision, flexibility and adaptability, and managing change;
- information: analytical skills, external focus, student, client and customer orientation;
- results orientation: motivation and drive, business awareness and technological awareness.

Each competence was associated with a list of positive and negative behaviours to make assessment easier. These competences supplied a basis for discussion of organizational objectives and the necessary managerial qualities and requirements and how these were interrelated. They were also used to understand and make explicit and manageable the implications of potentially radical organizational change for senior management roles and skills.

Why competences were used

At EducationCo competences were used to guide selection for senior management posts. The self-assessment of senior managers conditioned their development and training, allowed assessments for career planning and the identification of a pool of selected managers for succession planning. They enabled the design of an integrated competence architecture:

> It is embedded in a whole process of change, where things are building on each other, and gradually making the whole thing more systematic, rational, and describable.
>
> (Vice-chancellor, EducationCo)

At CosmeticsCo, competences were launched as an integral aspect of a new appraisal system. At workshops participants were informed of the required competences for each role, and asked to consider their relevance and application to the organizational mission statement, departmental objectives and key tasks in order to forge a connection between role content, the behaviours or competences of each role, and organizational objectives. Although they were initially used as a way of making performance appraisal more systematic and better aligned with corporate goals, it was expected that the competences would soon be incorporated into guidelines for selection and succession planning:

> People are very excited about it, the ability to tie it in with the values process. How do we train all the values, how do you integrate it into daily life? There was a very favourable reaction to the possibility of integrating that initiative into the competence programme. It is almost a very subtle, imperceptible change. It is imperceptible from day to day, but you would expect some of that kind of level of values and social changes. Whether it would be worth the investment, or the training process involved, I don't know, but then again it is about how you change people's fundamental nature.
>
> (Head of Corporate Services, CosmeticsCo)

The design and deployment of competences in these organizations reveal a number of important developments.

First, in all research organizations senior management were clear that the design and installation of competences represented an attempt to engage deliberately with the subjectivity of their managers:

> We'll be explaining the model in terms of the importance of behaviour, and how it is important to consider the way you do things, as opposed to just doing them.
>
> (Senior Manager, HealthCo)

Concentration on the attitudinal aspects of managing implied that functional control and hierarchical command were no longer a sufficient basis for management control, if they ever were. Foucault has argued that forms of power become effective when forms of subjectivity are constructed which are consistent with the logic of the form of power (Foucault 1980). Competences illustrate this. What was required was self-control, self-regulation in the service of organizational purpose. The competence project illustrates this but adds the further refinement that managers become responsible for ensuring their compliance with the new competences: with self-regulation. It seems that 'becoming a competent manager is equated with becoming a better, more autonomous, accountable self' (du Gay *et al.* 1996: 275).

Further, competences could be used to erode undesirable sectional affiliations and to replace them with organizational commitment. Managers at HealthCo perceived competences as a means of weakening the professional identity of some employees, such as information technology (IT) workers. They were expected to 'move from expert to market focus', as part of the organization's reorientation towards the customer.

Second, as part of the focus on subjectivity, competences were seen to allow organizational expectations to be more clearly allocated to individuals, and to enable individuals to be assessed and described in terms of organizational goals. They supplied a relay between organization and individual whereby organizational requirements and priorities could be transmitted to individuals by defining, measuring, developing and assessing individuals in terms of characteristics and attributes (behaviour) which are closely derived from wider organizational values and priorities:

> I am looking to use competencies as a means of having a much clearer idea about what we expect of people. Organizations generally are nowhere near specific enough…[we need] to be far more specific about what we are looking for and targeting, so that it can be assessed.
>
> (Senior Manager, CosmeticsCo)

Competences make available a way of talking about what managers need to be able to do to manage well. This language is supported by an infrastructure of frameworks and processes of assessment, training, appraisal, recruitment, promotion, etc. It allows translation between individual and organization, while at the same time defining this process of translation (which of course displays the play of power and ideology) as a neutral and technical and authoritative process safely removed not only from the vulnerabilities of intuition or subjectivity but, more crucially, from politics or power. This language, once imposed and established, neutralizes politics in the name of science and expertise; eliminates sectionalism in the name of shared organization-wide goals and purposes; and replaces subjective assessment by universal criteria. Best of all, it requires that members of the organization become masters of the language which redefines them – fluent speakers – and by so doing ensures that they manage their own redefinition:

It takes away a lot of the subjectivity in terms of how people are perceived or judged, and it helps also identify negative staff. The other thing I like about competencies is that there are a lot of elements of attitude contained within it…it maybe sort of helps people to analyse themselves.

(Senior Manager, HealthCo)

Shared language not only makes things discussible; it also defines the language *group*: members and outsiders. Senior managers presented the implementation of competence frameworks as establishing an organizationally specific language, one which applied to the particular needs of the organization but which also established membership of the organization: it defined boundaries, and by 'ruling in' certain ways of thinking about and assessing managers it also 'ruled out' alternative means:

I believe that most employees ought to know where they stand from the organization in terms of the areas they need to develop, and in terms of the organization understanding them, for the organization to make best use of them. Competencies let you know that you are part of an organization.

(Senior Manager, HealthCo)

Third, in all the research organizations the management competences were clearly and centrally connected by senior management to their intentions to achieve wide-ranging organizational change, which in every case involved a move away from bureaucratic and centralized forms of control to self-regulation and empowerment within a market focused context.

The development of management competences by the central HR function of CommunicationsCo was a key response to newly established strategic business units (SBUs), which had been allocated a degree of autonomy managed through tightly defined performance criteria. The establishment of SBUs was recognized as a potential source of divisiveness ('silo thinking'), and the competence framework was intended to reduce this by the development of a single set of generic competences as 'a strong unifying factor' to establish a shared understanding of standards and expectations. The competences were presented as closely connected to the achievements of the strategic objectives; business targets were established within the business planning cycle according to a framework that supported the overall objectives through profit targets, cost ratios, business volumes and incomes, and customer and staff satisfaction levels. The competences were seen as a way of connecting individual behaviour to the achievement of these targets by defining and encouraging appropriate sorts of behaviour.

At CommunicationsCo, four objectives were used to ensure the value and relevance of the individual competences: that they enable the business to develop timely and appropriate training to support business objectives; that they encourage managers to develop a sense of 'ownership' of their own (appropriate) development; that they enable the effectiveness of training and development initiatives to be measured and assessed; and that they make available to staff a set of standards that enable them to 'know what they are there to do', as well as how to do it:

> At the point of privatization, we inherited an organization built on technical excellence – engineers, predominantly. Now the pressure is on because we have introduced performance related pay, which demands a lot of interaction. For people who in the past would have little or no contact on that basis, it is challenging. We had a totally new range of skills to acquire that we never needed before; we had a new management style. Managers were also involved in 'getting people out' and counselling, and again new skills were needed. There have been massive changes, and some managers are struggling to change. Hopefully the ones that are left won't find it too difficult.
>
> (Senior Manager, CommunicationsCo)

Similarly, at HealthCo senior managers were under pressure to respond positively to the internal market in healthcare provision. State policy changes brought devolved budgets and required a higher degree of management involvement in previously centralized planning and budgeting. At operational level employees were formed into independent multidisciplinary teams, and the new chief executive aspired to change the trust into an organization where, as he put it, 'people moved faster, were more flexible and less expensive'. He wanted to use competences to 'break down traditional demarcations, destroy bureaucracy and change the culture'. Competences were developed in an attempt to achieve the organization's goals by developing a basic guiding structure to align the organization's objectives with individuals' behaviours. The introduction of the framework was not welcomed through the organization:

> My [first reaction to competencies] was 'oh my God, not another thing'. When competencies were first talked about, we were in at the deep end in terms of development, new structures – a lot of changes.
>
> (Personnel Manager, HealthCo)

The competences framework was connected to the achievement of a fundamental change of strategic focus – 'from a professionally driven service to a customer driven service' (as the chief executive put it). Competences were presented as a means to encourage managers to focus on customers' needs, and to develop new, more flexible ways of working within reduced budgets. The 'new manager' – *pace* the competences – was someone who understood the vision of HealthCo, its strategies, and who could achieve high performance through the people s/he managed. The new values operationalized through the competences were seen as quite distinct from traditional, professional healthcare sector values:

> [The aim of implementing competencies] is to ensure that everyone within the trust is giving an effective contribution to the business of the trust, to change the culture of the organization from one of public body to a culture

which is more businesslike and more customer orientated. If we don't provide the service, then somebody else will and we will be out of business.

(HR Manager, HealthCo)

The development of competences at EducationCo was also explicitly linked to wider changes, among which were increased competition for students, new technological developments and increased cost pressures. Changes in the higher education market (*sic*) required a speed of organizational response which in turn made the link between senior management capability and sustained organizational performance all the more critical; it was thought that management competences enabled this linkage. The stated purposes of the competences were: to identify the qualities necessary for current and future university needs; to ensure that these formed the basis of assessment and development of senior managers; and to ensure 'the continuing capability and readiness of the university and its individual units and managers to manage effectively in a rapidly changing environment'. The market orientation of the competence framework was succinctly set out by the personnel manager at EducationCo:

> There are people around, senior managers, that are notorious for not declaring their incompetencies. It is only when you say, 'Describe what you are doing here', it is only when you actually say, 'Okay, explain it to me, what is meant by a balance sheet', you suddenly realize that these people have been using this language and they haven't a bloody clue what it means.
>
> (Personnel Manager, EducationCo)

At CosmeticsCo, the primary rationale given for the introduction of competences was to answer the need to build a coherent and equitable structure for a rapidly growing business. The competences were seen as a way of building an HR strategy, providing a unifying logic for the first time. Thus the competence framework was presented as a way of increasing overall organizational effectiveness by supplying a basis for the systematization of the organization's previously ad hoc recruitment, selection, assessment and appraisal. Again, as in all four of our case study organizations, the competent manager was defined through character. And character was defined in terms of accepting and taking responsibility for self-regulation within a competence framework:

> We have got 'personal quality' as one category. People talk about the need to be enthusiastic; if you want to be highly effective in your job, you need to take the initiative and be self-confident.
>
> (HR Manager, CosmeticsCo)

Management competences and the new organization

Managerial interest in identifying and implementing management competences was closely linked to organizational restructuring and change projects of different types, and in particular with programmes of culture change and attempts to make the organization more competitive, more efficient and more market focused. Attempts to move away from hierarchy and bureaucracy towards more responsive, client-centred, commercially focused forms of organization were described as being radically opposed to the previous emphasis on bureaucratic values of standardization, central control and uniformity. The managerial qualities previously valued were overturned and redefined by the newly defined and discovered competences, which were seen as seen as critical to the achievement of the new organization and the new strategy.

The link between competences and organizational change is highly political. One manifestation of this is the way the competences are defined by those who define and install them as entirely non-political. Competence frameworks disguise or assume key organizational assumptions, objectives and priorities. These become embedded within a framework, which is presented as neutral, technical, specialist and operational. The construction of the competence models carries organizational values and purposes, although these are denied and disguised by an emphasis on the scientific, technical research methodology, which 'discovers' the competences from the managers themselves. Thus any possibility of discussion or disagreement about these key values and objectives is ruled out. All that is allowed is technical discussion of definitions and standards. And to engage in this debate is to accept the reasonableness of the competence project as a whole.

The quasi-scientific status of competence frameworks may be employed to control and suppress discussion. The approach was presented as neutral, unquestionable and beyond debate, as it purportedly 'unearths' or 'discovers' the qualities underlying successful incumbency of key management roles. The competence required that the managers took responsibility for ensuring that they and their part of the organization changed as necessary to support the business strategy:

> It is them [the employees] that are driving the thing, driving the change; they are actually setting the standards which people have to try and achieve.
>
> (CEO, HealthCo)

The introduction of competence frameworks did not question (or encourage debate about) the underlying direction of change. The competence programmes in the four research organizations were largely successful – managers did not seriously question the basis of the competences or disagree with their intentions, tending instead to be positive about the idea, theory and indeed practice of competences.

The new manager: summary

The competence-based approached to the construction of the new manager reveals some important features.

First, the competences identified in the research organizations represent an attempt to redefine the nature of management through a series of integrated processes ('architectures'), involving reshaping selection, appraisal, training and performance management, in ways that are aligned with the 'new organization' and its redefined purposes. Competences permit the apparent integration and consistency of key HR frameworks and processes. A competence architecture is an example of the type of complex mechanism

> through which it becomes possible to link calculations at one place with action at another, not through the direct imposition of a form of conduct by force, but through a delicate affiliation of a loose assemblage of agents and agencies into a functioning network.
>
> (Miller and Rose 1993: 83)

Second, competences represent a three step process of *translation* from strategy, to organization, and to individual manager. These three levels and the possibility of links between them have been identified by Miller and Rose, who stress how overarching discourses of government and organization supply a means whereby links develop between 'changing political rationalities and objectives, the ceaseless quest of business for profitability and a basis for managerial authority, with interventions at the subjectivity of the worker' (Rose and Miller 1988: 173).

The competent manager is someone who displays at the micro level the qualities the organization must display structurally to achieve its strategy, and very often exactly the same terms are used at each level. They are a supreme example of reductionism. New organizational priorities required by the new business strategy, such as 'customer focus', 'market sensitivity', 'commercial awareness', strategic focus', a 'concern for quality', etc., are achieved not primarily through new organizational structures and processes but through the construction of new managers behaving in new ways with new attitudes. The competence frameworks offer a way of redefining managers and management as a means of redesigning organization.

More than this, this translation is achieved while the ambitiousness and enormity of the task are denied. All difficulties are defined as merely technical or problems of implementation.

Third, as well as defining the qualities of the 'new manager', competences emphasize improvement in the performance of the manager. In every organization the competences were centrally associated with the *intensification* of management work through clearer 'stretch' targets, personal development, assessment and monitoring of improvement. Competences once again supply a framework and process for the management of improvement: explicit standards, dimensions, measurement, monitoring and development support.

Fourth, in all the organizations the competence projects placed emphasis on the importance of managers accepting and identifying with the competences, and identified managers as responsible for defining and developing themselves in terms of the competences. The key priority of all the competence frameworks was that the manager was prepared and willing to accept the assessment of his/her competence standard and to take responsibility for improving this assessment. The first management competence is commitment to the competence framework itself and, thereafter, acceptance of responsibility for self-regulation and self-management in terms of these competences. There is no room for disbelievers.

Competences redefine the relationship between the manager and the employer. Previous models of the employment relationship placed emphasis on 'the psychological contract of security for long-term commitment and loyalty along with an infrastructure of training and development' (Mabey *et al.* 1998: 270). Now the managers' employment and security are dependent on them taking personal responsibility for identifying their own development needs (through feedback against job profile requirements) and successfully developing themselves (and others) in terms of the organization's requirements. In short, job and career security now come not only from managers displaying the competences essential to the organization's new strategy, but from them being able to relate to their employer in terms of these qualities. Managers are only secure as long as they manage their relationship with their employer in broadly the same way that the employer seeks to relate to its clients: through marketing, client management and customer focus, continuous improvement. The application of competences embodies the conversion of the employer/manager relationship into one of purchaser/supplier. The competent manager not only must be prepared to display the sorts of behaviours required for the achievement of the new business strategy, but must also adopt an attitude towards him/herself as if s/he was a microcosmic business – marketing herself, developing her assets, investing in herself, designing an improvement plan, developing a strategy to ensure career and job security.

Fifth, the competence projects required a great deal more of the managers themselves. Competences assign to the manager new responsibilities previously handled elsewhere by specialists such as HR. Not only do these projects seek to define the new manager in terms of the qualities required of the new organization and to delegate responsibility for ensuring the achievement of these competences to the new self-regulating manager, but they also require that the new manager is responsible for designing and achieving necessary change within his/her area of control. Within competence architectures in the research organizations the manager is responsible for change management at the micro, job, level. Managers become responsible for redesigning their roles and the roles of their staff, as well as redesigning themselves to fit these roles and designing development requirements for them and their staff on the basis of their assessments. Thus, one of the most significant aspects of the competence projects was the delegation of responsibility for the design and achievement of the new manager to the manager on a *continuing* basis. The new manager not only embodies the qualities required by the new organization through a process of alignment of individual with business strategy, but also must accept responsibility for continuously adapting, and the capability to continuously adapt, the management role in the light of changing requirements.

Earlier work on attempts to redefine (or 'make up') the modern manager has stressed the linkages between the thrust of such initiatives (towards creating more enterprising and entrepreneurial managers) and wider societal discourses of government and organization centring on the value of market relationships and structures. But senior executives are unlikely to devise and implement new approaches simply because they resonate with wider bodies of ideas; this helps, but it is not enough. Senior managers are pragmatic and practical. They are only going to be willing to accept new approaches to the definition of manage-ment if they think that it will help with the achievement of their purposes. The research reported here shows how the competence approach is seen to offer such assistance. This occurs on a number of levels. At an immediate level, senior executives believe that this approach enables them to achieve the sort of organi-zational change necessary to support a major strategic focus or shift.

But the wider attraction of the competence movement lies in its claim to solve the major historic problem of organization: how to ensure managers are committed, willing and able to pursue the changing priorities of senior manage-ment. But it does this in a striking new way: it claims to solve the problems of organization by avoiding them and by redefining management. Changing managers is easier than changing organizations. Designing and implementing the necessary organizational changes to achieve a more customer focused, commercially sensitive strategy (or even knowing what such an organization would be like) is inherently difficult. And currently it is far from clear how this would be done. Many recent structural programmes of change have proved disappointing or have produced new problems. A major part of the attraction of the competence movement is that it offers to solve these difficulties by offering a way of changing managers which makes up for or avoids these organizational complexities and difficulties.

Competences offer a striking example of new processes and structures of government within the enterprise – of 'political rationalities' (Miller and Rose 1993). Competence frameworks and the architectures which can be constructed around them represent a powerful new way of 'knowing' managers and enable a complex and comprehensive set of procedures for measuring, describing, talking about and assessing managers. Once described and measured, managers are conceptualized and understood in a manner which makes them 'amenable to intervention and regulation' (*ibid.*: 79).

More than this, one of the key assumptions and purposes of competences is to ensure that managers accept the good sense of the approach and accept responsibility for ensuring their development with the requirements ('standards') of their management role. As such competences become part of the government of the organization, since external requirements become personal issues and priorities, to the extent that competences allow the translation of organizational priorities into the preferences and priorities of individual managers in their professional lives and careers, to the extent that managers see themselves as responsible for ensuring their continuing marketability in terms of their employers' aspirations, then competences become part of managers' 'self-steering' mechanisms, an element in their own self-regulation. Thus, free and autonomous individuals can be managed while preserving their formal autonomy (*ibid.*: 92).

Leaders and leadership

The period of greatest interest in management competences occurred in the decade 1985–95. More recently attention has moved away dramatically – from management to leadership. Now leadership is seen as the source of organizational success and the key determinant of organizational performance, and lack of leadership is blamed for poor performance at business and even national levels. The Council for Excellence in Management and Leadership (2001, 2002) argues that current management and business leadership development is operating dysfunctionally and that, in consequence, Britain's economic performance is impacted adversely by the resulting shortage of skills. Never before has leadership been given such emphasis as a determinant of organizational performance. This switch in emphasis raises fascinating questions about the continued relevance of the competence approach.

The emphasis on leadership is revealed in a number of recent developments: one is the explosion of interest in hagiographic biographies (or ghosted autobiographies) of heroic charismatic business leaders piled high in airport bookstalls. These works celebrate the extraordinary contributions of specific remarkable individuals to the success of large formal organizations: aggressive, self-confident, macho, uncompromising, visionary. No wonder a recent global survey by an international consultancy placed 'leadership development' at the top of the list of priority issues for chief executives worldwide – a lead that has been eagerly grasped by many business schools.

In the UK, enthusiasm for leadership is revealed in an array of major initiatives, including the launch of the Council for Excellence in Management and Leadership; in government the Public Services Leadership Scheme; in education the Leadership Programme for Headteachers – possibly the world's largest leadership development initiative. The UK's National Health Service (NHS) has launched its own Leadership for Health programme, which is intended to identify and develop strategic leadership for health authorities in the new NHS. And in many other public sector areas – including the armed services and the prison service – major leadership development initiatives are underway.

This emphasis on leadership is distinctive not only for its pervasiveness and dominance but also for its distinctive and self-justifying approach to leadership itself. The way leadership is currently defined is revealing for the work it is expected to do. Always an elusive concept, recent approaches stress the contribution of leaders as supplying vision, designing change and generating mobilization – the 'transformational leader'.

Transformational leaders are defined precisely in terms of their claimed ability to overcome or compensate for (transform) organizational and individual limitations. Transformational leaders 'motivate others to do more than they originally intended and indeed often more than they thought possible.... Team spirit is aroused. Enthusiasm and optimism are displayed' (Bass and Avolio 1994: 3). Transformational leaders enable their staff to overcome, to break through, to see beyond the limitations of their organization: they 'stimulate their followers' efforts to be innovative and creative by questioning assumptions, re-framing problems, and approaching old situations in new ways' (*ibid.*: 3).

Such leaders are often portrayed in the business and airport bookstall press in terms of the unique and specifically personal contribution of the charismatic individual leader, on whom organizational success depends (and who should therefore receive a considerable share of the benefits of that success). They are defined as aggressive, confident, potent, iconoclastic, irreverent, full of energy and competitive aspirations, driving change within the organization and attacking the forces of conservatism and regulation outside it.

The new leader is, in short, defined not only as making up for ('transforming') the weaknesses and deficiencies of organization, but in many respects as *anti-*organizational: as emotional rather than rational, as hugely and distinctively personal and subjective rather than formal and procedural, as intuitive rather than systematic, as instinctive and sexual (at least metaphorically – see Guthey 2001) rather than cerebral and impersonal, and of course as charismatic rather than organizational. Such leaders are also anti-organizational in that their style and reputation frequently involve claims that they publicly oppose and seek to destroy and overcome sources of conventional internal or external (governmental or regulatory) constraint which seek to protect the interests of parties other than shareholders or CEOs: workers, consumers, citizens. For the new transformational leader nothing must be allowed to restrict his/her right to pursue the only legitimate business goal: profit and increases in shareholder value.

There are, of course, as academics will tell us, a number of definitions of leadership, but it is revealing that current approaches tend to focus on those that support an emphasis on the heroic, narcissistic, egotistical, charismatic individual – i.e. trait theory – rather than those which define leadership in situational terms, as a process, as being revealed in a number of different leadership styles or distributed models of leadership. And so we find that academic approaches to leadership are hijacked by prevailing and dominant approaches to leadership.

Leadership is no longer 'merely' of academic interest: it is also of interest to those who define and present themselves as corporate leaders (and their acolytes and amanuenses). And the way corporate leaders define themselves and their tasks raises some fascinating issues, not only of corporate values and corporate governance (for whom is the business run; to whom is it answerable?), but also for the relationship between corporation and state. As Guthey notes, an important feature of the way leaders define themselves and their purposes is that it conflates public and private, individual and the corporate, and justifies predatory market adventurism and the celebration of personal greed and celebrity with an attack on more alternative and more regulated forms of managerialism (*ibid.*: 140). The cult of the transformational leader is important not only for the sorts of excesses it has encouraged, but also for its role in attacking and sidelining alternatives models of corporate purpose and relationships between the corporation and the wider society.

It is easy to be cynical about the recent focus on leadership. The advantages to the leaders themselves are obvious and potentially self-serving in both egotistic and financial terms. And it is possible that recent developments in the US which have seen some quintessential business leaders humbled and disgraced as they are, it is alleged, revealed as fraudulent and corrupt may well have occasioned a crisis for contemporary approaches to and definitions of leadership. But current concern for organizational leadership raises some deeper questions: namely why did it occur and why does it need its distinctive partial and frankly empirically questionable conception of leadership?

This raises questions about the success of the competence project which preceded it. Of course, a decline in interest in competences may simply reflect the fact that most large organizations have now installed their competence architectures. But the fact that leadership must now be invoked as the new solution to issues of organizational performance and change ('transformation', 'turnaround') suggests at the very least that the competence project has failed to deliver its promise. This, of course, is hardly surprising, since the problems it promised to resolve are not capable of resolution and its promises consisted largely of a sleight of hand whereby organizational problems were simply restated as management responsibilities.

Interestingly, the current emphasis on leadership reveals some similar elements to those revealed by the earlier interest in management competences. First, and obviously like the competence movement, the enthusiasm for leadership stresses the importance of the individual, although here it is the single, unique individual rather than a class or category of individuals. But the function served is similar: yet again organizational problems and shortcomings are seen as solved by, or redefined in terms of, the individual. Leadership is imbued with almost magical qualities: whatever the structural or system weaknesses of the organization, if you simply add leadership these problems will disappear. Leadership – however loosely and vaguely defined – fills the gap left by problems of organization or by difficulties in conceiving of appropriate forms of organization. There is a crisis of organization, caused by the successive failure of various regimes of organizational reform, as delayering, decentralization, business process re-engineering (BPR), downsizing are seen to fail, and in many cases are acknowledged publicly even by their advocates to have failed. This crisis is not just a crisis of practice and performance (although it is certainly that); it is also a crisis of theory: what would an effective and efficient rail system look like? In the UK this crisis is compounded by the confusion caused by attempts to combine contradictory elements – to proclaim the importance of market forces but to install regulators, to urge privatization but insist on benchmarking or targets – which has led to a major confusion in discourses of organization. Such confusions and contradictions – the current inability to imagine an effective form of organization – are resolved not by fresh thinking about organizations, their structures and their purposes, but by invoking the crucial role of leadership. Leaders give us a way out of these complex contradictory issues: leaders will solve these problems for us – or they will make it unnecessary to solve them. The role of leadership is to make up for and solve organizational confusion and the poverty of organizational analysis, as did management competences. How? By 'transforming' the organization.

It is tempting therefore to speculate that although current forms of leadership are defined in stark, deliberate and polar contrast to management and organization – in terms of individual, anti-organizational qualities: unpredictability, emotionality, intuition, creativity ('vision'), iconoclasm, irreverence, personality – nevertheless ironically the function of this non- or anti-organizational conception of leadership is entirely organizational, in the sense that it involves acknowledging the inherent problems and contradictions of organization and raising the prospect that these can be solved by heroic charismatic leadership. No wonder leadership is so attractive.

But the current cult of leadership reveals two particular ironies which deserve attention.

Although leadership is invoked in the face of a recognized failure to identify organizational solutions to organizational problems, the focus on the cult of the charismatic individual leader as a solution to such problems has had unintended effects. It has actually further damaged confidence in current forms of organization. It has made matters worse. This has occurred because a number of high profile US leaders (many of whom have been lauded by biographers, academic commentators and the media) had begun to think that their personal greed was actually acceptable, even virtuous, and that their acknowledged charisma made them inviolable: they began to believe in their own publicity and to go to any ends in order to sustain the myth of their invulnerability. And the resulting fraud and corruption have shaken confidence in organization and structures of governance.

But this crisis in leadership and damage to organizational confidence have not undermined the emphasis on leadership, although it has changed its form. If leadership is seen as critical to organizational success but single charismatic leaders are seen as vulnerable and dangerous, then an obvious solution is to argue for the importance of leadership distributed throughout the organization. Such thinking lies behind the extraordinary explosion of interest in leadership training. Now everyone must be a leader. Middle managers in public and private sector organizations must become leaders:

> No more close supervision of workers, no more focus on data irrelevant to running the business, no more energy spent on defending turf. The role of managers becomes one of empowerment – providing workers with the information, training, authority and accountability to excel.... As workers take on more management tasks, *managers must take on more leadership tasks – holding a vision of the business, articulating it to workers and customers, and creating an environment that truly empowers workers.*

> (Champy 1994)

This sort of argument brings us full circle. The competence movement failed to deliver its promises. So it was replaced by the cult of the charismatic leader.

Each represents a distinctively individualistic way of defining and resolving organizational weaknesses. The cult of the charismatic leader too is being seen to fail; it's too dangerous. Yet the idea of leadership remains attractive as an individualistic way of solving problems of organization by avoiding them. Now leadership is defined as a necessary quality of managers at all levels. It is a feature of management, no longer a distinctive and clearly demarcated quality, and – wait for it – it is developed through new 'leadership competences', with all the associated architecture of competence features.

For what are the key responsibilities of leaders (who are now managers)? They are very similar in essence to the responsibilities of the competence approach to management: to take individual responsibility for ensuring that the organization is capable of achieving its objectives – designing and directing organizational change in pursuit of organizational objectives (Pettigrew and Whipp 1991: 143). Although the current cult of leadership may seem (and indeed present itself as) in marked contrast, even opposition, to management (hence the need for definitions to clarify the differences between the two), in functional terms they are remarkably similar in that both offer to resolve the failures of organization by avoiding and individualizing them.

Notes

1   The distinction between these two levels of analysis reflects that used by Paul du Gay (1991), who differentiates between the 'paradigmatic status' of the overall model of organization and government (in which enterprise currently plays a major role) and the 'action or project' level, where these ideas are worked out in terms of the necessary qualities of individuals. There is also a third level: the political. As Rose and Miller note, three levels of analysis are involved, which within any particular discourse become aligned and consistent: the political machine, the economic machine and the human machine (Rose and Miller 1988: 173).

2   As du Gay and others have noted, much academic and managerial attention has been paid to the varying ways in which, under different epochs of management thinking, attempts have been made to integrate the work-based human subject and the organization (du Gay 1991: 47).

3   In the four cases the launch and application of competence frameworks were tracked over a period of more than a year. Senior managers were interviewed at least once, and key HR staff were interviewed often and regularly throughout the research period. Interviews were also conducted with managers involved in the implementation of the competence frameworks, and HR consultants brought in to guide the processes of change.

4   A focus on competences as a 'language' does not imply that competences exist *only* at the level of representation. The language supplied by competences not only makes managers knowable, but also makes managers amenable to intervention and makes such intervention logically consistent and hence undeniable.

References

Bass, B.M. and B.J. Avolio (eds) (1994) *Improving Organizational Effectiveness through Transformational Leadership*, Thousand Oaks, CA: Sage.

Bendix, R. (1956) *Work and Authority in Industry*, New York: Harper.

Boyatzis, R. (1982) *The Competent Manager: A Model for Effective Performance*, New York: John Wiley & Sons.

Champy, J. (1994) 'Time to re-engineer the manager?', *Financial Times*, 14 January: 17.

Council for Excellence in Management & Leadership (2001) *Leadership Development: Best Practice Guide for Organisations*, London: CEML.

—— (2002) *Managers and Leaders: Raising Our Game*, London: CEML.

Du Gay, P. (1991) 'Enterprise culture and the ideology of excellence', *New Formations* 13: 45–62.

—— (1994) 'Making up managers: bureaucracy, enterprise and the liberal art of separation', *British Journal of Sociology* 45(4): 655–74.

—— (1996) *Consumption and Identity at Work*, London: Sage.

Du Gay, P. and G. Salaman (1992) 'The cult(ure) of the customer', *Journal of Management Studies* 29(5): 615–33.

Du Gay P., G. Salaman and Rees B. (1996) 'The conduct of management and the management of conduct: contemporary managerial discourse and the constitution of the "competent" manager', *Journal of Management Studies* 33: 3, 263–82.

Foucault, M. (1980) *Power/Knowledge*, Brighton: Harvester.

Guest, D. (1992) 'Right enough to be dangerously wrong', in G. Salaman (ed.) *Human Resource Strategies*, Sage: London.

Guthey, E. (2001) 'Ted Turner's corporate cross-dressing and the shifting images of American business', *Leadership, Enterprise and Society* 2: 111–42.

Jackson, B. (1996) 'Re-engineering the sense of self', *Journal of Management Studies* 33: 571–90.

Jacques, R. (1996) *Manufacturing the Employee*, London: Sage.

Lucia, A. and R. Lepringer (1999) *The Art and Science of Competency Models: Pinpointing Critical Success Factors in Organizations*, San Francisco: Jossey Bass Pfeiffer.

Mabey, C., J. Storey and G. Salaman (1998) *Human Resource Management: A Strategic Introduction*, Oxford: Blackwell.

McClelland, D. (1961) *The Achieving Society*, New York: Van Nostrand Reinhold.

Miller, P. and N. Rose (1993) 'Governing economic life', in M. Gane and T. Johnson (eds) *Foucault's New Domains*, Routledge: London.

Pettigrew, A. and R. Whipp (1991) *Managing Change for Competitive Success*, Oxford: Blackwell.

Rose, N. (1990) *Governing the Soul*, London: Routledge.

Rose, N. and P. Miller (1988) 'The Tavistock programme, the government of subjectivity and social life', *Sociology* 22: 171–93.

Part III

The processes of leadership training and development

5 Methods of 'learning leadership': taught and experiential

Elena P. Antonacopoulou and Regina F. Bento

Introduction

Can leadership be taught? Can leadership be learned? For many years the answer to both questions was presumed to be yes. In countless business school classrooms and executive development seminars, 'experts' delivered lectures and presented examples that were supposed to 'teach' learners about the 1940s trait theories of leadership, the 1950s focus on tasks versus relationships, the 1960s identification of contingencies, the 1970s insights about leader–follower interactions, and the 1980s celebration of transformation and vision (Ferris 1998). This teaching paradigm is based on an instructor-centred approach, where an expert draws from an existing body of information to select some predetermined content and transmit it to passive students, whose 'learning' of this material is conceptualized in terms of memorization, abstract understanding and behavioural replication. The intellectual roots of this teaching paradigm can be traced back to positivism (an expert transmitting knowledge to a novice) and behaviourism (introduction of new behavioural patterns that are repeated until they become automatic), reflecting a 'banking' model of education, where information is deposited by the teacher into the learner, where it is accumulated (Freire 1970).

While the teaching paradigm was effective in the socialization process of a managerial elite (Grey 2002), providing them with the credentials for occupying positions of leadership and the language to talk about leadership, its emphasis on cognitive learning, tools and techniques often succeeded only in turning out 'highly skilled barbarians' (Bisoux 2002: 28).

There is a growing awareness of the limitations of these traditional approaches to teaching leadership (Kouzes and Posner 1995; Doyle and Smith 1999). While they might be useful in transmitting knowledge *about* leadership, they stop short at developing leadership per se.

When the study of leadership evolved, in the 1990s, to an understanding of the importance of credibility, soul, reflexivity, emotions, openness to experience, and values (Ferris 1998; Bolman and Deal 1995), exploring what McDermott (1994) calls 'leadership from within', there was a progressive shift from the traditional instructor-centred teaching paradigm to a learner-centred paradigm of personal transformation. The transformation paradigm, with intellectual roots in constructivism, social constructivism and interactionism, emphasizes co-creation, interpretation, discovery, experimentation and a critical perspective. Rather than learning 'leadership' as it is known by others, learners make sense of their own experiences, discover and nurture leadership in themselves and in each other, not in isolation but in community.

The premise of this chapter is that leadership is not taught and leadership is not learned. Leadership *is* learning (Vail 1996: 126). Whatever else leaders do, their primary role is to keep learning and to facilitate the learning of those around them. Immersed as they are in what Vail calls an environment of permanent white water, constant change requires something beyond managing to stay on a predetermined course. It requires leading, i.e. learning whether changing conditions are altering the landscape of needs and opportunities and requiring a change in existing plans or goals; learning which alternative courses might be possible or desirable; learning which direction to go; learning what it takes to get there; learning, learning, learning. In this sense, the crucial question in leadership development is not just *what* to learn, but how to *learn how to learn.*

This chapter departs from the dominant paradigm in leadership development research and explores the notion of 'learning leadership' as one which centres on the person discovering and experiencing leadership from within, as a continual learning process, rather than as something that can be simply granted by others. 'Learning leadership', therefore, is not the 'learning about leadership' that characterized the teaching paradigm. Rather, it is an approach to leadership that is rooted in the transformational paradigm, where leadership is a process of becoming, and learning is a way of being (*ibid.*: 126).

Whereas the teaching paradigm prizes and perpetuates the dominant conception of the leader as a fully competent, confident, knowledgeable, clear-sighted visionary,[1] the transformational paradigm sees the leader as being fundamentally a learner. In organizations immersed in continuous change, what matters most is not what a leader knows, but what he or she is capable of learning. This ability to learn, however, requires a leader who is willing to feel the vulnerability implicit in not knowing, an openness to experience that approaches each new situation as a circus artist who flies from one trapeze to the next, rather than clinging to the comforting security of the platform. Ironically enough, these are not qualities that are valued in the teaching paradigm, where not knowing is perceived as a weakness, and 'incompetence' is a dreaded state. By contrast, the experiential assumptions of the transformational paradigm foster the kind of leadership where one is perpetually a reflective beginner (*ibid.*) and 'incompetence' is just the exhilarating flight between competently holding the trapeze of the past and tentatively grasping for the trapeze of the future.

The analysis presented here is, therefore, a direct response to the need to explore ways in which management training and development activities can provide the space for leadership to emerge and be discovered. This can usefully be done both in the way individuals engage with their practice (self-learning) and in terms of the innovative ways in which individual learning can be supported.

The discussion is organized in three main sections. We begin with an overview of the main perspectives that have informed our assumptions and approaches to developing leadership so far. We make the case for 'learning leadership' as an alternative way to understanding leadership and explore leadership as learning practice. We analyse the relationship between learning (strategic learning) and leadership in highlighting two main principles which, we argue, underpin 'learning leadership'; namely *leadership as a window to inner learning* and *leadership as a relational process*.

The second section extends the illustrations of 'learning leadership' by considering approaches for developing 'learning leadership'. Examples from improvisational and image theatre are reviewed, as are approaches using arts and music. Both sets of examples help us distil more clearly the learning structures which can support leadership as learning practice.

The main learning structures and principles which underpin 'learning leadership' are reviewed in the last section of the chapter, in order to draw attention to the implications of this new perspective on leadership, both in terms of future leadership research and leadership development practices.

Perspectives on leadership development: the role of 'learning leadership'

The evolution of our thinking on how to develop leadership has paralleled the movement in theories of leadership. From trait theories of leadership came development efforts targeted at identifying and nurturing certain qualities and attributes associated with 'good leaders' (J. Gardner 1989; Wright 1996). The behavioural theories of leadership inspired development efforts directed at identifying and developing those behaviours that were most appropriate to each combination of leader, follower and situational characteristics (Hersey 1984; Sadler 1997). The more recent attention to the 'whole-person' aspects of leadership has promoted a variety of efforts towards the development of the physical, mental and spiritual dimensions of inner awareness (Ferris and Fanelli 1996).

In an extensive review of the development of thinking in leadership research, K.B. Boal and R. Hooijberg (2000) argue that the study of leadership has undergone fundamental changes in the last 20 years. Among other things, these changes reflect a shift in focus from 'supervisory' towards 'strategic' leadership, and from trait theories to a wider socio-cognitive analysis of the complexity of leaders and leadership, as a process of meaning creation and construction of reality, which they and their followers jointly negotiate (Smircich and Morgan 1982; House and Aditya 1997). The social constructivist view of leadership emphasizes both meaning construction and interaction. The interactionist view, in turn, emphasizes interpersonal relationships as a vital aspect of leadership. Some of the more recent theories of leadership have emerged from this perspective, emphasizing charisma, vision and inspiration (House and Aditya 1997; Hunt and Conger 1999). Although there is still little agreement as to the usefulness, or indeed appropriateness, of such value-laden terms to describe leadership (see Finkelstein and Hambrick 1990), the so-called 'emerging theories' of leadership, according to Boal and Hooijberg, hold great promise in furthering our understanding of what they see as the three cornerstones of strategic leadership; namely 'the capacity to learn, the capacity to change and managerial wisdom' (2000: 25–6). By drawing on Quinn's (1988) competing values framework and integrating themes such as behavioural complexity (e.g. Hooijberg and Quinn 1992), cognitive capacity (e.g. Jacques 1989) and social intelligence (e.g. Zaccaro *et al.* 1991), they put forward an integrative framework for exploring strategic leadership based on knowledge and cognitive structures, which are seen to have a bearing on the actions taken in line with one's ability to 'read' others' behaviours, perspectives and feelings. The ability to integrate and adapt the social conditions with the risks of environmental uncertainties and to make them interact with each other is seen to underpin strategic leadership. Therefore, the qualities of strategic leadership by necessity require strategic learning. As this chapter will argue, leadership research is more likely to move beyond the current paradigm if we explore leadership as learning practice.

Much current thinking propounds the view that leadership is central to organizational development and learning (Senge 1990; DeGeus 1997; DiBella and Nevis 1998). Yet the intricate relationship between learning and leadership has not been fully explored. We begin such an analysis by first unpacking the potential aspects of leadership if viewed as a *learning-supported process*. We focus, in particular, on recent debates which explore learning as a key capability.

The emphasis on learning capability as a key strategic resource has been increasing in recent years, as we come to appreciate learning as a key competitive resource for organizations. Learning is as much a cause as a consequence, and a context where effective practices which improve performance, enhance productivity and sustain innovation are embedded. In the strategic management literature much effort has been put on identifying the 'distinctive' (Selznick 1957) or 'core' (Prahalad and Hamel 1990) characteristics, referred to as 'competence(s)', that would be a differentiating factor for the organization in light of competitive pressures (Bogner *et al.* 1999). Terms such as 'organizational routines' (Nelson and Winter 1982), 'absorptive capacity' (Cohen and Levinthal 1990), 'organizational capability' (Grant 1996), 'transformative capacity' (Garud and Nayyar 1994) and 'dynamic capabilities' (Teece *et al.* 1997) are among the many conceptualizations to be found in our ongoing efforts to locate the key competitive differentiator. Recently, Zollo and Winter (2002) have taken the debate further in exploring the evolution of *dynamic capabilities*, suggesting that such capabilities can be learned.

This introduces a very promising perspective, as it opens up the possibility of exploring *learning as a dynamic capability*, an ability to respond to the unknown in ways that widen the scope of action to produce new solutions beyond what is currently known (Antonacopoulou 2003a). Learning is central to understanding how creative working conditions can be formed which allow managers the flexibility to respond to issues in ways that support sustained and sustainable innovation. Moreover, learning is central to adaptation and a necessary condition itself for implementing the changes needed to support innovation. Knowing (not just knowledge) therefore becomes a central learning dimension within communities of practitioners (Lave and Wenger 1991; Brown and Duguid 1991) in their particular cultural and political context, which would affect whether and how managers choose and learn from other's experiences and practices (Antonacopoulou 1998; Salaman and Butler 1990). Therefore learning itself can be seen as a dynamic capability because it is purposeful adaptation and reconfiguration of attributes (including knowledge and skills) and a capacity to renew previous competence to maintain congruence with changing requirements (Antonacopoulou 2003a).

The latter point is one that has not yet been fully explored in the existing leadership literature. We would argue, therefore, that if we are to explore the relationship between learning and leadership we can begin to explore both ways in which leadership capability can be supported and ways in which leadership may be learned. More importantly, in light of the emphasis placed on leadership as central to the development of 'learning organizations' (Senge 1990; Garratt 1990; Schein 1992) it is imperative to explore further the relationship between individual and organizational learning (Friedlander 1983; Kim 1993), a currently unresolved issue in organizational learning debates. In particular, what would appear to be critical in such analysis would be an integrative analysis of the *what, how* and *why* of individual learning in organizations if we are to address the challenges in the relationship between learning and educational interventions in organizations (see Antonacopoulou 2000b, 2002a) to support leadership development. Recent research exploring individuals' learning within organizations, using the manager as a unit of analysis (Antonacopoulou 1998, 1999a, 2001), highlights the contextual specificity of learning in the way the very processes intended to support learning are also frequently the ones restricting learning. In light of ongoing organizational changes, leadership development, at a minimum, would need to consider ways in which leadership capability can be learned. It can also be argued that this very approach of understanding leadership development – as learning practice – can be a useful point of departure, away from dominant assumptions about leadership and its meanings. This chapter, in particular, makes the case about 'learning leadership' not only as a prerequisite of developing 'learning organizations', in the same way as 'learning managers' would be a key ingredient (see Antonacopoulou 1998). More fundamentally, 'learning leadership' could be an avenue for rethinking and redefining leadership.

Rethinking leadership: defining 'learning leadership'

Leadership is a very fluid concept, as is the role of being a leader. The meanings vary with the multitude of conditions which shape the interrelationships between the diverse dynamic forces that define leadership in different contexts. Such forces could be factors like the persons, their beliefs, values, skills, resources, circumstances, power, organizational structure, etc. This very fluidity, therefore, calls for a paradigmatic shift, one that extends beyond a mode of thought restricted in a mentality of 'either/or' to one that embraces the possibilities embedded in the multiplicities of connections permitted even by seemingly oppositional forces (a both/and mentality). If one, therefore, were to rethink leadership as a process in search of questions rather than answers, then it would be possible equally to argue that leaders are defined by the questions they ask rather than the answers they seek to provide. It is possible to adopt a similar definition in relation to learning, consistent with recent definitions which propose learning as 'the liberation of knowledge through self-reflection and questioning' (Antonacopoulou 2001: 328). Learning, therefore, could be an avenue for rethinking leadership from a task, person or situation specific process to one that is defined by the lessons one creates as one discovers the inner meanings of leadership, in the way leadership provides and requires personal insight and acts as a window to inner learning (leadership from within). Moreover, learning could be another lens for exploring leadership as a relational and not simply transactional process. Particular attention here would be placed on the leader–follower relationship, a distinction of roles which from a learning point of view in the context of a community of practice may well prove to be unnecessary. Both sets of issues are discussed in more detail next.

Leadership as a window to inner learning: leadership from within

Lieutenant-General J.F. Deverell argues that '[l]eading is more than just doing; it is also about being. It's about who you are and what values you represent' (1999: 120). This assertion suggests that leadership is integral to the leader as a person; leadership *is* the leader in the way it allows that person to demonstrate insight not only about the issues at hand, but also about his/herself and his/her values. Leadership is, therefore, as much external in the actions one takes as it is internal in the way one *is* (in one's being and becoming). From this it follows that leadership has both explicit and tacit dimensions, which sensitizes us to the fact that leadership research and development have predominantly been focusing on the external, observable, explicit dimensions of leadership, captured in categories such as tasks and behaviours, at the expense of also exploring the tacit aspects of leadership, in such categories as one's identity, character and temperament. Posner supports this view and argues that the challenge of finding the leader within is about 'the exploration of the inner territory and the search to know more about the meaning of life and one's purpose in some grander scheme as the basis for developing leadership' (2002: 1). He emphasizes the importance of leaders knowing what they believe in, what their principles are and having unwavering commitment to them. He also explains that taking a journey into one's inner territory is about finding one's voice as deep down as one's soul.

Ferris and Fanelli take on board the debate about the role of leaders in 'learning organizations' and focus in particular on the role of these leaders, who they refer to as 'learning managers', in managing 'their own development, improvement and growth as well as that of their members' (1996: 66) as part of their leadership strategy, which would serve to establish a 'learning organization'. Their analysis explores the inextricable link between individual (leader and follower) and organizational development, and stresses the importance of being in touch with one's inner self as a condition for personal growth. They see the inner self as constituted by one's mental, spiritual and intuitive faculties, which at their most basic involve the 'reflective discipline of careful planning with a view of maximising available resources' (*ibid.*: 69). They also explain that accessing one's inner self could best be captured by such states as being 'in the zone', 'in flow', 'becoming one with the universe', 'infused with the excitement of being alive' (*ibid.*: 70). One could reach such a state through 'learned optimism' and 'ego energy' (*ibid.*: 71). Simply put, in practice this would mean 'seeing things with beginners' eyes', taking a fresh look as a 'naïve observer' would, 'cultivating a responsive awareness of the environment', and recognizing the 'dangers of ingrained mindless habits' and other factors which may inhibit learning from taking place (*ibid.*: 72). Learning leadership, therefore, depends not only on critical self-reflection, so that one is able to be reflexive, but more fundamentally it is about allowing our voice of consciousness to speak to us. In short, it is about recognizing individuality[2] as a condition of collectivity and connectivity.

Leadership as a relational process in a community of practice

The love of others is what drives leaders, according to Wakhlu (1999). By being compassionate and loving, leaders act as conduits for growth. This resonates with Ashkanasy and Tse's (2000) assertion that the power of transformational leaders lies in their ability to exercise control over their emotions, as well as the emotions of their followers. Effective leaders, therefore, care about others. Caring always involves personal risk. Jones explains that '[w]hen you show that you really care, you reveal a little bit of your self-identity and you may be rejected…it means putting a bit of yourself on the line' (1999: 107). This is in line with Posner's (2002) observation that caring is also associated with grief – 'the suffering of the mind'. He explains that 'deep within ourselves there is something we hold dear, and if it's ever violated we'll weep and wail…. Leadership begins with something that grabs hold of you and won't let go' (*ibid.*: 3). Jones also points out, drawing on Goleman (1997), that 'leaders use their emotions to liberate the *energy* of others' (Jones 1999: 107; emphasis ours). Leaders have relentless energy and they depend on high energy to keep them going (*ibid.*: 108). Leaders get people to act in a selfless way (Deverell 1999: 119).

Like a good gardener who nurtures the growth of his plants, a leader nurtures the growth of the people around him/her. They become a channel of nature's will and through the flow life finds expression in the totality of the collective achievement. Learning leaders, therefore, value learning with and from others and create a conducive learning environment where individual and collective growth can take place (Garratt 1990). Also referring to learning leaders, Schein argues that leaders 'have to set the example by becoming learners themselves and involving others in the learning process' (1992: 392). This would imply that traditional role distinctions between leaders and followers become unnecessary, particularly if one were to adopt the Royal

Military Academy motto 'serve to lead'. Lieutenant-General J.F. Deverell explains that 'those who lead are servants of those whom they lead. In order to lead one has to learn how to serve' (1999: 128).

The question central to learning leadership is, therefore, not what it takes to be a good leader, but what it takes to be a good follower. If one takes on board the ideas explored in the preceding paragraphs, it would appear that learning to adopt multiple perspectives (e.g. those of followers) rather than being self-diluted in one's own perspective and vision would be an important aspect of learning leadership. Another important aspect would be having the humility to recognize talent and allow it to grow, without setting boundaries or preconditions to self-development (see Antonacopoulou 2000a). What this means in practice is that it is critical to accept that there are people with more talent than oneself, as a reflection of one's commitment to learn from others, so that one can lead others. Learning from others also reflects a commitment to developing others. In other words, learning leadership is what community of practice (Lave and Wenger 1991) is; a way of exploring collectively the meanings of activities from which knowledge and learning derive and contribute to individual and collective development. Along the same principles, Raelin advances the idea of 'leaderful practice' in the way leaders who allow a team to thrive leader*less* is in fact leader*ful* in the way it maximizes leadership across team members 'concurrently', 'collectively', 'collaboratively' and with 'compassion' (2002: 6). The latter characteristic of leaderful practice emphasizes in particular the 'unadulterated commitment to preserving the dignity of others'.

Learning leadership revisited

Fundamentally, from the main principles of inner self and collective individuality one can appreciate that learning leadership is not simply about facilitating others' learning, or indeed being a skilful learner, as previously argued by proponents of the notion of learning leadership (Garratt 1990; Schein 1992). Learning leadership, as revisited in this analysis, is about acknowledging that *leading is learning*. This is not to suggest that the two terms are synonymous, but instead to encourage a stance which suggests that learning leadership begins with an appreciation that because leadership is ambiguous, as is learning, one has to start by exploring as much the external dimensions (explicit) which constitute leadership as the internal (tacit) dimensions. This would imply that critically reviewing how one thinks about leadership and learning is a fundamental principle of learning leadership (Alvesson and Deetz 2000). Equally fundamental is an appreciation of how one participates as a learner in collective leadership, as well as the way one participates as a leader in collective learning. In other words, by encouraging reflection and reconsideration of what one knows, one develops and is developed by others, one becomes a learning facilitator. In doing so, a leader is also learning about the process of leading; i.e. developing other leaders. Being a great leader, according to Hodgson (1999: 132), is about allowing yourself to be also vulnerable and having the humility to be willing to learn things that you often don't want to learn. In other words, confronting the dilemmas and challenges (of exploration and exploitation, as per March 1991) that learning presents is central to also addressing the paradoxical nature of what being a leader is about. This means that learning and leadership both require focus as well as flexibility. They require structure as well as agency. The flexibility and ability to move freely between apparently contradictory polarities requires an open mind. This is the art of 'wholesomeness' according to Wakhlu: 'Being wholesome as a leader is vital so that leaders can move freely as they discover and adapt their leadership instead of being fixed on any single idea of what a "good" leader should be' (1999: 208).

Approaches for developing 'learning leadership'

If we are to make the case that learning leadership provides the scope for moving away from the dominant paradigm of leadership research and development, a series of issues arise about ways in which learning leadership can be supported. In this section we explore the question of whether learning leadership can be developed.

Traditional questions around leadership development tend to be concerned with the extent to which leadership can be taught, or indeed whether it should be taught (in the way we understand teaching in the didactic training mode). There has also been concern with several questions: how might we justify investment in leadership development? What do we get from having effective leaders? And what is the return on investment in leadership development?

It is not hard to see that the traditional mode of researching and developing leadership is driven by a economic logic which sees learning and development as a means of improving financial performance. We would like to propose a different logic for understanding the importance of learning leadership. Our concern is with questions such as whether the leader is a learner, and whether leaders can and seek to learn from their followers. These questions essentially beg a more fundamental question: how can we develop learning leaders?

These questions require that we move away from an economic logic in justifying leadership development and instead adopt an affective logic, which places the emphasis not on the hard exchange (of give and take) between leaders and followers, but on the psychological contract that connects leaders and followers, based on their mutual respect, trust and commitment to collective learning and development. For instance, this would be the case in the psychological contract that binds a conductor with a group of musicians: other than a shared vision based on their collective experiences and the music which they jointly produce, they also rely on each other's artistic skills to produce good music, which is also the bond that connects and reinforces their interdependence. This is reflective of what Barry (1991) describes as 'distributed leadership' and Bradford and Cohen (1998) describe as 'shared leadership', the collaborative team process in which team members share key leadership roles. However, Houghton *et al.* (2003) argue that 'self-leadership' is at the heart of shared leadership. They define self-leadership as a 'process through which people influence themselves to achieve the self-direction and self-motivation needed to perform' (*ibid.*: 9). However, the ultimate state is what they call 'SuperLeadership'. Drawing on the work of Manz and Sims, they define SuperLeadership as

> an approach that strives to develop followers who are effective self-leaders…by helping, encouraging, and supporting followers in the development of personal responsibility, individual initiative, self-confidence, self-goal setting, self-problem solving, opportunity thinking, self-leadership, and psychological ownership of their work tasks and duties.
>
> (Manz and Sims 2001: 23–4)

Therefore seeking to develop leadership through definition, a didactic approach which restricts leadership to specific characteristics, would not support learning. On the contrary, it would seem to be more appropriate to create opportunities where leadership can be learned by exploring ways in which the risks of leading can best be managed. Hodgson emphatically argues that 'people who have learned leadership as a series of rules will have an inherent inflexibility that will eventually be their downfall. Leadership skills are learned by example and encouragement rather than by rote of rule' (1999: 129). He goes on to say that '[t]elling people how to lead is roughly equivalent to painting-by-numbers' (*ibid.*: 129). Along similar lines, Deverell (1999) emphasizes that art teachers can teach students to draw, but they cannot make them great artists. Great artists, he asserts, have to be born from within. Posner also uses the analogy of an artist's development to illustrate the point, suggesting that 'leadership development in the early stages is about painting exterior landscapes, copying other leaders' styles and trying to learn by mimicking great leaders' (2002: 5–6). The erroneous assumption, he argues, is that 'authentic leadership can come from the outside in. It cannot. It can only come from within…. You cannot lead through someone else's words nor someone else's experiences' (*ibid.*: 6).

Leadership, therefore, can be learned, and we would argue that learning leadership in turn can be discovered if one is committed as a learner to explore one's inner landscape. This is what learning leadership is about, the authenticity of leadership in action, interaction and transaction, which are fundamental aspects of the learning process if it were to act as a space in which the multiplicity of possibilities for growth can be identified and developed (Antonacopoulou 2002a, 2003a).

Therefore the kind of development that can support learning leadership is one that embraces one's practices as an arena of one's learning. Learning as a practice is not simply about using experiences in order to learn, or indeed learning by doing. It is essentially about practising one's practice, akin to saying *rehearsing* leadership, so that one is given the opportunity to learn by experience, to gain confidence in one's ability to lead.

Two examples that illustrate this rehearsing mode of learning leadership can be found in the way improvisational theatre techniques are used, as well as music and other arts. These artistic forms of learning leadership development not only break out of traditional didactic modes of development; they are also at the heart of exploring the art of leadership as personal insight, a mode of learning which, in our view, is consistent with Bateson's (1979) 'deutero learning' – learning how to learn.

Improvisational and image theatre

One of the major barriers for organizational learning and shared leadership is the difficulty in uncovering, interpreting and changing power imbalances in organizations. Those power imbalances drain the creative energy of organizations and often result in fear, defensiveness, lack of initiative and significant gaps between 'espoused theories' and 'theories-in-use' (Argyris and Schön 1974). One of the approaches that is increasingly gaining momentum as a means of identifying and working with power imbalances is theatre (see Ferris 2002; Moshavi 2001; Coopey 1998; Boje 1995). Whether it is radical, improvisational or image theatre, the common thread is providing a space where practice, experimentation, expression and discovery can take place; a space where creating a shared story and where reflection in action and interaction with others help produce surprising outcomes rather than pre-scripted solutions. Dealing with the unexpected is not a feature of testing situations but of everyday life. Justifiably, therefore, attention in recent years has been placed on dealing with the unexpected through improvisation as a natural part of both theatre and organizational life (Weick 1998). Researchers who have studied improvisation and its application in a range of contexts (Crossan *et al.* 1996; Crossan *et al.* 1999; Hatch 1998; Moorman and Miner 1998; Weick 1998) explain that some of the main principles of improvisation are:

- 'yes and-ing', never denying information and building on other's ideas;
- active listening;
- being open to various interpretations, thinking without criteria, going with the gut;
- tolerating mistakes and supporting others by not judging one's own and other's ideas;
- active participation of all involved in the act (spectators and actors).

Moshavi (2001) provides an interesting illustration of how these principles can be introduced in the management classroom through exercises which can enrich traditional teaching methods, such as class discussion and role playing. Among the learning points that the application of the improvisational theatre techniques help generate, explains Moshavi, are that 'there are not right or wrong answers or responses, but there are "better" and "worse" responses' (*ibid.*: 440). By shifting the focus from fact to experience and intuition, Moshavi argues that 'the fear of being "wrong" subsides' (*ibid.*: 444). He also explains that '[p]utting the "yes and" principle into practice builds teamwork and trust by enhancing student ability to both listen and communicate' (*ibid.*: 444). Perhaps more fundamentally, improvisational theatre techniques empower students to have control of their learning and the activities in the classroom, through the 'freeze tag'[3] format. Moshavi points out that '[e]ach and every student has the power to freeze a faltering scene and enjoy the feeling of "coming to the rescue". Students who are "rescued" come to see that trust is given as a gift' (*ibid.*: 444–5).

What this approach to leadership development emphatically demonstrates is that one can only explore multiple perspectives (in a 'yes and-ing' mode), listen actively, embrace different interpretations and engage with the internal and external aspects if one *cares*! The issue of caring, like the issue of compassion (see Frost 1999), reminds us of how critical it is to think and value others.

An equally powerful technique that reinforces the improvisational principles discussed in the previous paragraph is 'image theatre', based on Augusto Boal's 'theatre of the oppressed'.[4] Ferris (2002, 2001) has successfully adapted the techniques of image theatre for team and leadership development in a software and business solution company in the paper distribution industry. The company was having trouble with morale, employee relationships and customer service, and Ferris believed that image theatre could give organization members the opportunity to recognize and address issues that they might be unable or unwilling to identify in more traditional discussion formats. Ferris started by having the chief executive officer (CEO) and staff use image theatre techniques to represent family relationships in a warm-up exercise to acquaint them with forming tableaus, in a non-threatening context. He then challenged participants to form a tableau that would represent their current work relationships. They arranged themselves around the room, some sitting at different distances from the CEO at the head of the table, some standing up and facing the wall, and one person (who frequently worked offsite) even leaving the room entirely. Ferris asked them to silently assess whether the resulting tableau was an accurate representation of their current relationships, and after some rearrangements they achieved a tableau that they all agreed was accurate, which was captured in Polaroid pictures to represent their 'actual image'.

The same process was repeated to form a tableau of the 'ideal image' of their interpersonal relationships and power balances, and another tableau of the 'transitional image' of how they would get there, both captured in Polaroids. The three sets of photos (current, ideal and transitional) then formed the basis for an 18-month organizational change process, during which the tableaus served as a non-threatening, effective language for insight and feedback, reaching deeply into the truth and hopes of the organization, and helping to form and communicate shared meanings. The success of the intervention was measured not only through various standardized assessment surveys of group process, but also in a dramatic 84 per cent improvement in their most important measure of customer service.

Arts and music

Recent years have seen an increased interest in exploring and effort to explore the relationship between arts and management.[5] Beyond the aesthetic view of organizing (Strati 1999; Linstead and Hopfl 2000; Strati and Guillet de Montoux 2002), however, there has been a more explicit effort to engage with poetry, painting and music as means of illuminating management and leadership (Vriesendorp 2002; Lindkvist 2002; O'Doherty and Richford 2002; Marcic 2002).

A useful metaphorical approach to leadership development has been developed by Marcic (2002), using arts and music to help executives tap into their innermost resources and develop the courage and willingness to experiment that are so necessary to becoming learning leaders. Marcic argues that the traditional management paradigm underutilizes the multiple intelligences of organization members by only addressing rational approaches to leadership development and leaving aside the aesthetic and emotional dimensions that are so critical to self-awareness, motivation, creativity, vision forming and sharing, power dynamics, communication, conflict, fear and defensiveness, attitudes towards change, and other individual, interpersonal and organizational phenomena.

Marcic proposes a 'harmonics of management' model that uses arts and music to encourage executives to let go of the self-presentation routines they use in the workplace, which reward expertise and reliance on what they already know and are good at, and to put themselves in the vulnerable position of trying something outside their area of competence and experience. For example, Marcic might ask workshop participants to write and perform songs that reflect some aspect of organizational life (e.g. current leadership challenges, ideal state, etc.). Participants and facilitator then explore the content of the songs, achieving insights about individual characteristics, interpersonal relationships and organizational dynamics that might have remained buried or been too threatening to address in more traditional discussion formats. This exercise gives the executives a sense of the creativity and insight that can be unleashed when they deal with a challenge as whole human beings, simultaneously exercising their rational, aesthetic and emotional intelligences. Given that most executives lack skills in song-making and musical performance, this experience also triggers a feeling of 'shared incompetency' similar to what happens in the outdoor adventure approaches to leadership development (Schrank 1994). By allowing themselves to experience such vulnerability in a group context, executives develop and practice the ability to enter the cognitive, emotional and aesthetic state that Peter Vail (1996) refers to as the 'reflective beginner', so essential to becoming a learning leader.

Marcic suggests several other ways of using the arts to draw from multiple intelligences and generate this experience of 'shared incompetency', involving drawing, painting and sculpture. No matter what form of art is chosen, Marcic highlights the crucial role of the facilitator, the need to allow ample time for debriefing, and the importance of having those experiences planned in a way that makes pedagogical sense, rather than just performing them for the sake of fun and games.

Like image theatre, what arts and music based approaches to leadership development also confront is our very comfort zones. By being exposed to images one is not familiar or comfortable with one is not only exposed to the wide possibilities that exist, but also invited to reflect, leverage and reframe one's way of seeing the world. This process invites us to transcend time and space as we understand it, and explore the timeless qualities of learning leadership in the way learning acts as the space for growth.

The issue of timelessness can best be illustrated in the unique quality that all forms of art share; namely that their representations of reality have the capacity to transcend time. Paintings, for example, have an anachronistic quality which allows our appreciation of the work to mature over time (in the sense of the *aging* Dalí; see Antonacopoulou 2003b). For when we stand before abstract and surreal images (like leadership), and when we delve to explore the reality beyond what is visible within and around it, there are a number of lessons to be learned. A simple lesson could be the need to critically rethink what we see when we think we see leadership, and to assess how we react to what we see. These issues are critical, because the way we choose to see and react to images (including paintings and other forms of art) tells us more about *us* than it tells us about the object.

Learning leadership: implications for future research and practice

The analysis of learning leadership presented here, together with the examples of developing learning leadership by employing improvisation and image theatre techniques, as well as arts and music, helps us distil a number of learning structures around the two main principles which we argue underpin 'learning leadership'; namely *leadership as a window to inner learning* and *leadership as a relational process*. By 'learning structures' (Antonacopoulou 1999b) we do not mean boundaries or restrictions in the way procedures may act as structures indicating the limits of action. The notion of structure in the context of learning leadership is akin to the notion of routine/rehearsal which we indicated earlier. What this view suggests is that one learns from experiences of experimenting/improvising leadership behaviour and actions to the extent that one also generates patterns of what works and does not work, so that one is able to bring those lessons to bear in informing and improving one's practice. Learning structures therefore, intended to support inner learning and a relational mode of practice as essential principles of leadership, act as flexible frameworks for providing social meaning and value to acts of leadership, which emerge through social interactions that allow one to reflect, reframe and leverage one's learning capability. It is, in other words, what Weick (1993) refers to as the 'grammar' through which actions are interpreted.

Characteristics of the learning structures embedded in improvisation and image theatre, as well as arts and music, include the following:

1   Awareness, alertness and attentiveness to one's own and other's learning and leadership needs.
2   Shared learning and leadership responsibility, by alternating complementary roles (teacher/learner, leader/follower).

3　The incorporation of discontinuity as a necessary feature of building a sense of continuity in the actions taken in relation to learning and leadership – one can learn from situations one does not initially perceive as adding learning value in the same way as leadership emerges out of situations which are unknown as much as familiar. Discontinuity reminds us that surprise is an integral part of learning and leading.

4　Mutual cooperation and agreement to deal with issues being presented in a spontaneous and flexible way which allows the adding on of what is being offered rather than seeking to judge whether it fits with one's existing framework. By adding to what is happening one lets things become what they can become, rather than limiting them to be what we perceive they ought to be.

5　Tapping into one's own and others' cognitive processes as a way of *leading out* the thinking processes that define leadership and learning.

These five learning structures are a window to inner learning through critical self-reflection (Merizow 1991; see also Yukl 1998), and they are a space in which leadership can be practised. It is through rehearsing multiple images of one's learning and one's leadership in relation to other's learning and other's leadership that one emerges as a learning leader. Kets de Vries (1989: 9) refers to leaders' 'inner theatre', which affects the courses of action they choose to take, which in turn hold the key to success and failure as a leader. Therefore, one of the fundamental issues that this analysis brings to the forefront is that, essentially, images of leadership can be accessed internally and not learned by rote externally.

This suggests that one of the most fundamental implications for leadership research is the need to recast the focus from one which represents leadership as a landscape of ideal practice to one which abstracts leadership as a context of learning practice. In other words, leadership can be conceived of as surreal – a super-reality which defies objectivist representations, but which affords multiple interpretations; that is, if we learn to see beyond what we expect to see or assume there is to see. Learning leadership, therefore, presents a fluid image beyond attributes and tasks, beyond behaviours and situations. Learning leadership is the coming together of all these features in a complex blend of colour that stimulates our senses to learn to feel the impact of leadership rather than simply insisting on seeing it if we are to testify to its existence.

This phenomenological, interpretivist view of learning leadership not only extends the current constructivist perspective of leadership, but also enriches it by drawing attention to the importance of discourse. Sensitivity to discourse in the way the languages of leadership and learning are being spoken and enacted reveals the emotional and cognitive structures that provide learning and leadership with their social meanings.

Taking this view a step further enables us to acknowledge that one of the main implications of learning leadership for management development practices is the need to reinstate *education*[6] (see Antonacopoulou 2000b, 2002c) as a fundamental feature of management development programmes. In the most basic sense, leadership development programmes need to encourage greater attention to self-learning as part of discovering the inner meaning of leadership. It could be argued that it is only through self-learning that learning how to learn is possible and that it is by 'learning how to unlearn' that learning leadership can be 'developed'.

Conclusions

The analysis in this chapter has sought to promote new ways of understanding leadership by advancing the notion of 'learning leadership' both as an alternative image of leadership and as a method of learning to discover leadership. Fundamentally, learning leadership invites us to explore different ways of seeing leadership, learning and their relationship. Therefore the notion of learning leadership and the main principles that underpin it remind us that learning structures which provide freedom to practise leadership are necessary as an avenue of self-learning and learning how to learn. Moreover, the examples of image and improvisational theatre, as well as the use of art and music to support leadership development, also encourage us to critically reflect on our representations of leadership, which may limit the possibilities to view leadership by learning to engage with the emotional and cognitive complexity it entails. The beauty of embracing learning leadership as a new paradigm for exploring leadership is that it effectively highlights the vast array of possibilities for learning that leadership entails, in the same way that learning is a space for new *leads* in one's being and becoming.

Notes

1　John Storey, personal communication.
2　'Individuality' refers here to one's unique qualities, which need to be identified and utilized. It would be argued that it is in our unique characteristics as individuals – what makes us different – that our leadership may lie, i.e. our difference makes the difference. The meaning of individuality, however, extends here to embrace the other meaning of what being individual means; namely un-divided, an inseparable part of the social whole.
3　Moshavi explains the characteristics of the freeze tag format and provides an illustrative example as follows:

> In freeze tag, two actors engage in a scene based on physical positions suggested by the audience (kneeling, hands on hips, etc.). As the actors begin to move about and create a dialogue, another actor can freeze the action. He or she then assumes the physical position of one of the actors on stage and then unfreezes the scene and redirects the action by creating a new scene. In the classroom, variations on freeze tag can be particularly useful for reinforcing and applying different theories relating to a specific organizational behaviour concept, such as leadership, motivation or power and politics…. Ask the class for a place of business. Accept the first response that reasonably fits the request. Typical responses are banks, stores, restaurants, hospitals, and factories. Next, ask for a type of business relationship between two people that are employed in this setting (rather than for the physical positions requested in the theatre version). Responses are

often based on the place of business suggested and include such relationships as: employee/supervisor, bank manager/teller, doctor/nurse, and so forth. After restating the theory, place of business and the type of relationship, tell the class that based on this information, two student volunteers will create a scene. Ask for two volunteers. Explain that when the scene begins to stagnate or the student volunteers begin to falter, someone in the class should stop the action by yelling, 'freeze.' Let them know that in your experience, this faltering often occurs within 15 to 30 seconds and almost always within 1 minute. The person who yells freeze then makes his/her way to the front of the room, taps one of the two student volunteers on the shoulder, and replaces him/her 'on stage'. The two remaining students then pick up from the point where the previous scene stopped and continue to advance the action until the scene is once again frozen and a student volunteer is replaced. (The instructor should be prepared to call out the first 'freeze' and join a scene if students are initially hesitant.) After there have been four or five 'freezes,' stop the action and ask for a new place of business and a new type of business relationship and repeat the exercise. This allows the class to apply the chosen theory in a different business context.

(Moshavi 2001: 442–3)

4   The 'theatre of the oppressed' is a form of theatre created by Brazilian director Augusto Boal (1979). In the 1960s, Boal subverted the traditional roles of actors and audience, moving from a model where spectators are expected to behave as passive 'reactors', separate from the actors (play as monologue), to one where 'spectators' are encouraged to become 'spect-actors', equal and active co-creators with the actors (play as dialogue). It all started innocently enough, with audiences being invited to discuss the play at the end of the performance. This soon evolved into a bolder process, where members of the audience could actually interrupt the performance and suggest different courses of action for the actors, who would then act out these suggestions. One day, a woman in the audience became so frustrated by an actor's inability to understand her suggestion for a change in the play that she stormed the stage and demonstrated what she meant. This incident was a watershed moment for Boal, who started doing by design what had just happened by chance (a living example of learning leadership!). He developed a form of theatre where members of the audience were expressly invited to go on to the stage to demonstrate their ideas and suggestions for change, thus becoming 'empowered not only to imagine change but to actually practice that change, reflect collectively on the suggestion, and thereby become empowered to generate social action' (Paterson 1999). Later on Boal extended this technique to use theatre as a form of social activism, where spectators are encouraged to comment on the social situations represented in the play and propose directions for change (A. Boal 1979). Boal's 'theatre of the oppressed' encompasses a variety of expressions (image theatre, forum theatre, rainbow of desire), all based on the idea that human relationships involve real or perceived power imbalances, resulting in oppressor–oppressed dynamics. Improvisational theatre, according to Boal, exposes those power imbalances and makes possible a renegotiation of those relationships. The possibly threatening nature of this process requires creative approaches that allow both the 'oppressor' and the 'oppressed' to step outside the known boundaries of the relationship and conquer the fear of the suppressed or unspoken truths. In 'image theatre', for example, a non-verbal, metaphorical approach is used to portray the participants' views and opinions on a theme, such as the nature of the interpersonal relationships and power balances between and among the members of a group, organization or community. Participants are asked to represent those views and opinions by forming metaphorical tableaus without using any words, just facial expressions and the positioning of bodies, furniture or other props in space. By suspending verbal communication, image theatre hopes to elicit feelings

that may have been suppressed, and to decrease possible one-upmanship and misunderstandings. Once the tableaus are formed, participants are asked to observe the resulting arrangement, and to correct it as necessary to achieve a 'true representation' of the theme, i.e. the image that is most acceptable to all. Participants are then asked to reflect on that image (the 'actual image', what is), and to repeat the process to form a tableau that portrays the ideal state for the theme being represented (the 'ideal image', what should be). Following a reflection on the contrast between actual and ideal images, participants are asked to rearrange the tableau to represent a 'transitional image' to show how it would be possible to move from the current situation to the ideal one (*ibid.*: 135).

5   September 2002 saw the launch of the Art of Management and Organization Conference in London. It was the first of a proposed series of international conferences the aims of which are to explore the dramatic increase in recent years of the articulation of the humanities and the field of social inquiry into management and organization, as well as the utilization of artistic processes in the activity of managing. The conference was informed by the field of organizational aesthetics and its dramatic growth over the past 10–15 years, and focused on those dimensions of management and organization that render them an art, not purely a science. More information about this and future conferences can be found at: http://www.essex.ac.uk/AFM/emc/second_art_of_management_and_org.htm.

6   When one carefully examines the meaning of the word education – from the root '*e*', from '*ex*', 'out'; and '*duco*', 'I lead', so that it means 'leading out' – it becomes even more clear that the business ideology of *domesticating* knowledge for organizational ends, which is a central characteristic of management development programmes, hardly approves of questioning, experimenting and critical thinking, all of which reflect more aptly the meaning of education (for a more detailed analysis in relation also to the notion of '*ekpaideusi*', see Antonacopoulou 2002c).

References

Alvesson, M. and S. Deetz (2000) *Doing Critical Management Research*, London: Sage.

Antonacopoulou, E.P. (1998) 'Developing learning managers within learning organisations', in M. Easterby-Smith, L. Araujo and J. Burgoyne (eds) *Organisational Learning and the Learning Organisation: Developments in Theory and Practice*, London: Sage.

—— (1999a) 'Why training does not imply learning: the individuals' perspective', *International Journal of Training and Development* 4(1): 14–33.

—— (1999b) 'Learning structures and their social construction: a European perspective on management education', *Comportamento Organisacional e Gestao* 5(2): 69–86.

—— (2000a) 'Employee development through self-development in three retail banks', *Personnel Review* (special issue on 'New Employee Development: Successful Innovations or Token Gestures?') 29(4): 491–508.

—— (2000b) 'Reconnecting education, training and development through learning: a holographic perspective', *Education + Training* (special issue on 'Vocational Education and Training in SMEs') 42(4/5): 255–63.

—— (2001) 'The paradoxical nature of the relationship between training and learning', *Journal of Management Studies* 38(3): 327–50.

—— (2002a) 'Learning as space: implications for organisational learning', *Proceedings of the 3rd International Conference on Organisational Knowledge, Learning and Capabilities*, Athens, Greece, April.

—— (2002b) *Revisiting the What, How and Why of Managerial Learning: Some New Evidence*, Manchester Business School Research Paper series, No. 442, Manchester.

—— (2002c) 'Corporate universities: the domestication of management education', in R. DePhillipi and C. Wankel (eds) *Rethinking Management Education*, New York: Information Age Publishers.

—— (2003a) *Learning as a Dynamic Capability: Implications for Leadership Development*, Manchester: Manchester Business School, Working Paper.

—— (2003b) 'The persistence of memory', *Organisation Studies* (special issue on 'Time and Reflexivity in Organisation Studies') 26(3): v–ix.

Argyris, C. and D.A. Schön (1974) *Theory in Practice: Increasing Professional Effectiveness*, San Francisco: Jossey-Bass.

Ashkanasy, N.M. and B. Tse (2000) 'Transformational leadership as management of emotion: a conceptual review', in N. Ashkanasy, C.E.J. Härtel and W.J. Zerbe (eds) *Emotions in the Workplace: Research, Theory, and Practice*, Westport, CT: Quorum Books.

Barry, D. (1991) 'Managing the bossless team: lessons in distributed leadership', *Organisational Dynamics* 20: 31–47.

Bateson, G. (1979) *Mind and Nature: A Necessary Unity*, London: Fontana.

Bisoux, T. (2002) 'The mind of a leader', *BizEd*, September/October: 26–31.

Boal, A. (1979) *Theater of the Oppressed*, New York: Theater Communications Group.

Boal, K.B. and R. Hooijberg (2000) 'Strategic leadership research: moving on', *Leadership Quarterly* 11: 515–50.

Bogner, W.C., H. Thomas and J. McGee (1999) 'Competence and competitive advantage: towards a dynamic model', *British Journal of Management* 10: 275–90.

Boje, D.M. (1995) 'Stories of the storytelling organization: a postmodern analysis of Disney as "tamara-land" ', *Academy of Management Journal* 38(4): 997–1,035.

Bolman, L. and T.E. Deal (1995) *Leading with soul: an uncommon journey of spirit*, San Francisco: Jossey-Bass.

Bradford, D.L and A.R. Cohen (1998) *Power Up: Tranforming Organisations through Shared Leadership*, New York: Wiley.

Brown, J.S. and P. Duguid (1991) 'Organizational learning and communities of practice: toward a unified view of working, learning and innovation', *Organization Science* 2(1): 40–57.

Cohen, M. and D.A. Levinthal (1990) 'Absorptive capacity: a new perspective on learning and innovation', *Administrative Science Quarterly* 35: 128–52.

Coopey, J. (1998) 'Learning to trust and trusting to learn: a role for radical theatre', *Management Learning* 29(3): 365–82.

Crossan, Mary, H. Lane and R. White (1999) 'An organizational learning framework: from intuition to institution', *Academy of Management Review* 24(3): 522–38.

Crossan, M., H. Lane, R. White and L. Klus (1996) 'The improvising organization: where planning meets opportunity', *Organizational Dynamics* 24(4): 20–35.

DeGeus, A. (1997) *The Living Company: Growth, Learning and Longevity in Business*, London: Nicolas Brealey.

Deverell, J.F. (1999) 'Can you teach leadership?', in *The Royal Society (RSA) on Work and Leadership*, Aldershot: Gower.

DiBella, A.J. and E.C. Nevis (1998) *How Organizations Learn*, San Francisco: Jossey-Bass.

Doyle, M.E. and M.K. Smith (1999) *Born and Bred? Leadership, Heart and Informal Education*, London: YMCA George Williams College/Rank Foundation.

Ferris, W.P. (1998) 'Fear, stress and second-guessing in leadership decision making: using interior monologues, reflective nonfiction, and spiritual approaches', *Journal of Management Education* 22(1): 26–48.

—— (2001) 'An innovative technique to enhance teambuilding: the impact of image theatre', *Academy of Management Proceedings* : B1–B7.

—— (2002) 'Theater tools for team building'. *Harvard Business Review* 80(12): 24–5.

Ferris, W.P. and A.R. Fanelli (1996) 'The learning manager and the inner side of management', in S. Cavaleri and D. Fearon (eds) *Managing in Organisations that Learn*, Cambridge, MA: Blackwell.

Finkelstein, S. and D.C. Hambrick (1990) 'Top management team tenure and organizational outcomes: the moderating role of managerial discretion', *Administrative Science Quarterly* 35: 484–503

Freire, P. (1970) *Pedagogy of the Oppressed*, New York: Herder & Herder.

Friedlander, F. (1983) 'Patterns of individual and organisational learning', in S. Srivastva (ed.) *The Executive Mind*, San Francisco: Jossey-Bass.

Frost, P.J. (1999) 'Why compassion counts!', *Journal of Management Inquiry* 8(2): 127–33.

Gardner, J. (1989) *On Leadership*, New York: Free Press.

Gardner, H. (1997) *Extraordinary minds: portraits of 4 exceptional individuals and an examination of our own extraordinariness*, New York: Basic Books.

Garratt, R. (1990) *The Learning Organisation*, London: Fontana/Collins.

Garud, R. and P. Nayyar (1994) 'Transformative capacity: continual structuring by intertemporal technology transfer', *Strategic Management Journal* 15: 365–85.

Goleman, D.P. (1997) *Emotional Intelligence*, New York: Bantam Books.

Grant, R.E. (1996) 'Prospering in dynamically-competitive environments: organizational capability as knowledge integration', *Organization Science* 7(4): 375–87.

Grey, C. (2002) 'What are Business schools for? On silence and voice in management education', *Journal of Management Education* 26(5): 496–511.

Hatch, M.J. (1998) 'Jazz as a metaphor for organizing in the 21st century', *Organization Science* 9(5): 556–7.

Hersey, P. (1984) *The Situational Leader*, New York: Warner.

Hodgson, P. (1999) 'Leadership, teaching and learning', in *The Royal Society (RSA) on Work and Leadership*, Aldershot: Gower.

Hooijberg, R. and R.E. Quinn (1992) 'Behavioral complexity and the development of effective leaders', in R.L. Phillips and J.G. Hunt (eds) *Strategic Management: A Multiorganizational-Level Perspective*, New York: Quorum.

Houghton, J.D., C.P. Neck and C.C. Manz (2003) 'Self-leadership and superleadership: the heart and art of creating shared leadership in teams', in C.L. Pearce and J.A. Conger (eds) *Shared Leadership: Reframing the How's and Why's of Leadership*, Thousand Oaks, CA: Sage.

House, R.J. and R. Aditya (1997) 'The social scientific study of leadership: quo vadis?', *Journal of Management* 23: 409–74.

Hunt, J.G. and J.A. Conger (1999) 'From where we sit: an assessment of transformational and charismatic leadership research', *Leadership Quarterly* 10: 335–43.

Jacques, E. (1989) *Requisite Organization*, Arlington, VA: Cason Hall.

Jones, G. (1999) 'The leadership of organisations', in *The Royal Society (RSA) on Work and Leadership*, Aldershot: Gower.

Kets de Vries, M. (1989) *Prisoners of Leadership*, New York: John Wiley & Sons.

Kim, D.H. (1993) 'The link between individual and organisational learning', *Sloan Management Review*, fall: 37–50.

Kouzes, J.M. and B.Z. Posner (1995) *The Leadership Challenge*, San Francisco: Jossey-Bass.

Lave, J. and E. Wenger (1991) *Situated Learning: Legitimate Peripheral Participation*, Cambridge: Cambridge University Press.

Lindkvist, L. (2002) 'The art of leadership – the examples of Ingvar Kamprad, Ingmar Bergman and Sven-Göran Eriksson', *Proceeding of the Art of Management and Organisation Conference*, London, September.

Linstead, S. and H. Hopfl (2000) *The Aesthetics of Organizing*, London: Sage

McDermott, G.R. (1994) 'Partnering with God: Ignatian spirituality and leadership in groups', in J.A. Conger (ed.) *Spirit at Work: Discovering the Spirituality in Leadership*, San Francisco: Jossey-Bass.

Manz, C.C. and H.P. Sims, Jr (2001) *The New SuperLeadership: Leading Others to Lead Themselves*, San Francisco: Berrett-Koehler.

March, J.G. (1991) 'Exploration and exploitation in organisational learning', *Organisation Science* 2(1): 71–87.

—— (1996) 'A scholar's quest', *Stanford Business School Magazine* 64(4), available at http://www.gsb.stanford.edu/community/bmag/sbsm0696/ascholar.htm.

Marcic, D. (2002) 'Tuning into the harmonics of management', in T. Brown and R. Brown (eds) *The Encyclopaedia of Management*, London: Bloomsbury Publishing.

Meisel, S.I. and D.S. Fearon (1996) 'Leading learning', in S. Cavaleri and D. Fearon (eds) *Managing in Organisations that Learn*, Cambridge, MA: Blackwell.

Merizow, J. (1991) *Transformative Dimensions of Adult Learning*, San Francisco: Jossey-Bass.

Moorman, C. and A. Miner (1998) 'Organizational improvisation and organizational memory', *Academy of Management Review* 23(4): 698–724.

Moshavi, Dan (2001) 'Yes and…: introducing improvisational theatre techniques to the management classroom', *Journal of Management Education* 25(4): 437–49.

Nelson, R. and S. Winter (1982) *An Evolutionary Theory of Economic Change*, Cambridge, MA: Harvard University Press.

O'Doherty, H. and J. Richford (2002) 'The art of leadership: balancing and blending wisdom, courage and compassion', *Proceeding of the Art of Management and Organisation Conference*, London, September.

Paterson, Doug (1999) *Augusto Boal*, available at: http://www.unomaha.edu/pto/augusto.htm.

Posner, B.Z. (2002) 'The challenge of finding the leader within: committing to leadership', paper presented at the Academy of Management Annual Conference, Denver, August.

Prahalad, C. and G. Hamel (1990) 'The core competence of the firm', *Harvard Business Review*, May–June: 79–91.

Quinn, R.E. (1988) *Beyond Rational Management*, San Francisco: Jossey-Bass.

Raelin, J. (2002) 'Leaderful practice', *Executive Excellence* 19(11), November: 6.

Sadler, P. (1997) *Leadership*, London: Kogan Page.

Salaman, G. and J. Butler (1990) 'Why managers won't learn', *Management Education and Development Journal* 21(3): 183–91.

Schein, E. (1992) *Organizational Culture and Leadership*, 2nd edition, San Francisco: Jossey-Bass.

Schrank, R. (1994) 'Two women, three men on a raft', *Harvard Business Review*, May–June: 66–80.

Selznick, P. (1957) *Leadership in Administration: A Sociological Interpretation*, Evanston, IL: Row Peterson & Co.

Senge, P.M. (1990) *The Fifth Discipline: The Art and Practice of the Learning Organisation*, London: Century Business.

Smircich, L. and G. Morgan (1982) 'Leadership: the management of meaning', *Journal of Applied Behavioural Science* 18: 257–73.

Strati, A. (1999) *Organization and Aesthetics*, London: Sage

Strati, A. and P. Guillet de Montoux (eds) (2002) 'Organising aesthetics', special issue of *Human Relations* 55(7).

Teece, D.J., G. Pisano and A. Shuen (1997) 'Dynamic capabilities and strategic management', *Strategic Management Journal* 18(7): 509–33.

Vail, P. (1996) *Learning as a way of being: strategies for survival in a world of permanent white water*, San Francisco: Jossey-Bass.

Vriesendorp, S. (2002) 'The poetry of leadership', *Proceeding of the Art of Management and Organisation Conference*, London, September.

Wakhlu, A. (1999) *Managing from the Heart: Unfolding the Spirit in People and Organizations*, New Delhi: Sage

Weick K.E. (1993) 'The collapse of sensemaking in organizations: the Mann Gulch disaster', *Administrative Science Quarterly* 38(4): 628–52.

—— (1998) 'The attitude of wisdom: ambivalence as the optimal compromise', in S. Srivastva and D. Cooperrider (eds) *Organizational Wisdom and Executive Courage*, San Francisco: New Lexington Press.

Wright, P. (1996) *Managerial Leadership*, London: Routledge

Yukl, G. (1998) *Leadership in Organizations*, Upper Saddle River, NJ: Prentice Hall.

Zaccaro, S.J., J.A. Gilbert, K.K. Thor and M.D. Mumford (1991) 'Leadership and social intelligence: linking social perceptiveness to behavioural flexibility', *Leadership Quarterly* 2: 317–47.

Zollo, M. and S.G. Winter (2002) 'Deliberate learning and the evolution of dynamic capabilities', *Organization Science:* 13: 339–51.

6 Corporate universities and leadership development

Rob Paton, Scott Taylor and John Storey

This chapter describes and analyses the use of 'corporate universities' (CUs) to develop leaders. It examines these processes through a study of four large multinational companies: the Royal Dutch Shell Group, Cap Gemini Ernst & Young (CGEY), Barclays PLC and BAE Systems. Each of these companies operates across continents, each employs tens of thousands of people, and each has its own corporate university.

The chapter thus focuses on one particular, currently popular, structural form for the delivery and support of learning in large companies. We explore the extent to which leadership development is prioritized within companies with a CU initiative, and the methods commonly used for developing leadership within CUs. We suggest that CU approaches to leadership development have some distinctive features, and consider the tensions and uncertainties that are associated with them.

The corporate university phenomenon

As has been noted elsewhere (Blass 2001; Paton and Taylor 2002), there are numerous different types of CU with different missions, a variety of structures and potentially diverse contributions to the host organization. In this chapter, we focus specifically on CUs that are oriented towards selective development of current and future leaders. We note that such CUs also work within a mission framework that includes corporate values development, the maintenance of 'corporate glue' through transmitting those values, and personal development programmes dedicated to fast-track, high potential employees. This kind of CU is identified with selectivity, focus on an identified organizational elite, and often has a rural, 'stately home' location (*ibid.*).

As is outlined below and discussed elsewhere in this collection, languages of leadership have been very much to the fore at a variety of levels in recent years. Indeed, the rise of rhetorics of leadership as a commonplace within personal development has coincided with the growth of interest in CUs. In the early 1980s, fewer than 20 were identified in the US. This list included early CUs such as Hamburger U (McDonald's), the Disney Institute and, perhaps the best known of all, Motorola U. Less than 15 years later, the primary US-based CU consulting firm CU Xchange (see http://www.corpu.com) judged that there were more than 1,200 CU initiatives in the US alone. In addition to this, large European organizations across a range of industries began to develop CU initiatives: thus, for example, Unipart U liked to be known as the 'third university in Oxford', Cable and Wireless set up its own UK-based college (and subsequently embraced IT-enabled distance learning to such a degree that the college buildings could be sold off), and Lloyds TSB invested in a CU initiative.

It is significant that the rise of CUs as organizational innovations closely parallels the spread of leadership as a language and basis for practice. As this chapter will demonstrate, *leadership is a key focus of CU programmes* aimed at higher level and high potential staff. Currently, therefore, CU initiatives are an important vehicle for the delivery of leadership development. The chapter explores possible reasons for this, the ways in which leadership development provision is structured by CU initiatives, and what leadership development provision through CUs might mean for both the managers being developed and the leadership programmes.

The rest of the chapter is structured as follows. First, we examine the concept and outline the development of the corporate university phenomenon, from early roots in the US to its current global presence. Included in this is a discussion of the characteristics of CUs, a summary of the cases that form the empirical foundation of the analysis in this chapter, and the key differentiators of CUs as an innovation in the management of corporate training and development. This introduces the notion of strategic learning initiatives. Second, we explore the concepts and models of leadership that underpin leadership development in our cases, locating our analysis within contemporary understandings of leadership as a corporate and policy discourse. Third, we explore the pragmatics of leadership development programmes delivered by CU initiatives, focusing on the pursuit of strategic alignment, the methods employed, and operational issues such as costs, infrastructure and partnerships. Finally, we conclude with a discussion of the dilemmas and ambiguities associated with attempts to institutionalize leadership development in this way. In the process, connections are made to some longstanding debates about the place of leadership and leadership development in formal organizations.

What are corporate universities?

Early discussion of CU initiatives tended to focus first and foremost on the way private companies were seeking to appropriate the terminology and symbolism associated with institutions of higher learning (e.g. Eurich 1985; Craig *et al.* 1999). It is undoubtedly the case that there is a symbolic importance for established universities in the corporate trends of organizing training and development under a title such as 'University', 'College', or 'Academy'. Such symbolism operates both within the host organization and beyond into the wider society. However, for the purposes of conceptualizing CU initiatives the precise term a company may (or may not) use is less important than understanding both the continuity with and the differences from previous methods and structures for delivering workplace-based learning.

In our view, a corporate university is better understood as the most recent approach to providing a structure that enables important forms of work-related learning to occur within and for companies. This allows CUs to be seen as a pragmatic and practical development of notions such as the learning organization (Senge 1993) or the learning company (Pedler *et al.* 1991). But further, if we examine the history of training and development as an aspect of the industrial organization of work, then we can begin to see CUs as part of ongoing attempts by managers to structure employee engagement with knowledge and learning, and to incorporate such engagement within wider strategic concerns. In this perspective, CUs are less a new fashion than the latest manifestation of a long-standing effort to meet corporate learning requirements.

The emergence of CUs

'Corporation schools' began to emerge during the mid-19th century US, when large companies such as DuPont and Edison set up technical and liberal arts education for current and prospective employees (Eurich 1985). These institutions were intended to correct perceived inadequacies in state provision, as employers reportedly found it difficult to recruit employees with the requisite skills or attitudes. These early corporate education initiatives continued to train employees on this basis well into the 20th century, expanding to include the emerging profession of management. The structure of corporate education was changed radically, however, by technical colleges and universities willing to deal with business and management, both as consumers of education and as a subject area. The success of the first schools of commerce in the UK, in Birmingham and Manchester, was an early indicator of the potential in dealing with work organizations. This early faith has been borne out: business and management courses today are the single most popular subject in UK universities, and over 20 per cent of undergraduate courses contain a component relating to this area. Schools dedicated to the study of business and management are now found in most British universities.

Wiggenhorn (1990) indicates how such educational themes continue to be relevant in contemporary organizations. He outlines the managerial rationales behind restructuring employee education in Motorola, arguing that initial investment in Motorola U was stimulated by the need to implement new working practices requiring a more autonomous worker. Line managers found themselves unable to implement corporate directives on new methods of working with the large proportion of employees who were functionally illiterate and non-numerate or unable to follow instructions in English. According to Wiggenhorn, this 'discovery' resulted in two key innovations in corporate training. First, managers began to assess employees on a wide range of key skills that would normally have been taken for granted, and, second, Motorola representatives began to make more demands as to course content and delivery from third party suppliers.

From these roots, CU initiatives have spread across US industrial sectors and can now be found in manufacturing and services. In addition, in common with many managerial fads and fashions (Littler 1982), CUs have been exported across the Atlantic in the assumption that what is good for US business may be beneficial to UK and European organizations. This process has been in part driven by the development of a consultancy mini-industry around CU initiatives, led by Jeanne Meister (1998). Meister provides an outline of the business drivers for implementing a CU initiative, setting out changing conditions of organization (from bureaucratic to post-Fordist, emergence of the knowledge economy, replacement of lifetime employment with employability), and locates CUs within the learning organization discourse (asserting that a common goal of corporations with CUs is to sustain competitive advantage through lifelong learning). Finally, Meister codifies key aspects of CU initiatives: the commitment of senior management to the initiative, forming learning alliances with existing educational providers, increased use of technology to deliver learning experiences, and the operation of the CU as a separate cost centre.

We would suggest that two of the contexts that Meister outlines are paramount in understanding the recent rise of CUs. The first is the role of the internet and computer-based learning in the re-engineering of training and development activity. Inflated claims for e-learning during the dot.com boom have been replaced by more measured approaches in terms of 'blended learning', and the debate tends now to be about what sorts of 'blends' for what sorts of learning. In any event, the leaders of multinationals believe – on the basis, now, of considerable experience – that these technologies can support modes of learning that, for some purposes and contexts, are more timely, more accessible and more cost-effective than traditional approaches. And such views inform their learning strategies. Second, as we have suggested above, there is increasing emphasis on the role of learning both in managing work and in sustaining competitive advantage, following primarily from the work of Senge (1993). This chapter treats both of these dynamics as conditions within which CU initiatives are managed and experienced.

Table 6.1 attempts a brief summary of key aspects of the CU initiatives in the case organizations. It tries to capture the essential features of evolving corporate arrangements that were in all cases subject to significant change even during the course of the fieldwork. These features are: the strategic drivers for setting up and maintaining the CU, as expressed by senior managers within the CU structure; the form and approach that each CU takes; and the location of the initiative within the organization (whether physical or virtual, including the reporting relationship). In addition, the table outlines briefly the issues to which leadership development is perceived to be the solution, the scope and focus of programmes, and the methods that underpin the programmes.

Differentiating CU initiatives

From this brief outline of the development of contemporary CU initiatives and the representation of our cases in Table 6.1, we would suggest the following as the distinctive features of this method of organizing training and development, including leadership:

1 *Corporate level strategic initiatives.* First, CUs are intended to be both corporate and strategically oriented. A higher level of decision is evident in the management of the initiatives than is common in managing training and development, making CUs distinct from the human resource (HR) function within business units, and often distinct from HR altogether. CUs aim to deliver on a specific corporate contribution, such as re-engineering training and development provision through e-learning, outsourcing supply, or a broad rationalization of supply. In addition, CU managers focus more on the notion of providing a 'corporate value added', as one put it. This means avoiding the replication of what is done well at a local level, such as basic induction or skills training, while seeking to add corporate values such as a transnational approach or common cultural content. The scope of such content varies between organizations (and within them over time), but it is given high priority and significant resourcing within all of our case organizations.

2 *The pursuit of continuing strategic alignment.* Following from the above, a core differentiator in managing leadership through a CU is the intention to control more effectively training and development activities in relation to strategic priorities, whether they are group-wide integration, building customer loyalty, cross-cultural working, high flier retention and development, more cost-effective and timely staff development, or indeed leadership. Allied to this is an aspect of leadership development management that we explore in more detail below: as strategic priorities change, so must CUs and their programmes, meaning that everything about and in CUs is provisional.

3 *The attempt to raise standards, expectations and impact as regards training and development.* This aspect of CUs reflects the priority afforded to strategic learning, and may be seen in attempts to identify and engage the highest quality providers almost regardless of location; the development of sophisticated frameworks to increase consistency of provision; reinforcement of key messages and competences between levels and across diverse business and cultural settings; innovative programme designs, including much greater attention to pedagogy; the use of information and communication technologies (ICTs) through e- and blended learning and by fostering distributed communities of practice; and rationalization of the sourcing of education and learning services from external providers. Clearly it would be false to suggest that all of this is new and that all previous corporate training and development was non-strategic, unsophisticated, non-innovative and so on. As Eurich (1985) argues, corporate education has consistently adopted new forms and methods of educational provision before other providers. Nevertheless, what emerges from our case analysis thus far is the explicit aspiration of CU managers operating at very senior levels and from within

Table 6.1 Four corporate university cases and their primary dynamics

	Shell Group	CGEY	Barclays	BAE Systems
Strategic drivers	developing senior leaders; rationalization of global training spend; maintenance of health and safety standards globally; empowering individuals	post-merger integration; cross-cultural working; technological change; development of intellectual leadership and market positioning; customer relations; income generation	reorganization of business unit HR function; rationalization of training spend; increase in individual responsibility for career management	post-merger integration; development of learning organization; knowledge management across business units; internal benchmarking; more recent development focus on senior leaders
Form and approach	corporate ('global') learning remit includes OD and business improvement activities, as well as leadership development; these complement ICT-enabled technological and professional development (including some leadership) provided by major business units	'blended learning'; internal design of programmes – mix of internal and externally contracted provision; emphasis on communities of practice; complements training and development work undertaken by business units	dispersed small centres across the UK for lower level training; CU offers higher level training and development as 'quality assured'	small HQ staff provide basic e-learning, knowledge management services and infrastructure to group, and approve major learning providers; provide internal benchmarking/business improvement consultancy, bespoke programmes
Location in company space	within corporate HQ; purpose-built facility	purpose built facility near company HQ; reporting directly to executive board	administrative offices near corporate HQ; small sites around UK	no one central (bricks and mortar) learning facility; originally reporting to board, latterly reporting jointly to HR and technology vice-presidents

Issues to which 'leadership is the solution'	need for senior leaders of the highest calibre if the company's position in industry is to be maintained	need for consultants to cope with high levels of uncertainty and ambiguity, and show initiative and resilience	difficulty of differentiating service; need for cultural integration of traditionally autonomous business units	originally little consistency of approach across merged business; raising awareness of managers to corporate ethics and responsibility; to improve business performance
Scope and focus of leadership programmes	high potentials, through all management levels	all levels, including high potentials and potential 'thought leaders'	top tier of each business unit	top tier (currently)
Methods	A, B, C, E, F	A, B, C, D	A, C, E, F	A, B, C, D, E

Notes:

A   competence framework

B   coaching

C   use of e- and blended learning

D   networked community

E   business school consortia and partnerships

F   academic advisors (employed on CU board or as strategic advisors) the corporate centre to more closely manage standards in provision, in alignment with organizational strategy.

It is important to emphasize here that the notion of a corporate university remains loose and is still evolving. Even within the case organizations that form the basis for empirical analysis in this chapter there is a wide, disparate variety of managerial logics to the initiatives. In addition, organizational sponsorship and location of the initiative are diverse. These internal differences, combined with broader differences between the US and Europe, all indicate that an assumption of homogeneity is unwarranted. Nevertheless, we suggest that the aspirational characteristics listed above, in combination with the appropriation of educational symbolism and terminology in order to promote learning, can be found across CU initiatives. These characteristics express our working hypothesis as regards what is distinctive about CUs compared with more familiar approaches to training and development. They also provide the structure for describing and discussing how leadership development is provided through CUs in the rest of this chapter.

Leadership and its status in CU programmes

This section provides evidence for our claim that leadership development is a major focus and priority for CUs. It also describes some of the ways that leadership is discussed and operationalized in CUs.

Leadership as a corporate priority

The language of leadership heard within CUs is an aspect of two significant recent trends in managing people: human resource management (HRM) and competence frameworks. Within HRM, a shift towards transformational leadership and away from transactional line management is a key demand on line managers responsible for implementing new practices (Storey 1992). Similarly, many competence frameworks refer to leadership either in addition to or in place of 'management' as a key skill for the contemporary workplace. The embedding of leadership within frameworks focusing on everyday practice such as these indicates how much of a corporate priority it is, at all levels of organizations. From being a preserve of high fliers and those at the apex, leadership (or at least the language of leadership) appears to be percolating down through corporate hierarchies, in part through CU structures.

Parallel to these workplace developments, leadership also currently forms a central aspect of state policy towards management development. This is most evident in various government initiatives. First, the latest UK government review of management and management education in the UK sits under the title 'Council for Excellence in Management and Leadership'; it is the first such state sponsored committee to include leadership so explicitly within its remit. Second, the recently opened National College for School Leadership (which may be understood as, in effect, a CU for a particular part of the public sector; see Chapter 11) focuses on developing leaders from the school head population, with little mention of management. Third, as part of 'Modernizing Government' professional development programmes within the senior civil service are now highlighting the language and practice of leadership, rather than management or administration (e.g. the *PRIME: Leadership* online modules commissioned from within the Cabinet Office for the senior civil service).

Hence, as well as expressing the challenges of particular organizations and industries (as described above), the adoption of the language of leadership reflects broader currents in industry and government. These shifts in rhetoric and discourse would seem to provide further legitimacy and urgency to leadership initiatives. Indeed, some form of leadership development appears to be obligatory in contemporary organizations. This is in part manifest through high levels of economic investment. The Boeing Corporation may go further than most but it illustrates the point: according to a CU Conference presentation, programme participants at its large purpose-built facility eat in a five star restaurant, and, rather than watching film or video to dramatize corporate social responsibility issues, they enjoy the performance of a small troupe of actors regularly flown in from New York. Every month, too, main board members visit to contribute to leadership courses.

It is hardly surprising, therefore, that these trends are reflected in our case organizations – indeed, leadership development was seen as a core activity in all of the case CUs. The high priority afforded to leadership was revealed in different ways. It was made central to the operation of the CU at Barclays through the creation of a 'faculty':

> As part of the establishment of the university we've created four faculties. We've got one on leadership, we've got one on customers, we've got one on technology, and then [one on] reputation, which covers both the risk reputation side of banking, which is a traditional one, lending money, but also the brand and marketing side of reputation. We have deans of faculty in each case – each one of those people is a member of the executive committee, so they are significant players in their own right. The leadership faculty is supported by an external professor to give us some kind of benchmarking and to challenge some of our thinking.
>
> (CU Project Manager, Barclays)

The same manager later showed the priority he and others gave to leadership development in describing a choice he had made:

> A chief executive of a business unit wanted a leadership programme.... The director of OD [organizational development] said to the CU director, 'Look can you solve me a problem here? Pragmatically can you solve it?' Now if somebody else came to us from a team with a hundred people in an office in London and said, 'Will you develop such and such a programme for me?'

I'd say no, I can't do that because I've only got this much time and this much money. I'm going to divert that money on to that which I think is intrinsically high value.

(CU Project Manager, Barclays)

This manager also spoke of the effort that CU staff gave to making sure that the 'top leadership' team within the bank was involved in such programmes. Obviously, providing development opportunities for the highest levels in the organization ensures visibility, and potentially support, for the CU.

At Shell, leadership was on the agenda at both corporate and business unit levels. For the former, it was a very large part of the brief given to the Head of Global Learning by his manager:

[His] brief to me when I arrived was really two things: 'We need a learning strategy for the mid-term to underpin the people strategy, which makes reference to learning but doesn't really indicate where we are going....And very specifically within that, leadership development is already on the agenda because we know we haven't been doing anything in this area and we're getting concerned about identifying future talent – future potential talent – and what we should be doing to not only assess the talent that we have, but in fact developing that talent for the future'....So it was a great brief.... And very quickly, leadership development...was at the front of those two things.

(Head of Global Learning, Shell Group)

Concepts and models of leadership in CUs

Our case organizations grappled with the meaning of leadership even as they emphasized its importance. For example:

Shell was already using leader and leadership terminology, but when you asked what that meant there was relatively little understanding other than a replacement for the term 'manager' and 'managing'.... So the first thing we did was to work on the Shell Group leadership framework to give substance to our use of this language.

(Head of Global Learning, Shell Group)

Both he and the project manager for the Shell Open University emphasized that, without a common language to frame the notion of leadership, promoting a consistent concept of leadership across an organization is problematic. Often, diverse approaches to the area arise, dependent on the provider with whom different parts of the organization work. For such reasons all the case organizations had developed competence frameworks to provide a common language for discussing leadership issues and as an underpinning for leadership programmes. Nevertheless, such frameworks did not entirely resolve questions of meaning and usage:

What does leadership mean? To me there's a blend, isn't there, of tangibles and intangibles. That is what leadership is about. I think, from an organizational point of view, BAE Systems has put together a competence framework that is there to measure the tangibles. And the intangibles – the things like integrity, energy, inspiration – are still very important and somehow you still need to work out how those fit, and how you get that rounded individual.

(Leadership Development Director, BAE Systems)

This illustrates the tension between defining leadership in such a way that 'it' can be developed through an organization, measured and appraised for in terms of behaviour, and then further developed if necessary, and maintaining the more individual, mysterious element of leadership. This echoes the difficulties encountered in the UK in the 1980s, when the Management Charter Initiative proposed a set of management competences generic to organizations and management contexts.

A second feature of leadership discourse in the case companies was the way it was linked to current strategic issues – to an extent, it was a solution that was available for discussing or addressing a wide range of problems. For example, at BAE Systems post-merger integration was a key challenge, and it is interesting that 'leadership' provided a legitimate way for senior managers to express their concerns:

About 18 months ago we commissioned some focus groups with the top 600 [managers]. They were asked a number of questions about how they felt about the organization, how they felt the [recent] merger had gone, what they thought the issues were that needed to be addressed, and leadership came out as the key issue in that. Since that point it's become a pillar, one of the things that's been a hot topic. After the mergers I think the company had indigestion, it was so busy trying to get people into jobs and sort out what it owned and all those sorts of things. I think that feeling now has passed, and people have come to terms with it one way or the other. They've either got dissenchanted with it and left, or they've said, 'I can see what type of organization we are now', so now it's more about what type of leadership we want, what type of leadership we want to aspire to.

(Leadership Development Director, BAE Systems)

This challenge is echoed in the Cap Gemini Ernst & Young (CGEY) corporate university, under the heading of 'convergence' (indeed, assisting convergence is a major part of the CU's remit and not just as regards leadership):

When I joined the university [it] had lost its way a bit – it lost its footing within the organization and when the new [CU] president was brought in, he had the role of telling the CEO what we should do with the university. Either we turn it around and we make it a central player again or we close it down. This is when I was recruited – he brought me in to put into place the International Business School [for high potentials], which was the first programme that bridged the [two recently merged] organizations. It was the first group programme, the first time that we said, 'Okay, let's go and let's get our talent and let's create a bridge across these two parts of the organization.' At that time within the company the big buzzword was what we call 'convergence'.

(Director of Education, CGEY University)

CGEY has located leadership development within this broad remit of promoting a central, corporate understanding of values, approaches and methodologies.

Nevertheless, concepts of leadership within CUs are not simply a function of current management issues; they are also strongly related to the industries in which they are located, and the continuing challenges that parent organizations face. These influences show up in different ways. For example, the leadership competence framework at Shell includes the items 'demonstrates professional mastery' and 'demonstrates courage', both directly reflecting the advanced technological capacities and challenges that characterize the company's activities. As one informant put it reflecting on the strengths and weaknesses of leadership in Shell, as evidenced by benchmarking data:

It's very interesting having applied this now for the past two years to start to get the data about the leadership population as well as individual profiles.... We know that Shell is hugely strong on, erm, professional mastery. You don't get into the organization without demonstrating professional mastery and you survive on the basis of professional mastery. It's fascinating to see the evidence build up over time. Some *real* strengths and some significant weaknesses and some stuff we are getting better at. [We're] really quite courageous – [this] stems from, again, (being) at the frontier of technology, sometimes at the frontier of wilderness exploration, vast investment in platforms and drilling and so on, we know something about going for it with courage. And you can relate all this stuff to…the feel for the culture you get when you've worked in the organization for a bit.

(Head of Global Learning, Shell Group).

By contrast, CGEY managers working in information systems related to business consulting, process re-engineering and large-scale systems implementation, saw a need for employees to be able to tolerate high levels of uncertainty and ambiguity, to maintain a sense of direction and priorities, to take risks and to 'make things happen' without waiting for direction or approval. The culture of this industry is well captured in books like *Thriving on Chaos* (Peters 1987), as one informant pointed out. Another referred to *Leading the Revolution* (Hamel 2000), and went on to say:

> So many times in organizations everyone sits there and says, 'Well, if the top were giving us the strategic directions, if the board were telling us this or that', and, you know, it's never going to happen. Maybe we should just be adults and say, 'Well, maybe that's not where we should be looking for it. Maybe that's not what their job is.'... [What we try to do is] create bubbles of sanity and excellence within the organization...that means that a lot of that stuff isn't going to be coming from the top, it is going to be happening in the middle where people are actually interfacing and have those day-to-day interactions with the clients.... So we're saying, you know, 'Look, that's not just a bedside book anymore...it's life!'
>
> (Director of Education, CGEY University)

In sum, senior managers are promoting CU initiatives in order to enable organizational reflection on the meaning of leadership, and as structures within which methods to construct an agreed notion of leadership can be operationalized. Thus, a key contribution of CU structures in leadership development is the provision of frameworks and processes through which generic concepts of leadership can be understood, made locally meaningful, and then implemented more or less consistently across diverse settings. It appears, too, that considerable effort is invested by CU managers and senior executives in constructing a comprehensible language through which such leadership development can then be energetically pursued.

Approaches to leadership development through CUs

It is beyond the scope of this chapter to review in any great detail the ways in which the case study CUs have pursued leadership development in the various technical senses. This section attempts to highlight some recurring features, focusing on strategic alignment, the sorts of methods used, and how CUs are positioning themselves internally and externally.

Strategic alignment

It was argued earlier that a key purpose in creating a CU was to ensure continuing and close alignment with corporate priorities. This concerns *how* CUs operate, and not just the content of the programmes delivered. We can illustrate this by indicating how the case CUs addressed three interrelated and recurring strategic concerns – integration (some aspects of which have already been referred to), cost reduction/value for money, and building knowledge communities.

The rationalization of learning provision was a recurring theme in the accounts informants gave of the way their CUs contributed. As the CU director in Barclays related, the corporate group has been able to rationalize existing supply of training in two ways, the first of which is by taking stock of the training and development on offer across the business units, in order to centralize provision. This is exemplified in the area of leadership development: Barclays now offers one course in this area, where there used to be 12 different options for line managers across the group. Second, the 'headcount' in business unit support functions has been assessed and managed down. Comparable developments took place at BAE Systems, while at Shell and CGEY the focus was on identifying the best training and development professionals and facilities within the group and making them the basis for future provision. Such rationalizations were seen as delivering a combination of reduced cost, improved quality and greater consistency (through the promulgation of a common terminology and approaches across diverse locations). The delivery of e-learning resources across company intranets was another way of ensuring a shared vocabulary and consistent messages, and at the same time achieving cost savings (e.g. by reducing the need for expensive face-to-face elements with associated travel and subsistence).

A concern for integration was behind the explicit linking of leadership development with knowledge management and the building of company-wide professional networks and communities of practice. In other words, the concept of leadership was seen as relevant in professional and technological domains, as well as in business strategy and decision-making. Thus, at CGEY:

> This is the place where people come to build and to maintain their communities; this is the place where you're going to come and meet with your fellow specialists or the people that have a similar area of competence that you do, or that are on a similar track. If you start looking at things like – we call it talent development, but in other organizations it's called leadership development – if you look at that area, those are people that are on a similar track and they face similar challenges. What's interesting about them is that they form a microcosm of the organization because they cut through all the different professions, across the different countries, everything. [The] people that are in our high potential group are on a similar track so they need to be leveraging things across the organization. Those [two areas] are very important to the positioning of the university.
>
> (Director of Education, CGEY University)

Approaches to leadership development

The competence frameworks already referred to are central to CU efforts to engender a degree of coherence across very diverse cultural and operating environments. 'Coherence' here means vertical and horizontal consistency across business units, with a particular focus on transitions. Hence the companies use structured and stepped or staged development from first appointment leader through to senior executive. For example:

We have the top team and what we call the Performance Centred Leadership population – these are the strategic leaders – and the development of that group is very much supported by the CU. We also have leadership programmes in what we call executive development and functional development, and these are handled in the business units, as is the leadership development of our manufacturing and administrative staff.

(Leadership Development Director, BAE Systems)

And likewise:

We go through and we say, 'What's the competency level?' For talent development there are four key areas in our organization. There's 'Young Professional', between 12 and 24 months into the company; then Manager level; then Executive Proving Ground; then the 'Global Executives' level. This is going to be through the managers at foundation level.

(Director of Education, CGEY University)

Such programmes aim to promote distributed leadership and employee empowerment at the same time as giving renewed emphasis to high potentials and elite leaders. They are multi-track and multi-method, making commodified learning resources on leadership widely available, while also targeting high cost elements more selectively, on the basis of different forms of assessment – for example:

We took that leadership framework into an assessment setting and have extended Shell's experience with assessment centres for graduate selection – for which we're sort of world famous – into assessments for development at various stages in leaders' careers. And we now provide some of the most comprehensive data on personal strengths and weaknesses in terms of needs for development that I've ever seen in an organization....

[Later, pointing to diagram:] In the leadership assessment and development area [there are] four key leadership transitions: first, appointment leader – 10,000–15,000 of them around Shell; managers of managers; executives; and the senior executive group. A leadership framework underpinning all of this with assessment for development on this side of the framework and education on the other side. So educational activity responding to need via assessment.

(Head of Global Learning, Shell Group)

For high potentials, considerable effort is made to sustain and reinforce leadership development. The 'communities' at CGEY are one important means for this – but other methods are also used:

We organize learning events for the alumni on a regular basis. This is about developing them and their personal effectiveness – we have an 'Advanced Leadership Seminar' done with an external person, which allows them to talk about their careers, perhaps make connections to people that they didn't necessarily know beforehand because they were on a different programme. One of the things in that programme that we build in is coaching – it creates a buddy who you can reach out to and kind of say, 'I've got a question about this....' They really appreciate that sort of stuff.

(Director of Education, CGEY University)

Likewise, the alumni concept was taking root at Shell:

We're closely connected to INSEAD online because people who have been through a Shell/INSEAD programme basically say: 'Am I now part of an alumni network? Where's the continuous development? What's next? What access to resources do I get?' So we're using INSEAD online as an initial answer to that...in the same way Wharton has a thing called Wharton Knowledge, so everybody who has been through a Shell/Wharton programme gets access to Wharton Knowledge. IMD has a thing called IMD Wednesday Webcast that [is] only available to people issued with IMD passwords, so Shell alumni going through IMD programmes get access to that. So there are bits and pieces around at the moment, not separately developed but off the back of business school partnerships.... It's a bit fragmented but we're playing and experimenting. It's on the agenda.... What I'm trying to do – on the basis of cooperation between the schools – is to build the Shell alumni network irrespective of which school you've been to, drawing on the continued use of resources in schools. But that's more complex.... But the basis that anybody that has been through a Shell leadership programme – irrespective of level – becomes part of an alumni...a learning network...that's established.

(Head of Global Learning, Shell Group)

Another feature of the leadership development methods used by the CUs was their willingness to experiment sometimes with unconventional approaches. For example, within its consulting industry 'Thought Leadership' was an important concern for CGEY, and its University developed a programme – 'Guruschool' – specifically to support this. They were also prepared to create emotionally challenging activities for participants:

[We] have the 'Leaders of Leaders' programme – that's done externally. The facilitators discuss [issues] with the executives in our company, the global executives. For the teaching part of Leaders of Leaders we have quite a confrontational approach, so we want that to be done by someone externally.

(Senior manager, CGEY)

Organization and partnerships

CUs are generally comprised of a small core group of staff who variously design, commission or quality assure programmes, and who work with and through prestige partners and suppliers to deliver them. The most common business model is for some infrastructure and programme development costs to be covered centrally but for the main costs of programmes to be recovered from the business units who send participants. Three features of such arrangements need to be emphasized.

First, the CU itself is generally separate, or at least semi-detached, from HR and from the training and development function in business units. Thus:

> In reporting terms, there is a joint responsibility to the group HR director, the director for Technology and the director for Strategy – there are thus three key players to whom the Virtual University reports. But the HR function in the business units and the senior leaders of those units are our key cutomers and we need to ensure that the development solutions we provide meet the strategic needs of the businesses they work in.
>
> (Leadership Development Director, BAE Systems)

The position was more complex at Shell, where 'Global Learning' was part of a small corporate HR team. But the Shell Open University was a discrete entity with a separate reporting line:

> We are responsible for the technical, engineering training, and they [the central HR department] see themselves as responsible for generic management skills and the competencies, the top managers, and also the high flying youngsters who come in and want to get on the career ladder and do management training, leadership and coaching.
>
> (Head of Learning, Shell Exploration & Production)

However, both parties explicitly acknowledged that clear boundaries between technical and personal skill development would never be established; hence some blurring and overlap was inevitable, and the key was to ensure consistency through common frameworks.

Second, though a special corporate programme might be mandated at the most senior level, CUs were generally selling their frameworks and leadership programmes into business units. And in such cases the buying decision remained, ultimately, with the business unit. The arrangement at BAE Systems was described in the following way:

> There's nothing to stop a business unit going out and buying training from wherever it wants to – the only proviso to that is [exclusion of] the top 650 of the company we've determined as a corporate population, and they're all subject to the same sort of people processes like personal development reviews, 360 peer review, management review, career management, all that sort of stuff. It's kind of like a corporate framework, a corporate leadership framework. But below that, yes, you can go, theoretically, you can buy from who you want.
>
> (Head of Leadership Development, BAE Systems)

Of course, not all needs are met though in-house courses, so another important service provided by CUs is to identify and signpost quality provision for the centre and for business units:

> What I would be doing, rather than saying: 'Here's a brochure,' I'd be saying: 'We've done some research on this. We know who the providers are. This has been quality assured and I can tell you this is the best place we've come across for your particular need.'...Brokerage with quality assurance. Those days of 'Here's a catalogue...'. So we're really attempting to add some value even as the intermediary.... An example of that is when a senior leader comes along – as they quite often do in the early evening – drops by the office: 'I really recognize a particular area where I'm feeling more and more vulnerable. I really don't want to expose this on a Shell activity...but I need a programme or a workshop, or something.'...Or an executive coach, yep, that's a really good example: 'Erm, what's your advice Mike? Give me the best two or three to choose from.' That's happening all the time.
>
> (Head of Global Learning, Shell Group)

Third, CUs used external, often global, standards to define high quality for a given need, but often also as a means of benchmarking and driving down costs.

Thus, for example:

> [Our primary academic partner], yes, their research rating is important – they've got a five star, but usually it's personalities. It's like when you buy from a consultancy, my experience is you want to hire a top individual.
>
> (Head of Leadership Development, BAE Systems)

Likewise, at CGEY:

> When you get up here [to senior management level] it's almost all external people [delivering programmes], because we're pushing our high potentials to think 'It's not business as we do it today, it's how we could be doing business tomorrow.' The main content portions and the big pieces are almost all external, although when I say external it doesn't necessarily mean professors. It can be professors from business schools – we have professors from London Business School, from INSEAD, from Oxford, from North Western, but it can also be consultants that are from specialized consulting companies. So we have their critical messages [and] they work with a communications consulting company based in the UK that is specialized in communicating with the City and with the financial press, because that's what this is all about. It's about delivering business results – they are going to help them work on structuring their

messages just as they would help CEOs structure their message to the City or to analysts.

(Director of Education, CGEY University)

However, the CUs were not handing over control of the programmes to such suppliers. Rather, they were making very searching and specific demands on what were often elite partners – concerning content, case studies, timeliness, collaboration with other parties and so on.

Discussion: practical tensions, theoretical perspectives

The picture that emerges from our CU cases is of leadership development efforts that are increasingly comprehensive, sophisticated and sustained. This does not mean that they operate without problems. On the contrary, the challenges facing these CUs – particularly as regards the cultural, organizational and operational diversity their schemes had to encompass – are colossal, and tensions are inescapable. Relations with customers in business units could be bumpy, and all the longer established initiatives had experienced searching 'reviews' in which costs had to be justified and confidence in long-term benefits re-established. 'Eighteen more people at head office is not fashionable nowadays', as one manager put it. Moreover, those involved were often ready to acknowledge the limitations, dilemmas and difficulties involved:

> So, you know, is it perfect? No! Will it ever be perfect? No! And, you know, I would love to say that all the conversations are easy, but there are quite a few that aren't. But that's part of being in a professional position as well.
>
> (Director of Education, CGEY University)

Sometimes these tensions reflected different conceptions of development and how it was best undertaken:

> I think you can actually integrate learning into their day job, but when [the company has] an engineering base like us, we like to believe in things that are absolutely tangible. Naturally then the organization says, 'Well, tell me what training programmes there are, how long they will be, and how much they cost' – almost regardless of whether that's the right solution. We are starting to get people past that approach now, thank goodness.
>
> (Head of Organizational Learning, BAE Systems)

More specifically, the Head of Leadership Development at BAE Systems pointed to an issue at the heart of his role:

> The Stategic Leader Programme is about giving our senior leaders (many of whom do have a very similar profile, many of whom have been internally developed so they are homegrown senior leaders) an exposure to a different

worldview, a different perspective. And it's also about how they take that and translate it into how they are and how they behave. How that affects them in the way they lead. So that's what it's about. And a good way of helping them challenge their perspectives on how they see the world is by getting them to experience bits of the world and to run up against things that challenge their values and challenge their perspectives. For example, we took a group out a few years ago to Bosnia, and we went to Mostar, we went to Sarajevo. We did everything from meet the Prime Minister and have discussions with him, through to talking with artists and musicians. You know, when they walk through the streets they see the devastation ... each morning we ran a reflection session just about what's going on. For some people it has huge impacts, for some people it doesn't. When it was designed it was quite risky. It's not a 'tools and techniques' course – though there are some business-type inputs, so you've got some tangible parts. It's a programme that's been a bit of an investment of faith over the years. It's hard to measure.

(Leadership Development Director, BAE Systems)

The underlying issue here concerns whether and how far leadership development is a process that can be rationalized and institutionalized in a reliable fashion. The tension was experienced and expressed very acutely by an interviewee from another CU:

They [the company board] wanted the CU to be two things. They wanted it to become a project run in a particular fashion, and they wanted the leadership programme that they were running at the side of it to be run as a project. And I thought, 'We're talking about development as a project?' It was crazy – there was just so much effort put into the project formation that you were knackered before you started. It was supposed to run like a Swiss watch and yet it totally disengaged the individual.

(Project Manager, UtilityCo)

The point here is not just whether a particular event or programme is perceived by participants to be valuable and gives rise to indicators of company benefit (e.g. retention rates or differential rates of subordinate satisfaction, – generally, the CUs were conscientious and ingenious in gathering or identifying such data). It concerns whether such discrete events and courses can be coherently integrated and sustained across highly disparate and turbulent settings sufficiently to provide long-term corporate benefits in relation to a diffuse and notoriously elusive concept.

Indeed, one well established school of organizational analysis conceptualizes leadership in terms of charisma, and argues that it is antithetical to rational organization and always in tension with it. The processes of routinization that underpin organization, manifest in the problem of succession concerning the next leader and in the development of structure, are central to this tension (Bryman 1986). Perhaps, however, the development of a structure such as a CU which promotes leadership at all levels can reduce the problems of 'followership' that have undermined previous succession strategies. The *quasi-routinization* of leadership and its development in CU programmes may be seen as a method of ensuring succession while attempting to retain a sense of the charismatic nature of leadership.

Kanter's (1972) notion of 'institutionalized awe', whereby charisma is made to permeate a social entity rather than remaining lodged in an individual, also seems relevant here. She argues that routinized structures can become imbued with a sense of charisma – and arguably this can apply to a CU. For example, in our interviewing there was no doubting the respect that some alumni of the CGEY University had for their CU. It had been the context for formative professional experiences and they saw themselves as privileged in having been given the opportunity to pursue programmes through the university. The parallels here with the historic role of elite universities in providing leadership in ideas and thinking, and in educating the leaders of tomorrow, are obvious.

This opens up the possibility that CUs may be able to reconcile the Weberian opposition between leadership and organization. However, for this to happen CUs, or at least key aspects of their activity, will have to become institutionalized – that is, valued, more or less stable and enduring features of the corporate landscape. It is far from clear how this might happen. A central characteristic of CUs, we have argued, is their commitment to continuing strategic alignment, and this means their priorities must continually adapt to an evolving corporate agenda. Though in some respects a space apart from the turbulence of corporate life, in other respects they are at the heart of it. The continuity and longevity associated with elite universities could not be further from the experience of CUs, which in some cases have been substantially redesigned about every five years. Ensuring the necessary continuity and embedding of leadership programmes in such circumstances is thus likely to be a major and continuing challenge.

Conclusions

This chapter has argued that CUs and the renewed interest in leadership development are close cousins. Both are compensatory responses to the new forms of organization that have emerged from 20 years of global integration, industrial restructuring, and ICT-based re-engineering. CUs recognize the need for integration, culture building and knowledge management in order to realize the benefits of mergers and restore intellectual capital lost through delayering. The provision of explicit 'leadership programmes' is a recognition that corporations no longer generate enough of the sorts of people who can point the way ahead in the new turbulent, pressured and loosely structured corporate environments. Moreover, the requirements (for versatility, risk-taking, self-confidence, interpersonal skills, resilience, sensitivity to context and 'multi-lingualism', for example) are significantly different from what was sought through management programmes in the past. The required competences cannot be whistled up through a one-week course or two, or even by an analytically focused MBA. Hence, comprehensive and sustained leadership development programmes have become a priority for CUs.

The result of such efforts appears to be the emergence of a new process of leadership *formation* – in the sense of deliberate formative experiences being provided early in a career, with these then being extended and reinforced in a consistent way thereafter. It is too early to judge how successful these efforts are, and they face major challenges with regard to embedding and continuity. But, as we have shown, leadership development through corporate universities is being undertaken in earnest. In the cases considered, the initiatives have been well resourced and subject to sophisticated thinking using a wide combination of methods, and (in the main) with wide support and involvement from critical stakeholders at the most senior levels.

References

Blass, E. (2001) 'What's in a name? A comparative study of the traditional public university and the corporate university', *Human Resource Development International* 4(2): 153–73.

Bryman, A. (1986) *Leadership and Organizations*, London: Routledge & Kegan Paul.

Craig, R., F. Clarke and J. Amernic (1999) 'Scholarship in university business schools: Cardinal Newman, creeping corporatism and farewell to the "disturber of the peace"?', *Accounting Auditing and Accountability Journal* 12(5): 510–24.

Eurich, N. (1985) *Corporate Classrooms: The Learning Business*, Princeton, NJ: Carnegie Foundation for the Advancement of Teaching.

Hamel, G. (2000) *Leading the Revolution*, Cambridge, MA: Harvard Business School Press.

Kanter, R.M. (1972) *Commitment and Community: Communes and Utopias in Sociological Perspective*, Cambridge, MA: Harvard University Press.

Littler, C. (1982) *The Development of the Labour Process in Capitalist Societies*, London: Heinemann.

Meister, J. (1998) *Corporate Universities: Lessons in Building a World-class Work Force*, 2nd edn, New York: McGraw-Hill.

Paton, R. and S. Taylor (2002) 'Corporate universities: between higher education and the workplace', in G. Williams (ed.) *The Enterprising University*, Buckingham: Society for Research into Higher Education (SHRE) and Open University Press.

Pedler, M., J. Burgoyne and Tom Boydell (1991) *The Learning Company*, London: McGraw-Hill.

Peters, T. (1987) *Thriving on Chaos*, London: Book Club Associates.

Senge, P. (1993) *The Fifth Discipline: The Art and Practice of the Learning Organization*, London: Century Business.

Storey, J. (1992) *Developments in the Management of Human Resources*, Oxford: Blackwell.

Wiggenhorn, W. (1990) 'Motorola U: When training becomes an education', *Harvard Business Review*, July–August: 71–83.

7   Can leadership be taught?

Graham Mole

As noted in the introductory chapter to this book, the leadership training and development industry is big business. It is also an expanding business fuelled by a phenomenal growth in the demand for and the supply of leadership training and development programmes. This growth is associated with the increasing popularity of 'leadership' as a source of interest for organizations. This in turn is associated with the strength of contemporary belief in the magnitude of the effect of leaders on organizational performance. Underlying this belief appears to be another one, frequently revealed in popular managerialist literature, that leadership can be taught through the simple transfer of knowledge of its essential ingredients. The number of ingredients to be used varies depending on taste. From current book titles it seems there may be just seven 'habits' which need to be acquired, or 'nine leadership keys to success', or as many as '21 irrefutable laws of leadership'. This formulaic approach to training and developing leaders, of *teaching* people leadership in the same way one might teach geometry, is widely distributed and deeply embedded, and nowhere more so than in commercial training and development practice.

Many organizations working in this field use the word 'leadership' in their company name. Many more others include it in their menu of training offerings. Keying in the search command 'leadership AND training' to a search engine gave me 2,520,000 website hits from which to choose. We may infer from all this that we are meant to believe that leadership is capable of being transferred in a didactic way from the learned to the learner. As I have pointed out elsewhere (Mole 1996, 2000), it is in the interests of the training industry that we should believe this. The hallmark of leadership courses offered on the open market is their complete disregard for the organizational contexts in which their participants operate. A one-best-way approach is mightily convenient. There is no need to research the job content of the participants, the issues they face in their roles or the environments in which their organizations are operating. Instead, those who attend are likely be offered a fascinating voyage into self-insight, aided and abetted by the wisdom and self-report questionnaires of the likes of Bandler and Grinder, Berne, Covey, Goleman, Myers and Briggs and other luminaries from the world of popular psychology. The proposition here is that it is impossible to lead others without a deep understanding of oneself. It is a mantra which can be summed up by Zaleznik's somewhat eerie observation that 'leadership is a psychodrama in which a brilliant, lonely person must gain control of himself or herself as a precondition for controlling others' (1992: 127). Those who recite and adhere to this position might possibly be dismayed to learn of Dixon's view, based on his review of conspicuous examples of military incompetence, that 'some of the most effective leaders have been those who, merely through having more than their fair share of psychopathic traits, were able to release antisocial behaviour in others' (1994: 215).

Having learned more about their inner selves, it is likely that participants at our archetypal leadership training course will then be encouraged to learn about how to relate more effectively to others. What better way than to play competitive team games – crossing real or imaginary streams using only ropes, poles and oil drums, hunting for treasure, building paper towers or abseiling down cliff faces? The similarity between these activities and the actual challenges which the participants face in their jobs may be minimal or non-existent, but no matter – many will enjoy (as I admit I have) the experience of these games and feel affirmed by them. As Goffman noted:

> Another possibility is that games give the players an opportunity to exhibit attributes valued in the wider social world, such as dexterity, strength, knowledge, intelligence, courage, and self-control. Externally relevant attributes thus obtain official expression within the milieu of an encounter. These could even be earned within the encounter, to be claimed later outside it.
>
> (Goffman 1972: 61)

Woe betide those who do not enjoy such games because they find themselves intimidated or unfairly exposed by them. Again, I have witnessed this effect on people in leadership training situations. Perhaps this adverse experience makes them conclude that they are not, after all, cut out to be leaders, because they do not match the leader stereotypes portrayed by the trainers. Sadly, such a conclusion might be false but nevertheless career limiting for the individuals concerned.

The final main ingredient in the leadership training course recipe is likely to be a selection of better known – not to say overworked – frameworks from the world of organization development (OD). Old favourites include Maslow's (1943) hierarchy of needs theory as an explanation of individual motivation; Hersey and Blanchard's (1982) 'situational leadership theory'; and Senge's (1992) 'learning organization'. Regardless of the specific frameworks cited, however, the choice over citation will be that of the trainers, usually based on their own preferences, habits and comfort levels, and not on the job requirements of the trainees. At the end of their leadership training experience most of the participants – except, of course, those who feel puzzled, hurt or damaged by the experience – will go away feeling refreshed and quite good about themselves. But will this have any effect on the quality of their performance as leaders back in the workplace? Since this type of training is rarely evaluated and, when it is, the case for its efficacy is often found lacking (Tannenbaum and Yukl 1992;

Thomson 1998), few will know what its effect has been, and most will not be interested. Least interested of all will be the commercial training organizations, who, having provided the courses, waved goodbye to their charges and taken their fees, will probably never see them again – unless for a subsequent 'refresher' or 'advanced' version of the course. If my criticism here appears somewhat cynical, it is as nothing compared to the level of cynicism I have heard expressed by some commercial trainers. In one memorable instance I was advised by a trainer that the purpose of an initial outward-bound course was to 'hook' the participants and stimulate their demand for a subsequent more expensive, more exotic programme which involved scuba diving in the Mediterranean.

My primary aim in this chapter, however, is not to castigate ineffectual trainers, but to demonstrate that any attempts to teach people the universals – the 'irrefutable laws' – of leadership are most likely to result, using any sensible criteria for evaluating training effectiveness, in failure. In order that the reader is not left in total despair, my secondary purpose is to describe, largely out of personal experience, some ways and means of assuring and enhancing the effectiveness of leaders, in the context of the specific organizations in which they work.

Why can't leadership be taught?

Let me start by making clear that my position is not based on the nature versus nurture argument, as expressed in the tired old cliché 'leaders are born, not made'. This argument, which serves very well those people who have already attained a leadership position, is rhetorical rather than biological. It offers a model, which owes more to Nietzsche than to Darwin, of the genetically hardwired leader, the superman figure. Such individuals will always, regardless of social setting or the nature of current events, have both the motivation and the ability to assume the dominant power position in any group in which they find themselves. They are truly natural leaders, created for the purpose of leading herds of lesser mortals, and they are rare. It is hardly surprising that some of those in leadership positions wish to perpetuate this myth, since scarcity is equated with economic value and is used to justify large rewards. The power of the born leader myth is remarkably strong, despite its persistent inability to stand up to historical, actuarial, sociological, biological or psychological analysis. Indeed, the empirical *coup de grâce* should have been delivered more than 60 years ago. As Fraser notes:

> From what may well have been the first empirical studies of leaders by a psychologist (Terman 1904) onwards, great efforts were made to specify personality and social correlates of individuals identified as leaders. And such correlates were discovered in abundance. If anything, too many were discovered, in that different studies tended to produce quite different lists of characteristics, The nadir of the approach came with Bird's (1940) review of twenty studies of the traits of leaders. In all, almost eighty characteristics were reported, of which more than half were reported in only one study,

very few indeed were common to four or more investigations, and only one, intelligence, emerged from at least half of the studies.

(Fraser 1990: 191–2)

The fact that the quest to link leadership with certain personality traits or types has proved unremittingly fruitless (Landy 1989; Kniveton 1996) has been no deterrent for those who go on looking, relentlessly, for what Grint calls the 'alchemy of leadership' (1995: 124 *et seq.*). Whether they do so out of curiosity or the need for certainty, or any other reason, is not something I will examine here, though I have little doubt that the search for the universal, 'identikit' leader will continue. But if the essentialist notion on which it is based, that leadership is a fixed property of the individual, is fallacious, then one is forced to ask on what leadership *is* based, since that might help inform us about how easy or difficult it is to teach. One of the more promising areas of theory making in this area has been in what Landy (1989: 526) terms 'reciprocal' theories. Leadership does not exist in a social vacuum; it only exists in terms of the interaction between leader and followers.[1] Whether this phenomenon is entirely attributional, such that the construct of leadership is used retrospectively to account for events (Grint 1995), or there is an objectively measurable relationship between the variables of situation, leader behaviour and follower behaviour (as postulated, for example, in Hollander's [1978] social exchange theory of leadership) is immaterial so far as trying to teach it is concerned. The point is that the variables which can intervene in the relationship, or compact, between leader and followers are many and diverse, which renders them difficult to predict and control. Were this not so, Charles I and Louis XVI would have kept their heads, Churchill would have won the 1945 general election and Margaret Thatcher would not have been deposed by a putsch from within her own ranks. The disaffection of followers leads every day to the dethronement of surprised and hurt leaders – football managers, chairs of company boards, criminal gang-leaders, prominent holders of political office. It leads to mutinous or subversive behaviour by subordinates (Ackroyd and Thompson 1999). The great thing about leaders is that, because of their symbolic importance, the amount of attention given to them and the commensurate emotional investment in their performance (Schein 1992), when a badly performing one is discarded everyone else feels an instant sense of relief. Far easier to blame and eliminate one figurehead than share the responsibility and guilt among many. The execution of one messiah expiates a multitude of the sins of others, and allows the search for a new messiah to begin.

My contention, then, is this. No leader – even (or perhaps especially) a currently successful one – can predict with any certainty how changing circumstances and events might affect the relationship with his or her followers. S/he may have more experience of dealing with a variety of circumstances and events than others, and have learned from them, but still be limited by the bounded rationality which limits us all. S/he does not have perfect information, or an understanding of all the possible outcomes of any given situation. The most crucial aspect of leadership – how to keep it – simply cannot be taught. And even if it were possible to capture and transfer all the knowledge and experience of those who had been most successful in holding on to leadership, it would not be enough. Because leadership is a social phenomenon, it would never be enough to teach leaders to be good at leadership; we should also have to teach all their followers to be good at 'followership'. Admittedly, such an approach has been tried, by people we usually call dictators, using a teaching method we usually call indoctrination and for a purpose we usually call obedience. But obedience, though induced with relative ease, as Milgram (1974) found, can equally be easily diminished by social influence. Minority voices, when they are assured and consistent, are powerful sources of persuasion (Moscovici 1976). Attempting to counter these with the use of coercion can prove a costly strategy to sustain (Tedeschi 2001). Even in organizations which Goffman (1961) termed 'total institutions', such as prisons, prisoner of war camps and mental hospitals, a coercive leadership regime may be subverted by the inmates, sometimes quite openly and with the connivance of the staff.

From this, the conclusion must be that leadership cannot be taught as though it were a context-free subject. Context is not just important to the way leaders behave; it is axiomatic. Leadership cannot be treated as though it were a portable set of knowledge, skills and attitudes; what works in one context may be conspicuously unsuccessful in another. However, this does not mean that organizations are powerless to influence the quality of the work of those who perform leadership roles for them. I see no reason why the performance of leaders, in terms of the outcomes they achieve, should not be as subject to variation as any other occupation (Cook 1991). The trick is, as it usually is when it comes to human performance, to understand very precisely what the requirements are of the role concerned, in the specific context of the organization and the environment in which it is operating. As an analogy, think of two equally gifted and technically able pianists, except that one is classically trained and earns her living playing in a symphony orchestra, and the other earns his living playing in a jazz quartet. While both might be able to play each other's music, the classical pianist will rarely be expected to improvise and, even then, such improvisation will be within the narrow constraints determined by the composer. A good performance will usually be seen as her faithful adherence to the score. The jazz pianist, on the other hand, will be expected to improvise nearly all the time, only interpreting the score as a general guideline to melody, harmony and tempo, around which to use his imagination and experiment. Indeed, if he kept solely to the notes as written he would not be appreciated by jazz audiences. Talent is as people expect talent to be, and this applies conspicuously to those in leadership roles.

Understanding the leader's role

From the experience of facilitating numerous group processes and observing the behaviour of leaderless discussion groups in assessment centres, I find the model of role-sending and role-receiving (Katz and Kahn 1978: 190) appealing, and particularly so with respect to leadership:

All members of a person's role-set depend on that person's performance in some fashion; they are rewarded by it, judged in terms of it, or require it to perform their own tasks. Because they have a stake in that person's performance, they develop beliefs and attitudes about what he or she should not do as part of the role. Such prescriptions and proscriptions held by members of a role-set are designated role *expectations*; in the aggregate they define the role, the behaviours expected of the person who holds it.

> (Katz and Kahn 1978: 190; emphasis in original)

The dynamic process of creating expectations can be observed as a to-and-fro game between the emergent leader and the followers. According to Bion (1991), there is a general tendency for this process to be enacted by people in groups, even when there is no obvious, immediate purpose to be served by having someone perform a leadership role. Describing a situation where a group appeared to be desperately searching for a leader from within, Bion, with apparent exasperation, noted that either 'the desire for a leader is some emotional survival operating uselessly in the group as archaism, or else there is some awareness of a situation, which we have not defined, which demands the presence of such a person' (*ibid.*: 39). From this it follows that organizations could save themselves much time, and their employees much heartache, by defining their expectations of leaders as closely as possible. If done thoroughly and realistically, these definitions could serve a number of organizational purposes. They could be used, for example, to help select and recruit people who are likely to meet those expectations more effectively than others *within that specific organizational context*. Going back to the pianist analogy, does the organization generally do better with leaders who stick faithfully to a tightly written score or those who improvise – sometimes wildly – around it? If it is a large, multifunction organization it may well have different expectations of leaders, contingent on the functions performed in the different parts of the organization (Lawrence and Lorsch 1986). However, if the expectations are well defined, then the whole recruitment process becomes infinitely more realistic than a quest to find superman or superwoman, both for the questing organization and – crucially – for the applicant, too (Herriot 1991; Schuler 1989).

The same logic applies to other possible treatments of leaders, for example how they should be assessed in terms of their current performance (e.g. appraisal) or future potential (e.g. decisions about promotion, transfer, secondment or succession planning). It also applies to how they should be trained to enhance their abilities to perform their roles. In saying this, have I not just unwittingly destroyed my own earlier argument about the teachability of leadership? No; I am speaking here not of context-free 'leadership training' but of highly context-specific *job* training, where the leadership role has been defined in terms of its content, outcomes, and the knowledge structure, skills and attitudes which are most strongly predicted, on the basis of empirical evidence, to be associated with successful performance of that role. So, for example, the British armed forces do not teach leadership; they train people in how to perform as officers. And, as Hardinge (1992) points out, a substantial amount of that training is technical.

This is not surprising; in order to be a successful tank commander, a thorough understanding of tank technology should be a distinct advantage. Yet the technical content of the training required for the successful performance of leadership roles is rarely cited, and certainly not by those who make their living selling generic 'leadership training'. If one proffers one's product as a magic formula based on a finite number of laws, rules or successful habits, one could never admit that a large component of the training for a leadership role needs to be grounded in the specific technology of the organization in which the leader works. Over a number of years, I have observed one persistent Achilles' heel with leadership trainers. When one of them works with a group of executives from a single company, the trainer frequently receives criticism from participants for not knowing enough (and occasionally for knowing nothing at all) about their particular business. The basis of the criticism is twofold. First, trainers should not expect to receive a fee without doing some homework about their customer and, second, they should not make assumptions about the nature of leadership roles in the organization without a decent understanding of what the organization does.

So, in order to understand any leader's role we need to understand both the organizational context in which it exists and what the leader is expected to achieve in terms of outcomes – winning tank battles, winning elections or turning around the fortunes of failing hotel chains. These are in the nature of what Blum and Naylor (1968) term *distal* criteria of performance. But it would also help, particularly if we want to successfully recruit people for leadership positions, to assess their performance and to enhance their effectiveness as leaders, if we set out to understand the *proximal* criteria of effectiveness, which are concerned most with the processes which leaders use in order to achieve the distal outcomes. Effectively, this means – in simplistic human resources (HR) terms – creating 'job descriptions' for leadership roles, the validity of which will be dependent on the quality of the job analysis done to create them. But is this *too* simplistic? Is it possible to conduct sound job analysis for roles which are, in their nature, highly fluid and difficult to operationalize (Campbell *et al.* 1970; Cascio 1991)? Those who have attempted to do it, and I include myself among them, would not deny the difficulty, but might well, as I do, consider that it was worth the effort.

How can it be done? There are several job analysis methodologies available to practitioners (Pearn and Kandola 1988), but I am going to focus on one, the application of which I have described in detail elsewhere (Mole 2000). This is the development and use of competence frameworks. Salaman (Chapter 4) roundly – and in my view rightly – criticizes the claims of the so-called 'competence movement' to be able to use competence models to solve the problem of ensuring management commitment. He argues, and I agree, that competences were the great 1990s panacea, to be replaced by leadership in this decade. And it's entirely true that we no longer see competences prominently displayed on management and HR fashion rails. It would be easy to dismiss this as a failure of the concept rather than a failure of implementation, but I strongly believe it is the latter. Like it or not, many practitioners are susceptible to the promises of single-issue gurus and the movements they spawn, in HR as in other walks of organizational life

(Gill and Whittle 1993). Arguably, some practitioners are dependent on these promises as something they can use to sell to their sponsors to help justify their existence, in much the same way that data processing managers used to depend on a steady stream of new products from hardware suppliers. Worse than selling, they oversell, so that competences are elevated from being a job analysis technique to a recipe for organizational cohesion, commitment, culture change and anything else in that idealized model of organization where all the major features begin with the letter 'c'. When competences inevitably fail to deliver against these lofty promises they suffer the same fate as failed leaders, to be dropped, buried and forgotten with unseemly haste, and the quest for a suitable successor initiated. If competences were portrayed as the final HR solution that was a grievous fault, and grievously have competencies answered for it.

Although the idea of competences has been criticized on conceptual grounds (Cockerill 1989; Jacobs 1989; Reed and Anthony 1992), it has also received some acclaim (see particularly Boam and Sparrow 1992). My view, speaking as someone who has attempted to design and implement competence models in my organization over the last 10 years, is that the idea is sound provided that we keep it within the bounds of feasibility. Competences are a means of performing job analysis, at a relatively high level of abstraction, and nothing more. But their advantage lies in those cases, as Pearn and Kandola (1988) point out, where a relatively high level of abstraction of analysis is desirable, and leadership roles are just such a case. We cannot prescribe every method which a leader might use as means to various ends, but we can categorize them within a meaningful typology of constructs, such as 'ability to effect large-scale change in a manufacturing environment'. For each such construct, we can create an operational definition of what it means in terms of process and outcome. We can even define levels of competence and create a nominal scale so that these levels can be rated by direct observation, or on the basis of experience as, for example, by manager ratings or 360 degree feedback from multiple raters.

There is an the issue about the way that 'competence' is defined, and that, as for any other heralded source of salvation, has been the subject of some theological debate. I favour Woodruffe's definition of competence as 'the set of behaviour patterns that the incumbent needs to bring to a position in order to perform its tasks and functions with competence' (1992: 17). Though tautological, its value in a leadership context is that it does not imply or assume that the behaviour patterns are bound up with innate characteristics of the individual, but that they are purely requisites of effective performance of role. So, whilst we cannot teach leadership, we can identify and hold up models of what types of leader behaviour are more effective *in our own organization* than others. Again, I stress organizational context because there cannot be one set of behaviours which fits all organizational circumstances. Competences, if they are to have any value, have to be deeply and rigorously researched, tested and validated within the focal organization. The worst possible way of accessing them is to ask for an armchair design from the most senior people in that organization. You will probably end up with exactly the same set of attributes as if you had asked them for the qualities of an identikit leader. Worse still, you might generate a list of irreconcilable dichotomies: 'firm but flexible'; 'loose/tight'; 'quick to act, but reflective', and so on. We have all seen them.

If we can't teach 'leadership', can we teach the competences of leaders?

From the above, it can be seen that, by conceptualizing competences as a form of high level job analysis, I have assigned them the function of being predictors of successful performance in a leadership, or any other given, role. The use of predictors can be highly beneficial in selection and assessment, as it can in trainability testing (Downs 1992). But that is not to say that any behaviour which is highly predictive of effective performance can be readily taught. Suppose, for example, that years of patient gathering and analysis of bio data revealed that the most effective leaders in a particular organization, in terms of outcomes achieved, displayed very low levels of emotional stability. Extreme neuroticism, if that is how we might wish to label the source of such behaviour, is in that area which we would call 'innate characteristics'. However, it is conceivable that neurotic-looking behaviour can be modelled, observed, learned, imitated, practised and replicated if the observer perceives that doing so will lead to an efficacious outcome (Bandura 1977). Predictors of performance which are associated with particular abilities, such as intelligence, should, one might think, be extremely difficult or impossible to attain for certain individuals, but even then we should never underestimate the power of expectation. If analytical thinking ability becomes valued in an organization, for example because an incoming leader displays and promotes it, it might be surprising to find how much analysing ability is suddenly released among the rest of the work force.

From this, I would argue that many, and probably most, leader competences in organizations can be learned to some extent, though a few of them could prove painfully difficult, if not downright impossible, to teach. The value of competences, when they are well grounded and clearly articulated, is that they not only provide models of ideal behaviour, but also facilitate recognition of that behaviour. In other words, they create a *de facto* standard towards which people can be encouraged and guided to move. This is no more or less than a practical application of Bandura's (*ibid.*) social learning theory, which has been found to be an effective basis for management training design (Burke and Day 1986; Latham and Saari 1979; Latham 1989). For those, like myself, whose role requires them to improve leader effectiveness through 'training', it offers the best chance of achieving some meaningful outcomes. As I have made clear, the traditional approach to leadership training stands precious little chance of changing anything other than the participants' timetables, surroundings and diets for a few days. I would ask anyone who has experienced such training to try a simple test, by answering three questions. First, as a result of attending the training, can you recall how it changed the way you work? Second, can you recall how changing your work improved your performance? And, finally, compared to other learning experiences you have had, for example those which resulted from a change of role or receiving a bad appraisal, how powerful was it? I would predict that few readers will be able to give encouraging responses to these questions.

Implemented well, however, the use of job analysis as the basis for improving leader effectiveness – let us call it evidence-based learning – can also offer some other distinct practical advantages over traditional leadership training:

- It will almost certainly attract a lower cost. Because the focus is on real jobs in a real organizational context, there is little point in transporting participants to an offsite artificial environment, such as a residential hotel or an outward-bound centre. (It is high time we shifted our thinking away from the idea that training is some sort of 'break from real work'. It should be all about real work, and nothing else.) Similarly, it will not require the use of expensive 'know thyself' types of self-report questionnaire, or the expensive people who are brought in to administer and interpret these. Another costly and tiresome cliché which can be avoided is the ubiquitous after-dinner 'motivational speaker'. And so on.
- It can be delivered in relatively short sessions. Because it does not require time for spurious team games or the regurgitation of cherished OD frameworks, or travelling to and from offsite locations, the content can be delivered in short, sharp bursts of one day, a half-day, or sometimes even less. Participants and their managers tend to value this, as it is less disruptive to their work than longer residential programmes. Moreover, if it follows a spaced, rather than mass, training approach (Schendel and Hagman 1991) it is likely to produce better results in terms of learning retention. The intervals between training sessions can be used, as Latham and Saari in their classic study (1979) used them to good effect, for the participants to practice *in vivo* the behaviours they have learned, using their own work issues and situations as real-life cases.
- Finally, it will lend itself far better to meaningful evaluation, since the criteria of success will be based specifically on the extent to which the behaviour of the leader changes and what changes in performance outcomes can be attributed to these changes in behaviour. I am not suggesting that the evaluation process will be simple to construct or that valid pre and post measures of behaviour and results will automatically be easy to obtain. Training evaluation is a complex and slippery subject (Alliger and Katzman 1997). But I am arguing that the possibilities for meaningful evaluation will be infinitely greater than for a traditional leadership training programme, where it would be hard to conceive of how one would obtain any measure of effectiveness other than at the level of participant reaction immediately at the end of programme.

Conclusions

In this chapter I have questioned the wisdom of trying to teach leadership in the way that the main body of leadership training and publishers of leadership literature would have us believe possible. However, I have not sought to deny the phenomenon of leadership itself. Having spent my entire working life as an employee in large organizations, I am entirely sympathetic with those who claim to know when they are being 'well led' or 'badly led'. Equally, it is not unusual to detect a direct and sometimes rapid cause-and-effect association between a change in leadership and a change in the affective response (some might call this 'morale') of the followership. Such a change may well be followed by an objective change in the performance of the organization. Followers appear to understand whether and when their leader is doing a good job or not. And my point here is that leadership *is* a job, like any other, and jobs can be analysed. Once a job is analysed, whether we use competence modelling or any other reliable method, we can begin to understand what makes more or less effective performance of that job. Once we have that understanding, we have the basis for modelling it, in behavioural terms, as a vehicle for learning.

The type of leadership job analysis I have described above, as I have stressed throughout this chapter, will be strongly mediated by the organizational context in which the leadership job exists, particularly by the technology used to achieve results in that organization. The technical component of leadership – the specific knowledge and skills needed to improve profit margins in a financial services firm, or to wage successful jungle warfare, or to get trains running on time – is generally (and often deliberately) underestimated and understated. There is no single job model, no universal template, for leadership roles. There are no known keys to success or irrefutable laws, despite the ever-growing mountain of pulp and pointless training activity that is built on the misconception – and misrepresentation – that there are. As Salaman (Chapter 4) suggests, the 'problem' of leadership has become something of a fixation for many organizations. To believe that it can be solved through the teaching of specious recipes is absurd. It is like suggesting that the problem of world hunger can be solved by the publication of more cookery books. Unless and until this is grasped, especially by those who are responsible for providing training in their organizations, we shall continue to get what we do *not* deserve.

Note

1   How we define 'followers' presents difficulties in itself. Are followers only those individuals who are subservient to the leader, in terms of power and influence? Or do followers include all those, including superiors, peers and others, whom the leader needs to influence in order to implement his or her agenda? If the latter, wider, definition is favoured, it may be more appropriate to term such individuals 'stakeholders'.

References

Ackroyd, S. and P. Thompson (1999) *Organizational Misbehaviour*, London: Sage.

Alliger, G.M. and S. Katzman (1997) 'Reconsidering training evaluation: heterogeneity of variance as a training effect', in J.K. Ford (ed.) *Improving Training Effectiveness in Work Organizations*, Mahwah, NJ: Lawrence Erlbaum Associates.

Bandura, A. (1977) *Social Learning Theory*, Englewood Cliffs, NJ: Prentice-Hall.

Bion, W.R. (1991) *Experiences in Groups and Other Papers*, London: Routledge.

Bird, C. (1940) *Social Psychology*, New York: Appleton-Century.

Blum, M.L. and J.C. Naylor (1968) *Industrial Psychology: Its Theoretical and Social Foundations*, New York: Harper & Row.

Boam, R. and P. Sparrow (1992) 'The rise and rationale of competency-based approaches', in R. Boam and P. Sparrow (eds) *Designing and Achieving Competency*, London: McGraw-Hill.

Burke, M.J. and R.R. Day (1986) 'A cumulative study of the effectiveness of managerial training', *Journal of Occupational Behaviour* 6: 197–208.

Campbell, J.P., M.D. Dunnette, E.E. Lawler and K.E. Weick (1970) *Managerial Behaviour, Performance and Effectiveness*, New York: McGraw-Hill.

Cascio, W. (1991) *Applied Psychology in Personnel Management*, Englewood Cliffs, NJ: Prentice-Hall.

Cockerill, A. (1989) 'The kind of competence for rapid change', *Personnel Management*, September 1989: 52–6.

Cook, M. (1991) *Personnel Selection and Productivity*, Chichester: Wiley.

Dixon, N.F. (1994) *On the Psychology of Military Incompetence*, London: Pimlico.

Downs, S. (1992) 'Job sample and trainability tests', in P. Herriot (ed.) *Assessment and Selection Organizations*, Chichester: John Wiley & Sons.

Fraser, C. (1990) 'Small groups: structure and leadership', in H. Tajfel and C. Fraser (eds) *Introducing Social Psychology*, Harmondsworth: Penguin.

Gill, J. and S. Whittle (1993) 'Management by panacea: accounting for transience', *Journal of Management Studies* 30(2): 291–8.

Goffman, E. (1961) *Asylums*, Garden City, NY: Anchor Books.

—— (1972) *Encounters*, Harmondsworth: Penguin.

Grint, K. (1995) *Management: A Sociological Introduction*, Oxford: Polity Press.

Hardinge, N.M. (1992) 'Personel selection in the military', in P. Herriot (ed.) *Assessment and Selection in Organizations*, Chichester: John Wiley & Sons.

Herriot, P. (1991) 'Selection as a social process', in M. Smith and I.T. Robertson (eds) *Advances in Selection and Assessment*, Chichester: John Wiley & Sons.

Hersey, P. and K.H. Blanchard (1982) *Management of Organizational Behaviour*, Englewood Cliffs, NJ: Prentice-Hall.

Hollander, E.P. (1978) *Leadership Dynamics: A Practical Guide to Effective Relationships*, New York: Free Press.

Jacobs, R. (1989) 'Getting the measure of management competence', *Personnel Management*, June 1989: 32–7.

Katz, D. and R.L. Kahn (1978) *The Social Psychology of Organizations*, New York: Wiley.

Kniveton, B. (1996) 'Social influence', in D. Howitt (ed.) *Social Psychology: Conflicts and Continuities*, Buckingham: Open University Press.

Landy, F.J. (1989) *Psychology of Work Behaviour*, Pacific Grove, CA: Brooks/Cole.

Latham, G.P. (1989) 'Behavioural approaches to the training process', in I.L. Goldstein (ed.) *Training and Development in Organizations*, San Francisco: Jossey-Bass.

Latham, G.P. and L.M. Saari (1979) 'The application of social-learning theory to training supervisors through behavioural modelling', *Journal of Applied Psychology* 64(3): 239–46.

Lawrence, P.R. and J.W. Lorsch (1986) *Organization and Environment: Managing Differentiation and Integration*, Boston, MA: Harvard Business School Press.

Maslow, A.H. (1943) 'A theory of motivation', *Psychological Review* 50: 370–96.

Milgram, S. (1974) *Obedience to Authority*, London: Tavistock.

Mole, G.W. (1996) 'The management training industry in the UK: an HRD director's critique', *Human Resource Management Journal* 6(1):19–26.

——— (2000) *Managing Management Development*, Buckingham: Open University Press.

Moscovici, S. (1976) *Social Influence and Social Change*, London: Academic Press.

Pearn, M.A. and R.S. Kandola (1988) *Job Analysis: A Practical Guide for Managers*, London: IPM.

Reed, M. and P. Anthony (1992) 'Professionalizing management and managing professionalization. British management in the 1980s', *Journal of Management Studies* 29(5): 591–614.

Schein, E.H. (1992) *Organizational Culture and Leadership*, San Francisco, CA: Jossey-Bass.

Schendel, J.D. and J.D. Hagman (1991) 'Long-term retention of motor skills', in J.E. Morrison (ed.) *Training for Performance: Principles of Applied Human Learning*, Chichester: John Wiley & Sons.

Schuler, H. (1989) 'Some advantages and problems of job analysis', in M. Smith and I.T. Robertson (eds) *Advances in Selection and Assessment*, Chichester: John Wiley & Sons.

Senge, P.M. (1992) *The Fifth Discipline*, London: Century Business.

Tannenbaum, S.I. and G. Yukl (1992) 'Training and development in work organizations', *Annual Review of Psychology* 43: 399–441.

Tedeschi, J.T. (2001) 'Social power, influence and aggression', in J.P. Forgas and K.D. Williams (eds) *Social Influence: Direct and Indirect Processes*, Philadelphia, PA: Psychology Press.

Terman, L.M. (1904) 'A preliminary study of the psychology and pedagogy of leadership', *Journal of Genetic Psychology* 11: 413–51.

Thomson, I. (1998) 'Making the evaluation of training easier', *Banking and Financial Training* 102: 6–9.

Woodruffe, C. (1992) 'What is meant by a competency?', in R. Boam and P. Sparrow (eds) *Designing and Achieving Competency*, Maidenhead: McGraw-Hill.

Zaleznik, A. (1992) 'Managers and leaders: are they different?', *Harvard Business Review*, March–April: 126–35.

8 Innovative technologies and leadership development

Peter Scott

> Well, good afternoon to 'The Big Brother House'. At the end of this presentation you will be given the opportunity to vote as to whether I stay…or not.
>
> (Chief Executive of an NHS hospital trust)

Introduction

The quote above is the opening remark of the chief executive of an acute hospital as he began an interactive live webcast to his organization at the start of January 2002. In what was probably the first event of its kind in the UK health service, the chief executive's joke echoes many business leaders, being both enthusiastic to embrace the opportunities of innovative online technologies and yet anxious about its unknown threats. In some ways, it is clear that the webcast event did feel to him more like a challenging game show format than anything he had done to lead the organization to that date. We will return to this example later, to fill in the details and explain how it all turned out. The purpose of this chapter is to explore the newer online technologies that are starting to impact on the role and development of the corporate leader.

Many visionaries have predicted radical business change due to the current directions of technology. However, even the best and most entertaining of these (e.g. Levine *et al.* 2001) can show you an inevitable tomorrow and yet leave you without a clue about the reality of today. In this chapter, there will be no discussion about how the world will radically change in the next 10 years. The reality gap between what can be done now (and makes business sense) and what will be doable in the next 10 years is simply too wide. Instead, we will examine some technologies that have already made a big impact. The discussion will be about how these pose threats and offer opportunities to business leadership. Instead of a broad survey of new technologies, we will focus on one critical new concept, that of 'presence'.

We begin with a review of some studies in 'telepresence' that expose a range of key leadership issues. The remote 'being there' of the interactive live webcast is one innovation that is already having some business impact. Whilst most managers can immediately see the significance of a form of 'business television' that gives instant desktop access to allow them to 'talk to the troops', it is also possible to foresee more wide-reaching changes accompanying the widespread deployment of such technologies.

We will close with a brief examination of some other 'presence' technologies that have yet to make an impact. For example, the 'co-presence' technologies of instant messaging (IM) have been a big hit in emerging 'always on' broadband communities and are now starting to make a showing in some corporate systems. Finally, many Internet communities are developing strong new communities of practice around 'weblogs', simple forms of personal web page diaries and activity logs. However, there is little current evidence of real deployment of such technologies in industry – so-called 'business blogging'. We will argue that all these technologies will, clearly, have an impact and indeed that they all share a similar set of leadership threats and opportunities.

According to what could be termed 'classical diffusion theory' (Rogers 1995), the dilemma for the leader faced with any new technology is to decide which form of adoption is appropriate. For any decision about change the choice is to belong to one of these groups:

- innovators (those willing to commit now and take the risk);
- early adopters (respectable but adventurous);
- early majority (the deliberate decision-makers);
- late majority (sceptical and wary of change);
- laggards (a traditional community, reluctant to change).

Most leadership manuals will try to encourage the reader to spot the opportunity to join the 'early adopters' community, the advice being to get somewhat behind the 'bleeding edge' of the fully innovative risk-takers, but amongst those who encourage and foster innovations that are still (at least slightly) ahead of the competition. With each technology discussed below, you are invited to consider which group you and your organization would represent.

Case study: telepresence

In the Open University we have been webcasting for a long time (see, for example, the history of the telepresence project called Stadium – http://stadium.open.ac.uk). The technologies have been through many mutations and have been used in many corporate contexts. Critical to the concept of telepresence (remote presence – that is, the ability to feel that you are really there at a distant event) is to help the participant to 'be there' by enhancing interaction. Ergo, most of the webcasting that we have done is distinct from the broadcast of a rock concert or new-product launch, in that the participant must 'interact' both with the material of the event and with other participants (Scott and Eisenstadt 2000).

Let us take a typical business example. On 25 March 1999 the Stadium webcasting technologies enabled a project team from a British Petroleum (BP) oilfield facility in Dorset (UK) to achieve a key learning goal by sharing some valuable technical knowledge about oilfield equipment with colleagues within a BP community of practice. In two webcasts lasting 40 minutes each, three oilfield engineers spoke live from a working field stores shed, over the BP intranet, to over 50 colleagues seated at their desks around the world: from Bogotá, through Houston to London and Aberdeen. It had to be two events to reach the 'awake' parts of the world at their desks. Remote participants were able to see the presenters, interact with them via text chat, and interact with their presentation by clicking on animations and virtual-reality views – all this within a page of a web-browser on a standard desktop or laptop machine.

One participant in Aberdeen noted the transformational potential of the effective use of telepresence technologies such as this:

> The webcast was an excellent example of using new technology to distribute information, and I can see many applications for this approach in the future. I wonder how much it would cost to have the same 50 people in one room, in terms of expenses, never mind the man-hours!

This event and the activity around it had a number of transformational effects on the company. To give one example, it certainly forced their network to greater heights. One standard observation from any corporate information technology (IT) infrastructure professional is that 'no one is asking for that level of capacity and that level of support right now'. This sort of activity genuinely stretches that network and makes the lives of the support profession 'much more interesting'. In the case of webcasting, video to the desktop requires significant bandwidth per user, and this is synchronous use – i.e. many users requiring the same bandwidth at the same time. A corporate network designed to support email and the odd file transfer is rarely subjected to significant demands. In the case of BP, the desktop webcasting demand which was stimulated by such events caused them to put significant resources into researching 'multicast' – which is a computer networking technology that lets many users who are interested in connecting to a live service share the same bandwidth.

However, in most companies using webcasting technologies and systems their use is much more mundane. They are considered to be mechanisms for leaders to routinely use simple online (one-way) broadcasts to get a message out to their staff.

To explore the technology in some detail let us look at a recent example that has been the subject of extensive study at the Open University, the implementation of a set of leadership webcasts in a UK hospital.

As part of a large set of studies (Scott *et al.* 2001), a short series of webcasts were produced at a general hospital (Scott and Quick 2002). The topics of the events were chosen to be of direct relevance to the nursing staff across the hospital, and included presentations by a range of hospital leadership and management. Each presenter was briefed by the research team on the demand characteristics of the webcast medium and how to manage interaction with the staff who were likely to remotely attend.

The basic architecture of the system deployed is illustrated in Figure 8.1. For interest, the technical architecture deployed in the trust used three desktop computers and two servers. One desktop machine was used by the presenter, one by an event administrator and one further machine (actually a laptop, for simplicity, mobility and space) for the audio/video encoder. A separate audio/video server for the live events was not required – as these were multicast (see below). The two servers, one synchronizing events between all clients and the other serving up the pages and application, were both run on a single physical machine located in the hospital server room.

The client computers access the webcast via a Macromedia Shockwave applet (http://www.macromedia.com) embedded in a web page. They received the streaming video and audio, together with the presenter's slides (see Figure 8.2). Additionally, they could send text messages via the page application to all connected computers, including the presenter's.

All hospital webcast users (primarily the nurses in public spaces) were directed to a local web page on the hospital intranet web server. The Live Event page gave them some details of the timing and nature of the scheduled event. Near to the time of the event they could click a link on this page to get access to the webcast client applet.

The client applet (a Macromedia Shockwave web page plug-in) gave users a single window view which brings together and fully integrates controls, slides, text chat, etc. Users could talk to each other and send in questions to the

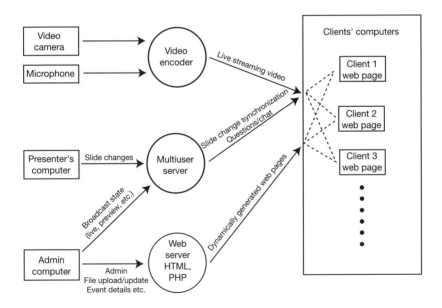

Figure 8.1 A technical view of the hospital webcasting architecture

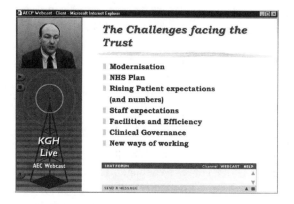

Figure 8.2 A user view of the first webcast live interface

presenter or support team via the chat form window shown in grey at the bottom of the figure. The input field only appears when 'send a message' is clicked, and the chat window can be expanded by dragging on its title bar. It can also be made semi-transparent to allow users to view the side beneath whilst typing.

The presenter used a 'standard' hospital desktop computer with web access, and, like the clients, connected to the same Shockwave application, but as a 'presenter'. The 'presenter' is allowed additional functionality, such as being able to control the slides currently being seen by the other clients. In addition to the 'presenter' and clients, an 'administrator' connects via the Shockwave application in an 'admin' mode. This gives the administrator the ability to change the state of the broadcast, e.g. preview, live, intermission, etc.

In the UK's National Health Service (NHS) economy is very important, so for the hospital events we used a low cost webcam and a tie-clip microphone. The audio and video from these were encoded using a single Sorenson Broadcaster encoder (http://www.sorenson.com) running on a laptop computer. The 'studio' room used was simply an ordinary 'naturally lit' office in the IT Department large enough to accommodate a few computers, some bright extra lights and a backdrop (a large sheet of plain blue paper attached to a poster display stand behind the speaker's head). Audio quality is the most important feature of such broadcasts – so a good quality, powered tie-clip mike was a critical feature of this mix. Lighting is the next most important feature – so the IT team invested in some large, diffusing uplighters for this office.

The live events were multicast over the hospital network. The multicast feature of the broadcast ensures that however many remote users connect to the event it consumes a fixed bandwidth of the corporate intranet. The multicast, being a single stream of network packets sent to all subscribing computers on the same network segment, did not require the use of a streaming server.

During the broadcast the video was also recorded to file, together with the timing of slide changes, and any text chat between participants. (A backup tape copy was also taken from a backup camera). Subsequently, a replay movie was created of the event (using Apple QuickTime), which can be launched by visiting an appropriate 'replay' web page and can therefore be viewed by people unable to attend the original live broadcast, or used as a resource for future training, education and knowledge management. Feedback from the staff indicates that these are particularly valuable for staff who normally feel excluded from such interactions – e.g. those who tend to work predominantly on a nightshift.

Initially, the format for a broadcast was for the presenter to give his or her talk, and at the same time the remote participants could submit any questions they had via the chat interface. At the end the presenter would scan through the text in the chat window and reply to the questions. It became obvious that there were some problems with this, as the viewers found it distracting to have to compose and type in questions, and the presenter found it difficult to scan and answer questions whilst still broadcasting. In previous deployments of the webcasting software (see http://kmi.open.ac.uk/stadium) the chat interface had been used extensively for general discussion purposes by remote users rather than for asking questions of the presenter, whereas within the context of the hospital webcasts it was used almost exclusively for direct questions.

As a result, the 'social' format of the broadcasts was modified, so that at the end of the presentation there was an intermission of several minutes, during which period the presenter could review any questions that had been asked, and the viewers had a period in which they could type in questions without missing the broadcast. At the end of the intermission the live video and audio would resume, and the presenter would then deal with the questions.

There was one test webcast event in 2001, which was followed by a series of further routine webcasts in 2002. Each webcast was given by a different hospital-based presenter and had a different 'leadership' topic. Attendance of each webcast varied; the largest audience (about 50 individuals) attended the chief executive's webcast.

Interview, survey and focus group respondents agreed that technical issues were a drawback of the webcasts – sound, in particular, is hard to get right in a busy NHS hospital. Indeed, this sort of multimedia technology is bound to be challenging to any busy information technology department and it can be difficult to prioritize the support issues alongside other demands. The issue of 'stretching' the technology support teams is a recurrent theme in such work. Indeed, the virtue of the detailed case study in this context is that it gave us the ability to raise a number of critical issues and explore them through the observation of participants.

Presence and absence

All forms of 'presence' technologies raise issues of presentee-ism. When staff can be present (and seen to be present) the social issues around who is and isn't visible can be more salient than in any conventional meeting.

I mean certainly it opened my eyes that, you know, [X] is our Head of Information Technology and yet he hasn't logged on.

(Nurse)

This issue is much more significant in some of the co-present technologies (discussed later), but even here the visibility of activity (not in itself necessarily a measure of real contribution or value) can appear as a negative metric. How, then, is a leader to ensure that the culture set around such events avoids inappropriate censure and yet rewards appropriate activity?

One of the problems with these sorts of event is getting people to attend in the first place. The novel style of the event will capture the imagination of some participants and instantly deter others. This is a significant barrier to the success of the webcast medium – especially in considering that those who did attend were committed to attending in the future. Indeed, 94 per cent of those attendees who were surveyed said that they would attend future webcasts. And yet those that did not attend seem to be quite content also to remain excluded.

Technology and use

There were many comments from the interviews and observations about the usefulness of the webcasts and this new type of communication. For instance, some of the health professionals surveyed felt that it was used as a 'public relations' exercise rather than a way of properly engaging with staff. But there was a widespread feeling that this was a much more powerful medium than the conventional chalk-and-talk sessions.

I think it's the way perhaps things are going to go. I think we'd be very naive to think we can just all go back to standing up with some acetates and doing a presentation.

(Sister)

Technology and accountability

One of the major strengths of the technology from a staff point of view was the ability to make their leaders directly accountable for their actions. When asked which was the most significant feature of the event, the 'direct questioning of senior staff' was popular comment. Many participants liked the ability to question and probe issues from behind the security of the computer screen:

Oh, and the interactive bit. And it was anonymous, so if you've got something contentious people can put their point of view over without feeling that they're being singled out, or that they're being labelled as a troublemaker. That's certainly a strength of it.

(Nurse)

In particular, the sort of open access to the leadership was highly rated:

> The good thing about it was likes of us being able to ask questions of the likes of him.
>
> > (A Charge Nurse commenting on the Chief Executive webcast)

Also, it is possible that innovation can, of itself, help an organization to welcome and stimulate essential change processes:

> It's about passivity...people don't feel able to control what's around them...people aren't at the moment yet positively buying in to change. Change is something that they don't drive; change is something that happens to them....What it is simply about is the challenge, the race, the aspiration, of providing high quality care to patients – and that people that are empowered do as much of that as they can.
>
> > (Sister)

Technology and two way communication

The complement of staff enthusiasm for accountability is a leadership enthusiasm for 'reaching out' to these workers:

> [The webcast was a] good opportunity for senior staff to communicate to a wide audience.
>
> > (Senior Nurse)

This can be part of a process of reaching out to staff who don't normally get close enough to engage with a leader:

> It's useful to be able to take the questions of people afterwards. So that it's just another way of people being able to raise some issues with you. I'm really passionate about that, about people being able to access me and ask questions; and do it in the way they want to.
>
> > (Director of Nursing)

Or it can be a recognition that some real issues for staff don't get enough attention until they appear, underlined, in a powerful context:

> being open to challenge and then prepared to do something – committed to do something about it. Because it's, you know, it would be quite easy to sit there and go: 'Oh that's terrible, yes, maybe we should have a look at that', and then actually not doing anything. I talk to staff, which I try and do as regularly as I can, You know, it's about finding another way to do that – so that you reach everyone.
>
> > (Chief Executive, NHS hospital trust)

Technology and empowerment

A major topic for most organizations is the 'empowerment' of staff and their integration into the decision-making process – indeed, giving all employees an ability to lead in their own way:

> Nurses have been told, 'This is what you are doing, and this is how it is changing', and now it's gone full circle and nurses are being asked, 'What do you think', well...they are not used to that. It's getting them used to being able to express an opinion, without having any come-back.
>
> (Sister)

In a modern organization the leaders must have effective channels of communication back from staff. For most organizations this has involved a significant investment in 'empowerment' of the workforce and the development of a culture of 'communication'. It seems likely that technology will have a big role to play in making this effective.

Technology and time

> I think it is good that you can come and have meetings, and share information, without pulling people out of clinical areas. I mean, if you go to a meeting that say lasts for quarter of an hour – you are 10 minutes getting there and 10 minutes back – that's three quarters of an hour out of the clinical area! Whereas, with the webcast, you are only taking up the 15 minutes. And if it is not a dire emergency you can say, 'Just a minute.'
>
> (Sister)

All new technologies tend to offer time savings. For instance, with the instant messaging technologies discussed below one concern is that the time involved is hard to account for. In telepresence the focus is usually a highly business-focused event, and so any saving of time is both accountable and a 'real' saving. But any innovation involves taking 'real' time from other activities, and the cost of the activity must be understood in the 'new' context.

Co-presence

The concept of co-presence is not so much about 'being there' (as in the remote presence at a meeting or presentation); instead it is about sharing information about the current status of members of an online community. Co-presence applications allow you to say something about yourself at the moment (e.g. 'I am busy', 'I am free for a text chat') and to observe and monitor those states in your 'monitored' community. Instant Messaging (IM) allows you to have instant text chats with others in your online community. IM really took off with the launch of the ICQ application (its name being a play on the phrase 'I seek you'). This was an instant hit with a dial-up community who wanted to know when they got online who else was online (family and friends) who they could have an instant and lightweight text chat with. Now the widely used desktop IM applications, like ICQ, MSN Messenger, Yahoo! Messenger, AIM, Odigo and Jabber, have mostly the same set of basic features, essentially showing who is online, with some indication of their 'state' (usually a self-declared status that is essential in an 'always on' broadband world). The handling of the different states differs superficially in most IM systems but, in essentials, users are invited to say that they are 'online', 'available for chat', 'busy' and so on. Some include more advanced communication capabilities, like voice chat and file exchange, whilst the most sophisticated provide powerful community visualization features such as interactive maps. For example, the BuddySpace system (Eisenstadt and Dzbor 2002) uses the concept of 'lights' distributed over maps to show location and state of 'buddies' or co-workers (see Figure 8.3).

This ability to see 'at a glance' the status of those around you in your 'virtual community' and to have a short and easy interaction with them is potentially very powerful, even if it is only a 'water cooler' or 'passing in the virtual corridor' text chat.

In a study of implementing the IM tool 'Rear View Mirror' in a multi-site multinational corporate context, Herbsleb *et al.* (2002) note that it was felt by early adopters to be a lightweight communication channel that enabled a team to find out who was available 'at that moment' over the disparate sites to trigger an opportunistic and rapid team communication. Anyone who is inundated with time-consuming, extended 'round robin' trails of email messages which

Figure 8.3 A view of the BuddySpace system

should have been resolved by a casual 'water cooler' conversation may share this enthusiasm.

At any rate, IM is set to be a powerful business force. For example, in an interview with Sharon Gaudin (2002), Jeremy Dies (Offerings Manager for Lotus Advanced Collaboration at IBM) notes that IM is rapidly becoming a critical tool for enterprise users. He asserts that internally at IBM about 270,000 people are already using it as a critical business tool.

The real power of such systems will only be revealed when they can effectively pick up and infer 'state' information automatically, to take this burden off the user. For example, the application could, in principle, know that you are in your office but busy, because your phone (in your pocket) is in your office too and you have switched it onto 'silent – I am in a meeting'.

Business blogging

If you have been snoozing though the technology pages of your newspaper for the last couple of years, the term 'blog' is a contraction of 'weblog' and the act of 'Blogging' is the making of said logs (see, for example, http://www.blogger.com). Some businesses are coming to understand that 'real' news isn't just a ticker-tape-like news feed from Reuters or the BBC. In business, the most significant news is what you and those you have reason to care about did yesterday, are doing today and plan to do tomorrow. If the people you want to know about are at your work, are in your supply chain (or are your customers), then you may have thought about business blogging. If telepresence is about sharing your company's live presentations and co-presence is about sharing your company's address book, then blogging is about sharing diaries and activity logs.

Essentially, blogging tools and portals have become a significant focus for a trendy vision of community publishing. They allow users to quickly generate simple web pages and link to others directly from within a public web page. In their simplest form they are used as stream-of-consciousness public web diaries or activity logs, hence 'weblogs'. They don't require expertise to use; they capture and share text easily and can even be extended to include images, sounds and movies. Members of your community can 'subscribe' to logs and upload comments to them – and even vote on the significance of the entries. In this way, this simple and yet pervasive set of tools has formed a large number of significant public 'communities of practice' around the bottom-up drive of community members.

One early corporate blogger and co-developer of some blogging portal work relates how the corporate blog called 'Stuff' became a knowledge management mainstay for the company Pyra Labs (now a part of Google):

> When new people joined our company, one of the first things folks did was read back through Stuff – all the way to the beginning. In a few hours they had a better sense of what Pyra was about than any mission statement could have hoped to communicate. We didn't need to tell anyone what our corpo-

rate values were; the spirit of the company was revealed through the posts available everyday in Stuff.

(Meg Hourihan, in Bausch *et al.* 2002: 214)

To give one example, consider a recent live audio blogging study conducted at the Open University. In August 2002 the contractor who maintains the pot plants in our research lab climbed the Matterhorn in Switzerland. As a member of our community, he took along a (then very new to the high street) mobile phone with built-in camera and used this to submit pictures and audio notes to a blog page. The whole world (or at least a few climbing enthusiasts) could track the activity, live, as it happened – and interact (via a little extra help) with the climber. The audio blog of this climb is captured on http://cnm.open.ac.uk/projects/matterhorn, along with links to other such activities (including an attempt on Everest). In Figure 8.4 the IM information about who is currently online, their state and what they are saying is at the bottom right of the screen. The audio blogs, with associated images, are listed in the middle and at the top of the image. The blue dots on the mountain ridge indicate an audio blog and/or image blog entry from this location on the mountain.

The blog pages generated in this example are not about 'leadership' per se; however, the opportunity is clear. As a team leader assessing energy efficiency on a remote chemical plant, how useful would it be to capture and share your thoughts about a damaging and expensive steam leak you see? What the simple phone to web to blog technology permits is for you to capture and share this experience right there and then – with an ordinary mobile phone, and with minimal technology in the way. The business blog would capture it to your website and your community could then share it. With some development in presence and instant messaging (and on a slightly smarter phone) you could pull

Figure 8.4 The Matterhorn live audioblog page

your team into a live meeting, there and then, to make a real learning impression. 'Hey team, who can tell me what is going wrong in this picture?'

Fin

Whilst it is clear that these presence technologies offer significant opportunities for leadership development, the threats are also substantial.

To return to Rogers' (1995) classic analysis, the important roles in the innovation process can be painted to include (at least) three different sets of innovators to complement the decision about technology adoption:

*   opinion leaders (who have relatively frequent informal influence over the behaviour of others);
*   change agents (who positively influence innovation decisions);
*   change aides (who have more intensive contact with clients, and a stronger safety and trust perspective).

In managing the risks inherent in any innovation the leader must also choose to lead from the front, as an 'opinion leader', or from behind, as a 'change aide'.

This final point brings us back to the telepresence example that we opened with. One comment from the hospital study nicely echoed the threat and opportunity theme:

> I think this is the future and we've just got to get used to it.
>
> (Nurse)

References

Bausch, P., M. Haughey and M. Hourihan (2002) *We Blog: Publishing Online with Weblogs*, Indianapolis, IN: Wiley.

Doctorow, C., R. Dornfest, J.S. Johnson, S. Powers, B. Trott and M.G. Trott (2002) *Essential Blogging*, Sebastopol, CA: O'Reilly.

Eisenstadt, M. and M. Dzbor (2002) 'BuddySpace: enhanced presence management for collaborative learning, working, gaming and beyond', JabberConf2002 Europe, Munich, Germany, 12–14 June.

Gaudin, S. (2002) 'IBM manager: IM muscles up for corporate users', *Datamation*, 16 August; available at http://itmanagement.earthweb.com/secu/article.php/1448271.

Herbsleb, J., D. Atkins, D. Boyer, M. Handel and T. Finholt (2002) 'Introducing instant messaging and chat in the workplace', CHI 2002, Minneapolis, Minnesota, USA.

Levine, R., C. Locke, D. Searls and D. Weinberger (2000) *The Cluetrain Manifesto: The End of Business as Usual*, Cambridge, MA: Perseus Publishing.

Rogers, E. (1995) *Diffusion of Innovations*, 4th edition, New York: Free Press.

Scott, P. and M. Eisenstadt (2000) 'Exploring telepresence on the Internet: the KMi Stadium Webcast experience', in M. Eisenstadt and T. Vincent (eds) *The Knowledge Web*, London: Kogan Page.

Scott, P. and K. Quick (2002) 'Technologies for electronically assisting nursing communication', in *Proceedings of IADIS 2002*, Lisbon, Portugal, 3–6 June.

Scott, P., K. Quick, F. Brooks and M. Macintyre (2001) 'Electronically assisting communication for health professionals: engaging with digital documents', in *Proceedings of WebNet 2001*, Orlando, Florida, USA.

9 Making leadership and management development measure up

Sheila Tyler

Organizations embark on leadership and management development programmes on the assumption that they will have a beneficial impact at one or more levels, from improvements in individual performance to changes in the organizational itself. Ideally, when they sponsor or implement such a programme they evaluate it. Typically, the most desirable question is deemed to be: 'What is the impact?' But is this the right question? This chapter argues that it is not. To explain why, the range of evaluation methods and key issues are reviewed in this chapter. The concept of building *organizational capacity* through evaluation is introduced. It is argued that, while leadership and management courses can build individual capacity which may benefit organizations, organizations themselves need to build their own capacity in order to leverage the new knowledge and thinking that are brought to the workplace.

Organizations use a variety of methods to achieve leadership and management development, ranging from formal classroom learning, through action learning via workplace projects, to outdoor training in which the course content and its presentation may bear scant similarity to workplace situations. These methods reflect not only the perspective of organizations on training and development and their resources (which also influence choices between in-house and outsourced provision), but also their views of leadership and management. While there are a number of models of leadership, the values-based or 'normative' approaches are popular. In these, management development may be regarded as educating individuals 'to do things right', while leadership development may be seen as enhancing individuals' ability 'to do the right things' (Bennis, cited in Loeb 1994). This ability is widely regarded as rooted in the personal attributes, knowledge and skills needed to set high goals and objectives and to influence others in order to achieve them. Thus, in leadership development there may be more emphasis on personal characteristics than in management development. These personal attributes have been interpreted by some as constituting 'emotional intelligence' (Goleman *et al.* 2002), covering self- and social awareness, self- and relationship management, and commitment to approaching people and situations with vision and command. As a result, the need for reflective learning, coaching and feedback is emphasized (Dearborn 2002). For many educators, however, the development of individual capabilities of any sort should embrace such practices to enable learners to acquire the skills necessary to use their new knowledge, to apply it in the workplace and to learn from feedback. These are vital for knowledge transfer and the *sustainability* of desired outcomes of training and development intervention. The brief 'buzz' of a weekend course may fail for lack of such practices, whether the focus of the course is management or leadership. Without doubt, implications arise from course content and the manner in which content is delivered – at the chalk face or the cliff face – and they have implications for the effectiveness of courses. However, they have little impact *per se* on *evaluating* effectiveness.

The classic work on evaluation of training or education outcomes is that of Donald Kirkpatrick (e.g. 1994). In 1959 he set out four levels of outcome which can be assessed:

- the reaction of learners to the programme (the 'happiness sheet');
- changes in learners' skills, knowledge or attitudes (test scores);
- behaviour change (application of learning in the workplace);
- the impact of behaviour change on the organization.

Phillips (1996) argues that return on investment (ROI) is the logical fifth level of the Kirkpatrick's model. This places a financial value on impact.

The attraction of Kirkpatrick's model is its apparent simplicity. Bernthal (1995) contends that this is because the model implies a standardized, pre-packaged process. Evaluators dive into the seemingly clear blue water, unaware of the thick mud of complexity beneath the surface. According to Bernthal, an advocate of the Kirkpatrick model, the primary problems are:

- a single evaluation will not provide definitive answers;
- learning is often confused with effectiveness;
- effectiveness is frequently not defined in terms of organizational, individual and training-related variables;
- there is an assumption that trainers or educators are accountable for effectiveness;
- there is an assumption that Kirkpatrick's four levels are related and that level 4 is superior because it's tough;
- there is often a failure to link outcomes at levels 3 and 4 with the original training or education;
- the type and quality of measures used are often poor.

Many of these criticisms can also be applied to 'level 5' – return on investment. At worst, all five levels will provide information which is narrowly limited to the consequences of decisions, with little explanation and no link to processes or organizational systems. Moreover, they may lack any strategic focus.

These problems can be exacerbated when leadership and management development is outsourced to providers of part-time vocational learning. This option can be a cost-effective means for continuing professional development. A key advantage is the combination of higher education with the immediacy associated with on-the-job training and development. Managers can bring their work experience to bear on their learning and their new knowledge to their daily workplace activities. Stakeholders focus on different types of outcomes, however. While educators may fully intend that learners will apply what they are taught, outcomes are judged in terms of course assessments which are likely to focus on evidence of learning, not workplace application of learning. For learners, a good outcome may mean being a better manager or exercising good leadership but, equally, it may be acquiring a qualification, career progression or a change of job. For their employers, desired outcomes are likely to be organizational ones – building capability by improving processes, systems and strategies. Alignment of aspirations may exist only at a rhetorical level. While education providers may evaluate programmes, rarely do they reach beyond the theatre of instruction to the Broadway of workplace performance. This can also be true of in-house provision, when even less evaluation may be carried out. Yet the reach of learning into the organization is the *raison d'être* for organizations that are serious about leadership and management education. Individual development is *supposed* to become organizational development (Mintzberg and Gosling 2002).

Within organizations, evaluation may take place at several levels, for example individual performance appraisals or the strategic balanced scorecard approach. However, these may not make the necessary causal links between education and impact, or provide the specific information needed to scrutinize the effectiveness of leadership and management education. Essentially, the question is not simply one of educational provision, quality and learning on the one hand (levels 1 and 2), and application and impact (levels 3 and 4) on the other. It is one of appropriation of knowledge, first by the learner then by the employing organization. However, the capacity to appropriate knowledge cannot be assumed either in the learner or in the organization.

What is capacity?

In the last decade, organizational capacity building has become a widely used concept in the management and development literature. Many organizations claim to pursue capacity building. But what is it? Writers embrace both the tangible, such as people, skills, resources, structures and systems, and the intangible, such as norms, values, culture and leadership, and, for individuals, commitment, attitudes, expectations and motivation. Thus 'capacity' differs depending on the 'level' at which it exists. There is at least some consensus about these levels – the individual, the organization and systems – and about the influence of factors such as the organization's level of development or evolution, and the wider context in which it operates (Lusthaus *et al.* 1999). In short, capacity is the 'wherewithal' to use and improve capabilities to achieve an individual or organizational goal. If this goal is competitive advantage and superior performance, then Day's (1996) definition of organizational capability as the source of these locates capacity in the intangibles, the 'glue', of organizational processes, knowledge and skills, technical and management systems, values and norms.

How is capacity built? Management and business writers place emphasis on people as the source of capacity building: writers from these disciplines appear to hold the position that training or educating individuals results in increased organizational capacity. The development literature, however, places emphasis on the systems level and holds the position that organizational capacity can be increased by intervention at group and organizational levels, and by processes. Examples of capacity building are often sector or even organization specific, e.g. health and safety concerns may be remedied by intervention which addresses risk assessment; fundraising capability may be increased by intervention that addresses planning. A more accessible example of a capacity building intervention at the organizational level is the implementation of quality assurance systems, such as Investors in People (IiP), a UK government sponsored initiative to improve training and development in organizations (although IiP is not without its critics, e.g. Ram 2000; Bell *et al.* 2002; Duckett 2002). The different positions adopted by the management and business literature, on the one hand, and the development literature, on the other, are not mutually exclusive. Capacity building can occur through influence at the systems level and through the development of individuals. Indeed, success is more likely if there is effort at both the individual and organizational levels. Mentz (1997) sees the relationship between individual capacity building and organizational change as operating through the normal interactions in organizational life. Individuals may seek to increase their own capacity for their own reasons, influenced by their own personal characteristics. The extent to which this personal development is translated to organization change and the achievement of wider development goals depends on the non-personal capacity of the organization: its norms, values, administrative and corporate capacity.

Clearly, there is no single process that will build capacity and there will be different pathways for different organizations. However, there are common themes: looking and learning; a supportive climate, but one that supports challenges to existing order; responsiveness. Hawe *et al.* (1998) believe that approaches to capacity building must engage people, challenge the way they think or act, be responsive to needs and issues as they arise, use the right language, build credibility skills and networks, and secure incentives, rewards and recognition for actions. Crucially, organizations must utilize individuals' new capacity (Rist 1995), but this may be inhibited by organizational policies and practices (Crisp *et al.* 2000). Significantly, Postma (1998) believes that assessment of capacity is itself capacity building.

Approaches to organizational capacity building refer to many characteristics associated with 'the learning organization'. Such organizations are said to be characterized by continuous learning at the systems level, knowledge generation and sharing, systemic thinking capacity, employees' participation and accountability, and the culture and structure for rapid communication and learning (Marsick *et al.* 2000). Senge *et al.* (1999) conceptualize three reinforcing processes which produce organizational learning capability (Figure 9.1). They envisage an increase in learning capability occurring first through individuals (1), diffusing via informal networks (2) and, finally, being established in new business practices (3) which then sustain growth in capability.

Senge *et al.* see the whole process being started by a core group of innovators 'starting small' but embarking on a purposeful change initiative. In reality, many leadership and management development programmes are the result of more prosaic considerations, and the notion of the learning organization itself can be easily problematized (Symon 2002). Nonetheless, for leadership and management development programmes to be optimally effective, organizations need to leverage new knowledge as it enters the workplace, or 'learn' to do so if the purpose of a programme is new knowledge rather than socialization and enculturation.

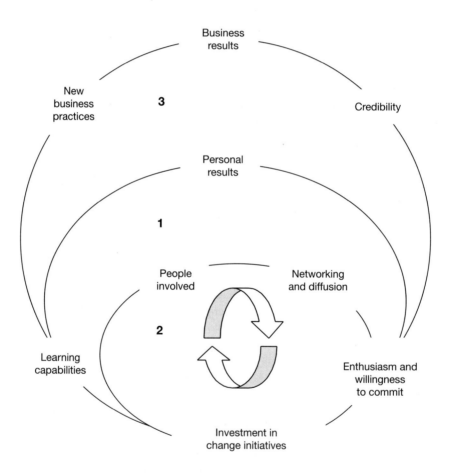

Figure 9.1 Three reinforcing growth processes

Source: adapted from Senge *et al.* (1999: 54).

Thus Roth and Marubecheck (1994) argue that transfer of knowledge into and within an organization needs to be complemented by organizational learning capabilities. Organizations need to understand the role of core knowledge in achieving their goals – the philosophy, systems, approaches to problem-solving and decision-making – as well as how to deploy skills to acquire, organize, codify and deploy knowledge. Roth and Marubecheck identified a number of key principles that organizations need to embrace to do this: a learning philosophy, stretched goals, opportunities for (low) risk-taking, systems for encouraging knowledge and learning, stimulating core knowledge processes, systems for crossing functional boundaries (e.g. teams and networks). Watkins and Marsick (1993, 1996) identified core practices which had an impact on performance: creating continuous learning opportunities; promoting inquiry and dialogue; encouraging collaboration and team learning; creating systems to capture and share knowledge; connecting the organization to its environment; and providing strategic leadership for learning.

The learner, the teacher and the workplace

The capacity of an organization to utilize new knowledge is but one part of the equation. According to Garvin (1993) the building blocks towards a learning organization are precisely those which pertain to the individual. These are:

- systematic problem-solving;
- experimentation with new approaches;
- learning from one's own experience and past history;
- learning from others' experience and best practice (e.g. benchmarking);
- transferring knowledge quickly and efficiently.

But how do individuals acquire these attributes? In those circumstances where learning is predominantly driven by course assessment (Gibbs 1991, 1995; Knight 2000) education programmes must be scrutinized in relation to these learner attributes. Without doubt, formal or academic learning is necessary for successful outcomes beyond the theatre of instruction, but it may not be sufficient to guarantee outcomes that are maximally beneficial to workplaces. Benefit results from learners applying their knowledge at work and this knowledge-in-action is of greater importance than reproducible knowledge-on-paper. But educators may fail to equip learners adequately for this, in the same way that organizations themselves may inadvertently inhibit learners from applying their knowledge. Educators need to help adult learners to 'learn how to learn': to acquire the disciplines and habits of critical analysis and reflection, sensemaking and search for meaning. This constitutes a 'deep' approach to learning (Entwistle 1988; Biggs 1987, 1999). However, this approach is context sensitive, influenced by the demands of assessment, time, workload, interest, age, anxiety and relevance of content (Fransson 1977; Entwistle *et al.* 1989; Biggs 1987, 1996; Richardson 1995, 2000; Sadler-Smith 1996). It is also related to educators' approaches to teaching. Thus, the educational provision must be effective in building the capacity of the learner, the learner must be sufficiently receptive (and motivated), and the context needs to be conducive to the 'right' sort of learning.

Attempting to move beyond the learning context is problematical, however. Learning is embedded in the context of learning (Lave 1985; Lave and Wagner 1991) and, according to Argyris and Schon (1996), further learning is needed to transfer learning from the educational context to that of the workplace. Transfer can be particularly problematical when the context of learning is far removed from that of application. This can be the case in outdoor pursuits courses designed to enhance leadership skills in the workplace, since, on the surface of things, the problems with which the learner is confronted can appear quite different. Educators may need to identify for learners the relationships between problems to be solved in each context. But even where the relationship between what is being learned and what must be applied is more obvious, a 'second loop' of learning is required. During this, values, beliefs and assumptions require scrutiny so that the learners are able to reframe their understanding of a workplace problem or situation. Clearly, some practices in both the learning environment and the workplace will facilitate this 'double-loop' learning better than others. Learner attributes are also implicated. Tracey *et al.* (2001) have identified the mediating role of characteristics such as self-efficacy and motivation in the relationship between job involvement, perceptions of the work environment and knowledge acquisition.

The extent to which new knowledge can be applied in the workplace will be influenced by organizational context and the affording of processes and systems through which skill and knowledge are exercised and embedded. Is the climate supportive and responsive enough to allow challenges to the existing order? Are systems capable of transforming individual knowledge into organizational results (Lusthaus *et al.* 1999)? Day (1996) believes that building capacity within externally focused organizations involves improving organizational capabilities for meeting client needs, and that this depends on internal responsiveness and flexibility. The capabilities of individuals alone are insufficient to 'locate' this capacity in organizations – organizations need to 'position' resources and ensure there is sufficient capability to use the resources effectively. What is clear is that such factors will render workplaces more, or less, capable and tolerant of managers applying their new knowledge at work. While some individuals in some circumstances may be able to create optimal conditions for the application of learning for themselves, many will not be able to do so. It will require the engagement of organizations in identifying and developing the key components of organizational capacity to appropriate new knowledge. Since Koys (2001) has established the direction of influence between human resources (HR) outcomes and business outcomes, it is likely to be the case that organizational policy and strategy, actioned through HR practices, will influence employee attitudes and result in positive business impact.

The missing links between education and workplace contexts

The literature reveals little systematic research on possible cross-context links between the formal study domain and application of learning outside the learning context. There are many concerns about the transferability of learning from the education domain to the workplace (e.g. Baldwin and Ford 1988). Research on knowledge transferability and usefulness in the workplace is sparse and has produced mixed findings (e.g. Shipper 1999; Liedtka *et al.* 1999). Relevant factors differ according to whether one consults the education or organizational literature. The dominant view in the capacity building and organizational learning literatures is that transfer is dependent on workplace factors, including an organization's propensity to detect, improve and change. In the field of education, the 'transfer' literature based on experiential learning (e.g. Kolb 1984) generally emphasizes the importance of practice, feedback and coaching – the provision of salient opportunities for concrete experience, support for critical reflection, and the provision of appropriate information for this and for reconceptualization and planning/trailing modified behaviour. However, opportunities to apply new learning may not be provided and may not always be recognized (Perkins and Salomon 1989).

For a number of years, the Open University Business School has been attempting to map learning outcomes in both the educational and workplace contexts. In doing so, we have attempted to move beyond the theatre of instruction to scrutinize the application of knowledge in workplaces and organizational support systems. In these studies, Sheila Tyler and colleagues Jenny Lewis, Suzanne Murphy, Alan Thomas and Hazel Johnson have followed part-time, mid-career management and development management students across both the learning and work contexts (e.g. Lewis and Tyler 1999; Murphy 2000). We find positive relationships between deep learning and application of learning in the workplace (and negative relationships between 'reproductive' learning and application) even where no relationship can be found between approaches to learning and course grades. Moreover, we find that deep learners take their new knowledge and skills further into the workplace by using techniques with others, including clients (Murphy and Tyler, forthcoming).

Our findings further suggest that challenges arising from organizational change and job change within the organization produce greater application of learning. The size of the organization is also a factor, with students from smaller organizations applying their learning more. This is consistent with Dodgson's (1991, 2000) view that small organizations may provide students with a wider range of experiences (opportunities) and that some features and requirements of small organizations are advantageous in knowledge application. These features include the quality of internal communications, responsibilities placed on employees, and the need to learn and react quickly. Other factors include students' own personal characteristics, which affect their resourcefulness. One of our studies found that both academic and work loci of control and work self-efficacy were related to various measures of application of learning, while 'good' approaches to learning were related to work self-efficacy (Tyler 2000).

Another of our studies (Ayele *et al.* 2002) revealed the ways in which development management students contributed to their employing organizations. Survey and case study data found three patterns. In small independent organizations learners were able to initiate and implement change. In large or bureaucratic organizations students were able to change *how* things were done but not *what* was done (changes to process). In organizations where learners were sponsored specifically to develop the capacity to manage change, they were able to bring about organizational change. Key factors in application of learning and organizational support for application of learning, regardless of context, were the relevance of course content, opportunities to apply learning and material support for study (e.g. study time and financial support), replicating earlier findings. The workplace impact of students' new knowledge was evident both at 'local' (personal and team management, relationships and performance) and organizational levels. Following Day's (1996) reasoning, the study also assessed the extent to which learners were able to have an organizational impact on processes and systems, strategies and structure. Students made their most major contributions in teamwork, managing information and communication, followed by impact on organizational culture, strategy, objectives and systems, with a lesser impact on organizational planning and budgeting, technology and organizational structure.

A framework from the literature

A conceptual framework can be derived from the literature to help to make sense of learning and capacity building at the various levels (Figure 9.2). Processes a, b, c and d are learning processes; 1, 2, 3 and 4 are sets of factors, relationships, and characteristics that influence a, b, c, and d. These are outlined below:

1   *Individuals* have experiences and personal characteristics that they bring to their learning; these include motivation and their own learning objectives (e.g. to improve the organization or to leave the organization).

- Process a is that by which the individual becomes 'educated', in the sense of developing knowledge. It is only part of the process of real learning – knowledge is not yet enacted.
- Process b is that of internalizing and personalizing knowledge and applying it (resulting in further knowledge gain). Whether this is 'turned' to the organization will depend on the objectives of the individual and the organization itself. Process b capacitates the individual as 'know-what' becomes 'know-how'.

2   *The organization.* This represents the organization with its hard and soft resources, expertise, practices, systems, characteristics, climate and motives, expressed as mission, aims and objectives.

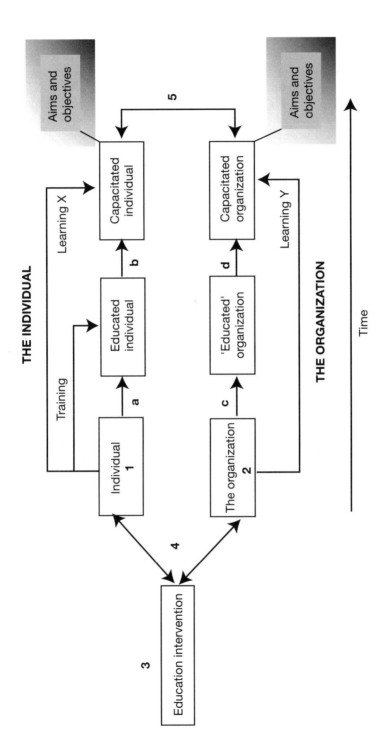

Figure 9.2 Capacity building: a framework

- Process c is the organizational equivalent of process a for individuals; an organization may know *about* organizational learning but not have the characteristics of one which is adept at it. It may have an espoused theory about itself as a learning organization but practices are not consonant with this.
- Process d is the organizational equivalent of process c for individuals. It leads to the development of practices conducive to sustainable organizational development which an organization has identified as essential to achieve its mission. Process d is Argyris's (2002) 'double-loop' learning.
- Learning X and learning Y represent, respectively, individual and organizational learning. These are different of course. Learning Y will result in knowledge that is embodied in hard and soft systems, organizational climate, attitudes and so on.

3   *Learning/education intervention.* 'Intervention' does not necessarily refer to training or education that has been outsourced, but is distinguished from learning simply by being at work. The key differences are that there is a learning intention; there is some kind of content and procedure, and a degree of learning support. (It is assumed that the organization has mapped the training or educational objectives to specific organizational needs.)
4   *The success of the intervention* will depend on its quality of content and delivery, on learners' objectives, needs and characteristics, and on the alignment between the intervention and organizational needs, and between these needs and its processes and systems.
5   *The desirable, ideal relationship* between the individual and the organization is the mutual capacitation of the individual and organization. However, an individual can become capacitated without support, organizations can become capacitated without carrying forward all their employees and, conversely, a capacitated individual could facilitate capacity building in an organization.

The area in the middle of Figure 9.2 represents the operational space occupied by everyday interactions between the learner and the organization. Figure 9.3 conceptualizes the learner as mediating between the learning and workplace domains. Causality and influences are bi-directional, with knowledge transfer by learners operating in both directions.

This conceptualization allows us to see that simple measures of the 'impact' of leadership and management development on an organization place undue focus on the learner and insufficient on the employing organization, the education provider and their respective capacities and systems. One needs to derive or map the following links:

1   Derive specific needs from organizational objectives and strategy.
2   Map specific needs to educational objectives (D; B).

3   Map educational objectives to individual objectives and characteristics (B; C).
4   Link workplace application of learning to micro context (C; D).
5   Map congruence between micro context and macro context (D; E).

(Links between Regions A and B are relevant, of course, but are beyond the reach of organizations.) The result of the mapping should be a value chain or system. The process is consistent with that suggested for the Kaplan and Norton (1996) balanced scorecard system and underlines complimentarity (Crandall 2002). All parties have accountability in different ways. The organization is accountable for the choice of educational provision and fitness for purpose, the education provider for the quality of its provision; the learner for learning, and the organization for ensuring that it has the capacity for appropriating the new knowledge learners bring to the workplace.

At the core of any evaluation will be three testable propositions:

1   The effectiveness of a learning programme will be manifest in the actions of learners at work.
2   These actions will have an impact on appropriate processes, systems, strategies and policies that position organizations to achieve their aims.

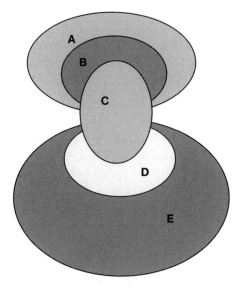

Figure 9.3 The learning and workplace contexts

Note: Regions A and B represent the learning domain, while D and E represent the work domain. Region A is institutional context of the education provider; B constitutes the learning support that the institution offers; C represents the learner; D represents the micro context in which the learner operates in the workplace; E represents the macro context of the organization.

3   The effectiveness of a learning programme will be dependent on the characteristics and practices of stakeholders at individual, systems and organizational
levels (those of both the employing organization and the education provider).

Evaluating leadership and management development programmes in a way
that appraises effectiveness and an organization's capacity to maximize return on
investment becomes possible with this 'multi-level' approach.

What a multi-level evaluation might look like

There are a number of ways in which multi-level evaluation can be achieved, but
there are some essential elements. These will require efforts which themselves
provide a basis for learning and capacity building within the organization. It is
assumed that specific organizational needs and objectives have been mapped to
the educational content and objectives of a particular leadership or management
programme. The key elements are as follows:

1   Link the formal learning objectives to the workplace behaviours expected.
One way of achieving this is to convert the detailed programme (learning)
objectives into behaviours expected as a result of learning and application.
This produces a set of statements which can be converted into a specific
performance appraisal for use pre- and post-programme. (Ideally this should
be a 360 degree appraisal, but in the case of leadership learning the 'feedback net' may need to be thrown wider, spanning more levels to avoid too
heavy reliance on a leader's followers.) The appraisal instrument links the
content of the programme with behaviour. It should be used pre- and post-
programme and with a control group in addition to the target group, but a
single before/after instrument presented at least two months after a
programme may be sufficient.

The next elements embrace factors which enhance or inhibit the application of
learning. They cover the extent and quality of learning and workplace support
both for learning and application of learning:

2   Identify key components of educational delivery and support systems
conducive to application of learning.
3   Identify specific support factors expected to enhance application and appropriation of learning (e.g. line manager support, provision of timely
opportunities, role expansion).
4   Identify generic support factors for professional development (e.g.
mentoring, coaching, job rotation).

The combined factors will provide the content for a short questionnaire to be
presented to learners after the course, along with questions about their motivation for learning and purposes.

Data from the performance appraisal (the pre- and post-course difference) can then be statistically related to support factors using correlation or regression techniques. (Alternative methods need to be used, or course, when sample sizes are insufficient for statistical techniques.) In addition to summary results, the evaluation findings will identify the relationships between use of new knowledge in the workplace and support systems that help learners to learn and to apply learning. They should highlight strengths on which to build and weaknesses to be remedied – and evaluated – next time.

Evaluations of this sort have the *potential* to be capacity building even before they are carried out because of the necessary preparatory process, which is likely to involve the education providers, the learner cohort, line managers and senior management. Evaluations are frequently used by HR managers and directors to justify training and development budgets. However, the mapping and linking required are a way of scrutinizing alignment between programme, learners, organizational systems and objectives. Areas of non-alignment become clear and action can be taken to maximize the benefits of a programme *before* it has begun. The preparatory process becomes a communication action in which people seek to understand a situation and clarify their plans of action in order to coordinate efforts (Cooper 2001). There is some evidence to show that this occurs. In an action-research project on return on investment involving a number of large European corporates (Tyler 2003), HR and finance directors and managers at various levels worked together closely for the first time. Once leadership and management development becomes embedded in policy, the use of evaluation to continuously justify expenditure becomes less compelling. Iles (1999), using data from Thomson *et al.* (2001), found that organizational policy contributed most to management development and that this in turn was related to the support of the board.

Moving on to ROI?

There are various methods of calculating return on investment (Phillips 1997) but very many problems with calculating return on 'soft' investment such as educational programmes. However, ROI calculations can be piggybacked on the method of evaluation set out above. Learners' performance improvements will provide the impact measure, on which a value can be placed. However, the resulting ROI figure will be retrospective and, while it appears to provide 'hard' financial facts, it hides what organizations really need to know. As Kanji (2002) points out, financial measures do not focus on processes that are at the core of management. What it is important to measure is not necessarily easy to measure technically or politically, but what gets measured speaks volumes about the real motives of management (Bradley 2002).

Are multi-level evaluations worth the effort?

Are multi-level evaluations worth the effort? Yes, but not for every cohort of learners on a programme. An initial multi-level evaluation can be followed by 'check-up' evaluations which use subsets of questions. The value of multi-level evaluations is that they do not pose the question 'What is the impact of a programme?' Rather they ask, 'Have we managed to appropriate the new knowledge brought to the organization?' Through the process of preparing for a multi-level evaluation, the alignment of purpose, strategies and systems within and between learning and workplace domains will be given appropriate attention. Accountability is also established. The question of impact is ultimately relative, while drawing a veil over the very factors that contribute to its relativity.

Particular implications for leadership development

There are some particular implications of multi-level evaluation for leadership development in organizations which embrace the notion of using it to build capacity. Predominantly, these concern the additional information organizations may need about learning processes in order to identify or create appropriate programmes, and the additional care needed regarding transfer factors.

The further removed training is from workplace contexts, the more difficult individuals will find it to make links between what is learned in one context and the context in which it must be applied. The more similar the contexts and the problems to be solved, the easier transfer becomes. For example, the links between an outdoor course and the workplace may not be immediately obvious: the point of the course may be to encourage individuals to identify leadership skills. These may then be further developed in other ways. It will be incumbent upon educators to help learners make the links, and upon organizations to ensure that all aspects of a phased programme are mapped and linked conceptually. The task of distinguishing transfer factors within the domain of the educators and learners from those that enable and enhance transfer in the workplace domain will probably be harder.

Further, learning objectives are likely to cover personal attributes which must then be 'translated' into expected workplace behaviours and activities. This will not only require particular care, but the effects of training will need to be distinguished from leadership qualities which were already present. Thus, pre- *and* post-course measures are necessary.

The major implication, however, is more fundamental. If the capacity building evaluative process is to begin with an analysis of needs and the alignment of these with educational objectives, organizations are likely to have to soul search more deeply when considering leadership than management development. It requires an organization not only to define leadership needs at different levels but also to define what it means by leadership and to explore beliefs about leadership. Current views of leadership are often not based on 'capitalist abstractions' – leadership as technique – with leaders attending to the bottom line, but on the normative approaches that invoke ideas of values, obligation, and of attending to the well-being and welfare of the stakeholder community (Harvey 2001). In reality, most leaders must face 'the Machiavellian dilemma' and strike a balance between being guardians of market value and shapers of community. But will this mean a requirement for leaders who *direct* or who *transform* by inspiring and motivating? Will leaders have to *generate* goals or simply *pursue* them? Will non-leaders play any part in the process? How much attention will be focused on non-leaders' interests and their personal growth? Each question is value laden, embracing even the morality of goals ('to what end and why'). As part of their capacity building, organizations may well have to become acquainted with models of leadership in addition to exploring how their initiatives are to bring about benefit at the levels required. Clearly, evaluation has the potential to propel organizations into becoming capacitated. But it may require some of the very leadership that an organization desires.

References

Argyris, C. (2002) 'Double-loop learning, teaching and research', *Academy of Management Learning and Education* 1: 206–18.

Argyris, C. and D.A. Schon (1996) *Organizational Learning II: Theory, Method and Practice*, New York: Addison-Wesley.

Ayele, S., S. Chiwara, P. Dzvimbo, H. Johnson, P. Kasiamhuru, J. Malaba, P. Manjengwa, F. Nazare, H. Potgieter, A. Thomas, S. Tyler and A. Woodley (2002) *Education for Development and Management Research Project. Final Report to DfID*, the Open University, UK; SAPES Trust; UNISA; Zimbabwe Open University. November.

Baldwin, T.T. and J.K. Ford (1988) 'Transfer of training: a review and directions for future research', *Personnel Psychology* 41: 63–105.

Bell, E., S. Taylor and R. Thorpe (2002) 'Organisational differentiation through badging: Investors in People and the value of the sign', *Journal of Management Studies* 39(8): 1,071–85.

Bernthal, P.R. (1995) 'Evaluation that goes the distance', *Training and Development*, September: 41–5.

Biggs, J.B. (1987) *Student Approaches to Learning and Studying*, Melbourne: Australian Council for Educational Research.

—— (1996) 'Enhancing teaching through constructive alignment', *Higher Education* 32: 347–64.

—— (1999) *Teaching for Quality Learning at University*, Buckingham: Open University Press.

Bradley, S.J. (2002) 'What's working? Briefing and evaluating workplace performance improvement', *Journal of Corporate Real Estate* 4(2): 150–9.

Cooper, D. (2001) *Performance Measures and the Rationalisation of Organisations*, CIMA Lecture, London School of Economics, 29 October.

Crandall, R.E. (2002) 'Keys to better performance measurement', *Industrial Management* 44(1): 19–25.

Crisp, B.R., H. Swerissen and S.J. Duckett (2000) 'Four approaches to capacity building in health: consequences for measurement and accountability', *Health Promotion International* 15(2): 99–108.

Day, G.S. (1996) 'The capabilities of market-driven organisations', in R. Paton, G. Clark, G. Jones, J. Lewis and P. Quintas (eds) *The New Management Reader*, London and New York: Routledge in association with the Open University.

Dearborn, K. (2002) 'Studies in emotional intelligence redefine our approach to leadership development', *Public Personnel Management* 31(4): 523–61.

Dodgson, M. (1991) 'Technology learning, technology strategy and competitive pressures', *British Journal of Management* 2: 133–49.

—— (2000) *The Management of Technological Innovation*, Oxford: Oxford University Press.

Duckett, I. (2002) 'Learning organisations, Investors in People and New Labour's learning society', *Journal of Further and Higher Education* 26(1): 61–74.

Entwistle, N.J. (1988) 'Motivational factors in students' approaches to learning', in R.R. Schmeck (ed.) *Learning Strategies and Learning Styles*, New York: Plenum Press.

—— (1998) 'Improving teaching through research on student learning', in J.J.F. Forest (ed.) *University Teaching: International Perspectives*, New York; Garland.

Entwistle, N.J., D. Hounsell, C. Macauley, G. Situnayake and H. Tait (1989) *The Performance of Electrical Engineering Students in Scottish Higher Education*, Edinburgh: University of Edinburgh, Centre for Research on Learning and Instruction.

Fransson, A. (1977) 'On qualitative differences in learning. IV – effects of motivation and test anxiety on process and outcome', *British Journal of Educational Psychology* 47: 244–57.

Garvin, D.A. (1993) 'Building a learning organization', *Harvard Business Review*, July–August: 78–88.

Gibbs, G. (1991) 'Using assessment strategically to change the way students learn', in S. Brown and A. Glasner (eds) *Assessment Matters in Higher Education*, Buckingham: Open University Press.

—— (ed.) (1995) *Improving Student Learning through Assessment and Evaluation*, Oxford: Oxford Centre for Staff and Learning Development.

Harvey, M. (2001) 'The hidden force: a critique of normative approaches to business leadership', *S.A.M. Advanced Management Journal* 66(4): 36–48.

Hawe, P., L. King, M. Noort and S.M. Gifford (1998) 'Working invisibly: health workers talk about capacity-building in health promotion', *Health Promotion International* 13(4): 285.

Iles, P. (1999) *Management Development and Lifelong Learning in the UK: Developing and Testing an Open Systems Model*, paper presented at the European Conference on Educational Research, Lahti, Finland, 22–29 September; available at http://www.leeds.ac.uk/educol/documents/000001145.htm.

Goleman, D., R. Boyatzis and A. McKee (2002) *Primal Leadership: Realizing the Power of Emotional Intelligence*, Boston, MA: Harvard Business School Press.

Kanji, G.K. (2002) 'Performance measurement system', *Total Quality Management* 13(5): 715–28.

Kaplan, R.S. and D.P. Norton (1996) *The Balanced Scorecard*, Boston, MA: Harvard Business School Press.

Kirkpatrick, D.L. (1994) *Evaluating Training Programs*, San Francisco: Berrett-Koehler.

Knight, P.T. (2000) 'The value of a programme-wide approach to assessment', *Assessment and Evaluation in Higher Education* 25(3): 237–51.

Kolb, D. (1984) *Experiential Learning*, London: Prentice-Hall.

Koys, D.J. (2001) 'The effects of employee satisfaction, organizational citizenship behaviour, and turnover on organizational effectiveness: a unit-level, longitudinal study', *Personnel Psychology* 54: 101–15.

Lave, J. (1985) 'Situationally specific practice', *Anthropology and Education Quarterly* 16: 209–13.

Lave, J. and E. Wenger (1991) *Situated Learning: Legitimate Peripheral Participation*, Cambridge: Cambridge University Press

Lewis, J.M. and S. Tyler (1999) *Why Managers Choose a Strategic Approach to Learning*, presentation to the British Academy of Management Annual Conference. Stirling, 1–3 September.

Liedtka, J., C. Weber and J. Weber (1999) 'Creating a sustainable executive education experience', *Journal of Managerial Psychology* 14: 404–20.

Loeb, M. (1994) 'Where leaders come from', *Fortune* 130(6): 241–2.

Lusthaus, C., M.-H. Adrien and M. Perstinger (1999) *Capacity Development: Definitions, Issues and Implications for Planning, Monitoring and Evaluation*, Montreal: Universalia Occasional Paper No 35.

Marsick, V. J., J. Bitterman and R. van der Veen (2000) 'From the learning organization to learning communities toward a learning society', *T*, Columbus, OH: ERIC Clearinghouse on Adult, Career and Vocational Education, Ohio State University.

Mentz, J.C.N. (1997) *Person and Institutional Factors in Capacity Building and Institutional Development*, Maastricht, Netherlands: European Centre for Development Policy and Management.

Mintzberg, H. and J. Gosling (2002) 'Educating managers beyond borders', *Academy of Management Learning and Education* 1(1): 64–76.

Murphy, S. (2000) 'Students' anticipated study approaches and preparation for study time and resource management', presentation to European Learning Styles Information Network (ELSIN) Conference, 26–27 June.

Murphy, S. and S. Tyler (forthcoming) 'The relationship between learning approaches to part-time study of management courses and transfer of learning to the workplace'.

Perkins, D.N. and G. Salomon (1989) 'Are cognitive skills context-bound?', *Educational Researcher* 18: 16–25.

Phillips, J.J. (1996) 'ROI: the search for best practice', *Training and Development* 50(2): 42–7.

—— (1997) *Return on Investment in Training and Performance Improvement Programs*, Houston, TX: Gulf.

Postma, W. (1998) 'Capacity-building: the making of a curry', *Development in Practice* 8(1): 54–63.

Ram, M. (2000) 'Investors in People in small firms: case study evidence from the business services sector', *Personnel Review* 29(1): 69–91.

Rist, R.C. (1995) 'Postscript: development questions and evaluation answers', *New Directions for Program Evaluation* 67, fall: 176.

Richardson, J.T.E. (1995) 'Mature students in higher education: II. An investigation of approaches to studying and academic performance', *Studies in Higher Education* 20: 5–17.

—— (2000) *Research Student Learning: Approaches to Studying in Campus-based and Distance Education*, Buckingham and Philadelphia: Society for Research into Higher Education and Open University Press.

Roth, A.V. and A.S. Marubecheck (1994) 'The knowledge factory for accelerating learning processes', *Planning Review* 22(3): 26–34

Sadler-Smith, E. (1996) 'Approaches to studying: age, gender and academic performance', *Educational Studies* 22: 367–79.

Senge, P., A. Kleiner, C. Roberts, R. Ross, G. Roth and B. Smith (1999) *The Dance of Change: The Challenges of Sustaining Momentum in Learning Organizations*, London: Nicholas Brealey.

Shipper, F. (1999) 'A comparison of managerial skills of middle managers with MBAs, with other masters' and undergraduate degrees ten years after the Porter and McKibbin report', *Journal of Managerial Psychology* 14: 150–64.

Symon, G. (2002) 'The "reality" of rhetoric and the learning organization in the UK', *Human Resource Development International* 5(2): 155–74.

Thomson, A.W.J., C. Mabey, J. Storey, C. Gray and P. Iles (2001) *Changing Patterns of Management Development*, Oxford: Blackwell.

Tracey, J.B., T.R. Hinkin, S. Tannenbaum and J.E. Mathieu (2001) 'The influence of individual characteristics and the work environment on varying levels of training outcomes', *Human Resource Development Quarterly* 12 (1): 5–23.

Tyler, S. (2000) *Management Development at IBM*, a longitudinal study of IBM, UK and European students following a first management course with the Open University Business School, confidential report for the Open University Business School.

—— (ed.) (2003) *ROI of Management Training and Development: An Innovative Approach to Measurement*, Brussels: European Foundation for Management Development.

Watkins, K.E. and V.J. Marsick (1993) *Sculpting the Learning Organization: The Art and Science of Systematic Change*, San Francisco, CA: Jossey-Bass.

—— (1996) *In Action: Creating the Learning Organization. Twenty-two Case Studies for the Real World of Training*, Alexandria, VA: American Society for Training and Development.

Zenger, J.H. (1996) 'Great ideas revisited', *Training and Development* 50(1): 48–51.

Part IV

Leadership in the public sector

10 Leadership in public sector organizations

Beverly Alimo-Metcalfe and John Alban-Metcalfe

Organizations across the public sector are facing enormous challenges in aiming to provide services of the highest standards to their clients and service users while operating with strictly limited resources.

In its recent report *Strengthening Leadership in the Public Sector*, the Cabinet Office Performance & Innovation Unit (PIU) (2001) places leadership at the core of its modernization agenda, and explains why:

> Britain's public services face unprecedented challenges at the start of the 21st century. They include: demands to modernise public services and orient them more closely to the needs and wishes of customers; higher expectations on the part of the general public, who expect public services to keep up with private ones; increasing opportunities, and requirements, for partnerships both across the public sector and with private and voluntary organisations.
>
> (Cabinet Office, Performance & Innovation Unit 2001: Key Findings, Section 1, p. 1)

However, the Cabinet Office is also aware of the confusion surrounding the study of leadership, and adds:

> There is little shared understanding of the qualities required for effective leadership in today's public services. Leadership theory is riven by conflicting interpretations, in a full spectrum from those which emphasise the primary importance of personal qualities to those who say systems are all-important. Leaders themselves often do not understand the reasons for their own effectiveness.... Fundamental to improved leadership is a clearer shared understanding of what leadership behaviours work in delivering today's services.
>
> (Cabinet Office, Performance & Innovation Unit 2001: Key Findings, Section 3, p. 1)

It is against this background that our interests and activities lie. We have spent over three years conducting one of the largest investigations ever undertaken of leadership, and the first major investigation in the UK public sector; more recently we have undertaken a corresponding study in the private sector. In both studies, we have adopted a different methodology from the studies which have gone before, and believe that the model to emerge is very different in tenor from those which currently dominate the literature.

The purpose and goals driving our research were not purely theoretical. The intention was to undertake an empirical study of the nature and assessment of transformational leadership in the UK, and to complement the findings with carefully thought-out development activities. The latter provide both benchmarks for best practice and support for individual and organizational development for those wishing to transform themselves and their organization, so as to deliver the best services, whilst sustaining the human efforts which will ultimately achieve the outcomes desired; in other words, to achieve 'best practice'.

In this chapter we describe the research in which we have been involved, which has led to both a greater understanding of what constitutes effective leadership behaviour and how it can be developed most effectively, and an understanding of why so many leadership development initiatives fail. We also provide examples of how we have supported leadership development across the public sector, including the National Health Service (NHS), local government, schools and areas of the criminal justice system. In some cases we cannot identify the organization, but can provide details of the initiatives.

Why the public sector needs more leadership

Under the government's modernization agenda, managers are being constantly evaluated in terms of achieving stringent targets – including Ofsted inspections in schools, 'starred status' of NHS trusts, comprehensive performance assessments in local government, key performance indicators in the prison service, and crime reduction figures in the police service – whilst at the same time being exhorted to encourage innovation and change, and to empower staff and create workplaces that support well-being.

It should be remembered that the tradition of management in most public service organizations has a relatively short history (for example only entering the NHS arena after the Griffiths Report recommendations of the mid-1980s); but leadership is an even newer phenomenon. One of the real dangers of becoming driven by targets is that managers can become so target focused that they behave in ways that can destroy the motivation and morale of their staff, which of course, in turn, deleteriously affects performance and leads to other costly outcomes.

Leadership is the process by which individuals' effectiveness is increased, while at the same time maintaining, if not increasing, motivation, job-related satisfaction and other forms of psychological well-being. It is *the only way* in which the government's multifaceted objectives for the public sector can be achieved. But this is not the only reason why leadership is so desperately needed in organizations.

One other crucial reason relates to the levels of stress being experienced in the public sector. One recent major study of levels of stress in the NHS concluded that stress levels were so high that probably about 27 per cent of staff in the NHS are minor psychiatric 'cases' (Borrill *et al.* 1998). Equally, the realization that your job, or indeed your organization or department, is under threat of takeover or reorganization if the range of challenging performance targets are not met leads to potentially highly stressful environments populated by highly stressed staff. Whilst threat of job loss might be a normal feature of life in most private sector companies, this is a relatively new experience for the public sector. A major difference between the two sectors is, however, that resources needed to cope with the increased demands have, typically, been far less readily available in the latter. So public sector managers have to manage with what they've got. This also means that staff should be provided with the highest levels of support from their managers to enable them to cope with the pressures of the complex challenges they face. Managers, in turn, need to be aware of the potentially positive, as well as negative, effects of their behaviour on their staff.

According to US psychologists Hogan, Curphy and Hogan, who reviewed the extensive findings from anonymous employee surveys to identify what staff perceive as the most stressful aspects of their job:

> 60% to 75% of the employees in any organization – no matter when or where the survey was completed and no matter what occupational group was involved – report that the worst or most stressful aspect of their job is their immediate supervisor.
>
> (Hogan *et al.* 1994: 494)

The researchers add that

> Good leaders may put pressure on their people, but abusive and incompetent management creates billions of dollars of lost productivity each year'. This lost productivity is caused by (high) turnover, insubordination, industrial sabotage, and malingering.
>
> (Hogan *et al.* 1994: 494)

Therefore, surely the first lesson of leadership must be to realize that leadership is not a choice, but a moral, and a financial, imperative for any manager of staff, and certainly for the most senior. We will return a little later to look at the importance of leadership among senior and top managers, but meanwhile, here are a few more thoughts on the relationship between leadership style and stress.

There is also good news. Several studies have been undertaken to identify what exactly are the managerial behaviours that can reduce the negative impact of environmental stress in organizations; the results are remarkably consistent. Three major variables emerge, consistently, as crucial in reducing stress (e.g. Bond and Bunce 2001a, 2001b). These are: a sense of high levels of autonomy or control one has in one's job; clear objectives and priorities; and 'social support'. This third factor is, in fact, an umbrella term to cover relatively small behaviours such as thanking staff for their efforts, empathizing with the pressures being experienced, providing timely feedback, and dealing with problems as they occur rather than avoiding issues. All of these behaviours come under the heading of leadership.

What is the nature of leadership in UK public services?

Dominant models of leadership have been based on US studies, and those which emerged in the early to mid-1980s, which have come to be referred to as the 'new paradigm' models, are no exception. These include the 'charismatic' models of Conger (1989) and House (1977), the 'visionary' models of Bennis and Nanus (1985), and the 'transformational' models of Tichy and Devanna (1990) and, perhaps most importantly, of Bass (1985).

What characterizes these models is their major focus on enabling organizations to deal with change, and even encouraging the change before it is imposed. This is a very different notion of leadership from the 'situational' models of the 1970s, which regarded leadership as essentially a combination of concern for people and a concern for task. These are now regarded as reflecting 'management', or what is sometimes described as 'transactional' leadership.

Despite the evidence that the transformational leadership approach is more effective than efficient management or transactional leadership alone (e.g. Bass 1998), we had several concerns about the relevance of these models to UK public sector managers. In brief, these concerns relate to the fact that these new paradigm models were:

- based on US studies;
- based on studies of 'distant' leaders, such as CEOs of large commercial organizations or senior military officers;
- based largely on the study of males;
- based on white populations;
- based, in the main, on the views of those occupying formal leadership positions.

These considerations raise questions as to how relevant were findings from these sources to the day-to-day leadership of managers and professionals at various levels in highly complex, highly politicized, UK public sector organizations delivering their services to an increasingly multicultural population.

We therefore set about undertaking two major research investigations, one of which was part-funded by the Local Government Management Board, into the nature of leadership as perceived by the arbiters of leadership – that is, direct reports, rather than by those who happen to occupy a formal leadership position. Thus, we sought the perceptions of male and female staff, from a range of ethnic groups and working at various levels, of their current or previous boss.

We wished to identify the leadership behaviours that staff had experienced with bosses with whom they had worked or currently worked. Another major difference in our approach was to focus on 'close' or 'nearby' leadership, rather than 'distant' leadership, such as that shown by outstanding chief executives. Research has shown (Shamir 1995) that 'distant' leadership is nearly always characterized by attributes of 'charisma', 'vision' and extraordinary communication qualities. In contrast, the study of 'nearby' leadership leads to the identification of the day-to-day behaviours of bosses who have an unusually positive impact on the motivation, job satisfaction, sense of self-efficacy (personal powerfulness), commitment and performance of staff and of the team or organization.

Details of the methodology are described in various articles and research papers (e.g. Alimo-Metcalfe and Alban-Metcalfe 2001, 2002, 2003a), but the final data set was based on responses from over 2,000 managers and professionals from middle to top levels in the NHS, and was found to generalize to staff working in local government ($n > 1,450$). We have since repeated the investigation in other public sector organizations, including schools and a major organization in the criminal justice field. Independently, a government department has conducted a validation study in a second organization, also in the area of criminal justice. The same model of leadership emerges consistently. The 14 dimensions that comprise transformational leadership are presented in Table 10.1.

Table 10.1 Scales measured by the transformational leadership questionnaire (TLQ)

LEADING AND DEVELOPING OTHERS (1)	
Showing genuine concern	Genuine interest in staff as individuals; values their contributions; develops their strengths; coaches, mentors; has positive expectations of what his/her staff can achieve
Empowering	Trusts staff to take decisions/initiatives on important matters; delegates effectively; develops staff's potential
Being accessible	Approachable and not status conscious; prefers face-to-face communication; accessible and keeps in touch
Encouraging change	Encourages questioning of traditional approaches to the job; encourages new approaches/solutions to problems; encourages strategic thinking
PERSONAL QUALITIES (2)	
Being transparent	Honest and consistent in behaviour; more concerned with the good of the organization than personal ambition

Table 10.1 continued

Acting with integrity	Open to criticism and disagreement; consults and involves others in decision-making; regards values as integral to the organization
Being decisive	Decisive when required; prepared to take difficult decisions, and risks when appropriate
Inspiring others	Charismatic; exceptional communicator; inspires others to join him/her
Resolving complex problems	Capacity to deal with a wide range of complex issues; creative in problem solving

LEADING THE ORGANIZATION (3)

Networking and achieving	Inspiring communication of the vision of the organization/service to a wide network of internal and external stakeholders; gains the confidence and support of various groups through sensitivity to needs, and by achieving organizational goals
Focusing team effort	Clarifies objectives and boundaries; team-oriented to problem solving and decision-making, and to identifying values
Building shared vision	Has a clear vision and strategic direction, which s/he engages various internal and external stakeholders in developing; draws others together in achieving the vision
Supporting a developmental culture	Supportive when mistakes are made; encourages critical feedback of him/herself and the service provided
Facilitating change sensitively	Sensitivity to the impact of change on different parts of the organization; maintains a balance between change and stability

The most obvious feature of this model is the staggering complexity of the nature of leadership in the UK public sector. What emerges is also of a very different tenor from the US 'new paradigm' models. Typically, the US models place an overwhelming emphasis on charisma and vision; that is, *on the leader as primarily acting as the role model for his/her followers*. One might speculate that this is the product of adopting research methodologies which focus solely on the views and/or observations of top managers.

In contrast, the results which emerge in our studies – based on asking the *recipients* and ultimate arbitrators of leadership effectiveness, namely the staff who work in the public sector, how they perceive leadership – present a very different model. What these staff are clearly stating is that the most important role for the leader is *what s/he can do for his/her staff*. This is very reminiscent of the model of *leader as servant*, which is described in the writings of Robert

Greenleaf (1970). However, leadership is not only about meeting staffs' needs; it is much more than that. The UK model suggests that leadership is fundamentally about engaging others as partners in developing and achieving the shared vision, and, as such, it relates to distributed leadership. The UK concept of leadership is also about creating a fertile, supportive environment for creative thinking, for challenging assumptions about how public services should be delivered. And it is about sensitivity to the needs of a range of internal and external stakeholders. It is about connectedness! How else, one might ask, can the daunting challenges of delivering modern public services be achieved?

Another very positive feature of the findings is that what emerges in the UK public sector significantly reflects aspects of the government's modernization agenda, including partnership working, valuing staff, aiming for best practice, removing the traditional barriers between agencies working together within the community. What is encouraging is that there would appear to be a high degree of congruence between what those who work across the public sector believe to be leadership and the espoused leadership tenets of the government.

How can leadership be developed?

Given the fact that leadership is ultimately a social influence process (e.g. Parry 1998), it is axiomatic that development must involve feedback from others as to the impact of the leader's behaviour. Thus, the use of 360 degree feedback is now regarded as an essential element in any leadership development initiative. Its use within organizations is increasing significantly, so much so that it has been described as one of the most important human resource interventions of the last decade (Wimer 2002). In a review of its use in the UK conducted by Warr and Ainsworth in 1999, it was found that 360 degree feedback was being used by approximately 50 per cent of large and medium-sized organizations in the UK, and that 74 per cent of the organizations surveyed expected its use to expand. At the time, 34 per cent of the organizations that were not currently using it planned to introduce it before the end of 2000. With respect to the proportion of managers at different levels who were using 360 degree feedback, the figures below show that it is mainly used by top managers, and that (directors excepted) the proportion decreased with level.

directors   57 per cent
senior managers 81 per cent
middle managers 67 per cent
junior managers 43 per cent
supervisors   17 per cent

Finally, with respect to how it was being used, it is heartening to note that 360 degree feedback was used to support individual development in almost all organizations, though 50 per cent of these organizations also used it for the purpose of performance appraisal. Only 7 per cent were using it for performance-related pay purposes.

The benefits of using 360 degree feedback to support leadership have been documented in several studies, with several concluding that it led to increased self-awareness and more effective managerial behaviour (Hazucha *et al.* 1993; London and Wohlers 1991).

A recent study of its use in a US private sector organization (Sweeney 2002) found that it led to increased performance and productivity. The greatest improvement in performance was found in two areas of behaviour: leadership (including coaching and motivating staff, providing feedback and empowering others) and management (including clarity of goal-setting, organizing people to work on the goals, monitoring progress, and problem solving).

In a study of bank managers (Barling *et al.* 1996), the use of anonymous feedback of leadership style from staff (which is sometimes referred to as 180 degree feedback) was not only found to increase the effectiveness of the managers with respect to their transformational leadership behaviour, but also led to an increase in the staff's levels of commitment to the organization and to their performance. Moreover, the changes were not short lived, and were found to be sustained two years later. However, this study also pointed to the fact that 360 degree feedback (or in this case 180 degree feedback) on its own is of little use. The study involved two groups of managers, who were randomly allocated to either the 'control group', which only received the feedback report, or the 'training group', who also received some post-feedback support. This support included a one-day workshop on the nature of transformational leadership, a personal goal-setting meeting with an experienced management development consultant, and three monthly review discussions around the individual's personal development plans. No changes were perceived in the leadership style of those who only received the report, or in the effects on their staff's commitment or performance.

From such research, several important principles of the use of 360 degree feedback to support leadership development have emerged. These include the crucial importance of the following:

- ensuring the anonymity of raters;
- providing a one-to-one discussion with an experienced development professional;
- encouraging the individual to seek specific examples from colleagues of how they can be more effective;
- turning the information gathered into no more than two or three priority development areas;
- ensuring these are translated into 'SMART' objectives;[1]
- regularly reviewing progress.

For a fuller description of the essential ingredients for using 360 degree feedback to support leadership development, see Alimo-Metcalfe (1998), Antonioni (1996) and the British Psychological Society's (BPS) *Best Practice Guidelines* (2000).

Given the potentially considerable power of 360 degree feedback, it is of crucial importance to be aware of circumstances when it is entirely inappropriate or inadvisable, and to note that several factors must be considered before an organization, or an individual, is encouraged to undertake 360 degree feedback. These require, at the very least, a one-to-one discussion with an experienced person. A range of other factors to consider are listed in the appendix, and are also discussed in various publications, including the BPS's *Best Practice Guidelines* (available from its website: www.bps.org.uk). The public sector is increasingly adopting 360 degree feedback to support leadership development, as the next section suggests.

How is leadership development being approached in the public sector?

There is an enormously wide range of activities being undertaken by organizations in the public sector. We would like to describe some in which we have been involved.

Case study 1: leadership development for headteachers – the National College for School Leadership (NCSL) Transformational Leadership in Schools (TLiS) Project

The NCSL is a unique organization, created by the UK government 'to provide a single, national focus for school leadership development, research and innovation'.

The TLiS project was commissioned to evaluate the use of the public sector version of the transformational leadership questionnaire (TLQ) among senior staff who had recently obtained the National Professional Qualification for Headteachers (NPQH). The NPQH qualification, which will become a prerequisite for entry into headship, can be seen to focus on the managerial/leadership competences required, while the TLQ can be seen as a next stage in their continuing professional development. This is consonant with the view adopted here and elsewhere (e.g. Bass 1998; Kotter 1990) that leadership competences and transformational leadership are complementary.

A major consideration was how to maximize development opportunities and support for a large group of participants (circa $N = 350$) spread throughout England, with limited financial resources available. The content of the project was to include the following:

- didactic input on the latest research on leadership, and how leadership can be developed using 360 degree feedback;
- an individual diagnostic process to support the creation of personal development plans to support participants' leadership, based on the use of the TLQ, which is a 360 instrument;
- local peer group support for programme participants;
- robust, independent evaluation of the process;
- the creation of 'project associates', who are experienced headteachers currently in post and seconded to the NCSL on a part-time basis (15 days

over the 15-month project), or recently retired, and who are provided with support in acting as facilitators of one-to-one discussions with each of the programme participants following receipt of their TLQ report, helping them to identify areas for further discussion with colleagues who had rated them and to begin to construct personal development plans;

- training of the project associates as facilitators for local 'peer support groups', which would serve as action learning sets for the participants for the duration of the programme;
- the creation of 'research associates', also experienced serving headteachers seconded on a part-time basis (15 days of the 15-month project), to conduct a range of research projects to evaluate the impact of the project, including the 360 degree feedback process, with supervisory support from Leadership Research and Development Ltd (LRDL);
- a two-day research methods workshop to support the research.

Selection of participants for the TLiS project

Owing to the demand for places far exceeding availability, the project was almost doubled in capacity, and a selection process was constructed. This process was designed to ensure that the final group of participants included, as far as possible, equal gender representation and minority ethnic group representation, and reflected the variety of different types of schools and regions across England. Applicants were also required to submit a 'case' for why the project would be of particular benefit to them and their school.

Selection of 'research associates' and 'project associates'

An Assessment Centre was conducted jointly by NCSL and LRDL to reflect the agreed criteria for these posts.

Elements of the leadership development programme

STAGE 1: THE MASTERCLASS

A series of 10 'masterclasses' for all participants was held across England, with participants encouraged to bring a colleague with them, who would be involved in their TLQ 360 assessment and post-feedback development support. The content of the seminar included:

- the background to leadership research;
- an explanation of the UK investigation of leadership that led to the development of the TLQ;
- the difference between transformational leadership and management (transactional leadership), stressing that both are required for effectiveness;
- the value of 360 degree feedback in supporting leadership development;

- the importance of post-feedback development plans;
- examples of sample TLQ 360 degree feedback report;
- important considerations in selecting one's raters;
- the structure of the development programme;
- discussion group exercises on the potential benefits of transformational leadership in the context of the participants' jobs, and for their schools;
- the relationship between leadership and organization culture.

At the end of the workshops the TLQ was distributed.

STAGE 2: ONE-TO-ONE DISCUSSIONS WITH PARTICIPANTS AND PERSONAL DEVELOPMENT PLANNING (TWO MONTHS AFTER STAGE 1)

The 'project associates' arranged individual appointments with the programme participants, at which they were offered a 1½ hour discussion to enable them to identify key themes for follow-up with colleagues who had rated them, and guidance in creating personal development objectives.

STAGE 3: ATTENDANCE AT THE PEER SUPPORT GROUP (SIX TO EIGHT WEEKS AFTER STAGE 2)

At the time of writing, local peer support groups are about to be arranged, which will operate under the principles of action learning sets, to support participants in discussing the progress on their personal development plans, and to share and to explore the challenges they face. While it is suggested that these groups meet every six to eight weeks over the remaining duration of the project (seven months), the first two and the last meeting will be facilitated by the project associates.

Ongoing research projects undertaken by the research associates

Each of four research associates has selected one of several topics determined by LRDL in consultation with NCSL. These focus on the evaluation of the leadership development programme, and include the following:

the evaluation of the programme (including the effect of the 360 degree feedback on individuals' personal development as school leaders);
the content and relevance of the 'masterclasses';
the impact of the programme on the individuals and on their schools;
a qualitative study, using the technique of repertory grid interviewing, to compare feedback received from the TLQ with a wide range of other sources of support for development, including appraisal; feedback from colleagues, students, and parents; academic courses being undertaken; the NPQH process; discussions with the local education authority (LEA) adviser

and governors; personal reading and academic qualifications being pursued, etc.;

a quantitative survey of the comparison between the feedback received from the TLQ 360 degree feedback process and the formal performance management review;

the impact of being a project associate on the personal and leadership development of these individuals.

The project is currently ongoing, but the results to date suggest that the participants are finding the 360 degree feedback extremely valuable, and the teachers who are providing one-to-one support following receipt of the 360 report (project associates) are finding the experience of this role invaluable.

The key role of senior and top managers

One of the most important considerations of any leadership development initiative in any organization is the degree of support from the most senior managers. There is an inextricable link between the leadership style of the top group of managers and the culture of the organization. Therefore, before introducing any major leadership activity is it crucially important to try to ensure the commitment, and, ideally, the active involvement, of these managers. This can, however, be problematic.

A few years ago, one of the authors was commissioned to undertake an investigation into why, despite the substantial expenditure on leadership development initiatives by both private and public sector organizations, most failed after a few years. Together with colleagues at the University of Leeds, we undertook an investigation of the major factors that impede success, involving a survey and several case studies in a range of organizations. Several findings emerged, but among the most formidable barriers identified were the attitudes of the most senior managers, in particular in relation to three aspects (Alimo-Metcalfe *et al.* 2000).

The first was their reluctance to participate themselves, believing that they had little need for such support. However, they thought that managers at lower levels did need such development. This lack of commitment to continuous self-development is anathema to the notion of transformational leadership. The second barrier was created as a result of middle level managers' greater understanding of the nature of leadership as a result of their development experiences, and a heightened awareness of the lack of appropriate role models amongst the top managers. The behaviour of the top managers virtually destroyed the potential benefits to the organization of the development investment.

The third impediment was the lack of general support by the top managers for the initiatives, and in particular a lack of support for the proposals made by those managers who had participated in such programmes or initiatives. As a result, cynicism amongst those at lower levels increased, and enthusiasm for applying the development acquired waned.

How to get top managers on board

The ideal situation is, of course, to begin the leadership development initiative with the wholehearted support of the board and other senior and top managers, who then themselves participate actively in the intervention. Unfortunately, this is not always the case. The following case study describes how we typically deal with such a situation.

Case study 2: getting top managers on board

This case study involves a large local authority that was seen as clearly 'failing' in terms of government evaluations of the performance of a range of the services it delivered to the community. This failure was attributed largely to its lack of leadership.

It was decided by the chief executive and the local councillors (persons elected by the local population to represent them, and usually attached to a political party) to introduce a major leadership development initiative across the population of 120 senior managers. We were told that the top managers were not intending to participate, however. We refused to be involved in the initiative unless they at least attended the 90-minute introductory seminar.

The chief executive was asked to introduce this seminar by explaining to the audience of managers why the development initiative was being introduced, and together with the top team colleagues he was to remain at this session to join a panel at the end of the seminar to answer questions raised by potential participants.

We have found that eight topics are particularly valuable for increasing the potential effectiveness of an introductory session:

- The reason why management is no longer sufficient, and that leadership is essential for sustained success of individuals and organizations; research findings on the superiority of leadership, whilst emphasizing the crucial complementary importance of management/transactional leadership.
- The essential role of 360 degree feedback for supporting leadership development, including an explanation of the 'Johari Window'; showing examples taken from anonymous individual reports.
- A description of the typical findings from research on 360 degree feedback, including evidence that managers tend to rate themselves higher in leadership effectiveness than do others, particularly their staff; recent findings relating to the predictive validity of staff's ratings of a manager's future effectiveness.
- The importance, and moral responsibility, of using 360 degree feedback only if there is a real commitment by managers themselves, their boss and the organization to supporting post-feedback development.
- Research findings relating to the potential benefits of using 360 degree feedback in increasing leadership effectiveness.

- The inextricable link between the leadership style of the most senior managers and organization's culture.
- The value of combining individual reports anonymously, to form an organizational group report which is some measure of organization culture.
- Discussion among groups of participants given sample anonymous 360 degree feedback group reports, and asked to reflect on the possible culture of the organization from which they came and to consider the reasons for the differences in the ratings of various rater groups (e.g. managers rating themselves, versus their staff's ratings, their bosses' ratings, their peers' ratings, and their 'others' ratings – e.g. partners in other agencies).

So far, we have found this to be particularly successful in gaining the involvement of top managers in leadership development initiatives, even when they were initially reluctant.

Case study 3: a new chief executive wanted to transform the organization's culture

We are increasingly being invited into organizations when a new chief executive is appointed, possibly to take over an organization that is regarded as being 'in trouble'.

One recent example was the case of a chief executive newly appointed to a large local government organization which had been managed for over 10 years by a highly transactional predecessor. The new chief executive was extremely keen to transform the culture from one that was highly bureaucratic and transactional in style to one that encouraged innovation, an entrepreneurial approach and was based on principles of valuing and developing people, in order that the services provided would be of the highest standard, and would increase morale and encourage pride in working in the organization.

The top management team comprised eight directors, five of whom had worked in this capacity within the authority for over six years, and one who was a relatively new appointee. Four of the longer serving directors were rather autocratic in their style, three were highly transactional and managerial, and one appeared to resent the appointment of the new chief executive 'over her head', as she saw it.

It was decided that the chief executive would hold one-to-one discussions with each of her directors to explain her vision for the organization as embodying a transformational culture, whilst acknowledging the crucial importance of managerial efficiency and effectiveness. She outlined her timescale for transformation, starting with leadership development support for the top managers, followed closely by support for the next layer of 40 or so heads of service, and within eight months moving to the next layer of 140 or so managers heading large teams and departments.

At these discussions, she wanted to share these ideas with her board level colleagues and to encourage the managers to offer suggestions, as well as any concerns they might have. She encountered particular problems with a couple of her board level colleagues, who were not enthusiastic about the proposed changes. Nonetheless, after exploring the issues, she had made it clear to them that she was determined to see significant changes within the organization, and that if they would not support this initiative with active personal commitment they could not remain in their posts. If, however, they were willing to give the initiative a try – which included their full participation in their own development as a first stage – she would offer them as much support as she could from internal and external resources.

Together with the chief executive, we proposed a programme, which is outlined below.

STAGE 1: LEADERSHIP AND CULTURE CHANGE SEMINAR FOR
THE TOP MANAGEMENT TEAM (CHIEF EXECUTIVE PLUS EIGHT
BOARD LEVEL DIRECTORS)

The content of this was similar to the content outlined in case study 2. It was emphasized that the culture change was dependent on the wholehearted commitment of each member of this team. The evaluation of the council in relation to Audit Commission criteria for comprehensive performance assessment (Audit Commission 2001), acted as the background to this seminar. The authority had been assessed as 'poor' in several areas, and with respect to leadership in particular.

The intention was to use a process of 360 degree feedback, and the model of leadership the chief executive wanted for her authority was the transformational model on which the TLQ is based. At the end of the seminar, which was highly interactive, the principles and conditions for using 360 degree feedback and the TLQ were explained, including the conditions: that the reports generated are owned by the 'target' manager, and confidential to them; that raters would be selected by the managers; that ratings by others of the manager would be anonymous and would be combined with others' ratings and shown as an average; that the purpose of the exercise was individual and team development; and that support for individuals would be provided by both external and internal sources. We suggested that it would be a good idea to involve all the staff whom the directors managed directly in completing their questionnaires, so that individuals did not feel 'singled out' or excluded. (This also acts as an excellent model of transformational leadership.)

Since the success of the initiative was significantly dependent on the preparedness of the managers at the most senior levels to modify their attitudes and style, it was crucial that they undertook some form of leadership development, and this should involve gathering anonymous feedback from colleagues, including their staff. While the chief executive wished the managers to use the TLQ as the 360 degree feedback process, a condition of its use was that participation must be voluntary. Individuals were given the choice of suggesting an alternative process of gathering feedback from their colleagues, but this had to be consistent with the transformational behaviours that the chief executive sought to encourage in the authority.

Apart from the provision of confidential individual reports, a group report would be produced, which included the data from the chief executive's TLQ along with the others. There would be a team development programme, together with provision for individual development support. The team development would be closely linked to the organization's strategic plan, which included much closer multi-agency working, and might well therefore involve working with partners in other agencies in the community, and quite possibly local councillors (elected members).

In the event, all the directors chose to undertake 360 degree feedback using the TLQ.

STAGE 2: ONE-TO-ONE DISCUSSIONS OF THE 360 DEGREE FEEDBACK REPORTS (EIGHT WEEKS AFTER STAGE 1)

These discussions provided an opportunity to discuss the individual's report (if they chose to show it to the one-to-one discussion facilitator) and to help them identify themes in the data of which they may not have been aware. Some of these themes may be in areas of strength, others in areas for development. We also explored how they could get 'behind the data' to clarify the reasons why certain colleagues perceived them in a particular way, and how they could check out any assumptions they were making.

It is useful to explain that at this stage individuals are encouraged to try to make sense of the reasons behind the perceptions others have of them; that is, they are *generating hypotheses* as to the reasons for the perceptions of others. However, the next stage, *testing these hypotheses*, can only be achieved by seeking specific examples from others of behaviours which have a positive impact, and those which have a negative impact.

The end result of these discussions was the creation of a schedule of meetings with colleagues to seek examples of more effective behaviours and to ask for examples of current ineffective or inappropriate behaviour of which they may be unaware. We emphasized that at these meetings it is good practice to summarize what they thought the other person had said, so as to reduce the effect of 'selective perception'. Doing this would also increase the other person's belief and confidence in the willingness of the 'target' manager to understand the impact of his/her actions on others.

We encouraged the managers to spend some time in reflection on patterns in the data, and to complete the exercises contained at the back of their reports, which include a grid to be completed by the manager which encourages her/him to look for similarities and differences in self-ratings and ratings by others. In this way, the disparity between self-perceptions and the views of others become more clear.

In this meeting we also discussed managers' feelings about the 360 process. Finally, a follow-up one-to-one discussion was agreed and diarized.

STAGE 3: GROUP FEEDBACK WORKSHOP (AS SOON AS POSSIBLE
AFTER STAGE 2 IS COMPLETED, TYPICALLY A DAY OR SO)

This stage sometimes comes before stage 2, but in this instance, given the possibility of reluctance to share feedback and impressions in a group setting, we decided to reverse the order. This also enabled us, as external consultants, to establish a personal relationship with each individual.

At this session, which lasted around 2½–3 hours, we began by asking if anyone in the group wished to express their feelings or impressions of the process so far. We were pleased to note that two of the directors who had initially appeared somewhat reluctant to participate were more relaxed and more positive towards the process than we had assumed they would be. This therefore challenged the assumptions that we had held about those individuals. On the whole, the managers stated that the exercise had been interesting and valuable, and had encouraged them to reflect, sometimes for the first time, on the way in which they related to their staff, colleagues and external partners.

After some discussion we moved on to a didactic seminar, at which we summarized the different but complementary nature of transformational leadership and transactional (management) leadership, and then focused on research findings concerning the potential benefits of 360 degree feedback in supporting greater leadership effectiveness. The crucial importance of follow-up of the 360 degree feedback was emphasized strongly, not least because top managers should be exemplary in reflecting the role model of leadership in seeking feedback from colleagues. We also emphasized that the data in the reports are based on perceptions, and that these are potentially influenced by bias and may contain some inaccurate reflections on behaviour. Nonetheless, we also emphasized that the very nature of leadership is to do with how others perceive us and the impact that our behaviour has on others.

We described the list of principles for maximizing the value of 360 degree feedback to support leadership development, namely:

- letting colleagues know a week in advance about which particular dimensions of leadership they wished to seek specific feedback on;
- seeking specific examples of behaviour (effective and non-effective) from colleagues in a one-to-one discussion;
- summarizing back what one has heard, and checking out understanding;
- agreeing a review date with the colleague to check progress;
- diarizing the date;
- gathering the feedback and identifying no more than two or three major themes on which to focus;
- turning these themes into 'SMART' objectives;
- regularly reviewing progress.

We then had a brief look at the group report, which was constructed from the aggregate of the anonymous individual reports, and which showed the average of self-ratings by the managers and the average of other raters, separated out by direct reports; bosses (the chief executive in this instance, but also including some elected members with whom they worked closely); peers (most of whom were themselves); and 'others', who included partners in other agencies and/or elected members. Their scores were juxtaposed with the norms for each of these rater groups, established from the use of the TLQ in local government. (In some organizations we are asked to provide normative data from other comparable organizations in the public sector.)

At this stage, we showed the team the summary scores they had obtained on the 10 'leadership impact measures', which were average scores taken from their staff's ratings of them on the variables included in the TLQ, each of which has been found to affect morale, performance, general psychological well-being and other outcomes, such as turnover and absenteeism. These include:

- stress
- motivation to achieve
- job satisfaction and satisfaction with the leader's style
- job commitment
- organizational commitment
- motivation to achieve beyond expectations
- self-confidence and self-esteem.

We were then able to show them the results of analyses we had conducted on the relationship between each of the 14 scales and each of the leadership impact measures. These data are also broken down by the level and gender of staff on whom they have an impact. Table 10.2 shows the results that emerged from a sample of 1,400 managers in local government.

To understand the possible impact their behaviour was having on their staff, and probably on the culture of the organization, we summarized their areas of strength (as rated by their direct reports) and the impact these dimensions of leadership behaviour have on the measures of psychological well-being described above. But the most powerful effect was when we showed the table of their areas of weakness, and how these significantly predict a range of the outcome measures listed above.

It then became clear that there was a need to do something about the quality of leadership in the team. This then became the focus for discussion.

It was decided that the most important priority for the team was to undertake their discussions with their colleagues, although we also decided that there was a need for some shared team development activities.

The discussion became more focused on specific leadership dimensions at this stage, and, within these dimensions, on particular behaviours. So we divided the complete group report among the eight directors, with each couple taking one 'cluster' of scales on the TLQ. Participants were then asked to identify any 'surprises', including 'good news' and 'not so good news'. The ideas which emerged from these in-depth inspections were shared in a plenary session.

From this group session, a list of priorities was identified for team develop-ment action, and a decision was made to diarize three days over the next four months in which one area for development would be explored by the team, facilitated by ourselves. It was heartening that the directors also suggested that in-house training and development staff be involved in supporting these events. Differences between the perceptions of these groups of raters were discussed, particularly where the differences were quite large and where there were surprises. The latter were also explored in terms of possible consequences for the organization's culture. Not surprisingly, this kind of discussion can be a very powerful experience for the group.

STAGE 4: INDIVIDUAL REVIEWS

While it was very important to support the team's development, it was also crucial to support the individual managers. Thus we scheduled a series of four follow-up one-to-one coaching and review sessions with each of the managers, which were two months apart. One of the most common reasons for the failure of leadership development initiatives is lack of continued support for development. Another potential problem can be the cynicism of staff if they see no noticeable effort being made by their manager to do anything about responding to their feedback.

At these follow-up meetings with the managers we discussed progress since the previous meetings, and crucially they were asked to report back on the evidence they could present of how their personal development plans had had some observable impact. Such impact ranged from much more productive departmental meetings and regular individual and team briefings with their staff, to the creation of personal development plans for each of the people they managed directly, and to some planned secondments, shadowing activities and more frequent joint projects, for example with the local primary care trust, with whom they were achieving a much more effective relationship.

One of the managers who had initially shown the most resistance made considerable progress in changing his style, and he had inaugurated some significant changes in his department, including regular brainstorming sessions with his managers, and much more thoughtfully planned, developmentally oriented delegated activities, which staff had responded to with enthusiasm. He had also introduced regular fortnightly lunches with his immediate team, which take place in a local pub. He requested from us a monthly telephone conversation to discuss developments in his personal development plan, and became enthusiastic about offering similar development opportunities to his staff.

One manager has left the team, not because of his lack of support for the culture change, but because he has successfully moved into a chief executive's post.

STAGE 5: SEMINAR FOR ALL MANAGERS IN THE COUNCIL

The first priority had been getting the top managers to identify the behaviours that were having a negative impact on their staff, and in some cases on their colleagues. Equally important was supporting this team of top managers in becoming more collaborative and in acting in a corporate manner. This was not

Table 10.2: The impact of the scales measured by the transformational leadership questionnaire (TLQ) on male and female staff at middle to top management level in local government

SCALE/ CRITERION VARIABLE		Reduced stress		Motivation		Achievement motivation		Job satisfaction		Satisfaction with leadership	
		Levels 1, 2 and 3	Level 4	Levels 1, 2 and 3	Level 4	Levels 1, 2 and 3	Level 4	Levels 1, 2 and 3	Level 4	Levels 1, 2 and 3	Level 4
Showing genuine concern	M	-	0.13	0.38	0.18	0.64	0.11	0.40	0.06	0.31	-
	F	0.46	0.24	0.29	0.09	0.47	0.06	0.36	0.06	0.32	0.09
Enabling	M	-	-	-	0.16	-	-	-	0.06	-	-
	F	-	-	-	0.08	-	0.06	-	0.05	0.26	0.09
Being accessible	M	-	0.13	-	-	-	0.11	0.29	0.05	-	-
	F	-	-	0.30	-	0.39	-	0.27	-	0.26	-
Encouraging change	M	-	0.17	-	0.17	-	-	-	-	0.29	-
	F	-	-	-	-	-	0.05	-	0.05	-	0.09
Being honest and consistent	M	0.51	-	0.33	-	-	-	-	-	0.29 -	0.13
	F	0.44	0.20	-	-	-	0.05	-	0.05	-	0.09
Acting with integrity	M	-	-	-	-	-	-	-	-	-	-
	F	-	0.18	-	0.07	-	0.05	-	0.06	-	0.09

		C1	C2	C3	C4	C5	C6	C7	C8	C9	C10
Being decisive	M	-	0.15	-	-	0.40	0.10	-	-	-	-
	F	-	-	0.28	-	-	-	-	-	-	0.09
Inspiring others	M	-	-	-	-	-	-	-	-	-	-
	F	-	0.07	-	0.07	-	0.05	-	0.05	0.29	-
Resolving complex problems	M	-	-	-	-	0.39	0.11	-	0.04	-	0.14
	F	-	0.07	-	0.07	-	0.05	-	0.06	-	0.10
Networking	M	-	-	-	-	-	-	-	-	-	-
	F	-	-	-	0.07	-	-	-	0.05	-	0.09
Focusing effort	M	-	-	-	-	-	0.10	-	0.04	-	-
	F	-	-	-	-	-	-	-	0.05	-	0.18
Building shared vision	M	-	-	-	-	-	-	-	0.04	-	-
	F	-	-	-	-	-	0.05	-	0.06	-	-
Supporting a developmental culture	M	0.54	-	-	-	-	-	-	-	-	-
	F	-	0.07	0.27	0.07	-	-	-	-	-	0.10
Facilitating change sensitively	M	-	-	-	-	-	-	0.27	-	-	-
	F	-	0.07	-	0.07	-	0.05	-	0.05	-	-

simply because of their seniority *per se*, but because of the potentially dysfunctional effect their behaviour could have on the rest of the organization. Having succeeded in getting the top managers committed to their leadership development, and that of the organization, the intention was to move on rapidly to widening the programme to managers at levels below the board.

It was felt that it was crucial that everyone should be aware that the leadership intervention was occurring. This was, not least, because of the strong view of the chief executive, and of ourselves, that everyone in the organization has the potential to show leadership, and that cultural change needs to be understood and supported by everyone in an organization. It was also evident that staff at middle to junior levels were practising more effective leadership than many of the senior and top managers, and that they needed to have this fact affirmed, and to be encouraged and valued.

It was decided, therefore, to have a lunchtime seminar on leadership and its importance for the organization, and to open this to all staff in the organization. Three such seminars were organized to accommodate all staff. Each seminar lasted one hour and was attended by the chief executive, who also opened the event and explained the reasons for the initiative and the programme for rolling development out, eventually, to all managers in the organization. She emphasized that the process had started with herself and the directors, and she shared some of the benefits they had achieved.

Time was allowed for small group discussion among participants, who addressed three questions, which were:

1   In what way might this organization benefit from becoming more transformational?
2   In what way could I benefit?
3   How could it benefit the community we serve?

A plenary session involved staff feeding back comments from the discussions. The chief executive then described the rollout programme for leadership development in the organization. She explained that colleagues from the training and development team would be facilitators on future programmes, and that future programmes would offer staff development support from the establishment of peer support groups/action learning sets. These sets would focus on combining individual development needs and specific challenges and/or projects in which individuals were involved within their department.

The chief executive asked for any individuals who would be interested in being trained as peer support group facilitators to approach the training and development team for more information.

Finally, she asked if anyone had noticed any difference in the culture. It was fascinating to hear at least six individuals offering their perceptions of positive change. One person also made the suggestion that there should be more frequent seminars such as this one, and that suggestions for how the organization could be more effective could be shared on a staff intranet.

STAGE 5: MOVING THE PROGRAMME TO THE NEXT LEVEL IN THE ORGANIZATION

This programme began six months after starting the programme with the top team. It is very similar to the top team's programme; however, we are only partly through this stage of the project.

We have been working with internal training and development staff to support their skills in sharing the individual and group sessions that arise from the use of the 360 degree feedback process. As soon as they feel confident in taking over these responsibilities we will take a much smaller role by only occasionally offering sessions when their resources are stretched. In addition, some managers have been invited to offer time for co-counselling support for colleagues.

STAGE 6: THE CREATION OF ACTION LEARNING SETS

As more managers are becoming involved in the development initiative, the model of transformational leadership is becoming increasingly embedded in the organization. It is crucially important that the momentum be maintained. Of course, as more managers undertake the development initiative there will be a need for more support for development. This is one of the major benefits offered by peer support groups/action learning sets (ALS).

ALSs will be organized once there has been discussion around the potential benefits they could offer in relation to the most important organizational development needs. This may be by arranging groups of individuals who are linked by common development needs, or by combining individuals in a group who have complementary strengths and development needs, so that there are resources available within each group for mutual support. However, given that one of the organizational development priorities to emerge at this stage of the intervention is the need to create more cross-department working, this should be another criterion for the possible structure of some groups. Other factors being considered include the benefits of creating groups of managers from different levels, as well as from different departments; another is the pressing need for wider development experiences to be afforded to black and minority ethnic managers (Alban-Metcalfe 2003).

The first few sessions of the ALS will be facilitated by a mixture of internal human resources and organizational development staff and external consultants, but the hope is that the sets will become self-supporting within two or three sessions. Sessions will probably be offered every six to eight weeks, with information about shared learning gathered by the training department, who will also create a website to enable staff to advertise a development need, or an interesting project or activity that can be offered to a staff member. In this way, the council is moving towards the creation of a 'transformational learning organization'.

A core activity which it is hoped will be adopted by the ALSs is the regular review of personal development plans, and encouragement of the identification of objectives that will support the strengthening of a transformational organizational culture, as well as those meeting individuals' leadership development needs.

STAGE 7: THE EVALUATION

We have already discussed the evaluation of this organizational leadership intervention. One suggestion is the re-run of the TLQ after about 18 months. However, this will only cover part of the evaluation. An additional source of information on what is changing is a survey of staff attitudes. Another is the ideas that are shared on the new staff intranet. Given that the purpose of supporting the leadership of staff is ultimately to improve the services offered to the community, focus groups can also be run which include members of the community, including local users' groups and organizations. The senior managers are also considering a request for a peer review to offer feedback from an outsiders' group perspective.

Case study 4: a national leadership programme across the public sector – the Cabinet Office-sponsored Public Service Leaders Scheme (website: www.publicserviceleadersscheme.gov.uk)

This programme is the first major cross-public sector leadership development initiative sponsored by the UK government. The partners in this joint venture are the Cabinet Office, the Association of Chief Police Officers, the Improvement & Development Agency, and the NHS. The programme is delivered by a consortium of staff from the civil service, the university sector and the police service.

The current proposal is to have an intake of 100 participants per year for three years. Participants are initially self-selecting, but there is a quota allocated to each of several public sector sponsors, including local government, the NHS, the police and Criminal Justice Service, and central government Departments. A selection process is undertaken which includes in its criteria, evidence of skills in change management and the ability to influence management practice within the applicant's sector. Participants come from middle to senior positions and are expecting to move into a more demanding role in the next three to five years.

The inclusion of participants is constructed to achieve a certain composition:

- 50 per cent civil servants and 50 per cent public sector employees;
- 50 per cent female;
- 6 per cent from minority ethnic groups;
- a geographical representation.

The programme is viewed as a 'leadership journey' which links a personal learning contract with organizational challenges in modernizing the public services.

Elements of the programme[2]

The programme is made up as follows:

- Foundation event: (three days residential) for groups of 15–20 people to start networking, developing self-awareness and clarifying leadership learning needs; and to start to construct the framework for their personal learning contract.
- Network learning events (NLE): three of these per year to bring together all participants for two or three days: comprising networking opportunities, workshops and expert presentations.
- Action inquiry groups (AIG): facilitated and geographically based events for groups of 12 participants, who set their own agenda in a confidential environment for learning.
- Mentoring: participants can choose whether they wish to have a mentor during the scheme, and beyond. The programme secretariat has a pool of mentors from senior levels in the public sector, and will match a choice of three mentors, from whom they can choose, or they bring their own mentor into the programme.
- Interchange: the only compulsory element of the programme, which involves spending time with another public sector organization in activities such as a secondment, shadowing, project work or training; it must last for a minimum of 444 hours.
- E-learning: a platform is available on a secure part of the Public Service Leaders Scheme (PSLS) website to share information and experiences between participants; it has chat rooms and a library resource.

STAGE 1: A THREE-DAY FOUNDATION MODULE

The participants are introduced to the design and content of the programme, and personnel and organization development staff (PODs) work with each participant to begin the outline of a personal learning contract (PLC), which identifies possible areas of strength, as well as those for development. These contracts will be tightened up after the participants have had a one-to-one discussion with a programme tutor following receipt of their feedback from the TLQ at their first network event. Participants undertake a case study, which involves taking on the role of someone who has a responsibility for an area of public policy. Feedback from this exercise is included in their discussion of their PLC with a POD.

Between this event and the first network event (described below), a POD will visit the participant's place of work to meet with them and one of their managers and help construct their PLC. Part of the POD's responsibility is to constructively challenge some of the individual's assumptions and opinions, so as to enable them to construct a more focused and relevant PLC.

Since this leadership development programme is seen as a 'personal journey' for the participant, it may take months before the final PLC is constructed; furthermore, it will be regularly reviewed throughout the course of the programme.

All participants in the particular cohort attend at least three two- or three-day network events. At this first event we introduce the subject of leadership, including its research history and the reasons why we undertook our UK study of 'nearby' leadership and the construction of the TLQ, since it provides a key element of the leadership framework for the programme. The relationship between leadership and organization culture is explored, along with principles of using 360 degree feedback to support development.

Each participant also has a one-to-one discussion of their TLQ report with a tutor, which, again, is related to their PLC. Time is also set aside for participants to meet in their AIGs.

There is other didactic input from other speakers, plus some time for personal reflection. At previous events, a recent head of the civil service and his successor have joined the programme as after-dinner speakers outlining the challenges for the service and for the government's public sector reform agenda.

Subsequent events include a presentation relating Shakespeare's *Henry V* to different classical styles of leadership. On one network event a 'question time' forum was arranged, which included panel members who may be regarded as representing a range of such styles of leadership. Other events have included intensive workshops on dimensions of the TLQ, where there are several people who share a similar leadership development need, and input on the ethics of leadership.

STAGE 3: ACTION INQUIRY GROUPS

This is not a single event, but a support process which runs throughout the programme for groups of around 12 participants, in which individuals can debate and share experiences, describe challenges they face or report on activities in which they have participated which may be of interest to colleagues. They are facilitated by specifically qualified programme tutors.

Certain crucial principles are strictly adhered to in these groups, including total confidentiality and the fact that the agenda is self-determined. The environment is safe for experimentation and the content of the discussions is determined by the members of the group.

These groups meet between five and six times per year, including time being provided at each of the three network events for these to take place.

THE PSLS WEBSITE

Some of the components of the PSLS website are accessible by the general public, including the framework for the PSLS and its underpinning themes. There is also the facility to download an application form. Programme participants can also use the website to access a hyperlink to online discussion groups, notice boards of future events and, importantly, an e-learning platform developed by Durham University, which offers a range of resources, including articles and references.

A mentor is not compulsory for programme participants, but is often chosen. S/he may come from the same organization or a different organization in the same sector, or from a very different one, such as the commercial or voluntary sector. The PSLS also provides a workshop for mentors which enables them to share learning, challenges and gain some mutual support, and to hear more about the mentoring process, the transformational leadership model adopted by the programme, and how leadership impacts on public sector reform.

'THE INTERCHANGE': STEPPING INTO THE SHOES OF ANOTHER

One of the key themes of the PSLS is to cross organizational boundaries, and one of the vehicles for this is to undertake at least 444 hours in the 'interchange' process. This may involve a specific project, or other activities such as work-shadowing, attending meetings in another organization, twinning or job-swapping. The intention is to see public services from the perspective of a very different provider. These activities are arranged by the provider and supported by the programme secretariat. The process is one of the compulsory elements for every participant.

ORGANIZATION 'RAIDS'

These may be proposed by participants, either as a visit to their organization or a suggestion of a 'raid' on an entirely different organization.

One such 'raid' was initiated by a speaker who happened to be a relatively newly appointed chief executive to a city council that needed radical reform. He was determined to 'be leading edge and transformational, learn from the mistakes of others and leapfrog the rest'. Following a robust question session, he invited members of the PSLS to visit his organization. A number of participants took up the offer, and each spent a day in a particular service offered by the council, from a community regeneration team to a day with the local police service, including attending a 'drugs raid'.

The group spent the evening preparing presentations to their colleagues and sharing their experiences and reactions. The following morning some of the group got together to construct a final presentation on their impressions to the chief executive whose initial invitation they had accepted.

Programme evaluation

The PSLS is currently completing its list of participants on the third annual cohort of the scheme. Interestingly, those who joined in the first year can remain on the programme for the length of the scheme, and the second year's cohort can stay for a second year. Their network events are usually of shorter duration, but their PLCs and AIGs continue.

It has been recognized that it may take a few more years for the potential benefits of the programme to be evidenced in the public sector organizations in which the participants will practice their leadership. However, one evaluation process which is now in place is the repeat of the TLQ for participants of the first cohort, which started some 20 months ago. It has been realized that the individuals' jobs and the organizational context in which they work have no doubt also changed, but it may provide some interesting data on areas of greatest and least change, and on the effects on the psychological outcome variables measured by the TLQ.

This has been a courageous and undoubtedly exciting programme for most participants. Several have documented their experiences in articles published in the PSLS newsletter *Leading Edge*, and tutors and AIG facilitators will have anecdotal comments to offer. It remains to be seen whether the sponsors believe that the investment has been worthwhile.

Concluding points

This chapter has sought to explain the rationale behind a new UK-developed model of 'nearby' transformational leadership, and the practices being adopted to support the leadership development of individuals and organizations in the public sector.

The range of case studies was chosen to explain some of the varied uses of leadership development initiatives within the public sector, including their use in supporting top team development; organization culture change; transformation across a subculture of the public sector, and across the general public sector. The initiatives have emphasized that, while it is crucial to try to gain the commitment of the most senior managers, it is also extremely important to enable everyone in the organization to understand the reasons why leadership development is key to achieving the modernization agenda, and why simply focusing on management will not be sufficient to sustain change. The role of 360 degree feedback in the development process has the benefit of actively seeking the support of managers' staff and their colleagues in providing more senior managers with both feedback and practical suggestions of how they can role model leadership in their day-to-day practice.

We stress, however, that 360 degree feedback is merely the start of the development process, and that new initiatives must be embedded in real challenges, supported by well facilitated action learning groups. We also believe that it is essential for managers to identify personal objectives relating to leadership development, but also to identify objectives which focus on supporting the leadership of their staff and a transformation of the organization's culture. Without the support of the organizations' processes, such as selection, appraisal, performance management and other development initiatives, leadership will be seen as detached, rather than embedded as a theme running through the core of these activities.

We are very aware that the new model of leadership adopted in these programmes requires the development of new ways of supporting the transformation of organizations, and that many of the initiatives we have described are still 'experimental', although nonetheless undertaken by real people in some of the most demanding jobs. But, given the extraordinarily complex challenges, and resultant demands, faced by managers and professionals delivering public services, one thing we are certain of is the need for more leadership. While this chapter has been devoted to leadership development within the public sector, we hope the ideas presented in this chapter will stimulate constructive debate in the wider organizational arena.

Notes

1   SMART: specific, measurable, achievable, realistic, within a timescale.
2   Taken from the PSLS Application Guide with permission from the Cabinet Office PSLS Secretariat

References

Alban-Metcalfe, J. (2003) 'It don't matter if you're black or white? Not according to 360 feedback', *Proceedings of the Annual BPS Occupational Psychology Conference*, Bournemouth, 8–10 January.

Alimo-Metcalfe, B. (1998) '360 degree/feedback and leadership development', *International Journal of Selection & Assessment* 6(1): 35–44.

Alimo-Metcalfe, B. and J. Alban-Metcalfe (2001) 'The development of a new transformational leadership questionnaire', *Journal of Occupational & Organizational Psychology* 74: 1–27.

—— (2002) 'The great and the good', *People Management*, 10 January: 32–4.

—— (2003a) 'Gender & leadership: a masculine past, but a feminine future?', *Proceedings of the BPS Annual Occupational Psychology Conference*, Brighton, 8–10 January: 67–70.

Alimo-Metcalfe, B., J. Ford, N. Harding and J. Lawler (2000) *British Companies at the Beginning of the 21st Century: Factors that Impede Leadership Development Initiatives*, London: Careers Research Forum.

Antonioni, D. (1996) 'Designing an effective 360-degree appraisal feedback process', *Organizational Dynamics* 25(2): 24–38.

Audit Commission (2001) *Change Here*, London: Audit Commission/PIU.

Barling, J., T. Weber and E.K. Kelloway (1996) 'Effects of transformational leadership training on attitudinal and financial outcomes: a field experiment', *Journal of Applied Psychology* 81(6): 827–832.

Bass, B.M. (1985) *Leadership and Performance beyond Expectations*, New York: Free Press.

—— (1998) *Transformational Leadership: Industrial, Military, and Educational Impact*, Mahwah, NJ: Lawrence Erlbaum Associates.

Bennis, W. and B. Nanus (1985) *Leaders*, New York: Harper & Row.

Bond, F.W. and D. Bunce (2001a) 'Mediators of change in emotion-focused & problem-focused worksite stress management interventions', *Journal of Occupational Health Psychology* 5(1): 156–63.

—— (2001b) 'Job control mediates change in a work reorganisation intervention for stress reduction', *Journal of Occupational Health Psychology* 6: 290–302.

Borrill, C.S., T.D. Wall, M.A. West, G.E. Hardy, D.A. Shapiro, C.E. Haynes, C.B. Stride, D. Woods and A.J. Carter (1998) *Stress Among Staff in NHS Trusts. Final Report*, Sheffield: University of Sheffield, Institute of Work Psychology; and Leeds: University of Leeds, Psychological Therapies Research Unit.

British Psychological Society (2000) *360 Degree Feedback: Best Practice Guidelines*, Leicester: BPS.

Cabinet Office, Performance and Innovation Unit (2001) *Strengthening Leadership in the Public Sector*, London: HMSO.

Conger, J.A. (1989) *The Charismatic Leader: Behind the Mystique of Exceptional Leadership*, San Francisco: Jossey-Bass.

Greenleaf, R.K. (1970) *The Servant as Leader*, San Francisco: Jossey-Bass.

Hazucha, J.F., S.A. Hezlett and J. Schneider (1993) 'The impact of 360-degree feedback on management skills development', *Human Resource Management* 32(2–3): 325–51.

Hogan, R., G.J. Curphy and J. Hogan (1994) 'What we know about leadership', *American Psychologist* 49: 493–504.

House, R.J. (1977) 'A 1976 theory of charismatic leadership', in J.G. Hunt and L.L. Larson (eds) *Leadership: The Cutting Edge*, Carbondale, IL: Southern Illinois University Press.

Kotter, J.P. (1990) *A Force for Change*, London: Free Press.

London, M. and A.J. Wohlers (1991) 'Agreement between subordinate and self-ratings in upward feedback', *Personnel Psychology* 44: 375–90.

Parry, K.W. (1998) 'Grounded theory and social processes: a new direction for leadership research', *Leadership Quarterly* 9: 85–105.

Shamir, B. (1995) 'Social distance and charisma: theoretical notes and an exploratory study', *Leadership Quarterly* 6: 19–47.

Sweeney, T. (2002) '360 (degrees) feedback leads to improved productivity', *Credit Union Management* 25(8): 50.

Tichy, N. and M. Devanna (1990) *Transformational Leadership*, 2nd edition, New York: Wiley.

Warr, P. and E. Ainsworth (1999) '360° feedback – some recent research', *Selection & Development Review* 15(3): 3–6.

Wimer, S. (2002) 'The dark side of 360-degree feedback', *Training & Development* 56(9): 37–42.

11 Leadership and leadership development in education

Ron Glatter

Introduction

Remarkable growth has occurred in England within the space of little more than a generation in what is now commonly referred to as leadership development for staff in the education service. The first master's level courses were offered during the 1960s in what at that time was called 'educational administration', following usage in North America, where there had been provision since the late 19th century. The term 'management development' was probably first applied within the education context by the present author (Glatter 1972: see Bolam 1997) following a development project at the University of London Institute of Education which included courses run in collaboration with the London Business School. Central government interest in the area began in 1983 and has grown steadily since then, culminating in the establishment of the National College for School Leadership (NCSL) in 2000 and, more recently, a leadership college for the postcompulsory or 'learning and skills' sector.[1]

The present chapter will concentrate on contemporary issues relating to leadership and leadership development, focusing primarily on the schools sector. As a backdrop to this it is important to appreciate the profound structural transformations (or 'reforms') which the English schooling system has experienced since the 1980s. These have had a very significant impact on the work of school staff, perhaps most notably those with leadership and management responsibilities. Space does not permit a full discussion (see, for example, Riley 1998; Tomlinson 2001), but four elements, which interact with one another, seem of particular importance in relation to educational leadership and management:

- A sharp process of centralization and attendant detailed prescription, turning the English system from one of the least to one of the most centralized in the world within a period of a dozen years, from the Education Act of 1986 to the School Standards and Framework Act of 1998.
- Perhaps paradoxically, a concomitant process of 'devolution' to institutions, involving, in the schools sector, the exchange of powers over the curriculum (which schools largely lost to the centre) for powers over resources (where they made significant gains): or, in Simkins' (2002) terms, the exchange of

criteria power, concerned with the 'what' and 'why' of service provision, for *operational power,* concerned with the 'how' of service delivery.

- The introduction of incentives to institutions to compete for students, and the encouragement of choice for 'consumers', thus creating a quasi- or public market (Woods *et al.* 1998), complemented in recent years by a strong policy aspiration for institutional collaboration and systemic improvement (DfES 2003).
- The establishment of strong accountability regimes based on technical-rational performance management principles.

Against the background of these developments in governance and policy, the remainder of this chapter will present:

- a brief discussion of the increasing prominence of the discourse of 'leadership';
- consideration of three important contemporary perspectives in educational leadership analysis and research;
- issues and tensions in educational leadership and management development;
- conclusions and implications.

'Leadership' takes over?

Although discussions of the uses and meanings of terms such as 'leadership', 'management' and 'administration' can often be tedious and appear like semantic quibbles,[2] it is worth commenting on the recent rise of 'leadership' in relation to education. This trend is evident in the US as well as the UK (Gronn 2002b). At times it almost appears as though 'management' has been totally eclipsed. Although much of the trend in the UK has been driven by official formulations, it was prefigured in an influential academic book of the mid-1990s entitled *School Leadership – Beyond Education Management: An Essay in Policy Scholarship* (Grace 1995). This asserted the moral superiority of the concept of school leadership over that of educational management and identified the latter term with the competitive market culture which central government attempted to introduce through the Education Reform Act of 1988 and subsequent legislation. There is a certain irony in the fact that a proposal to privilege a term on the basis of a critique of government policy was in effect then appropriated by the government. The present author cautioned against injunctions upon us 'to breathe the purer air of leadership, *beyond* education management' (Glatter 1997: 189), arguing that this position tended to disregard the messiness of the real world, its dilemmas, ambiguities and constraints:

> Erecting this kind of dichotomy between something pure called 'leadership' and something dirty called 'management', or between values and purposes on the one hand and methods and skills on the other, would be disastrous. It

would create exactly that divorce between values and methods which the critics claim to abhor.

(Glatter 1997: 189)

Sergiovanni argued that the challenge of school leadership was 'to make peace with two conflicting imperatives, the managerial and the moral' (1991: 329). Schools had to be run effectively, but 'for the school to transform itself into an institution, a learning community must emerge' (*ibid.*). Introducing the notion of 'institution' is important here because it arguably takes us to the heart of what may be a distinctive (if not unique) feature of leadership and management in the educational context, where the task may be seen as relating to institutions rather than organizations (W.R. Scott 2001). Peter Scott has suggested that we already understand a great deal about what he called the 'public life' of educational institutions, for example how they should be planned and organized, but too little about their 'private life':

> how they work to educate people, how they successfully transmit social and cultural values, how they model the conduct of modern society. Yet it is in this second context, of institutions as moral entities, that the most important issues of accountability, responsiveness and responsibility arise.
>
> (P. Scott 1989: 22)

If educational leadership is concerned with effectively reconciling the 'public' and 'private' lives of educational institutions, there is little agreement on how to achieve this. The UK government (whose education remit is, following devolution, largely restricted to England) frequently refers to 'strong' leadership and employs transformational discourse (see, for example, DfES 2003). One well publicized example was the Fresh Start scheme, the policy designed to 'save' failing schools through formal closure, staff and name changes and, crucially, through bringing in a new headteacher. The approach bore a close resemblance to Goddard's characterization of 'white knight leadership', where 'a leader is "parachuted" in to a school in order to "fix" real or perceived problems'. If wholesale staff changes are needed, 'the metaphor changes from chivalry to the wild west' as the new leader 'cleans up the lawless town' (Goddard 1998: 6–7). The Fresh Start policy suffered a series of high profile disasters and resignations and it was substantially withdrawn.

The transformational rhetoric often employed is difficult to reconcile with the tight central control and close specification of performance targets and requirements that are dominant features of current governance processes. These features reflect an aspiration to create schools in the image of what Leithwood and his colleagues, who have conducted extensive empirical research on school leadership, have termed the 'high reliability organization' (HRO), which responds to the public expectation of dependable performance and guaranteed effectiveness (Leithwood *et al.* 1999). Their other two images of future schools are 'school as community', focusing on the school as a social institution, and 'school as learning organization', focusing on innovation. They argue that, although the three images are based on substantially different assumptions, each contains a partial solution to the dilemmas schools face and a synthesis can and should be achieved.

The image that is most strongly reflected in the section on leadership and management in the government inspection agency's framework for conducting school inspections (Ofsted 2000) is that of the high reliability organization. The emphasis is on tight coupling, rigorous target-setting and monitoring, and clarity of roles and responsibilities (see also Levačić *et al.* 1999). Some attention is, however, given to the 'school as community', with references to aims and values, good relationships, equal opportunities and inclusive policies. 'School as learning organization' is notably absent; in fact identifying solutions is treated as unproblematic: 'You need to evaluate how far the staff know the right things to do to improve performance and whether or not they do them' (*ibid.*: 8). Leadership and management are treated as largely separate, though there is acknowledgement that they overlap. On this basis the chief inspector has reported that the quality of the leadership and management of headteachers and key staff has been improving (Ofsted 2003a).[3]

Thus, while leadership has risen to prominence conceptually and rhetorically, management in its technical-rational manifestations has become an increasingly powerful force (Glatter 1999).

Leadership in context

Despite substantial empirical work both in the UK and elsewhere, the impact of leadership on school effectiveness and student outcomes is still poorly understood. From a review of some 20 years of research in the UK, Hall and Southworth concluded: 'The idea that powerful and visionary heads enhance the school's effectiveness is…a continuing belief in the research and the teacher profession generally. Yet beyond this assertion surprisingly little else is known' (1997: 164). Despite a great deal of empirical evidence from many countries, there is no consensus about what constitutes effective school leadership practice (Harris 2003).

Hallinger and Heck (1999) undertook a rigorous review of more than 40 predominantly quantitative studies from 11 countries conducted between 1980 and 1998 in an attempt to answer the question 'Can leadership enhance school effectiveness?' Their conclusion was that school leaders – especially headteachers – do make a difference to outcomes, but they enter two important caveats. First, the influence of leadership is *indirect* rather than direct: 'Skilful school leaders influence school and classroom processes that have a *direct* impact on student learning' (*ibid.*: 185). In other words, their actions are mediated by others. Second, school leaders are themselves heavily influenced by the norms of the school and by its external context. The authors state that the image of the heroic school leader is not supported by the findings. 'School leaders do not *make* effective schools. Rather the image we draw from this review is that of school leaders who are able to work with and through the staff to shape a school culture that is focused yet adaptable' (*ibid.*). This 'working with and through staff' involves fostering the development of a collaborative school culture in which the staff 'find meaning in their work and are motivated to learn and solve problems' (*ibid.*).

Broadly similar conclusions emerged from a conceptually and methodologically sophisticated study of leadership influence conducted in Canada, in which the dependent variable was 'student engagement' rather than the narrower and more common measure of outcome in terms of student attainment in tests or examinations (Leithwood and Jantzi 1999). The significance of context is emphasized by the finding that a substantial proportion of variation in student engagement was explained by family educational culture, but, as the authors suggest, the 'good news' is that this context variable may be susceptible to leadership influence through improving the school's relationships with parents.

The implications of such an analysis have been well set out by one of the best-known writers on educational leadership and change, the Canadian author Michael Fullan. He has worked in this field for over two decades at national and international levels. His book *Leading in a Culture of Change* (Fullan 2001) provides a number of insightful pointers about effective leadership practice in education which appear to the present author to be in accord with the research literature. They include the following:

- moral purpose is critical to long-term organizational success;
- change cannot be bulldozed – it takes time and must be organic: develop capacity and secure internal commitment to solve complex problems;
- detailed sets of prescriptions are unhelpful in conditions of complexity – living systems cannot be directed along a linear path;
- '[t]he soft stuff is really the *hard* stuff, and no-one can really "engineer" it' (Pascale *et al.* 2000: 12);
- in a culture of frenetic change, there is a dangerous appeal in off-the-shelf solutions;
- relationships and emotional development within the organization are of key importance;
- visions need to be shared and emerge from experience rather than being imposed;
- the demand for charismatic leadership is a delusion born out of the confusion we feel in complex times.

Three aspects of such a formulation are worth particular attention: moral purpose, environmental complexity and 'quiet' leadership.

Moral purpose

This has already been touched on in the previous section. A study for the Department for Education and Skills (DfES) conducted case studies of 10 schools whose leadership and management was rated as 'excellent' or 'outstanding' by inspectors. A key feature of these schools was said to be that the school leaders 'held a number of clear – and shared – educational values and beliefs.... They were concerned with such matters as inclusivity, equal opportunities and equity or justice, high expectations, engagement with stakeholders, co-operation, team-work, commitment, and understanding' (Earley *et al.* 2002: 89). The authors refer to this as 'values-driven leadership'. A similar conclusion was drawn from a study of 12 schools deemed effective: 'Good leaders are informed by and communicate clear sets of personal and educational values which represent their moral purposes for the school' (Day *et al.* 2001a: 53). These authors also comment that the values 'were often part of strong religious or humanitarian ethics which made it impossible to separate the personal and the professional' (*ibid.*: 45).

A similar emphasis is evident across the Atlantic. For example, Furman (2003), in her 2002 presidential address to the (North American) University Council for Educational Administration, refers to the 'new' scholarship focusing on the purposes of leadership, such as social justice, democratic community and learning for all children. In an era when political, instrumental and account-ability purposes tend to dominate, she cautions against conflating student learning with measurable student achievement.

Environmental complexity

The significant impact of the environment upon school leadership has only begun to be recognized relatively recently (Glatter 1989), a recognition that is closely related to the structural transformations referred to earlier. Thus educa-tional leadership can now be conceptualized as involving 'the complex interplay of the personal/biographical, the institutional/organisational, and the broader social, political and economic context' (Christie and Lingard 2001: 5). It must be said, however, that most research and writing still focuses on the first two dimen-sions to the relative neglect of the third.

The significant devolution of powers, particularly over resources, coupled with the new quasi-market dynamic with its associated rhetoric of 'consumer choice', has introduced a focus on strategic thinking and strategy development (see, for example, Davies and Ellison 1999; Fidler 2002; Preedy *et al.* 2002). The centralization of the system has led to a continuous flow of initiatives that need to be negotiated and adapted to the school's values and ethos. 'Policy eclecticism' (Leithwood 2001) and work intensification produce a series of tensions and dilemmas for school leaders. For example, the strong current policy thrust towards partnership and collaboration between schools has been injected into a system in which there are powerful incentives towards competition, and the tensions between these countervailing forces need to be resolved at the level of the school. A paradox of contemporary school leadership is that, while many powers have been delegated to schools, they are still highly dependent on their environments. As Bolman and Deal point out, state schools 'have low power with respect to external constituencies and struggle to get the resources they need.... An organization such as Harvard University is insulated from its environment by its size, elite status and large endowment' (1997: 52). This does not simplify the task for schools: if anything it makes it more complex.

'Quiet leadership'

In these conditions it may be thought that effective school leadership may often be close to the characterization put forward by Mintzberg *et al.*: 'Real leadership is often more quiet than heroic. It is connected, involved and engaged. It is about teamwork and taking the long-term perspective, building an organization slowly, carefully and collectively' (2002: 71). Of particular relevance here is the recent growth of interest in 'distributed leadership' in relation to schools; that is, leadership seen as the product of concertive or conjoint activity rather than as a phenomenon which arises from the individual (Bennett *et al.* 2003).[4] Despite the sharp focus on the 'headmaster' (Baron 1956), and more recently the 'headteacher', in the history and culture of British schooling, the management structure of secondary schools has at least since the growth of comprehensive education in the 1970s been more elaborate and explicit than in many other countries. More recently the structure of primary schools has become more elaborated too. There is now a strong focus of attention on 'middle leaders' (previously 'middle managers'), for example subject and pastoral leaders and special educational needs coordinators (SENCOs). The interest in distributed leadership implies a belief that leadership is an attribute not just of headteachers and the numerous other post-holders in schools, but even of those without formal posts of responsibility. Gronn (2002a), writing from an international perspective, considers that distributed leadership has grown because of increased work intensification and complexity in schools – distributing leadership is essential for survival. For example, he draws attention to the data-rich task environment found in schools today, and this certainly matches the experience of English schools, where the generation and analysis of data, whether relating to pupil attainment or to finance and budgeting, are far more substantial activities than they were a decade ago.

Leithwood argues that 'distributed orientations to leadership are the antithesis of "great man" orientations, assuming as they do that leadership is shared by many people' (2001: 231). However, Bennett *et al.* (2003) point out that there is no necessary contradiction between the concept of distributed leadership and strong senior leadership: disparities of power may still exist even where leadership is distributed. The key point for them is that distributed leadership is defined as 'an emergent property existing in relationships, rather than an activity carried out by an individual or individuals' (*ibid.*: 11). On this view, leadership is fundamentally relational. Leaders 'both shape and are shaped by their constituents... Leadership is not simply a matter of what a leader does but also of what occurs in a relationship' (Bolman and Deal 1997: 296).

A striking development of this approach is seen in Robinson's (2001) depiction of leadership as embedded in the performance of tasks. Leadership is identified with making contributions that are seen *by others* as progressing tasks or problems which *they* perceive to be important in a manner consistent with their understanding of those problems. It is therefore identified by the reaction of others, particularly where individuals are perceived as repeatedly making such contributions. In attempting to progress or resolve problems, constraints have to be specified and integrated. These constraints will arise both from the preferences of the 'problem solvers' and from features of the environment which they cannot control but which they think need to be taken into account. Constraint specification and integration are therefore key processes of leadership.

Presenting a vignette designed to illustrate her central proposition, Robinson comments: 'In this scenario, leadership has gone underground because it is embedded in the task, rather than floating above it as a meta-level commentary' (2001: 93). The scenario is of a school trying to decide how to monitor and report on the collective achievement of students. It shows how emphasizing task performance in this way focuses attention on the key tasks of schools concerned with learning and teaching, as well as the central role of professional expertise and understanding in educational leadership. This conception has a close affinity with the portrayal by Eraut of *deliberation* as a process containing elements of both analysis and intuition which

> may involve turning things over in one's mind, looking at the situation from different angles; trying to make sense of many viewpoints, many sources of information and many theoretical perspectives; searching for ways to frame the problem; trying to reconcile conflicting factors; developing a new approach; or exploring possible scenarios.
>
> (Eraut 2000: 128)

This section will hopefully have conveyed something of the complexity of educational leadership and also its contextualized character. Against the background of this brief discussion of analytical frameworks and evidence relating to educational leadership, we move in the next section to examine leadership and management development for education.

Leadership development: issues and tensions

The focus here will be on longer programmes of leadership and management development offered by the new NCSL and by higher education institutions. As in other sectors, there is a great range and variety of shorter offerings and forms of school-based development.

The NCSL

Proposals for a national staff college for school leaders have been around in the UK at least since 1967 (Michael 1967) but were often received with considerable scepticism: 'Underlying these doubts was a justified fear that a single orthodoxy about administrative practice would develop' (Glatter 1972: 52). Following increasing central government involvement in school leadership training, plans to establish in England a National College for School Leadership were announced in 1998 by Prime Minister Tony Blair as a major initiative of the new Labour government (DfEE 1998). The college formally opened in 2000 and moved into an impressive £28 million new building located on the campus of the University of Nottingham in 2002. Its remit from the government included providing 'a single national focus for school leadership development and research' (Blunkett 2000: 2). By 2002–3 its government grant was £60 million (NCSL 2002) and its staff had grown to some 150.

In 2001 the college issued its *Leadership Development Framework*, identifying five stages of school leadership:

* emergent: those who are beginning to take on formal leadership roles or would like to do so;
* established: experienced deputy and assistant heads who have decided not to pursue headship;
* entry to headship;
* advanced: those with four or more years' experience of headship;
* consultant: headteachers with a proven track record of success who wish to develop others.

Formal programmes are being developed or have been taken over from the Teacher Training Agency (TTA) and the Department for Education and Employment (now the Department for Education and Skills, DfES) for staff at each of these stages, and there are other programmes as well, for example for school bursars.

In the *Framework* document the college committed itself, among other things, to 'the principles of blended learning, whereby development activity is composed of a complementary mix of private study, e-learning and face-to-face interaction' (NCSL 2001: 6). Such an approach appears essential in view of the scale of the operation. As will have become clear, the college's remit covers everyone in schools who holds or aspires to a formal leadership position, not just headship. The target audience of emergent (middle) leaders is well in excess of 100,000. In terms of scale the individual programmes related to each of the stages must compare with, if not exceed, the largest leadership development programmes anywhere. Even before the college had been established, national programmes for aspiring, new and experienced headteachers instituted by the government during the 1990s were regarded by Brundrett as representing 'a grand design on a scale which had not been attempted anywhere else in the world up to that time' (2000: 86). He enumerated some of the criticisms which had been made of these programmes, including a lack of reference to theoretical perspectives, insufficient use of research, an excessively bureaucratic approach and insufficient articulation with university higher degree systems (*ibid.*).

We will focus attention here on one of the college's many programmes, the National Professional Qualification for Headteachers (NPQH). This is arguably the most important programme and unusual within the total offering in that it includes extensive assessment and leads to a national qualification. It is designed for those wishing to become heads. Introduced in 1997 following a decision by the previous Conservative government, it was reduced in length and made less demanding in 2001 in the face of concerns about a growing shortage of applicants for headships. Possession of NPQH is about to become a requirement for everyone appointed to a headship. By 2003 there had been around 8,000 NPQH 'graduates' and 7,000 were registered on the programme.[5]

There are limited out-of-school attendance requirements for face-to-face sessions. The programme involves mainly school-based work, self-study and e-learning. There are three routes. The first, for those with limited senior management experience, is expected to take a maximum of two years, while the third, for those assessed by a tutor as close to being ready for headship, may require as little as four months. There are four modules but candidates only take what they are considered (via a personal training and development plan) to require depending on their previous knowledge, experience and skills. The module areas are:

- strategic direction and development of the school;
- teaching and learning;
- leading and managing staff;
- efficient and effective development of staff and resources.

Assessment is a two-stage process. First, a 'tutor' (perhaps more accurately an assessor) visits the candidate in school to verify that they have completed their training and development plan, to review and discuss points from a learning journal they have been expected to keep, and to assess written and oral evidence of required school improvement work and of their capability against the National Standards for Headteachers (see below). If they are successful in this school-based assessment they can proceed to the final stage, which is hosted by the college but held in regional centres. It begins with a two-day residential course covering leadership and vision, future schools, national priorities and personal effectiveness. This is followed by a one-day assessment based on critical incident-type exercises and a personal interview. Successful candidates may attend an award ceremony to receive their NPQH certificate.

The National Standards for Headteachers (DfES 2000) against which candidates are assessed is a 16-page document containing a highly detailed specification in five sections: core purpose; key outcomes; professional knowledge and understanding; skills and attributes; and key areas (those covered by the modules). Gronn criticized the standard-setting approach to educational leadership development, which is evident in other countries too, notably the USA, and linked it to the ideology of the new managerialism: 'The introduction of standards creates a regime of compliance and an industry of verification' (Gronn 2002b: 556). He argued that bodies such as government agencies were 'customising their requirements by accrediting individuals according to standards-determined profiles of preferred leader types'. Hence he characterized the approach as 'designer leadership' (*ibid.*: 558).

More pragmatically perhaps, the present author has warned of the danger of such standards 'fostering an excessively atomised and disaggregated approach which would not reflect the reality of the job' (Glatter 1999: 259). There is no indication of any research basis for the standards. Conducting a literature review of school leadership research for the college, Bush and Glover (2003) comment that the approach taken in the standards, particularly the section on skills and attributes, is similar to trait theory. They also observe that it pays little attention to different school contexts. Such criticisms appear to have had some impact, as the standards are under review at the time of writing.

Taken on its own, this account would raise major questions about the college's stance and focus. However, it must be pointed out that the standards pre-date the college's establishment, having first appeared in 1997. As indicated previously, the college also provides a growing range and variety of development programmes, for example one for black and minority ethnic teachers designed to support equal access to promotion. Further, a significant programme of research was built into the design from the outset. One of the major strands of this is concerned with investigating the impact of leadership development, an area seriously neglected by the traditional providers (Bennett and Marr 2002). It has also promoted the production of literature reviews in the school leadership field. Such reviews were previously extremely rare. Links with universities have been developed through contracted research projects and funded practitioner research associateships, and also through the college's Universities Partnership Group, consisting of 10 universities with nationally recognized educational leadership centres.[6] Through this group and other channels, the college has been proactive in seeking to establish accreditation routes from its programmes to master's degrees in universities and vice versa. Finally, considerable emphasis is given to international activity. Some of the leading international scholars in the field are directly associated with the college and there is a substantial international research associateship programme linked with the partner universities. There is much interest in the college in a number of other countries.

Higher degrees

The master's degree with a named specialization in educational leadership and management and related areas is widely available in the UK. In 1994 Lawrence conducted a survey and found 53 institutions offering such degrees in England alone (Lawrence 1994). A later study (Brundrett 1999) produced a total of 63 for England and Wales. The great majority are offered by schools and departments of education, though a handful are provided by schools of business or management. Most are designated MA, MEd or MSc, but a few are entitled MBA (Education). Generally this specialization has been one of the most popular routes among education master's degree options. A significant development in the past decade has been that of the taught doctor of education degree (EdD), which normally involves a thesis of about half the length of that for a PhD. Here again specialization in leadership and management has accounted for a substantial proportion of the total take-up.

The advent of the national programmes referred to earlier, closely tailored to assumed career and professional needs, creates a significant challenge for conventional broadly focused higher education provision of this kind, and there is anecdotal evidence of some reduction in take-up. However, the longer-term prognosis is unclear. The national programmes could generate in many more teachers and school leaders an interest in leadership learning, and this, together with the development of accreditation links of the kind discussed earlier, could increase the numbers seeking higher degrees. In order to meet the challenge successfully, however, universities would need to engage more strongly with and seek to complement the national and professional agenda. Some – or even many – may find this difficult because of the heavy emphasis placed in recent years on the production of original research and traditional academic forms of dissemination.[7]

Eraut (2000) has distinguished between *codified knowledge* and *personal knowledge*. Codified knowledge is subject to quality control, for example by peer review and academic debate, and is explicit by definition. Personal knowledge includes codified knowledge in a personalized form, but also process and experiential knowledge and impressions in memory, and it may be explicit or tacit. The expertise of universities is predominantly related to codified knowledge. This knowledge is extremely important for developing our understanding over the longer term, but on its own it may have limitations for current leadership development. A survey of school leaders reported that higher education institutions were viewed 'as better at "pushing back the frontiers of knowledge" rather than providing training and development which focused on the needs of school leaders' (Earley *et al.* 2002: 58). This is perhaps not surprising since, as Bolam has commented, 'We have a multiplicity of theoretical perspectives, which at best provide illumination and insight but few guidelines for action' (Bolam 1997: 275–6).

Drawing on his concept of *deliberation* referred to earlier, Eraut suggests that school leaders aspire to a maturity of judgement sometimes referred to as wisdom, which is neither purely analytical nor purely intuitive but conveys 'an ability to deliberate about issues and problems, to see how different people might be affected and to put them into longer-term perspective' (Eraut 1999: 122). A key challenge for higher education institutions may be the extent to which they are able and willing to extend their expertise beyond codified knowledge to offer leadership development that, through developing a wider range of capabilities, more fully prepares school leaders to operate in a complex world. Many institutions have sought to grapple with this key issue since educational management was first established as a field of study in universities in the UK more than 30 years ago. In this connection it is potentially significant that the Quality Assurance Agency for Higher Education (QAA) has explicitly included capabilities related to originality, initiative, problem solving and decision-making in complex and unpredictable situations alongside skills related to codified knowledge in its qualification descriptors for master's level programmes (QAA 2001a, 2001b). It is not clear though how far and by what means the institutions are seeking to meet these requirements or how their performance in this regard is to be monitored.

Conclusions and implications

Leadership in education is seen here as embedded in relationships, context and task performance and operating in conditions of complexity and ambiguity. In these respects it may have much in common with leadership in other fields of activity, but it is exercised within a specific, transformed governance context which has been referred to in terms of the paradox of 'decentralized centralism' (Karlsen 2000: 529). Generally the nature of the governance context is an important influence on school leadership: on whether, for example, the skills required are primarily those of an entrepreneur, a director and coordinator, a networker or a production manager (Glatter 2002).

Educational leaders are expected to foster simultaneously high reliability organizations, social institutions and creative learning communities. Wallace (2002) has argued that an unintended consequence of UK central government education policy designed to reduce ambiguity (for example through rational planning and performance management) has been to increase it because of the complexity of the change process required for implementation. As a result of the pervasiveness of ambiguity, much leadership and management practice necessarily consists of attempts to resolve a series of intractable tensions and dilemmas – for example over control and flexibility, innovation and stability – which present themselves in different combinations in specific decision situations (Cuban 1992; Glatter 1996; Day *et al.* 2001b).

The future is likely to be even more opaque. The Organization for Economic Cooperation and Development (OECD 2001) has published six contrasting possible scenarios for the future of schooling, each of which would imply significantly different sets of leadership requirements. In this general context, leadership development policy and practice might well take full account of the view that 'in today's complex organisations, models based on linear and rational problem-solving do managers a tremendous disservice. Managers need to recognise, become comfortable with, and even profit from tensions and the anxieties they provoke' (Lewis 2000: 765). However, this should not be interpreted as a recipe for nihilism or lack of purpose. The central remit of educational leaders is to secure the improvement of teaching and learning, sometimes in extremely challenging circumstances. Education is a value-laden activity, and so personal and educational values and the exercise of leadership may be considered inseparable.

Some implications of the foregoing analysis are tentatively offered below.

The limits of prescription

Detailed standards and specifications are not the way forward. As Fink, in offering trenchant advice to the NCSL, has noted, 'combining extensive lists of expected proficiencies with elaborate accountability procedures' (2003: 25) is more likely to inhibit leadership than to develop it. In interpreting its brief, the college will hopefully shun over-prescription and, where it does prescribe, ensure that it can demonstrate convincingly the rationale and evidence for the prescriptions. Also, it should celebrate and promote genuine debate and pluralism because this is the stance that is most likely to bring well founded advance in leadership development and research. Creative and dynamic partnerships with universities in leadership development would be one important means of ensuring that school leaders have access to perspectives that are not tied to specific government agendas.

The limits of disaggregation

Closely related to the above, educational leadership and management should be viewed as an integrated, holistic activity infused by values, rather than an atomized series of disconnected tasks. Of particular importance for leadership development in this context are the 'higher order capacities' such as 'reading the situation, balanced judgement, intuition and political acumen' identified by Cave and Wilkinson in their insightful study (1992: 40).

Leading people

A focus on leadership as embedded in relationships (as in the distributed leadership perspective) would suggest that the leadership of people should feature prominently in leadership development. Surprisingly for a 'business' that is centrally concerned with people and their development, the human resource aspects of education have received limited attention in either policy or research in the UK, except (in the case of policy) in the arguably narrow and mechanistic sense of performance management. Fortunately there is now at last serious engagement with this area, at least for teaching staff (Johnson and Hallgarten 2002), prompted largely by the emergence of severe problems of staff recruitment and retention. As the Audit Commission has noted with reference to the public services generally, 'recruitment and retention go to the heart of the way that organizations are managed and led' (Audit Commission 2002: 4). Dysfunctional practice in this area can have particularly debilitating effects. Special emphasis might be placed on promoting leaders' capabilities in supporting the learning of others and creating a climate that enhances informal learning, given that 'formal education and training provide only a small part of what is learned at work' (Eraut *et al.* 2002: 91).

Leading partnerships

The strong current policy emphasis in England, covering all levels of the education system, that institutions should 'play to their strengths' by specializing and at the same time cooperate with one another has significant leadership implications. The implementation of this policy will be challenging in a context in which institutional autonomy and separateness are deeply rooted in history and culture. Research in this area is just beginning in education (Jones and Bird 2000), although studies in other sectors have been undertaken for some time (for example Alter and Hage 1993). A key difference in education may be that institutions which are expected to collaborate are often also competing for the same market. As Huxham and Vangen report, '[u]nderstanding how to manage across organizational boundaries has been argued to be almost as significant as knowing how to manage within organizations' (2000a: 772). Moreover, research covering mainly the public and voluntary sectors suggests that somewhat distinctive capabilities may be required for leading partnerships (Huxham and Vangen 2000b). This form of leadership therefore merits special attention in educational leadership development.

A focus on learning and enquiry

Educational leadership development has taken insufficient account of adult learning theory (Hall 1998). The rhetoric of 'best practice', transformation and school effectiveness in policy discourse has militated against an orientation towards open-ended learning and enquiry. That education has not been alone in this neglect is suggested by the conclusions of a study of the learning processes of managers, professionals and technicians in the engineering, financial services and healthcare sectors. The authors' conclusions regarding the limitations of much existing policy and practice could be applied with equal force to education:

> Problems are treated as well defined and readily soluble, and therefore susceptible to formal, standardised types of training to clearly specified targets. Yet the concept of a knowledge-based economy and the metaphor of a learning organisation derive from recognition of the complexities and uncertainties of the modern world. Public discourse about training not only neglects informal learning but denies complexity by over-simplifying the processes and outcomes of learning and the factors that give rise to it.
>
> (Eraut *et al.* 2002: 108)

It is in this domain that the most important challenges for leadership development in education arguably lie.

Notes

1   See Brundrett (2000) for a detailed overview of the developments.
2   For a discussion of these terms in the context of education, see Bush and Glover (2003).
3   The most recent version of the framework (Ofsted 2003b) has, at the time of writing, been published but not yet implemented. It maintains the separation between leadership and management but makes specific reference to the concept of a learning organization.
4   This publication provides a review of relevant literature.

5   Personal communication from the NCSL, March 2003.
6   The Open University and the universities of Bath, Cambridge, Hull, Leicester, London, Manchester, Nottingham, Reading and Warwick.
7   For discussions of the application to educational leadership of recent national debates about educational research, see, for example, Ribbins and Gunter (2002) and Levačić and Glatter (2003).

References

Alter, C. and J. Hage (1993) *Organizations Working Together*, London: Sage.

Audit Commission (2002) *Recruitment and Retention: A Public Service Workforce for the Twenty-first Century*, London: Audit Commission.

Baron, G. (1956) 'Some aspects of the headmaster tradition', in P.W. Musgrave (ed.) (1970) *Sociology, History and Education*, London: Methuen.

Bennett, N. and A. Marr (2002) 'Leadership development and school middle management: problems in judging its impact on practice', paper presented at the 2002 Annual Conference of the Canadian Society for the Study of Educational Administration, Toronto, 24–28 May.

Bennett, N., C. Wise, P.A. Woods and J.A. Harvey (2003) *Distributed Leadership*, Nottingham: National College for School Leadership.

Blunkett, D. (2000) *National College for School Leadership: Tasks and Responsibilities* (attached to letter to Richard Greenhalgh, chair of the College Governing Council, 25 September), London: Department for Education and Employment.

Bolam, R. (1997) 'Management development for headteachers', *Educational Management and Administration* 25(3): 265–83.

Bolman, L. and T. Deal (1997) *Reframing Organisations: Artistry, Choice and Leadership*, 2nd edition, San Francisco: Jossey-Bass.

Brundrett, M. (1999) 'The range of provision of taught higher degrees in educational management in England and Wales', *International Studies in Educational Administration* 27(2): 43–59.

—— (2000) *Beyond Competence: The Challenge for Educational Management*, Dereham: Peter Francis Publishers.

Bush, T. and D. Glover (2003) *School Leadership: Concepts and Evidence*, Nottingham: National College for School Leadership.

Cave, E. and C. Wilkinson (1992) 'Developing managerial capabilities in education', in N. Bennett, M. Crawford and C. Riches (eds) *Managing Change in Education*, London: Paul Chapman Publishing.

Christie, P. and B. Lingard (2001) 'Capturing complexity in educational leadership', paper presented at the Annual Meeting of the American Educational Research Association, Seattle, 10–14 April.

Cuban, L. (1992) 'Managing dilemmas while building professional communities', *Educational Researcher*, January: 4–11.

Davies, B. and L. Ellison (1999) *Strategic Direction and Development of the School*, London: Routledge.

Day, C., A. Harris and M. Hadfield (2001a) 'Challenging the orthodoxy of effective school leadership', *International Journal of Leadership in Education* 4(1): 39–56.

—— (2001b) 'Grounding knowledge of schools in stakeholder realities: a multi-perspective study of effective school leaders', *School Leadership and Management* 21: 1, 19–42.

DfEE (1998) *New National College for Headteachers*, press notice 477/98, London: Department for Education and Employment.

DfES (2000) *National Standards for Headteachers*, London: Department for Education and Skills.

—— (2003) *A New Specialist System: Transforming Secondary Education*, London: Department for Education and Skills.

Earley, P., J. Evans, P. Collarbone, A. Gold and D. Halpin (2002) *Establishing the Current State of School Leadership in England*, Research Report 336, London: Department for Education and Skills.

Eraut, M. (1999) 'Headteachers' knowledge, practice and mode of cognition' in T. Bush, L. Bell, R. Bolam, R. Glatter and P. Ribbins (eds) *Educational Management: Redefining Theory, Policy and Practice*, London: Paul Chapman Publishing.

—— (2000) 'Non-formal learning and tacit knowledge in professional work', *British Journal of Educational Psychology* 70: 113–36.

Eraut, M., J. Alderton, G. Cole and P. Senker (2002) 'The impact of the manager on learning in the workplace' in F. Reeve, M. Cartwright and R. Edwards (eds) *Supporting Lifelong Learning: Organizing Learning*, London: Routledge/Falmer.

Fidler, B. (2002) *Strategic Management for School Development: Leading Your School's Improvement Strategy*, London: Paul Chapman Publishing.

Fink, D. (2003) 'How to grow a leader', *Times Educational Supplement*, 17 January.

Fullan, M. (2001) *Leading in a Culture of Change*, San Francisco: Jossey-Bass.

Furman, G. (2003) 'The 2002 UCEA presidential address', *UCEA (University Council for Educational Administration) Review* 45(1): 1–6.

Glatter, R. (1972) *Management Development for the Education Profession*, London: Harrap.

—— (ed.) (1989) *Educational Institutions and their Environments: Managing the Boundaries*, Milton Keynes: Open University Press.

—— (1996) 'Managing dilemmas in education: the tightrope walk of strategic choice in more autonomous institutions', in S.L. Jacobson, E. Hickox and R. Stevenson (eds) *School Administration: Persistent Dilemmas in Preparation and Practice*, Westport, CT: Praeger.

—— (1997) 'Context and capability in educational management', *Educational Management and Administration* 25: 2, 181–92.

—— (1999) 'From struggling to juggling: towards a redefinition of the field of educational leadership and management', *Educational Management and Administration* 27(3): 253–66.

—— (2002) 'Governance, autonomy and accountability in education', in T. Bush and L. Bell (eds) *The Principles and Practice of Educational Management*, London: Paul Chapman Publishing.

Goddard, J.T. (1998) 'Of daffodils and dog teams: reflections on leadership', paper presented to the annual conference of the British Educational Management and Administration Society, Warwick, 18–20 September.

Grace, G. (1995) *School Leadership – Beyond Education Management: An Essay in Policy Scholarship*, London: Falmer Press.

Gronn, P. (2002a) 'Distributed leadership', in K. Leithwood, P. Hallinger, K. Seashore-Louis, G. Furman-Brown, P. Gronn, W. Mulford and K. Riley (eds) *Second International Handbook of Educational Leadership and Administration*, Dordrecht: Kluwer.

—— (2002b) 'Designer leadership: the emerging global adoption of preparation standards', *Journal of School Leadership* 12: 552–78.

Hall, V. (1998) 'We are all adult educators now: the implications of adult learning theory for the continuing professional development of educational leaders and managers', paper presented at ESRC seminar on 'Redefining Educational Management', the Open University, Milton Keynes, 4–5 June.

Hall, V. and G. Southworth (1997) 'Headship', *School Leadership and Management* 17(2): 151–70.

Hallinger, P. and R. Heck (1999) 'Can leadership enhance school effectiveness?', in T. Bush, L. Bell, R. Bolam, R. Glatter and P. Ribbins (eds) *Educational Management: Redefining Theory, Policy and Practice*, London: Paul Chapman Publishing.

Harris, A. (2003) 'Distributed leadership in schools: leading or misleading?', *Management in Education* 16(5): 10–13.

Huxham, C. and S. Vangen (2000a) 'Ambiguity, complexity and dynamics in the membership of collaboration', *Human Relations* 53(6): 771–806.

—— (2000b) 'Leadership in the shaping and implementation of collaboration agendas: how things happen in a (not quite) joined-up world', *Academy of Management Journal* 43(6): 1,159–75.

Johnson, M. and J. Hallgarten (2002) *From Victims of Change to Agents of Change: The Future of the Teaching Profession*, London: Institute of Public Policy Research.

Jones, K. and K. Bird (2000) '"Partnership" as strategy: public–private relations in Education Action Zones', *British Educational Research Journal* 26(4): 491–506.

Karlsen, G.E. (2000) 'Decentralised centralism: framework for a better understanding of governance in the field of education', *Journal of Educational Policy* 15(5): 525–38.

Lawrence, I. (1994) 'Master plans', *Times Educational Supplement*, 18 November.

Leithwood, K. (2001) 'School leadership in the context of accountability policies', *International Journal of Leadership in Education* 4(3): 217–35.

Leithwood, K. and D. Jantzi (1999) 'The relative effects of principal and teacher sources of leadership on student engagement with school', *Educational Administration Quarterly* 35(supplemental): 679–706.

Leithwood, K., D. Jantzi and R. Steinbach (1999) *Changing Leadership for Changing Times*, Buckingham: Open University Press.

Levačić, R. and R. Glatter (2003) 'Developing evidence-informed policy and practice in educational leadership and management: a way forward', in L. Anderson and N. Bennett (eds) *Developing Educational Leadership: Using Evidence for Policy and Practice*, London: Sage.

Levačić, R., D. Glover, N. Bennett and M. Crawford (1999) 'Modern headship for the rationally managed school: combining cerebral and insightful approaches', in T. Bush, L. Bell, R. Bolam, R. Glatter and P. Ribbins (eds) *Educational Management: Redefining Theory, Policy and Practice*, London: Paul Chapman Publishers.

Lewis, M. (2000) 'Exploring paradox: towards a more comprehensive guide', *Academy of Management Review* 25(4): 760–76.

Michael, D.P.M. (1967) *The Idea of a Staff College*, London: Headmasters' Association.

Mintzberg, H., R. Simons and K. Basu (2002) 'Beyond selfishness', *MIT Sloan Management Review*, fall: 67–74.

NCSL (2001) *Leadership Development Framework*, Nottingham: National College for School Leadership.

—— (2002) *Corporate Plan 2002/06*, Nottingham: National College for School Leadership.

OECD (2001) *Schooling for Tomorrow: What Schools for the Future?*, Paris: Organisation for Economic Cooperation and Development.

Ofsted (2000) *Inspecting Schools: Handbook for Inspecting Secondary Schools with Guidance on Self-evaluation*, London: Stationery Office.

—— (2003a) *Annual Report of Her Majesty's Chief Inspector of Schools*, London: Stationery Office.

—— (2003b) *Inspecting Schools: The Framework for Inspecting Schools in England from September 2003*, London: Stationery Office.

Pascale, R., M. Millemmann and L. Gioja (2000) *Surfing the Edge of Chaos*, New York: Crown Business Publishing.

Preedy, M., R. Glatter and C. Wise (eds) (2002) *Strategic Leadership and Educational Improvement*, London: Paul Chapman Publishing.

QAA (2001a) *The Framework for Higher Education Qualifications in England, Wales and Northern Ireland*, Gloucester: Quality Assurance Agency for Higher Education.

—— (2001b) *The Framework for Qualifications of Higher Education Institutions in Scotland*, Gloucester: Quality Assurance Agency for Higher Education.

Ribbins, P. and H. Gunter (2002) 'Mapping leadership studies in education: towards a typology of knowledge domains', *Educational Management and Administration* 30(4): 359–85.

Riley, K. (1998) *Whose School is it Anyway?* London: Falmer Press.

Robinson, V.M.J. (2001) 'Embedding leadership in task performance', in K. Wong and C.W. Evers (eds) *Leadership for Quality Schooling: International Perspectives*, London: Routledge/Falmer.

Scott, P. (1989) 'Accountability, responsiveness and responsibility', in R. Glatter (ed.) *Educational Institutions and their Environments: Managing the Boundaries*, Milton Keynes: Open University Press.

Scott, W.R. (2001) *Institutions and Organizations*, 2nd edition, London: Sage.

Sergiovanni, T.J. (1991) *The Principalship: A Reflective Practice Perspective*, Needham Heights, MA: Allyn & Bacon.

Simkins, T. (2002) 'Reform, accountability and strategic choice in education', in M. Preedy, R. Glatter and C. Wise (eds) *Strategic Leadership and Educational Improvement*, London: Paul Chapman Publishing.

Tomlinson, S. (2001) *Education in a Post-Welfare Society*, Buckingham: Open University Press.

Wallace, M. (2002) 'Managing the unmanageable? Coping with complex educational change', inaugural lecture given at the University of Bath on 23 May, 2002, Bath, Department of Education, University of Bath.

Woods, P.A., C. Bagley and R. Glatter (1998) *School Choice and Competition: Markets in the Public Interest?*, London: Routledge.

Part V

Leadership and career development

12 Positive career development for leaders and managers

Wendy Hirsh

Introduction

This chapter addresses the place of career development within the overall challenge of developing managers and leaders in organizations. It does so from a predominantly practical point of view, using illustrations from a number of major UK employers. It is written with large employers in mind, but many of the same ideas are applicable, albeit in a pared down and less bureaucratic form, to smaller organizations.

Managers and leaders do nearly all of their developing through the sequence of work experiences that they have – in other words their careers. So this and other books on management development should arguably be 90 per cent about career development, with small sections on all the other interventions we use to try and improve the skills of managers. All the more curious then that the career development of most managers – while strongly espoused in theory – is often seriously neglected in practice.

Some of the reasons for this difficulty relate to a problematic career context and struggles to find a clear strategy. These are issues we look at later. But there are also some more straightforward reasons why career development is especially challenging with regard to its implementation. First, career development is not a clear-cut development intervention which can be bought off the shelf or delivered by consultants. It relies on a complex web of people management practices, often mainly designed to achieve other purposes, such as resourcing, training or performance management. Second, it has to deal with tensions between the needs of the business and the interests and aspirations of individual employees. This means talking to employees about very personal things, such as how they see themselves and what they want from work. Organizations are pretty inept at dealing with their employees as real people – it is a messy, challenging and therefore uncomfortable thing to do. Third, effective career development requires persistent and consistent attention over fairly long periods of time. Human resources (HR) departments are always under pressure to produce quick fixes and HR directors often stay in post only a short time. Employees and line managers have often become cynical about career development because initiatives in this area come and go so frequently.

Ways of looking at careers

Before we address the practical problems of the career development of managers and leaders, it may be helpful to identify some more general ideas about careers and career development. There are a number of different start points for looking at this field, and these are reflected in its rich but fragmented literature. Arnold (1997) provides a most useful account of the varied definitions of 'career' and the development of career theory. Social scientists, especially psychologists and sociologists, have long been interested in the meaning which individuals attach to their careers and the many factors which influence their choices of work. These factors include abilities and interests, social background and relationships, and the way they approach career decision-making itself. Schein's well-known career anchors (1990) are one example of how ideas about personal career values can be useful to individuals in considering their own careers.

The idea of career as a way in which people tell the story of their working lives has led to a strong interest in career as narrative. Researchers also recognize the powerful emotions involved in career choices, and the emotional work involved both for individuals and those advising or counselling them (Kidd 1998). Indeed, the whole idea of the subjective aspect of the career (i.e. how the individual perceives and feels about his/her career) is as important as the objective career (i.e. the actual series of jobs someone has held). Working lives are just a part of our whole life experience, and are affected by the different preoccupations and feelings which people may have at various times in their lives. Sheehy (1974) observed the importance of life-career stages in signalling typical career concerns, which relates to the more recent interest in work–life balance (Kodz *et al.* 2002).

Economists see careers in the context of an ever-shifting labour market, with shortages or surpluses of people with different kinds of skills. This perspective emphasizes career decisions as rational responses to the opportunities and risks the labour market presents. These risks and opportunities need to be understood by both employees and employers.

Those engaged in professional career guidance or counselling have often used their experience to produce frameworks and self-help materials to support individuals going through the process of career review or decision, and the practical process of job search (Bolles v.d.; Hopson and Scally 1993; Hawkins 1999). Although written primarily for those job hunting on the external labour market, much of this self-help material is just as relevant to those making internal career moves, and has been incorporated into tools more recently developed for employees, as in several of the company examples in this chapter.

In comparison with this very extensive literature on individual careers, that on organizational careers is more limited. Schein (1978) and Hall (1976) highlighted the need to manage both organizational and individual needs. We have very few studies of the actual career patterns of managers in the UK, although Nicholson and West (1988) provide useful insights into the career transitions of managers. The politics of organizational careers, especially at senior levels, has also been the subject of study (Kets de Vries 1998).

The HR literature on career development tends to focus on the formal processes which HR people design to manage careers (Mayo 1991; IPD 1998; IDS 1999). The idea of the psychological contract is directly related to organizational careers, adapted by Herriot and Pemberton (1995) into the idea of a 'career deal' offered to employees. There is also strong interest in the careers of particular groups, especially the way in which women have found it difficult to progress in organizations dominated by men (White *et al.* 1992).

Conflicting attitudes to career development in organizations

In looking at career development for managers, we need to recognize that organizational careers have been going through turbulent times. Careers in organizations are seen simultaneously as a problem, a necessity, and a way of attracting the best employees.

Careers as a problem

In normal English usage, the word 'career' has been used for centuries to talk about occupations or types of work, and also progression or pathways from one job to another. Posters advertising educational courses still stress the career doors they will open. Actors on chat shows talk about the highs and lows of their careers. The idea of career has been especially important to those in managerial jobs, as management responsibility is usually seen as an upwards career step from whatever came before.

Likewise, and especially in the second half of the 20th century, organizational careers were an accepted phenomenon, with some organizations (e.g. ICI, Shell, the UK civil service) developing ambitious approaches to the careers of their employees, especially managers.

A number of factors came together around the early 1990s to challenge the organizational career. Significant levels of white collar redundancies took away the employment security which large organizations had provided. Partly as a result of this, there was more acceptance of skilled employees moving from one employer to another. Various forms of organizational change, especially 'flatter' structures with fewer, broader grade bands, appeared to reduce promotion opportunities and made career paths more difficult to see (Holbeche 1998). At the same time, personnel functions were cut in size, rechristened HR, and devolved most resourcing and development responsibility to line managers. The old mechanics of organizational career planning and managed moves was largely dismantled except at very senior levels.

There was a lot of talk about the loss of 'careers for life' and the development of more free-wheeling careers. Terms like 'portfolio' and 'boundaryless' were used to describe these (Arthur and Rousseau 1996). Some even foresaw the possible disappearance of organizational employment (Bridges 1994). Alongside all this doom and gloom there was also a more productive debate about self-managed careers, put into practice at the Career Action Center in California (Waterman *et al.* 1994) and some organizations in the UK. This image of a more flexible and self-managed career sat well with parallel notions of self-managed learning (Pedler *et al.* 1988) and a wider societal shift towards self-determination and personal choice in all areas of life, employment included.

The predominant organizational response, however, was to back off all talk of careers except in negative terms. Career development strategies in the mid-1990s seemed to list what was *not* on offer – no jobs for life, no career paths, less upward movement and, above all, no promises (Hirsh and Jackson 1996). What was on offer instead was 'development' – such a vague term that it can mean anything, or nothing. Although some organizations are now taking a more positive view of careers again, HR professionals still feel career development is a problem area, and line managers often don't know how to 'help employees develop their careers'. Many employees still find the strategic messages about careers rather contradictory and overall rather negative. So career development for managers takes place against a somewhat problematic backcloth where the 'C' word (career) makes many people in organizations rather nervous.

Careers as a necessity for the organization

However, organizational careers developed for good reason. Those reasons have been present in large organizations for many hundreds of years, and they are too fundamental to simply go away, especially for managers and leaders. Large organizations still aim to grow the majority of their managers from their employees. This means those employees moving from one job to another with increasing amounts of management responsibility. Although recruitment from outside at all levels is healthy, it is too risky to rely on the external labour market for all the management skills needed. Anyway, at least some managers need to know something about the organization and the nature of the work it carries out.

So managerial careers serve two fundamental functions, and have to do both at the same time. Career moves pull in to jobs people who have most of the skills they need to carry out those jobs. While working in any job, employees are also gaining experience and learning some new skills and knowledge which will equip them better for future job roles. These two fundamentals – careers as resourcing and careers as learning – are what career development is there to do for the organization.

Careers as attractive to employees

Employees, especially those confident of their own ability and with high aspirations, see positive career development as one of the most important aspects of their employment package. Especially in early career, opportunities for varied and stretching work, rapid promotion and individual attention paid to their careers are all highly attractive (Winter and Jackson 1999).

So employers want to make a positive career offer and a promise of personal career attention as a way of winning their fair share in the 'war for talent' (Chambers *et al.* 1998) and of keeping the best employees with them for longer (Winter and Jackson 1999).

Even though the word 'career' has become problematic, organizations know they do need to do something about the career development of their staff. The rest of this chapter will look at the three levels on which this task is approached:

- the strategy level – what is the overall intention for the career development of managers and leaders?
- the process level – what mechanisms can we see which facilitate career development?
- the implementation level – how do we make these mechanisms effective in practice, and especially who needs to do what?

Career development strategies for managers and leaders

There are many ways of looking at career development strategy, and here we choose just two of its dimensions. A career development strategy for managers and leaders should be based on the kinds of careers we expect managers to have, so the first dimension we look at here is the changing career needs of the rather diverse group of people we call 'managers'. The second dimension is what we might call the 'career deal' – the balance between employer and employee responsibility and what is really being offered and expected on both sides of that relationship.

The changing career needs of managers and leaders

This book shows the increasing demands being made on managers and leaders. The term 'leadership' in itself signals some shifts in skill needs which the word 'management' does not seem to embrace so clearly (see the discussion in Chapters 1 and 2).

In the context of careers, there is an ever growing list of the career experiences seen as desirable for senior managers and leaders in order to develop the ever widening range of skills and knowledge required. The list includes:

- broad business experience – especially of different products or markets, the wider political and economic context, and sometimes experience of other organizations or sectors;
- cross-functional experience;
- direct line responsibility for staff – often including staff of varying kinds, e.g. professional staff versus clerical or shop floor staff;

- strategic experience – often this means head office roles;
- delivering major projects – especially those crossing organizational boundaries;
- managing in particular situations, e.g. start-ups, mergers, joint ventures;
- initiating and leading people through major change;
- working in other cultures, especially in other countries;
- staying in some of these roles long enough to show real delivery of business goals!

This list is by no means exhaustive but it is still potentially exhausting to achieve. Organizations do have the strategic aim of offering wider career experience to those likely to reach senior general management positions (e.g. managing director of a business stream or country). This broadening is perhaps the clearest strategic intention of the corporately managed approaches to career development we discuss later. Such careers are very likely to include lateral or diagonal moves and project working, as well as promotions.

However, we must not only think about management careers in terms of the tiny minority who will reach the very top of the organization. The first move into managing other people is a key career step both for the organization and the individual. It is too easy to promote people into management roles who do not have the necessary potential or attitudes, simply because they have been good at doing the job below. The transitions between broad levels of management work – often junior (or first line), middle, senior, plus sometimes a small 'top' tier – each require significant changes in skills and attitudes. The career strategy needs to support each of these major career transitions and build in ways of checking that the right decision is being made both for the organization and the employee. Recruitment is also a critical career transition and can occur at any level. Recruits at professional and managerial level are often brought in to fill a particular job without much thought as to their future career.

The 1980s and 1990s saw a preoccupation with 'general managers' – people who are both senior and manage multifunctional teams. Good general managers were seen as being a cure for all ills. This obscured for a while the varied management roles which large organizations have, and the diverse career paths they imply.

Functional managers and leaders are far more numerous than general managers. Nearly all first line managers have a strong functional focus to their work, i.e. they are responsible for a particular type of work. At middle management levels, functional managers head up a department or division which often has a particular functional focus (e.g. research and development), production, sales or marketing, finance, information technology), HR, etc.). Even at board level, many jobs are what we might call functional leadership roles (finance director, marketing director, etc.). These jobs combine a strong element of professional judgement with the need for many of the generic leadership skills required by general managers. The career paths of functional leaders need to develop both breadth and depth within the function across business units, with perhaps some excursions into other functions.

So career development for managers and leaders needs to recognize the diversity of managerial careers both by level and by career path. BP, for example, has recently strengthened technical as well as general management careers. General managers, functional leaders and also high level specialists are all seen as contributing to the leadership capability of the business. Figure 12.1 shows how this is expressed in terms of both professional/functional and general management career paths.

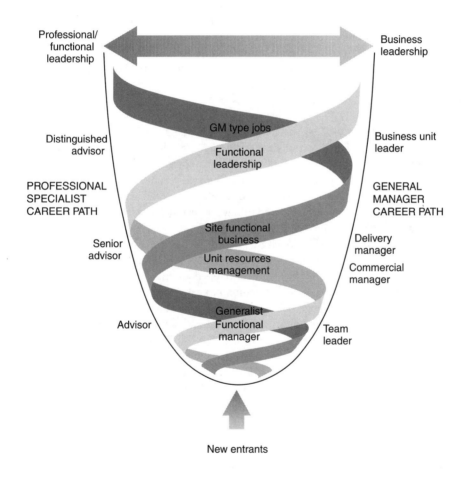

Figure 12.1 Career paths in BP

Source: BP plc, 2003

BP

BP, a global energy company with around 116,000 employees, has all the challenges of developing managers and leaders in a complex business with a large geographical spread.

It has a long-established approach to the active career development of managers seen to have potential for the most senior roles. Although the precise approach has been modified over the years, it has always had an emphasis on giving such people a wide range of career experience. The premise is that this varied experience in challenging roles equips them for general manager and functional leadership roles. The career experiences embrace varied functions, types of business and also international moves. In its current form the Group Executive Development Programme covers about 140 people, selected through assessment centres in their late 20s to early 30s, and manages their development for 7–10 years. As BP has become more truly global, selection for this programme now looks for cultural awareness as well as people awareness skills, along with a strong track record of performance.

Since the early 1990s, BP has emphasized the management of people as a crucial part of business performance. Line managers are expected to be strong both on the performance management and the development of their staff. With a well-qualified workforce, the employee is also expected to take the initiative in his or her own career and development. Below the very top levels, jobs are internally advertised and staff apply. Staff who are seeking to develop their careers are expected to have a personal development plan and to discuss this with their boss.

In addition to developing leaders who are general managers or functional heads, BP also needs excellent specialists. Recently a Professional Recognition Programme has been developed to encourage and recognize functional excellence. A grade structure and generic job titles emphasize the increasing value through career of someone's ability to give specialist advice, rather than to manage increasing numbers of staff. So there are now three different types of career path in BP, and individuals may choose the kind of career path which best suits their aspirations and talents. A career development workshop offered at mid-level in the organization helps individuals think about their leadership skills and future direction. Within limits, individuals can move across career paths as the needs of the organization and their own ambitions change.

The career deal for managers and leaders

The types of careers we need managers to follow need to be linked to a second key aspect of strategy – the nature of the career development 'deal'. The model shown in Figure 12.2, developed by the Institute for Employment Studies,

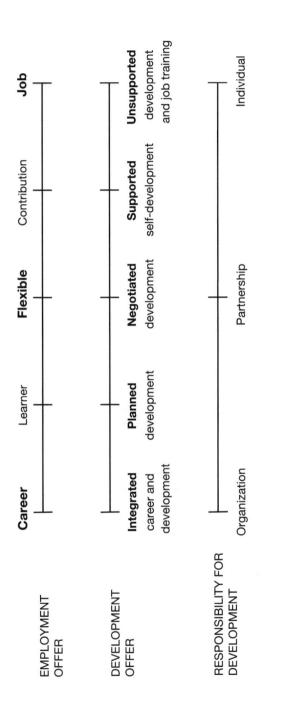

	Career	Learner	Flexible	Contribution	Job
EMPLOYMENT OFFER	⊢─────────┼─────────┼─────────┼─────────┤
DEVELOPMENT OFFER	Integrated career and development	Planned development	Negotiated development	Supported self-development	Unsupported development and job training
RESPONSIBILITY FOR DEVELOPMENT	Organization		Partnership		Individual

Figure 12.2 The career development continuum

Source: Institute for Employment Studies (Hirsh and Jackson 1996).

illustrates a range of career development deals in terms of the extent to which the organization takes responsibility for proactive development (Hirsh and Jackson 1996).

Positions to the left hand side of this diagram are ones in which the organization is taking the main role in career planning and offering development which is highly integrated with future career possibilities. We see this deal most clearly for 'high potential' and senior managers. At the right hand extreme we see no career development offered by the organization. This does not preclude proper training for the current job, but skill or job progression is simply not on the agenda. In the middle we have a term now in widespread use – 'career partnership'. In this deal, the employer and employee have pretty equal responsibility for development, which is explicitly negotiated as part of the employment relationship. Valuable specialists often come closest to the partnership deal because their power to leave the organization is often high, and so the employee can negotiate over both the job role he or she has and the training they receive. Some organizations offer a positive career deal to the whole workforce. For example, the Nationwide Building Society offers significant support for career development to all its employees as part of its business strategy.

Nationwide Building Society

The Nationwide Building Society has about 14,000 employees, many of whom work in local branches. So the organization needs managers at local level, as well as corporate leaders and functional specialists. It has linked its career development strategy to one of its key business goals: having employees who feel proud to work for the organization. The strong emotional engagement of all staff with the organization is seen as central to business success.

Career development was identified several years ago through staff surveys as an area of relative dissatisfaction for staff. Employees were unclear about the nature of the career development offer and also the processes by which their careers might develop. Nationwide now makes a positive career offer to all staff who wish to further their careers. Individuals are expected to make the most of their talent, and the organization undertakes to facilitate their development through information and advice. Staff surveys provide regular feedback on how well the organization is delivering on this promise.

Individuals are encouraged to discuss their career with their line manager, using a simple framework of questions. This takes place alongside the annual performance review, but in a separate discussion. Other channels for career information and advice have been developed independent of this reporting relationship. The intranet makes available a wide range of career facilities, including self-help career planning tools, information on job opportunities and specific vacancies. Individuals can search for particular kinds of job vacancies or register their interest in the kind of job which interests them. Considerable effort is going into making these systems convenient and attractive for busy staff to use.

Queries on career issues can also be sent direct to the central Career and Leadership Development Team, who offer personal advice to employees. As the workforce is geographically dispersed, telephone and e-mail are used to offer such support.

These universal approaches to career development are augmented by the more targeted development of existing and potential managers. As well as corporate succession planning, local areas and functions are responsible for identifying talent and developing it. Personnel consultants work with the line to facilitate developmental job moves for individuals identified as meriting proactive development. This active career development of the broad populations of junior and middle managers at local level ensures the business has a continuous flow of new managers coming through.

Most large organizations operate a segmented career development strategy, with some staff getting more proactive development and career attention than others. This segmentation may indeed be an appropriate strategy, but it is very seldom honestly reflected in those vague policy statements about employees developing within business needs.

The career continuum model has particular relevance to managerial careers in two ways. First, the overall career development climate of an organization is set by the career deal offered to the majority of staff. There is a big difference in management climate between an organization which shows no interest at all in the careers of most staff, compared with one offering some career support to all staff who are interested. Second, the diagram helps us see how much the career deal for an individual manager can yo-yo around. If employees come in as a graduate recruit, they will be on the planned development or 'learner' deal for a while, with their work experiences largely planned by the organization. When they finish the graduate scheme, they fall off this deal and return to whatever degree of career support everyone else gets – usually pretty far to the right hand side of the diagram. If they are picked up later by some management development or fast-track scheme, they find themselves moving left again. If they reach a career ceiling, or even if their career slows down, they move back to the basic deal. If or when they enter senior management, they may feel their career is planned again, but not always. At the very top, board members can have a 'job' deal again, and chief executive officer (CEOs) can just have short-term contracts – in career terms a move back to being an office temp. Little wonder that many managers feel very confused about the issue of career ownership and whether the organization is any consistent kind of partner in their career.

Something closer to the middle ground 'partnership' strategy would seem to make basic business sense for the majority of professional and managerial staff. As a group which is relatively expensive to employ and replace, it should repay the organization to have a strong interest in the deployment and career direction of these individuals. This strategy does not imply all managers being told they are promotable, and indeed naturally emphasizes lateral career moves. The partnership strategy does expect the employee to make much of the running in career terms, and so does not take us back to the idea of the organization planning an individual's career for him or her. Rolls-Royce comes close to implementing this partnership strategy through its Development Cell process, described later in this chapter.

The other advantage of upgrading the deal and adopting a true partnership approach for all managers, is that a rather more strongly planned approach for selected groups (e.g. graduate trainees, high potentials, senior managers) can more easily overlay it. The yo-yo experience is reduced, and rather more individual responsibility is expected even in the 'special' populations. BP, for example, carries much of its philosophy of self-development into its high potential development programme.

Career development processes for managers and leaders

So how do these strategies manifest in practice? As we have discussed, career development strategy for managers and leaders is tending towards varying blends of support for employees in managing their own careers, plus more organizationally planned careers for selected sub-groups of managers. It should be no surprise then that the formal processes for developing managers' careers operate in a similarly two-legged fashion. This can be seen in handbooks for practitioners and reviews of current practices (e.g. IDS 1999; IPD 1998). In this section we will look briefly at practical approaches to supporting self-managed careers for managers, then at more corporately planned careers and, finally, at how these two can work together.

Supporting the self-managed career

The extreme models of 'manage your own career' seem to be giving way to a greater emphasis on the support an organization needs to give employees to enable them to develop their own careers. The recognition that self-managed careers require support from employers was advocated by Waterman *et al.* (1994) in their influential exposition of the need for 'career resilience'. However, organizations have been rather slow to admit it, and much slower to act on it. Of course its implication is that the organization has to *do* something with and for the majority of employees. It is the strategic arguments around attraction, retention, skill development and motivation which have persuaded organizations like Lloyds TSB and Nationwide to offer some career support to all staff.

There are many possible processes for supporting individuals in managing their own careers, but a simple way of looking at them is through the underlying functions these processes support, as shown on Figure 12.3.

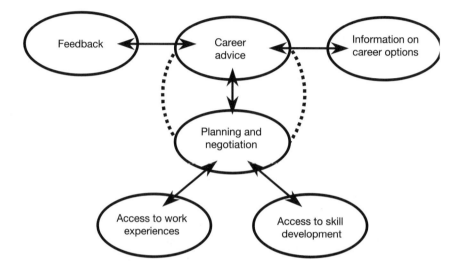

Figure 12.3 Supporting individual career development

The top left hand function – that of feedback to individuals on their performance, skills and potential – supports individuals in understanding themselves. The top right hand function of providing information on career options informs the employee about the structure of the internal labour market. The two central functions of advice plus planning and negotiation support individual career planning and decision-making. They help to answer the question 'where am I going?' They are shown as two separate but closely linked functions, as advice can aim to be impartial, but planning and negotiation are about finding solutions which meet the needs of both the organization and the employee. In the career partnership strategy, the planning and negotiating function is critical. The bottom two functions – giving access to work experiences and skill development – address the 'how do I get there?' question. They are shown separately here because offering access to skill development (for example through e-learning or even qualifications) does not necessarily give employees access to varied or progressive work experiences.

Just to illustrate what this all looks like in practice, most organizations are operating mainly with only a few core processes, which only partly address the needs for support. Other organizations are starting to offer a richer range of support mechanisms.

Access to skill development is often extensive, but for most employees focuses only on training for their current jobs. Organizations can often block employees accessing the training they will need to progress to other jobs. For example middle managers would often appreciate more exposure to business strategy. Employees who study in their own time are often seeking to gain a qualification which they hope will open up new career options. Thompson *et al.* (1998) certainly found this a key motivation for MBA study.

Appraisal is assumed to be the main way of giving feedback to support career development. In fact it does this rather poorly, often addressing performance but not potential or suitable career directions. In a study of effective career support at work among a largely professional and managerial population, appraisal accounted for a very small proportion (about 7 per cent) of useful discussions individuals had about their careers (Hirsh *et al.* 2001).

An open internal job market is seen as the main process for employees to move from one job to another. Internal job vacancies are advertised to employees, who then apply for the next job they want, and it is up to the line manager concerned to select the successful candidate. Hirsh, Pollard and Tamkin (2000) found rapid growth in open internal job advertising, increasingly through corporate intranet sites. The process of internal job application in effect becomes the main process by which employees manage their careers. It does not normally cover the very top of the organization, but has extended well into management in many organizations. It can cover project assignments as well as permanent job moves. Although a popular process with employees, there is a hidden trap. If the appointing managers always select the 'best fit' candidate for internal job moves, then it is difficult for employees to achieve a change of career direction within an organization. The Catch-22 is that you will only be selected for a new job if you have done a job very like it before. This makes self-managed cross-functional or cross-unit moves particularly difficult.

Companies are starting to recognize the need for overview information on job options and for career advice. Organizations usually advocate some form of personal career plan, often incorporated into a personal development plan (PDP). It is usually assumed that such planning is facilitated by a dialogue between the individual and his or her line manager, either in the annual appraisal or in a separate development review. Managers do not find that these processes really address their career issues (Hirsh *et al.* 2001), and the boss is often not the person they need to speak with.

Two further types of support are therefore becoming more prevalent. Tools which employees can use for themselves to think about their career plans are available through workbooks and, more recently, intranet sites. Nestlé, Nationwide, Lloyds TSB and Rolls-Royce all offer self-help career planning materials in some form. The second option – more personal one-to-one support – poses a greater challenge. Some organizations, such as Sun Microsystems, run career workshops to help a group of employees work together over a day or two on their self-assessment and career planning. BP offers something similar to middle managers. 'Career coaching' has recently become a fashionable term for one-to-one career support, but it is applied both to external professionals and to an additional role taken on by some managers internally, who may receive special training (e.g. Lloyds TSB). Sometimes the HR function offers more in-depth support, as in Rolls-Royce and Nationwide.

Lloyds TSB

Lloyds TSB Group has about 80,000 employees. It has strongly espoused the idea of self-managed development, and has had a corporate university since 1999. The same philosophy extends to employees managing their own careers. In common with many other organizations, Lloyds TSB has found that employees then need information and support to make the self-managed career a reality. Many aspects of HR have moved into a 'shared services' model, with employees and their managers accessing information and advice via both intranet and Internet sites and an HR call centre. Support for career development has followed this strategy, and the Centre for Career Management website was launched in 2000. Employees can access information and use the Job Shop for internal vacancies. The Developing Managers and Leaders website provides managers with information on management skills and development opportunities, while the Developing Trainers and Coaches site provides support for people across the Group who are responsible for training and developing others.

The company has a sophisticated set of self-help career tools which employees can obtain on disc and workbook from the HR call centre. The decision to provide an individual disc is a conscious one to preserve confidentiality and also to allow employees to use it as they wish. More personal support is provided by a group of career coaches. These are mainly HR people, who offer one-to-one career support to individuals referred to them by the HR call centre. They do this in addition to their normal job, taking a few cases each month and seeing them once or twice, normally face to face. They are not designed to be ongoing mentors, but to offer an in-depth career discussion. The career coaches are trained to a level recognized by the Institute of Career Guidance.

The careers of the most senior people – roughly the top 160 – are more proactively managed by the company, and they are given internal secondments and placements as well as leadership development. Local business units, especially in retail banking, have their own processes for identifying potential managers and giving them appropriate career experience. In addition to the general graduate intake, a small number of group management trainees are recruited, and their careers are managed on a faster track.

Informal support for individuals is a crucial part of the jigsaw. Some of the most important advice comes from managers other than the direct boss, and arises naturally in work situations. Sometimes long-term informal mentoring relationships result. The importance of informal networks in getting access to jobs is also important. Even where more formal processes govern the selection process, personal knowledge and the judgements of others will inform the decision, perhaps especially so at management levels. So employees do need to make themselves visible, and this is much more difficult early in one's career than for senior managers. One of the reasons that internal secondments so often lead to career moves is because they simply make an individual more visible to and better known by another part of the organization. When a vacancy arises, they are much better placed to get it.

The big gap in this collection of practices is a real opportunity for the organization to understand and support the career plans made by the individual. Even if the line manager tries to do this in appraisal, it does not give any collective management support for bringing that plan about.

Corporately managed careers

It is interesting that the prevalent strategy of largely self-managed careers has not led to the demise of corporately driven career planning. Organizations still seek to plan ahead for some of their employees and to proactively facilitate career moves as well as skill development for them (Gratton and Hailey 1999). The populations which receive this higher degree of investment from the organization are usually senior managers and those seen as having potential to fill these jobs in future.

The term most often used for planning of this kind is succession planning (Eastman 1995). It is a slightly misleading term, as, in its modern form, it is likely to put emphasis not just on planning for specific posts, but rather on identifying and then developing various 'talent pools' in the organization (Hirsh 2000). The database resulting from succession planning is often used to identify possible candidates (usually several) for senior job vacancies. Talent pools by function can link up with the diverse career paths discussed earlier. It is an important aspect of succession planning that it is a collective management activity – that is, groups of managers discuss and agree plans, and take some collective responsibility for supporting the implied development for individuals.

Succession planning and high potential development can be devolved in large organizations, reflecting the different locations at which appointment decisions are made. The very top of the organization is still usually handled at the corporate centre, as are often the top teams at divisional, country or subsidiary levels. However, at layers of senior management below that a similar and linked succession planning process might plan for jobs critical within countries, divisions or functions. Nestlé, for example, has processes within the UK, at European level and corporately. Although many organizations operate a fairly simple process for the very top of the organization, this more ambitious devolved model takes a lot more discipline and effort to implement.

Nestlé

Nestlé is a Swiss company with about 250,000 employees worldwide, of whom about 8,000 work in the UK, at several sites including the UK head office. Nestlé has operated a rather paternalistic approach to employment, including career development, which was very much driven by the company rather than the employee.

Nestlé is now making its approach to careers more of a partnership and giving employees a much more positive role in developing their own careers. Nestlé UK has been in the forefront of this change, in particular making career development much more transparent to employees. Among a range of tools and information on the intranet, Nestlé lists 'career contacts' in various jobs and locations who can give any employees information about the job they do themselves. Other popular areas of the Career Connections site explain the various HR processes involved in careers, such as succession planning, appraisal and job filling.

The approach to career development within the annual performance review has changed from one focused on collecting data on promotability (which was never systematically used) towards the encouragement of a more meaningful conversation between the individual and his or her boss.

Nestlé, in common with most large corporations, has a 'nested' approach to succession and high potential development. Within the UK there are three levels of 'Resource Groups' operating on a functional basis to identify and develop talent, including a fairly small group seen as 'high potential'. These UK processes link into succession discussions at European level where developmental job moves may be agreed on a regional basis. International career experience is an increasingly important requirement for those aspiring to senior roles. The most senior managers are appointed and developed corporately on a worldwide basis. For the UK, the top 200 jobs (out of about 2,000 managers) are appointed by the company rather than applied for by the individual. In a mature market – such as the UK – where management jobs are not expanding, the company feels it is important to retain and promote the best managers by continuing to plan the career moves of senior people.

The Rolls-Royce example shows the use of a process called Development Cells, which is a form of succession planning taken much further down the organization – into most of the professional and management population. It gives company attention to the careers of far more junior managers.

A process which often sits very close to that of succession planning is high potential (sometimes called fast-track) development (Corporate Leadership Council 1997). The proactive career development of high potential staff often grows naturally out of their identification as longer-term successors to senior posts. These people are then given career opportunities to broaden their career experience. These days they also are likely to have a raft of other development support, often including mentors and/or coaches, as well as training, secondments, sometimes an MBA course and so on. Such special treatment of the people who should be most able to manage their own careers does raise some interesting paradoxes (Viney *et al.* 1997). The HR function usually works very closely with senior management to facilitate the delivery of high potential development. One difficulty of high potential development is that it often requires considerable geographical mobility and expects people to be working very hard indeed. However, it takes place between the ages of roughly 30 and 40 – a time at which employees of both genders are often raising families and managing two careers.

Sometimes, high potential development is more open and visible as a development 'programme' or scheme. Individual managers are nominated and then go through an assessment centre to check their suitability (as in BP). In other organizations, employees can apply for an accelerated development programme themselves, but normally would have to seek approval from their manager before going forward for selection.

The same idea can apply much lower in the organization, in the form of management development programmes of various kinds, including ones within a function (e.g. finance managers). After selection, a group of people at one level is given planned development to position them for jobs at the level above, often including work experience as well as training. Graduate development programmes may do something similar right at the start of the career. Within clerical or shop floor workforces, formal or informal development schemes are often used to prepare prospective candidates for supervisory jobs.

Just as self-managed approaches fail to get buy-in for an individual's plans from wider management, so the big challenge for corporate processes is to get close enough to the individuals they are planning for. Many are the high potential managers who have left the organization before anyone gets round to telling them how good they are! In theory, succession processes should feed back to the individuals concerned, but often this does not happen in practice. Again, sensible management development or HR directors talk to high potential staff to keep in touch with any issues or concerns. This should complement the discussions they have with their own line managers.

Combining self-managed and corporate career development

Figure 12.4 shows just a few of the wide range of processes which play a part in career development for managers and leaders. Those towards the left tend to be corporately driven, and those towards the right tend more towards supporting self-managed careers. Some processes in the centre of the diagram – such as appraisal, compétence frameworks and development centres – can support both aspects.

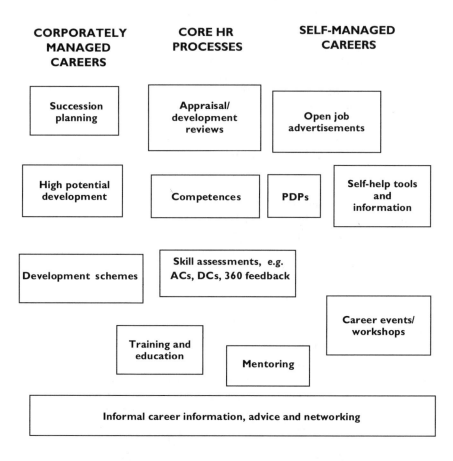

Figure 12.4 Some career development processes

Notes:
AC   assessment centre(s)
DC   development centre(s)

As we have seen, the biggest challenge is to get serious dialogue between the organization and the individual. It is not clear who speaks for the organization in this relationship, as bosses come and go and are often not there to help the individual action an agreed development plan. This is most critical when it comes to supporting lateral or unusual career moves. Rolls-Royce attempts to use its Development Cell process to achieve a more thorough sharing of understanding between the individual and the organization.

Rolls-Royce

Rolls-Royce operates in a very competitive global market. It has about 38,000 employees, of whom roughly 60 per cent are now in the UK. Although the company's staff turnover in the UK is relatively low, skill needs are changing all the time. Career development is seen as central to both the deployment and development of skills, especially among professional and managerial employees. Managers have careers which often start in a technical or functional area of expertise. Careers paths have to take into account the complex structure of the organization, with business stream, functional and geographical axes.

There has always been a strong emphasis on development in Rolls-Royce, and this has increasingly emphasized management and leadership as well as technical expertise. To quote the chief executive:

> It is one of our fundamental company values that achieving business success and promoting individual development go hand in hand. The Rolls-Royce name is recognized internationally and we operate worldwide. Our management development policy will make us a world-class business through having world-class people.

A process called Development Cells drills a succession and development approach right down through the managerial and professional populations. Development Cells are, in essence, meetings of groups of managers to discuss the careers and development of those they manage. They are used to discuss skill needs and to identify people who need a move or some particular development. Job moves are often lateral, for example from one area of engineering to another, or into the commercial functions. At their best, Development Cells help to establish a strong development environment which is both business focused and interested in each individual. Although this approach has been in operation for 15 years or more, the global business expansion over the last five years has made it more important and increased its visibility with the Group Executive Team.

The HR function works very closely with the line over matters of career support and career moves. Some HR professionals offer in-depth career advice to employees who ask for this or who are referred by their line managers.

One of the challenges is to link individual employees into the Development Cell process. Some employees are proactive in this by, for example, booking discussions with their manager when they know a cell meeting is coming up, and asking for feedback afterwards. A second interesting challenge is to link such company-led development with an increasingly open internal job market. The engineering culture does not readily accept the elitism of overt "high potential schemes', especially if it leads to a loss of good engineers to the general management stream. Interestingly, an engineering fast-track scheme is proving to be much more acceptable. The business docs also identify managers in all functions with potential for very senior roles, but seeks to accelerate their development without managing their careers in a completely different way.

Implementing career development for managers and leaders

Even if the strategy and processes are articulated, actually delivering career development requires persistent hard work. Most large organizations load most of the responsibility for career development onto line managers. This is often taken to mean the immediate line manager, a less than satisfactory solution. The immediate boss is often not well placed to be the main facilitator of career development. There are many tensions between keeping a good team member and encouraging them to move on. The employee may also not wish to 'rock the boat' by raising career issues with his or her boss. In addition, bosses often know little more about career opportunities than those they manage, and may have little power to facilitate developmental opportunities beyond the current job. So career development needs to be a responsibility of the whole management community, not just the immediate boss. The boss's boss, for example, can play a key role in spotting potential and opening up opportunities.

Nor can the HR department just design the appraisal form and sit back. Career development is only partly facilitated by formal processes. HR managers can play a number of important roles. In terms of planning processes, such as succession, HR needs to make sure key information is challenged, shared, then acted on and reviewed. In terms of offering support to individual employees, HR managers often have a much better overview of opportunities than local line managers. They can also network with their HR peers in other parts of the organization and find out about opportunities or facilitate developmental experiences such as secondments, job swaps, etc. HR managers can also make an important contribution to career advice, especially when employees need a more confidential discussion. Of course, an HR function which sees itself as too strategic to talk to employees, or conversely which does not know how to handle sensitive information, will not fulfil this role.

Career development makes distinctive demands on those involved both as 'givers' and as 'receivers' of support. Some of the generic skills needed to do this apply to many aspects of developing other people, but these generic skills are not enough (Hirsh *et al.* 2001). Employees need to know how to manage their own careers and those who help them need to feel they have adequate skills, knowledge and confidence to take on this role. Many organizations now train managers in aspects of performance management (objective setting, giving feedback, etc.) and some in coaching skills. It is high time that career development skills were added to the mainstream agenda for management training. There is interesting evidence from Yarnall (1998) that if we give employees the skills to manage their own careers they extract better career support from those who manage them. In terms of management employees, this means giving such training early in career, which is what BP has started doing for its first line managers.

A positive approach to career development for managers

This title of this chapter refers to 'positive' career development for managers and leaders because it is my personal view that a more positive approach is what most organizations now need. The negative lessons of the 1990s served a useful purpose in highlighting that employees can't expect employers to manage their careers for them, and that they are likely to experience major and unforeseen career changes from time to time. But the 1990s also left us with an unhelpfully negative message about careers in organizations and a lot of demotivated managers (Herriot *et al.* 1996). Most of the time, careers for managers are better thought of as a joint responsibility than just something the employee does in spite of the organization.

Getting positive means a much more up-front and realistic career message which says what the organization *can* offer, rather than dwelling on what it can't. The career message for managers also needs to clarify the deal for all managers (and probably at least for professionals too) and not just focus on the small numbers of corporately identified high potentials or the most senior layers of management.

Getting positive also means explaining to employees what formal and informal processes they can use to develop their careers. These processes need to build in real dialogue and provide opportunities for in-depth discussion of career issues. If corporate career planning processes, such as succession planning, are used, then all employees should understand their objectives and how the process works.

Getting positive also implies equipping employees and those who manage and support them to discuss career issues properly and act on their discussions. The active role of HR as broker and adviser – not just systems designer – is crucial. Individual managers, or potential managers, should have access to a range of people who can help them with their career issues.

Effective career development is not just vital for growing good managers and leaders at all levels; it is a remarkably cheap and powerful way of motivating and retaining good people. More than anything else, effective career development really calls upon employees to understand the changing needs of the business, and seriously engages the organization with the people it employs. That engagement is what counts, and that is why career development is not amenable to a quick fix.

References

Arnold, J. (1997) *Managing Careers into the 21st Century*, London: Paul Chapman.

Arthur, M.B. and D.M. Rousseau (eds) (1996) *The Boundaryless Career: A New Employment Principle for a New Organizational Era*, New York: Oxford University Press.

Bolles, R.N. (various dates) *What Color is Your Parachute?*, Berkeley, CA: Ten Speed Press; updated annually.

Bridges, W. (1994) *Job Shift: How to Prosper in a Workplace without Jobs*, London: Addison-Wesley.

Chambers, E., M. Foulon, H. Handfield-Jones, S.M. Hankin and E.D. Michaels (1998) 'The war for talent', *McKinsey Quarterly* 3: 44–57.

CIPD (2002) *The Future of Careers*, London: CIPD.

Corporate Leadership Council (1997) *The Next Generation: Accelerating the Development of Rising Leaders*, Washington, DC: Advisory Board Company.

Eastman, L.J. (1995) *Succession Planning*, Greensboro, NC: Center for Creative Leadership.

Gratton, L. and V.H. Hailey (1999) 'The rhetoric and reality of "new careers"', in L. Gratton, V.H. Hailey, P. Stiles and C. Truss, *Strategic Human Resource Management*, Oxford: Oxford University Press.

Hall, D.T. (1976) *Careers in Organizations*, Glenview, IL: Scott, Foresman & Company.

Hawkins, P. (1999) *The Art of Building Windmills: Career Tactics for the 21st Century*, Liverpool: Graduates into Employment Unit, University of Liverpool.

Herriot, P. and C. Pemberton (1995) *New Deals*, Chichester: John Wiley.

Herriot, P., C. Pemberton and E. Hawtin (1996) 'The career attitudes and intentions of managers in the finance sector', *British Journal of Management* 7: 181–90.

Hirsh, W. (2000) *Succession Planning Demystified*, IES Report No. 372, Brighton: Institute for Employment Studies.

Hirsh, W. and C. Jackson (1996) *Strategies for Career Development: Promise, Practice and Pretence*, IES Report 305, Brighton: Institute for Employment Studies.

Hirsh, W., C. Jackson and J.M. Kidd (2001) *Straight Talking: Effective Career Discussions at Work*, Cambridge: NICEC/CRAC.

Hirsh, W., E. Pollard and P. Tamkin (2000) *Free, Fair and Efficient? Open Internal Job Advertising*, IES Report No 371, Brighton: Institute for Employment Studies.

Holbeche, L. (1998) *Motivating People in Lean Organizations*, Oxford: Butterworth-Heinemann.

Hopson, B. and M. Scally (1993) *Build Your Own Rainbow*, Leeds: Lifeskills Associates; first published 1984.

IDS (1999) 'Career management', *IDS Studies, Personnel Policy and Practice*, Number 678, London: Incomes Data Services.

IPD (1998) *The IPD Guide on Career Management in Organisations*, London: IPD.

Kets de Vries, M.F.R. (1998) 'The dark side of CEO succession', *Harvard Business Review* 88(1): 56–60.

Kidd, J.M. (1998) 'Emotion: an absent presence in career theory', *Journal of Vocational Behaviour* 52: 275–88.

Kodz, J., H. Harper and S. Dench (2002) *Work–Life Balance: Beyond the Rhetoric*, IES Report 384, Brighton: Institute for Employment Studies.

Mayo, A. (1991) *Managing Careers: Strategies for Organizations*, London: Institute of Personnel Management.

Nicholson, N. and W. West (1988) *Managerial Job Change: Men and Women in Transition*, Cambridge: Cambridge University Press.

Pedler, M.J., J.G. Burgoyne and T.H. Boydell (1988) *Applying Self-development in Organizations*, Hemel Hempstead: Prentice-Hall.

Schein, E.H. (1978) *Career Dynamics: Matching Individual and Organisational Needs*, Reading, MA: Addison-Wesley.

—— (1990) *Career Anchors: Discovering Your Real Values*, San Francisco: Pfeiffer, Jossey-Bass.

Sheehy, G. (1974) *Passages: Predictable Crises of Adult Life*, New York: Dutton.

Thomson, A., J. Storey, C. Mabey, R. Thomson, C. Gray and E. Farmer (1998) *Management Development. The Views of the Membership of the Association of MBAs*, London: AMBA.

Viney, C., S. Adamson and N. Doherty (1997) 'Paradoxes of fast track career management', *Personnel Review* 26(3): 174–86.

Waterman, R., J. Waterman and B. Collard (1994) 'Towards a career resilient workforce', *Harvard Business Review*, July–August: 87–95.

White, B., C. Cox and C. Cooper (1992) *Women's Career Development*, Oxford: Blackwell Business.

Winter, J. and C. Jackson (1999) *Riding the Wave*, Oxford: Career Innovation Research Group.

Yarnall, J. (1998) 'Line managers as career developers: rhetoric or reality?', *Personnel Review* 27(5): 378–95.

13 The individualization of the career and its implications for leadership and management development

Jane Sturges

Introduction: the career as a context for leadership and management development

Organizations seek to manage the development of individuals to fulfil their requirements; individuals seek to find work situations and developmental opportunities which suit their needs. A key problem for employers, therefore, is how to align these respective wants. The concept of the 'career' offers a useful means of exploring how this matching might best take place, because the concept of career 'has meaning to both the individual pursuing an occupation – the "internal career" – and the organization trying to set up a sensible developmental path for employees to follow throughout their working life in the organization – the "external career"' (Schein 1978: 1). The career therefore provides a framework within which leadership and management development might be viewed, since it is within the context of organizational needs (for example environmental or strategic) and individual competences (for example sensemaking and ability to deliver change) that this development must take place.

A career has been defined as 'the sequence of employment-related positions, roles, activities and experiences encountered by a person' (Arnold 1997: 16). As this definition suggests, a career is not simply an occupation, but a personal sequence of employment-related events. As such, it may include self-employment and freelance work, as well as education and leisure activities which relate to a person's work life in some way. It is also closely related to the non-work aspects of a person's life upon which it impinges. As long ago as 1937 it was pointed out that the career has two aspects: the objective career, the series of positions or offices ('statuses') which the person holds – that is, the career as perceived by external observers; and the subjective career, which is the individual's view of his or her own career experiences (Hughes 1937). Hughes' notion of the subjective career as 'the moving perspective in which the person sees his life as a whole and interprets the meaning of his various attributes, actions and the things that happen to him' (*ibid.*: 413) continues to provide an important context for development from both the individual and the organizational perspective.

Indeed, this view of the career as an entity which has both a personal and an organizational context is necessary to understand the course of a person's work life; both the subjective and the objective careers must be considered together as two facets of the same process. It can be seen as providing a link between the individual and the social structure, which melds observable facts and individuals' interpretation of their experience (Derr and Laurent 1989). The two dimensions of the career are 'inseparable and interactive elements in the social construction of career reality' (*ibid*.: 454), as the model in Figure 13.1 indicates.

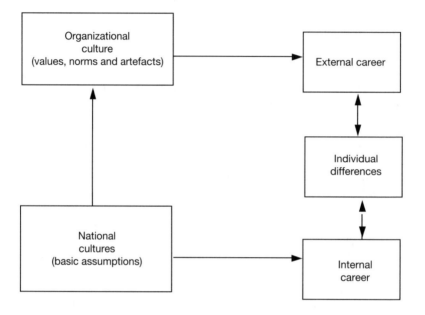

Figure 13.1 Derr and Laurent's cultural model of career dynamics
Source: Derr and Laurent (1989).

This chapter explores career theory as a framework which provides an important context for leadership and management development. In particular, it focuses on the individual perspective of the career, which traditionally has received less theoretical attention than the organizational dimension. Yet it is of vital importance to consider this dimension if organizational and individual needs are to be matched. For it is not just individuals' competences which matter in terms of the identification and development of leaders and managers, but their career-related preferences and dispositions, which may (or may not) dispose them towards leadership in general and specific types of leadership roles in particular. In the sense that individual career orientations are a powerful influence on how individual careers develop, traits, in the form of inclinations towards certain kinds of career, do matter.

The way in which a person's career unfolds – *career development* – is a process which has value both for the organization, which wishes to maximize the contribution that an individual makes at work, and for the individual, who has career-related aspirations which he or she wishes to achieve. Attempts to influence the career development of individuals – *career management* – can also be undertaken by the organization and by the employee, both of whom have different but related interests in this development process. Ideally this development benefits the organization, in terms of the contribution which the individual makes at work, and the individual, in terms of job satisfaction and self-fulfilment. For leadership and management development to take place successfully it is important that both perspectives are properly understood and assimilated.

The individual perspective of the career has increased in importance with the emergence of the so-called 'new' career, a phenomenon which will be discussed in detail below. Amongst other things, the concept of the new career has led to an increased emphasis on individual (rather than organizational) management of the career, an erosion of careers bounded by a single organization and a focus on the development of individual career competences. This chapter argues that, amongst other things, this has resulted in an 'individualization' of the career which has important implications for management and leadership development. One aspect of this is an increased focus on individual career orientations, for example Schein's (1978) career anchors. The existence and value of such orientations are discussed in the next section. Briefly, career orientations theory implies that individuals may be suited to different styles of leadership and indeed to different leadership roles (Nicholson 2000: 69). Therefore a better understanding of such orientations is likely to inform more efficient selection of potential leaders, as well as more effective leadership and management development.

Second, the individualization of the career is a consequence of the necessity for individuals to take responsibility for managing their own careers and build career competences which will enhance career portability and development in an environment where they can no longer look to their employer to provide security and a predictable career ladder. Increased individual responsibility for career management may appear to be at odds with organizational efforts to develop leaders and managers successfully. It is therefore important to understand what this kind of individualization means and to what extent it exists, if leadership and management development are both to reflect and to enhance individual behaviour in a 'boundaryless' career environment. Indeed, in a boundaryless environment where organizations offer a shorter career ladder, the main focus of development may be on the learning of 'near' leadership skills, that is empowering and team building skills, rather than 'distant' leadership skills, which may be less appropriate for this kind of organizational context.

Third, the individualization of the career is further augmented by the increased diversity of the workforce, an acknowledgement of differences in individual values, especially according to generational cohort, and growing individual interest in balancing work with the rest of one's life. A desire for work–life balance both affects what individuals seek to achieve in their career and how they seek to achieve it. Thus it is increasingly something which organizations must take into consideration in terms of individual development at work.

Furthermore, if increasing numbers of individuals have values at odds with those traditionally espoused in organizations or are choosing to subordinate the development of their career to an emphasis on more rounded life goals, then the pool of potential organizational leaders may in the future be considerably smaller than it has been in the past.

Individual career orientations

The subjective meanings which people ascribe to their careers are often described in terms of their *career orientations*. Such orientations affect the kind of career choices which individuals make – where they work, the kind of jobs they want to do, and the kind of education and training they undertake. Understanding career orientations can therefore be a useful means of discovering what kind of management and leadership roles suit individuals in terms of personal preferences and capabilities. Career orientations can also offer useful insights into how individuals might best be developed in terms of leadership competencies.

Schein (1978) described career orientations in terms of *career anchors*. This concept refers to individuals' conceptions of themselves in terms of an occupation. Career anchors are based on individuals' talents and abilities, motives and needs, and attitudes and values. Five career anchors were originally identified by Schein's research: a *technical and functional competence* anchor, where the individual's career is guided by a desire to emphasize the functional specialism of a job; a *managerial competence* anchor, where the individual's career is motivated by a desire to rise to positions of managerial responsibility; a *security and stability* career anchor, where the individual's career focuses on securing long-term stability; a *creativity* career anchor, where the individual's career develops from a desire for self-expression at work, for example through the creation of a new business which can be closely identified with their own efforts; and an *autonomy* career anchor, where the individual's career is driven by a wish to be as free from organizational constraints as possible. Later research led Schein to add three further career anchors to his list: a *sense of service, dedication to a cause* anchor, where the individual's career is shaped more by strong values than actual talents and competences; a *pure challenge* anchor, where the individual's career is dominated by a desire to seek high levels of challenge in their work; and a *lifestyle* anchor, where the individual's career is seen as an integral part of their total lifestyle (Schein 1993).

Since the career anchors concept was developed in the 1970s, the popularity of different anchors has shifted away from an emphasis on managerial competence and technical and functional competence anchors towards autonomy and lifestyle anchors. In the 1970s and 1980s roughly 25 per cent of the populations Schein studied espoused a managerial competence career anchor and a further 25 per cent were anchored in technical and functional competence. By the 1990s the popularity of these career anchors had waned and as many as 50 per cent of those surveyed considered their career anchor to be lifestyle (Schein 1996). This may reflect generational differences, as well as the changing nature of work, with the prevalence of downsizing and restructuring threatening the nature and longevity of the managerial career. It also poses questions for organizations which may still wish to develop individuals for senior management or specialist roles, since it appears to suggest that fewer individuals may aspire to traditional leadership roles within organizations.

Other researchers (e.g. Derr 1986; Driver 1982) have produced similar classifications of individual career orientations and patterns. Driver, for example, identified four different career development patterns or 'career concepts': the *steady state* career concept, where an individual selects a job or profession early in their career and remains within it, with little suggestion of hierarchical movement, for example medicine; the *linear state* career concept, which corresponds to the traditional hierarchical career within an organization; the *spiral state* career concept, which consists of a succession of 'separate' careers in different fields; and the *transitory state* career concept, where an individual never settles on a set job or field but changes jobs in a random way (*ibid.*).

It has been suggested that this typology might be used to inform a pluralistic approach to management development, giving individuals the opportunity to pursue different kinds of career paths which reflect their personal orientations, rather than simply adhere to a traditional hierarchical career structure. As well as better meeting individual preferences, this approach would allow employers to cultivate a more diverse range of skills and capabilities within their workforce, thereby offering them a potential source of competitive advantage (Brousseau *et al.* 1996). Such an approach would be reflected in a range of career track options, development systems and training opportunities offered by the organization. As such, it may also be used to support the development of individuals in a range of 'near' and 'distant' leadership roles, to suit the organization's strategic requirements.

It is important to note, first, that an individual's orientation towards particular kinds of careers may change over the course of their lifetime and, second, that individual career orientations have become more even more diverse because the traditional career 'ladder' no longer exists in many organizations. This could operate to employers' advantage; for example, individuals with a 'creativity' career anchor may be deemed to be better leadership material during times of turbulence, change and shortened product life-cycles. As part of their career orientation, individuals are also likely to have their own subjective definitions of what career 'success' means to them. While organizations tend to measure success in objective terms, such as hierarchical status, these criteria on their own do not appear to be sufficient to make many people feel that their careers are actually successful (Scase and Goffee 1989; Korman *et al.* 1981). A better understanding of what success means to individuals is important because traditional models of leadership are based on the assumption that people aspire to fill senior roles in the management hierarchy. If this is not in fact the case, then it may be much harder to interest many staff in taking on such leadership roles. In fact, recent research has shown that many people incorporate other, more subjective criteria, such as recognition, influence and personally defined achievement, into their own definitions of career success, and that these criteria can change as individuals grow older and their careers develop. Four types of individuals have been identified in terms of how they define career success (Sturges 1999). These are outlined below.

The climber

The climber is the type of manager who describes career success very much in terms of objective criteria, such as hierarchical position, promotion and reward. Their view of success is thus closest to the 'traditional' concept of organizational career success and is often expressed as reaching the most senior levels of leadership or management. Climbers not only aspire to move up the organizational hierarchy but also seek the status which they believe this will bring. Being in a position of influence at work is not sufficient to make them feel successful; they have to achieve a perceived status as well. Climbers tend to be very goal oriented in terms of their attitude to their career progression: they set themselves regular stretching goals and targets relating to their level of pay and their position in the hierarchy. Linked to this emphasis on career goals, climbers often have a strong competitive instinct. However, climbers also need to enjoy their work to feel that they are successful. In fact, they frequently believe that any material success they achieve is meaningless if they do not enjoy their work. It is the climber's notion of success that has traditionally underpinned models of 'distant' leadership in organizations.

The expert

For the individual who defines career success as an expert, success is seen in terms of achieving a high level of competence at their job and being recognized personally for being good at what they do, in terms of being seen to be an expert or winning the respect of the people they work with. Affirmation of what they accomplish at work is central to the expert's perception of career success; this affirmation can take many forms, such as being given positive feedback, being thanked for their efforts or winning awards. For many experts, hierarchical position is not part of their definition of success at all. Other experts, especially younger ones, do include grade, promotion and reward in their definition of career success, but only because they see them as another form of personal recognition, not because they value them for their own sake. To experts, the content of the job they do is more important than their position in the hierarchy or their status within the organization. They often indicate that they not prepared to sacrifice a job they enjoy doing for advancement within the organization. The expert's emphasis on personal competence may mean that individuals with this success orientation are well suited to supportive and empowering 'near' leadership roles, where they are well placed to lead by example.

The influencer

To the influencer, career success means being able to do things at work which have a tangible and positive effect on the organization they work for, regardless of their position in the hierarchy. The influencer's idea of career success is thus grounded on criteria such as leaving a mark or having an impact on the business. The way in which the influencers think they might achieve influence varies. For older influencers in particular, the idea of leaving a mark on their organization is extremely important, and often linked to gaining autonomy at work, particularly for those managers who have not reached senior levels in the managerial hierarchy. For younger influencers, or those who wish to progress up the hierarchy, influence is frequently seen as attaining a level of responsibility within the organization, and, as such, something to aspire to as their career develops. Influencers commonly try to make an impact at work, sometimes by getting involved in activities outside the normal remit of their job, which allows them to attain greater levels of influence than their position in the hierarchy might permit. Influencers who believe that their grade in the hierarchy is important do so for the influence this allows them, rather than for the status which it endows. Individuals with an influencer career success orientation may be well suited for senior leadership roles, but will be motivated to seek these for the power and influence they permit, rather than the hierarchical status which they entail.

The self-realizer

For the self-realizer, career success is very much an internal concept, based on the idea of achievement at a very personal level, sometimes in a way which means little to other people. Self-realizers' definition of success is thus as far removed from objective hierarchical success as possible and closest to the notion of personal fulfilment. Self-realizers often value being good at their job, because this can lead to a sense of achievement. However, while success for self-realizers can be the result of specific job-related achievements, they frequently have difficulty in describing their very personal idea of career success in organizational terms at all. Self-realizers find it essential that their work is challenging at a personal level in some way. Meeting a challenge not only adds to their sense of achievement but is also seen as helping them develop as managers, something which the self-realizers value. For self-realizers, their definition of career success often includes achievement of balance between their work life and their home life; it matters to them that they succeed in both spheres of their life on their own personal terms. Individuals who subscribe to a self-realizer career success orientation may be suited to certain types of leadership roles which offer them the kind of very personal challenges they enjoy.

Career orientations theory offers insights into the diverse meanings individuals ascribe to their careers and what success might mean to them on their own terms. Such insights might usefully inform organizational policy and practice regarding leadership and management development. Understanding such individual orientations and conceptions of success is important because if organizations wish to motivate and develop their staff they must take heed of their career preferences. Furthermore, individuals may be suited to different roles and models of leadership, appropriate in particular organizational circumstances (for example change or innovation), depending on their career orientation. Without consideration of an individual's career orientation, their inclination to certain types of roles may be hard to identify. The literature on career orientations also suggests a more pessimistic perspective on leadership, in that the popularity of senior management positions may be limited if people do not necessarily aspire to positions of management responsibility. Evidence of difficulties filling senior roles in fields such education and health in the UK may support this conclusion.

The new career and its impact on individuals

Despite an acknowledgement that organizations must engender some kind of stability in their human resources in order to meet strategic needs, many senior teams have been rethinking what kind of 'careers' they wish to offer their employees. In order to remain competitive in a business environment dominated by globalization and rapid advances in technology, firms have restructured, delayered and been through mergers and acquisitions programmes. This has reduced the opportunities for hierarchical progression in many organizational structures. In addition, the continuing insecurity of the environment and the perceived need to be able to respond quickly to business imperatives has meant that employers are questioning whether it is in their interests to offer long-term career opportunities to their staff. Potentially this could have important implications for the development of leaders within organizations, in that if fewer opportunities are presented employees will not only look to develop their careers elsewhere but may also see less reason to aspire to senior management roles at all.

In fact, it has been suggested that, for many people, 'traditional' organizational careers may soon cease to exist. The consequence of this for individuals is that careers will no longer be 'bounded' by the organization, but instead will become 'boundaryless' and 'portable' (Mirvis and Hall 1994; Kanter 1989). This new type of career is said to be boundaryless because it can no longer be defined within the confines of one company. It is described as portable because an individual's success will depend on his or her ability to transfer skills from organization to organization (*ibid.*). The absence of boundaries is also sometimes depicted in terms of a 'new deal', where the psychological contract which exists between employer and employee has shifted to reflect the fact that there is no longer a promise or an expectation of a career for life (Herriot and Pemberton 1995). The dissipation of traditional organizational boundaries implies, amongst other things, the emergence of a new set of leadership skills suited to an environment where networks and coalitions need to be managed.

The notion of the 'new' career has two crucial implications for individuals and organizations. The first key implication of the new career relates to individuals' career-related behaviour, in particular the management of the career. If organizations can no longer offer individuals a career for life, then it is argued that nor do organizations have any responsibility to manage careers for their staff. In the past, the process of career management in organizations was seen as predominantly the responsibility of the employer (Orpen 1994). While individuals acted to further their own careers – performing activities such as setting career-related goals and devising appropriate strategies to achieve them (Noe 1996), this was more in support of their employers' career management activities than a substitute for them. The new career implies that the balance between organizational and individual responsibility for career management has shifted to a position where the onus for managing the career now rests with the individual. Therefore, many organizations now stress that their staff must 'manage' their own career – that is, find themselves suitable roles, make sure they get the training they need, and promote their own interests at work. Amongst other things, this approach further encourages the individualization of the career, as individuals are expected to take responsibility for the management and development of their career. As such, the notion that career management has become the responsibility of the individual rather than the organization also appears to be at odds with the aims and process of leadership and management development. It is potentially difficult to see how companies can orchestrate individual career management and organizational leadership development without compromising either or possibly both of these activities.

Career self-management is said to consist of gathering 'information and plans for career problem solving and decision-making' (Kossek *et al.* 1998: 938). As a concept, it may be more complex than some commentators would suggest. A study of graduates working for large UK organizations showed there to be two quite different kinds of career management activities, those primarily aimed at furthering the individual's career within the organization and those aimed at furthering it outside the organization (Sturges *et al.* 2002). Furthermore, the graduates practised two distinct kinds of internal career self-management behaviour, one kind focusing on networking activities, such as getting to know the right people at work, and the other on visibility activities, such as drawing attention to achievements at work.

The research also showed that there is a close reciprocal relationship between the things people do to manage their own careers and the career development help which they receive from their employer. Organizational career management help appears to encourage practice of career self-management, and practice of career self-management leads to further experience of organizational help. This suggests there may be the potential for employers to create a 'virtuous circle' of career management activities in which individual and organizational activities complement, rather than contradict, each other and help to build organizational commitment (*ibid.*). If this is the case, then it may well suggest a means of resolving the contradictions posed by the 'new' career's emphasis on individual management of the career in the context of the need for organizations to identify and develop leaders and senior managers.

Indeed, organizations traditionally had an interest in 'managing' their employees' careers – placing them in jobs, giving them training and development, and establishing career 'paths' for them to follow – in order to maximize the contribution they made at work. It would appear that the wholesale rejection of this approach in favour of an overemphasis on career self-management could endanger organizational attempts to secure any kind of employee development at all. Promoting career 'self-management' unreservedly is likely to encourage individuals to try to further their careers elsewhere, as well as undermine organizational leadership development initiatives. It is clear that if employers do not make a contribution to their employees' career development this may weaken their commitment to the organization, since there will be little incentive for them to remain there for more than a very short period of time (Sturges *et al.* 2000).

The second key implication of the 'new' career relates to the skills necessary to secure career development. Development within the new career scenario no longer implies hierarchical progression, but rather a succession of roles across a number of organizations, possibly including periods of self-employment. 'People may still have a job, but they no longer have a career, at least in the traditional ladder sense…. Climbing the corporate ladder is being replaced by hopping from job to job' (Kanter 1989: 299). The implied portability of the new career means that an individual's success depends on the transfer of skills from organization to organization. Therefore if individuals can no longer count on a long-term career with their employer they will have to focus on developing skills and competences which will make them employable elsewhere, rather than just able to do current or future jobs with their existing employer. (These skills and competences may of course include leadership capabilities.)

The new career also has implications for individual skill development within organizations. If it entails an overall erosion of organizational boundaries, then managers and leaders in organizations may need to develop new collaborative knowledge and skills. Such skills include *referral skills*, the ability to diagnose situations and act as a broker between individuals and resources; *partnering skills*, the ability to create relevant networks and contractual arrangements; and *relationship management skills*, the ability to prioritize the needs and preferences of customers and partners (Miles and Snow 1996).

It has been argued that a resource-based theoretical perspective is a useful means of conceptualizing how individuals might facilitate their career development in a boundaryless environment (Jones and Lichtenstein 2000). Taking such a perspective, the career is conceptualized as a repository of knowledge (Bird 1994) or an accumulation of capital (Inkson and Arthur 2001). Within this framework, it is suggested that in order to secure career development individuals must cultivate career competences – that is, skills and know-how which build career capital. Thus, through the acquisition of career competences, individuals put themselves in a position where their careers can prosper in the boundaryless career environment. Three key forms of career competence have been identified: *knowing-how* competences; *knowing-why* competences; and *knowing-whom* competences (*ibid.*).

Knowing-how career competences reflect career-relevant skills and job-related knowledge needed for competent performance in work roles. As such, they relate to tacit as well as explicit knowledge, and soft skills as well as technical expertise.

Knowing-why career competences relate to values, meanings and interests that shape the way in which an individual's career develops. Such values and meanings relate to the career orientations, such as career anchors (Schein 1978; Derr 1986), and can be expressed, for example, as a desire for autonomy, security or challenge. Knowing-why career competences also relate to having the confidence, motivational energy and self-assurance to pursue a desired career path (Inkson and Arthur 2001). *Knowing-whom* career competences involve the creation of social capital by gaining proximity to those who may provide opportunities and resources to aid career development. It has been shown that managers with greater numbers of external ties earn more (Belliveau *et al.* 1996) and secure jobs more easily (Granovetter 1974). The scope for and importance of such networking activities are clearly more important in a boundaryless career environment where individuals must facilitate their own career development.

As well as giving a focus for individual development, career competences might also provide a useful framework for the development of leadership capabilities from the perspective that both the individual and the organization should benefit from this process. *Knowing-why* career competences allow both the individual and the organization to understand better to what kind of leadership roles and situations a person is suited. *Knowing-how* career competences allow potential leaders and managers to develop the kind of leadership capabilities needed to deliver 'accomplished performances'. *Knowing-whom* career competences may help provide the networking skills necessary for leaders operating in a boundaryless environment.

Interestingly, there is little real evidence to suggest that the 'new' career, as described by Mirvis and Hall (1994), Kanter (1989) and Herriot and Pemberton (1995), has actually had a major impact on UK workplaces as yet. The indications are that organizations remain committed to retaining valuable staff and are keen to help develop the careers of those whose performance is especially likely to benefit them, such as managers. While some changes in career practices and attitudes have undoubtedly taken place, there is no indication that these have been on the scale proposed, especially by US commentators (e.g. Kanter 1989). In a UK study of eight large organizations conducted in the late 1990s, career self-management emerged as little more than a rhetorical idea (Gratton and Hope Hailey 1999). That is, while these employers endorsed it as a concept and advocated its practice to their employees, they did little to encourage or support them to manage their own careers. This conclusion is supported by the findings of a study of the early years of UK graduates' careers, which found that individuals still expected and received a great deal of career management help from the organizations which employed them (Sturges *et al.* 2000).

This may be an indication that, while restructuring and downsizing have had an impact on job security, employers still realize that it is in their interests to retain some involvement in the management of their employees' careers if they wish to secure their development and commitment. What may have changed is the emphasis of organizational career management activities, in that many organizations now aim to offer their staff 'employability', rather than a career for life; that is, the acquisition of skills and experience which will enable them to move jobs as and when necessary, as well as perform effectively in the roles individuals undertake for them.

Changing values and the desire for work–life balance

The career has been individualized further as a result of a growing expression of interest by individuals in balancing work and career with other aspects of life, such as family, friends and personal interests. For example, a survey of UK managers conducted by *Management Today* magazine indicated that nearly half of them would accept lower pay in return for more personal time (Rice 2001). For some time it has been argued that achieving a balance between home life and work life is increasingly a priority for many people. As long ago as the late 1980s it was suggested that UK managers were becoming less interested in career success as it has been traditionally understood and more interested in career advancement as a means of enhancing personal lifestyles which are separate from, rather than subordinated to, work roles. They were more drawn to their families as a source of satisfaction and less prepared to sacrifice their lifestyles for their careers (Scase and Goffee 1989). It was likewise proposed that individuals in the US were adopting 'a more individualised "protean" definition of success which stresses autonomy, flexibility and balance between home and work' (Sekaran and Hall 1989: 176). These conclusions are borne out by Schein's (1996) research findings, which show that growing numbers of people are endorsing a 'lifestyle' career anchor, discussed earlier in this chapter. It is this aspect of career individualization which most threatens the identification and development of leaders and senior managers, in that it implies that such roles, and indeed the work environment itself, may be far less attractive to many individuals in the future than they are assumed to be at present.

A number of factors have been identified as contributing to this growing interest in work–life balance. The entry of women into the workforce has made issues concerning balancing home and work more relevant for more people. The UK is typical of Western countries, in that women now comprise 50 per cent of those at work. Some have concluded that this could mean massive change for organizations, in that they may have to rethink completely the way work is structured in order to accommodate the competing demands of individuals' non-work responsibilities. At the very least, employers are under pressure to recognize the importance of families and out-of-work responsibilities to individuals, by offering benefits such as parental leave and part-time working, as increasing numbers of women work and men become more inclined to play a greater role in bringing up their children.

Yet the increasing availability of such 'family-friendly' policies on their own does not seem to have secured greater equality for women at work. For example, women managers' careers continue to look very different from those of their male colleagues. They are still likely to occupy 'specialist' support roles, in functions such as personnel and marketing, rather than 'generalist' line management roles. They remain clustered in certain business sectors, such as the public sector and service organizations, like retailers. They reach fewer senior positions, are paid less and have more complicated career paths than their male counterparts. Research has also shown that women's ideas of what career success means to them differ from those of their male colleagues, being more based on personal recognition and achievement than objective measures of pay and hierarchical position (Sturges 1999). Failure to respect any difference in women's values may be an important reason why the contribution they could make at work remains unfulfilled. Research has shown that women tend to endorse more inclusive and empowering management styles (Ferrario 1994); a reluctance to acknowledge this may also limit the contribution women can make to senior management roles at work.

It is argued that those aged 35 and younger – sometimes known as Generation X (Cannon 1995) – form a distinctive cohort within the workforce. They are said to hold work-related values which differ from those held by previous generations, because of formative influences in their youth, such as media technology, globalization, economic instability and AIDS (Tulgan 1996). In particular, it is argued that they wish to develop and manage their careers on their own terms, as opposed to those suggested by traditional organizational norms (Cannon 1995). An important part of their career individualism is said to be an aspiration to achieve balance between the work and non-work aspects of their lives. Recent research supports these conclusions. Smola and Sutton (2002) concluded that so-called Generation X-ers had different values from those of the same age a generation earlier, in that they were less likely to feel that work should be an important part of life. Their conclusion is borne out by Lewis *et al.* (2002), who, in a study of young people's values across four European countries, found the existence of a strong desire to lead a balanced lifestyle. If younger workers are keen to achieve success on their own terms, not those of organizational norms, and to seek a good balance between work and the non-work aspects of their lives, then one cannot necessarily assume that traditional leadership roles in organizations will be attractive to them.

The long-hours culture which prevails in many countries has also focused interest on the topic of work–life balance. For example, the majority of British managers work far more than 40 hours a week (Worrall and Cooper 1998), despite European legislation which attempts to limit the number of hours worked. This long-hours culture is partly perceived to be the result of downsizing and the more demanding workloads with which those who remain in employment must contend (McGovern *et al.* 1998). It may also be a consequence of the widespread belief that in order to succeed individuals must demonstrate an indefatigable commitment to their work, regardless of personal cost (Anderson-Gough *et al.* 1998). Pressure to demonstrate commitment by working long hours is likely to have a particularly strong impact on individuals at the start of their career (Coffey 1994), at the point when competition to succeed in the promotion tournament is fierce (Rosenbaum 1979). This may reinforce younger individuals' desire to seek a balance between home and work.

Lack of balance between work and home caused by excessive work demands is conceptualized either as work spillover – that is, 'the degree to which workers feel their work is invading their non-work life' (Wallace 1997: 228) – or, more commonly, as work–family conflict, 'a form of inter-role conflict in which the general demands of the job interfere with performing family-related responsibilities' (Netemeyer *et al.* 1996: 401). More recently, it has been argued that a broader definition of this term, such as work–non-work conflict, is necessary in order to encompass aspects of non-work lives others than family responsibilities (Wallace 1999). Research has identified several factors which can cause individuals to experience an imbalance between work and home life. These include biographical characteristics, personal characteristics, hours worked, organizational experiences and family experiences.

Biographical influences which have an effect on work–family conflict include family circumstances and gender: women are more likely to experience work–family conflict than men (Gutek *et al.* 1991). Personal characteristics related to experience of work–family conflict are job and life involvement; individuals who are more involved in their job or more involved in their out-of-work life are more likely to experience conflict between the two domains (Parasuraman *et al.* 1996). Not surprisingly, the number of hours an individual works has been shown to contribute directly to feelings of imbalance between work and home life (Frone *et al.* 1997). However, the relationship may not be quite as straightforward as it may seem. It has been suggested that the number of hours worked does not necessarily produce feelings of work–family conflict, because feelings of strain depend on an individual's values, beliefs and orientations towards work, especially the salience they attach to work, as well as external work pressures (Greenhaus 1988). Organizational experiences which have been shown to cause (or alleviate) work–family conflict include work stress and organizational policies regarding out-of-work responsibilities (Thompson *et al.* 1999).

The effects of imbalance between work and home occur chiefly in three areas. These are: job satisfaction and life satisfaction; organizational commitment and intention to leave; and psychological and physical health. Lack of balance between home and work has a negative effect both on job satisfaction (Netemeyer *et al.* 1996) and life satisfaction (Carlson and Perrewé 1999), as well as leading to psychological and physical ill health (Frone *et al.* 1997). For employers there are potentially serious consequences, since lack of balance has been shown to have a detrimental effect on how committed individuals feel to them and how inclined they may be to move jobs (Thompson *et al.* 1999).

Taking Arnold's broad definition of the career as 'the sequence of employment-related positions, roles, activities and experiences encountered by a person' used at the beginning of this chapter (Arnold 1997: 16), one can see how career theory has utility as a framework which can elucidate attitudes to and behaviour concerning work–life balance. It has long been recognized that career roles, activities and experiences impinge upon the non-work domain as well as the work domain (Barley 1989). Indeed, it has been suggested that individuals' work and non-work lives are inextricably intertwined (Sekaran and Hall 1989). If this is the case, then concepts relating to work–life balance may be considered to be career phenomena. Treated as such, they impinge crucially upon the issue of leadership and management development.

The case for considering them as such is strengthened by the emergence of the 'boundaryless' career. This implies an enlargement of the 'career space', since work and non-work roles are likely to overlap and intermingle to the extent that they jointly shape a person's career identity and sense of self (Mirvis and Hall 1994). This overlapping and intermingling are significantly reinforced by the widespread use of technologies which 'invade' the non-work sphere, such as laptops, virtual networks and mobile phones. Thus, any notion of a 'boundaryless' career which overlooks the boundary between work and non-work is likely to be incomplete (Fletcher and Bailyn 1996).

This suggests that the importance that an individual ascribes to work–life balance will both influence and be influenced by a broader range of attitudes, dispositions and orientations through which they pursue the nature, direction and progress of their career. In this sense, attitudes relating to work–life balance will contribute to the individualization of the career. In particular, what individuals seek to achieve in their career and how they define career success for themselves is likely to affect and be affected by the meaning they ascribe to work–life balance. Their disposition and attitudes relating to leadership roles will be similarly affected. Furthermore, this implies that individuals' career-related behaviour will both influence and be influenced by activities concerned with managing the relationship they seek to achieve between the work and non-work domains. Behaviour aimed at managing this relationship could be considered to be an integral part of the broader range of activities which an individual pursues in order to manage the nature, direction and progress of his or her career. Thus, individual and organizational behaviours aimed at assisting the management of the balance between home and work can be seen as part of a wider range of personal career management behaviour.

This has implications for employers, who must acknowledge this aspect of the individualization of the career, if they are to recruit, retain and develop their staff. This means they need to be concerned not just with offering employees 'family-friendly' policies, but with recognizing the impact of a desire for work–life balance on employees' career orientations and behaviour and to take this into consideration with regard to the management and development of their careers. An individual's orientation towards demanding and time-consuming leadership roles at work is likely to be influenced considerably by the extent to which they wish to lead a 'balanced' life. Increasingly, for many people aspiring to such roles may entail sacrifices which they do not wish to make. Organizations can therefore no longer necessarily assume that those with identifiable potential will aspire to the management positions they would like them to occupy.

Conclusion: the individualization of the career and its implications

As was identified at the beginning of this chapter, a key challenge for organizations wishing to establish developmental pathways for leaders and managers is how to match individual needs with organizational requirements. The career can provide a useful framework through which to view this matching process. However, the challenge which this presents is being exacerbated by the increasing individualization of the career, a phenomenon discussed in detail in this chapter. What is meant by 'individualization' in this context is the manifestation of the career as an individual rather than an organizational property. This reflects both the growing importance of the individual perspective on the career and an acknowledgement of the diversity of this perspective. In a practical context, it means that the focus of career sensemaking, decision-making and activity is increasingly at an individual level. This is important for the context of leadership and management development, because such individualization fundamentally challenges organizational 'control' over the determination of who should be developed for positions of senior responsibility and how this development should take place.

As this chapter has discussed, a number of factors are influencing the emergence of career individualization. The phenomenon is partly a result of changes in organizations, in particular the emergence of the new career ideology. The main theme of this rhetoric is that the career is no longer primarily an organizational entity, but the responsibility of the individual, who must take charge of its development and management. Career individualization is also partly a result of a growing awareness that individuals have diverse career values, wants and needs and an acknowledgement that these differences matter and should be respected in the workplace. These two important influences are probably mutually reinforcing, in that by placing greater responsibility for career management and development on the individual the new career rhetoric encourages the individual to reflect on and pursue his or her own, rather than the organization's, values, wants and needs.

Career individualization manifests itself in a number of ways. It is demonstrated by the diverse range of career orientations which individuals espouse, for example personal definitions of career success which incorporate criteria other than the objective measures of success currently emphasized by most organizations. It is apparent in the now widely held view that the career is just one part of life, of which other aspects such as family and personal life may be equally or more important, depending on the individual's circumstances and preferences. It is exhibited in an acceptance of what the boundaryless career implies. This leads individuals to realize the need to take personal responsibility for management of the career (sometimes to the detriment of loyalty and commitment to the organization) and to acquire portable skills, rather than those only useful in their current job, with the aim of building career capital of value across boundaries.

From the perspective of career theory, the emergence of career individualization means that more research is needed to explore and define individual, as opposed to organizational, dimensions of the career. Organizations need to know more about what people think and how they behave with regard to their career if they are to delineate and respond to increasing individualization. In particular, research is needed to investigate the personal and subjective dimension of the career, and the meanings people ascribe to their own career-related values, wants, needs and behaviour. Research is required which examines the sense people make of the work and non-work aspects of their lives and how the two parts of their life should and do fit together. There is also a need to acknowledge the personal subjective dimension of the career more fully in other studies. For example, despite evidence that individuals ascribe diverse meanings to career success, researchers still frequently operationalize success only in terms of objective criteria such as hierarchical level and pay.

From the individual perspective, a wider acceptance of the individualization of the career gives people's career-related values, wants and needs more latitude and more credibility. If people are motivated by personal models of success and cultivate skills which are meaningful for the kind of career which they want rather than to suit an organization's requirements, then this could make conventional career norms less relevant. Traditional hierarchical organizational careers may not be so attractive to many people; long hours may become otiose and intolerable; people may choose increasingly to pursue individual developmental paths and fulfil leadership ambitions in other, less conventional, ways, possibly even outside the organization altogether.

From the organizational perspective, the individualization of the career has important implications for leadership and management development. In a bid to match individual and organizational needs more carefully, employers may be obliged to endorse different models of leadership and multifarious career paths. This may both suit individuals' diverse aspirations and respond to the reduced opportunities for hierarchical advancement restructured organizations can offer. Different developmental processes and experiences may be appropriate, based on diverse models of success and individual career orientations. Less traditional models of leadership – for example roles which offer short-term specific challenges or roles based on expertise in a particular situation – could be endorsed if organizations acknowledge that the status of leadership may be derived from a personal preference for success in terms of expertise or influence as well as hierarchical position. Such roles may not only add to an organization's strategic capabilities but also provide the basis for new career paths that will motivate and secure the commitment of employees.

It is clear that organizations cannot abnegate all responsibility for career management with impunity, especially if they wish to retain the right to select and develop leaders of whatever kind. The potential conflict inherent in such an approach is massive. Individuals need help to help themselves in terms of managing their careers: organizational career management and career self-management are not mutually exclusive; the former may aid the promotion of the latter, as discussed earlier in this chapter. Moreover, if organizations do not provide help with career management they are likely to undermine employee commitment and lose valuable staff as a result, negating any attempts to develop a leadership cadre. Absence of career management and development help may set in place a vicious circle where the employee becomes more inclined to leave than to stay, just as provision of help can promote the establishment of a virtuous circle where the individual willingly engages in activities aimed at furthering their development within the organization

As discussed in this chapter, the 'career competence' model could provide a useful framework for organizational developmental practice in an environment where the career is increasingly indvidualized (Jones and Lichtenstein 2000). This acknowledges the kind of career capital individuals need to accumulate for their careers to develop in a boundaryless career environment, and ascribes the importance it deserves to the individual dimension of the career in the form of knowing-why career competences (Inkson and Arthur 2001). Reference to it could help organizations gain insight into what individuals want from their careers and what kind of roles they are capable of filling, as well as what skills and developmental experiences will be required to help them achieve them. Traditional career interventions such as assessment centres, career planning workshops, career counselling and mentoring schemes could all be used to help ascertain individuals' personal career and leadership preferences, facilitate career self-management and plan future development.

It is necessary to strike one further note of caution amongst the positive implications of the individualization of the career. With the upbeat rhetoric of the new career and the acknowledgement of individual notions of success it is easy to overlook the possibility of individual failure. Yet, paradoxically, failure may be both more common and more painful in an environment where individuals are encouraged to seek success on their own terms rather than perhaps not expect to succeed according to criteria set by the organization. Organizations therefore must endeavour to set realistic expectations and deal sensitively with individual failure as part of the establishment of new developmental pathways and processes.

References

Anderson-Gough, F., C. Grey and K. Robson (1998) 'Work hard – play hard: an analysis of organizational cliché in two accountancy practices', *Organization* 5: 4, 565–92.

Arnold, J. (1997) *Managing Careers into the 21st Century*, London: Paul Chapman.

Barley, S. (1989) 'Careers, identities and institutions: the legacy of the Chicago School of Sociology', in M.B. Arthur, D.T. Hall and B.S. Lawrence (eds) *Handbook of Career Theory*, Cambridge: Cambridge University Press.

Belliveau, M., C. O'Reilly and J. Wade (1996) 'Social capital at the top: effects of social similarity and status on CEO compensation', *Academy of Management Journal* 39: 1,568–693.

Bird, A. (1994) 'Careers as repositories of knowledge: a new perspective on boundaryless careers', *Journal of Organizational Behavior* 15: 325–44.

Brousseau, K., M. Driver, K. Eneroth and R. Larsson (1996) 'Career pandemonium: realigning organizations and individuals', *Academy of Management Executive* 10(4): 52–66.

Cannon, D. (1995) *Generation X and the New Work Ethic*, London: Demos.

Carlson, D. and P. Perrewé (1999) 'The role of social support in the stressor–strain relationship: an examination of work–family conflict', *Journal of Management* 25: 4, 513–40.

Coffey, A. (1994) 'Timing is everything: graduate accountants, time and organizational commitment', *Sociology* 28: 4, 943–56.

Derr, C.B. (1986) *Managing the New Careerists: The Diverse Career Success Orientations of Today's Workers*, San Francisco: Jossey-Bass.

Derr, C.B. and A. Laurent (1989) 'The internal and external career: a theoretical and cross-cultural perspective', in M.B. Arthur, D.T. Hall and B.S. Lawrence (eds) *Handbook of Career Theory*, Cambridge: Cambridge University Press.

Driver, M.J. (1982) 'Career concepts – a new approach to career research', in R. Katz (ed.) *Career Issues in Human Resource Management*, Englewood Cliffs, NJ: Prentice-Hall.

Ferrario, M. (1994) 'Women as managerial leaders', in M. Davidson and R. Burke (eds) *Women in Management: Current Research Issues*, London: Paul Chapman.

Fletcher, J. and L. Bailyn (1996) 'Challenging the last boundary: reconnecting work and family', in M. Arthur and D. Rousseau (eds) *The Boundaryless Career*, New York: Oxford University Press.

Frone, M., J. Yardley and K. Markel (1997) 'Developing and testing an integrative model of the work–family interface', *Journal of Vocational Behaviour* 50: 145–67.

Granovetter, M. (1974) *Getting a Job: A Study of Contacts and Careers*, Cambridge, MA: Harvard University Press.

Gratton, L. and V. Hope Hailey (1999) 'The rhetoric and reality of "new careers"', in L. Gratton, V. Hope Hailey, P. Stiles and C. Truss (eds) *Strategic Human Resource Management*, Oxford: Oxford University Press.

Greenhaus, J. (1988) 'The intersection of work–family roles: individual, interpersonal, and organizational issues', *Journal of Social Behavior and Personality* 3: 23–44.

Gutek, B., S. Searle and L. Klepa (1991) 'Rational versus gender role explanations for work–family conflict', *Journal of Applied Psychology* 76(4): 560–8.

Herriot, P. and C. Pemberton (1995) *New Deals: The Revolution in Managerial Careers*, Chichester: John Wiley.

Hughes, E.C. (1937) 'Institutional office and the person', *American Journal of Sociology* 43(11): 404–13.

Inkson, K. and M. Arthur (2001) 'How to be a successful career capitalist', *Organizational Dynamics* 30(1): 48–58.

Jones, C. and B. Lichtenstein (2000) 'The "architecture" of careers: how career competencies reveal firm dominant logic in professional services', in M. Peiperl, M. Arthur, R. Goffee and T. Morris (eds) *Career Frontiers*, Oxford: Oxford University Press.

Kanter, R.M. (1989) *When Giants Learn to Dance*, London: Simon & Schuster.

Korman, A.K., U. Wittig-Berman and D. Lang (1981) 'Career success and personal failure: alienation in professionals and managers', *Academy of Management Journal* 24(2): 342–60.

Kossek E., K. Roberts, S. Fisher and B. Demarr (1998) 'Career self-management: a quasi experimental assessment of the effect of a training intervention', *Personnel Psychology* 51: 935–62.

Lewis, S., J. Smithson and C. Kugelberg (2002) 'Into work: job insecurity and changing psychological contracts', in J. Brannen, S. Lewis, A. Nilsen and J. Smithson (eds) *Young Europeans, Work and Family*, London: Routledge.

McGovern, P., V. Hope-Hailey and P. Stiles (1998). 'The managerial career after downsizing: case studies from the "Leading Edge"', *Work, Employment & Society* 12: 3, 457–77.

Miles, R. and C. Snow (1996) 'Twenty-first century careers', in M. Arthur and D. Rousseau (eds) *The Boundaryless Career*, Oxford: Oxford University Press.

Mirvis, P.H. and D.T. Hall (1994) 'Psychological success and the boundaryless career', *Journal of Organizational Behaviour* 15: 365–80.

Netemeyer, R., J. Boles, and R. McMurrian (1996) 'Development and validation of work–family conflict scales', *Journal of Applied Psychology* 81: 4, 400–10.

Nicholson, N. (2000) 'Motivation–selection–connection: an evolutionary model of career development', in M. Peiperl, M. Arthur, R. Goffee amd T. Morris (eds) *Career Frontiers: New Conceptions of Working Lives*, Oxford: Oxford University Press.

Noe, R. (1996) 'Is career management related to employee development and performance?', *Journal of Organizational Behaviour* 17: 119–33.

Orpen, C. (1994) 'The effects of organizational and individual career management on career success', *International Journal of Manpower* 15(1): 27–37.

Parasuraman, S., Y. Purohit, V. Godshalk and N. Beutell (1996) 'Work and family variables, entrepreneurial career success, and psychological well-being', *Journal of Vocational Behaviour* 48: 275–300.

Rice, M. (2001) 'Great expectations', *Management Today*, June; available at sss.clickmt.com.

Rosenbaum, J.E. (1979) 'Tournament mobility: career patterns in a corporation', *Administrative Science Quarterly* 24(6): 220–41.

Scase, R. and R. Goffee (1989) *Reluctant Managers: Their Work and Lifestyles*, London: Routledge.

Schein, E. (1978) *Career Dynamics: Matching Individual and Organizational Needs*, Reading, MA: Addison-Wesley.

—— (1993) *Career Anchors: Discovering Your Real Values*, San Diego: Pfeiffer.

—— (1996) 'Career anchors revisited: implications for career development in the 21st century', *Academy of Management Executive* 10(4): 80–8.

Sekaran, U. and D.T. Hall (1989) 'Asynchronism in dual career and family linkages', in M.B. Arthur, D.T. Hall and B.S. Lawrence (eds) *Handbook of Career Theory*, Cambridge: Cambridge University Press.

Smola, K.W. and C. Sutton (2002) 'Generational differences: revisiting generational work values for the new millenium', *Journal of Organizational Behavior* 23: 363–82.

Sturges, J. (1999) 'What it means to succeed: personal conceptions of career success held by male and female managers at different ages', *British Journal of Management* 10(3): 239–52.

Sturges, J., D. Guest and K. Mackenzie Davey (2000) 'Who's in charge? Graduates' attitudes to and experiences of career management and their relationship with organizational commitment', *European Journal of Work and Organizational Psychology* 9(3): 351–70.

Sturges, J., D. Guest, N. Conway and K. Mackenzie Davey (2002) 'A longitudinal study of the relationship between career management and organizational commitment among graduates in the first ten years at work', *Journal of Organizational Behavior* 23: 731–48.

Thompson, C., L. Beauvais and K. Lyness (1999) 'When work–family benefits are not enough: the influence of work–family culture on benefit utilization, organizational attachment and work–family conflict', *Journal of Vocational Behaviour* 54: 392–415.

Tulgan, B. (1996) *Managing Generation X: How to Bring out the Best in Young Talent*, Oxford: Capstone Publishing.

Wallace, J. (1997) 'It's about time: a study of spillover of hours worked and work spillover among law firm lawyers', *Journal of Vocational Behaviour* 50: 227–48.

—— (1999) 'Work-to-nonwork conflict among married male and female lawyers', *Journal of Organizational Behavior* 20: 797–816.

Worrall, L. and C. Cooper (1998) *The Quality of Working Life*, London: Institute of Management.

Part VI

How does leadership fit with business strategy?

14 Strategically aligned leadership development

Martin Clarke, David Butcher
and Catherine Bailey

Introduction

The widespread recognition of business leadership as a pillar of organizational success and the subsequent growth and investment in the executive development industry have resulted in businesses being faced with a diversity of approaches to leadership development. By which criteria, therefore, should those intent on developing leadership capability value one approach over another – business impact, individual behaviour change, novelty? And, with such an array of different offerings, is one approach more effective in certain circumstances than others? These questions are ever more pertinent given the substantial investment of time and money that executive development typically involves. A two-week senior executive programme at a UK business school can cost around £10,000, and at Harvard a nine-week leadership programme costs around $50,000. In the US it is estimated that the costs of developing in company programmes can run from $100,00 to $250,000, and it can cost from $50,000 to $150,000 per session to deliver (Fulmer 1997). It is not surprising therefore that *Training* magazine estimated that in 1998, US companies were spending around $60 billion on training each year (Fulmer *ibid*. 2000). And in the UK, business schools are reported as being among the UK's top 50 exporters, attracting over $640 million a year from other countries (Crainer and Dearlove 1999). Thus, for senior managers the choice is wide and the stakes are high. But it is easy to get it wrong.

Take the example of a high tech company (TechCo), where a series of developmental activities for a cadre of high potential managers were designed to enhance the company's succession planning. Many best practice features of leadership development were incorporated in the process. Thus the content was crafted around a detailed corporate-wide management competence framework. Senior executives joined the group at various points during the development process to demonstrate their support for the initiative. Immediate operational issues were identified for the high potential managers to tackle as 'action learning' projects in order that they would be able to translate the content of the programme into a real-life work context. The participants worked on these projects in small autonomous teams with access to an internal facilitator. Each individual also had one-on-one professional feedback on his or her psychological profile, and all attended 'masterclass' sessions on key business issues delivered by external experts.

The whole process was designed and coordinated by a management development manager who was considered by many to be influential in the business.

However, it became apparent that the programme had no lasting impact on individuals or on the company. Several critical thinkers amongst the cohort of high potential managers claimed that they did not really know why they had been selected, what they were supposed to do differently as a result of the programme, or how it fitted with the company's overall business strategy. The action learning projects were regarded by most as an imposition on their day jobs. The psychological profiling results were routinely greeted with a 'so what?', and participants regularly complained that the external tutors did not sufficiently understand their business. The management development manager had little choice but to return to the drawing board.

Contrast this experience with that of FinCo, who approached the issue of succession planning from a notably different temporal perspective. As with TechCo, a competence framework was also used, but it focused on developing competences that directly reflected the future direction of the business. A similar cadre of high potential managers were asked to create their own personal development plans to acquire these 'new to the business' executive capabilities. In contrast to TechCo's internally driven approach, external coaching and business school programmes featured heavily in the methodologies chosen to meet these needs. Although it is early days, the company is already beginning to see a noticeable shift of approach in some of its senior managers, reflecting a longer-term view of the business and a flow of talent around the organization, indicating positive progress in succession planning. So why did this approach work whilst the great effort expended in TechCo amounted to so little?

Put simply, in TechCo the issue of 'fit' between strategy and leadership development was subsumed by concerns over immediate learning transfer, whilst FinCo benefited from a strategic, long-term view of leadership development that was fundamental to ensuring future business renewal. Recent research we have undertaken into current practice in leadership development suggests that FinCo's success is the exception rather than the rule. In a two-year study of business leadership development involving 400 executives in a wide range of organizations, we found instances where leadership development had a confused and often short-term strategic focus, the methodologies used were of questionable relevance to business needs and lacked any real personal or business impact. We concluded that achieving an integration of leadership development with business strategy is problematic, despite the wide choice of methods available to human resource (HR) and development professionals. Others, too, have noted a gap between the theory and reality of leadership development. As one leading author in the field comments, 'we know very little about the processes in leadership and management training that contribute to organizational performance' (Fiedler 1996: 244). This gap between the theory and practice of leadership development marks our starting point in this chapter.

We present findings from our recent research, which specifically investigates innovative practice in business leadership development (Butcher *et al.* 2002). We of course recognize that as organizations embrace a logic of self-organization (Galunic and Eisenhardt 2002) in an effort to deal with increasing uncertainty and complexity, the opportunity for managers to exert strategic influence in many different organizational arenas is now a reality (Wall and Wall 1995), and therefore that the idea of 'leadership at all levels' is becoming an organizational necessity (Tichy and Cohen 1997). However, for the purposes of investigating the critical alignment between leadership development and business performance we have focused on the development of leadership for those roles that reflect general management content and which have the greatest potential to impact directly on business strategy. We reasoned that this would enable us most readily to examine the relationship between organizational performance and leadership whilst also permitting a consideration of how these findings may be generalizable to the wider practice of leadership development.

Through the chapter we explore the gap between the theory and practice of business leadership development. We look at how this can be overcome in order that organizations can make informed choices about development methods and create more strategically aligned leadership development processes. Our findings have significant implications for both senior executives and HR/development professionals, and we offer specific recommendations on how they can make a much greater contribution to business success by realizing the strategic potential of leadership development.

The problem

Much helpful advice is available to HR/development professionals seeking to review and improve leadership development in their organization. This typically emphasizes the importance of strategic alignment, gaining high level support, a partnership between HR and line management, the use of competence frameworks, action learning, evaluation, and a focus on succession planning and home-grown talent (Fulmer and Wagner 1999; but see also Zenger *et al.* 2000; Cacioppe 1998; Fulmer *et al.* 2000). However, some research findings and much anecdotal evidence suggest that this is much easier said than done and that organizations often struggle to implement these principles successfully. What, then, explains this gap between the espoused theory of leadership impact and the realities of leadership development delivery? The literature on organizational leadership and its development offers three particular reasons, which are outlined below.

Confusion about the nature of leadership and its distinction from management

As is pointed out in other chapters within this book, reviews of leadership theory over the past two decades demonstrate that there is little agreement about the nature or role of leadership, and even its definition (Barker 1997). Wide conceptual differences exist encompassing a broad church of untested assumptions about the relationship between strategic leadership, leadership development and business performance. The same may be said about the distinctions between business leadership, supervisory leadership and management (House and Aditya 1997). Given the plethora of research and published material in the field of leadership, it is remarkable how little conceptual convergence is to be found (see Lowe and Gardner 2001 for a helpful example of the current breadth of leadership research). On these grounds alone a gap between the rhetoric of business leadership and effective leader development can be expected. If there is not yet a coherent theory of leadership and its significance for business performance there is unlikely to be an understanding of how to develop business leaders effectively (Barker 1997).

Poor development evaluation

Surveys repeatedly report inadequate assessment of development activities (Axel 1999; CEML 2001). Lack of clear objectives and the difficulty of establishing quantifiable results have been cited as significant reasons for this shortfall (Cairns 1997). If the level of evaluation is inadequate how can we be sure which methods are really making a difference to business performance? For example, Zenger *et al.* (2000) suggest that public or open programmes tend to have little impact on leaders' ability to produce better results. However, in an Institute of Management Development (IMD) study (Cairns 1997), only 27 per cent of organizations evaluated open programmes and half of those evaluations focused on immediate post-programme effects. Only 6 per cent evaluated programme effectiveness one year later. Tailored in-company programmes faired little better in this regard: only 18 per cent of organizations assessed their impact one year after the event. These kinds of studies draw attention to the questionable application of evaluation criteria, with the inevitability of inappropriate evaluation processes leading to unusable results. They also question the basis on which decisions about different methodologies are made.

Concerns over HR/development capability

The ability of an organization to establish clear linkages between its business strategy, leadership development and the appropriateness of different methodologies will be in part dependent on the quality of the HR and management development professionals working in the area. Meldrum and Atkinson's (1998) study of the effectiveness of management development activity found that only 35 per cent of line managers surveyed believed that management development managers added significant value to their organization. In particular, management was critical of the ability of HR and development professionals to act as effective role models, to influence the business and to take a strategic overview. Likewise, Mole's (1996) training and development industry review criticized the quality of such professionals, and their bias towards efficiency rather than inno-

vation. Thomson *et al.*'s Institute of Management study of over 900 organizations also supported this view:

> there was not a great deal of evidence of deep thinking about management
> development, either in terms of learning processes or in respect of an oper-
> ational model or in how to link it to organizational strategies. Indeed, from
> our case studies we got the feeling that management development is lagging
> behind and derived from change rather than helping to shape it.
>
> (Thomson *et al.* 1997: 78)

Exploring the problem

These issues illustrate the difficulty practitioners can face in attempting to establish a strategically oriented approach to leadership development. Our own
research of business leadership development (BLD) strategy and practice was
designed to create greater understanding of why such difficulty arises, so as to
bridge the gap between development activity and business outcomes.

The theoretical assumptions implicit in the literature that underpin the
importance of the strategic alignment of BLD can be thought of as a virtuous
cycle of development (see Figure 14.1). Business strategy implies leadership
requirements, which in turn imply activities to deliver enhanced leadership capability. Resultant improved leadership capability is assumed to make a measurable
difference, both to current business performance and to future strategic position.
Our research explored the extent to which the theoretical linkages exist in practice between business strategy, future business requirements, BLD strategy and
BLD practice.

In order to understand the organizational complexities associated with the
gap between BLD and business outcomes, we explored the virtuous development
cycle by soliciting views from four distinct managerial roles: senior business
managers, managers who had been recipients of BLD, senior HR/development
professionals responsible for BLD, and management development practitioners
responsible for implementation.

Two broad messages emerged from this. First, and generally consistent with
theoretical assertions (Fulmer and Wagner 1999), the data revealed widespread
consensus about the business leadership capabilities required by organizations in
the future. We summarized these capabilities as 'future oriented' leadership
behaviours (see Table 14.1).

Second, and more importantly, it was clear from our research that many organizations are struggling to develop and benefit from these behaviours in practice.
More often than not, BLD appears to be an unfocused and diffuse activity.
Respondents found it difficult to differentiate between BLD and other types of
management development, and to distinguish between the needs of different
populations. Less than half believed their organization to have a strategy for
BLD, and even when strategies were perceived to exist the quality and clarity was
highly variable. There was in consequence little perceived linkage between BLD

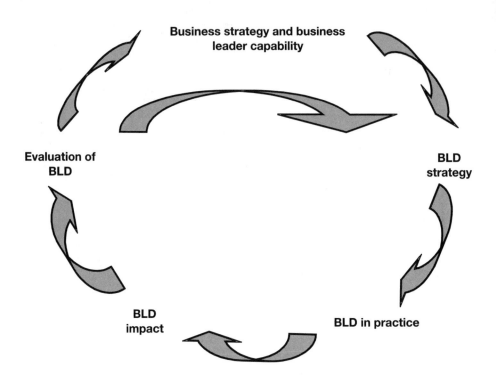

Figure 14.1 The virtuous development cycle

Note:
BLD   Business leadership development

Table 14.1: The transition to 'future oriented' leadership

Less	More
Problem-solving	Innovating in networks/partnerships/market
	Handling ambiguity
	Lateral thinking
	Anticipating the future
Complacent	Asking difficult questions
	Risk-taking
	Entrepreneurial
	Willing to exceed organizational boundaries
Defensive	Confident
Narrow	Open, demonstrating people are key
	Listening, involving, participative
Managing output/utilization	Managing the how
	Longer-term approach
	Acclimatizing people to change
	Building trust

and the business. Less than 1 per cent of respondents could identify any bottom-line impact, and 54 per cent reported no measured business impact. In such circumstances it is unsurprising that organizations struggle to identify the most appropriate and effective BLD methods.

In seeking to understand this lack of coherence we found four complementary explanations. First, it appeared that BLD strategy is often derived without sufficient reference to business needs. Notably, this disconnection seemed more likely when BLD took best HR/management development or industry practice rather than medium- and long-term business needs as its reference point. Second, there was often no business value or binding clarity guiding the design and implementation of BLD. In the absence of senior management vision for BLD, the process of management development itself often provided its own *raison d'être*, without consideration of business needs. For example, BLD was frequently simply seen as an output of appraisal activity or an input for succession planning. Third, the overall approach to BLD was often subject to a range of competing political agendas that prevented a more coherent strategy developing. Finally, in line with previous research, BLD strategy formulation, communication and implementation were often perceived to be poor. There was frequently a lack of understanding within HR about how their activities connected to business strategy and about which BLD activities were appropriate for different management groupings.

Although each explanation may have an impact in its own right, of greater significance is the organizational Catch-22 that arises when they combine to block successful development and to create an 'unvirtuous circle'. For example, the ability of HR/development managers to promote greater coherence for BLD can be constrained by their lack of understanding of its business relevance. This may then be compounded by a lack of understanding by senior management of the potential business contribution of BLD, resulting in an inability to evaluate effectively the case being put by HR. Thus, far from reflecting a virtuous circle, the influences on BLD practice combine to create a negative 'unvirtuous' circle. This finding suggests that trying to break the negative cycle by attending only to one component explanation, such as improving the quality of the HR input, is unlikely to be effective. Moving beyond this stalemate requires that positive linkages be made between business strategy, BLD strategy and executive development methodologies.

With this in mind, our research also addressed, through an executive survey and detailed case analysis, practical questions about the way BLD is used in organizations in order to discover how businesses can successfully create these positive linkages (see Figure 14.2).

Survey results

Three significant themes emerged from this analysis: a marked lack of understanding of the value of BLD at executive level, the poorly discriminated focus of BLD, and HR thinking that is often at odds with the business. We next consider how these themes hold the key to creating strategically aligned BLD.

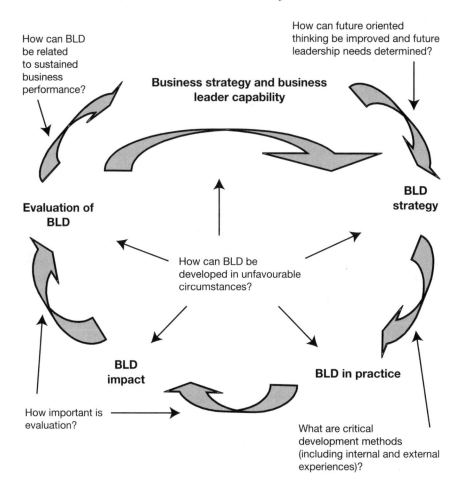

Figure 14.2 Questions to create a virtuous development cycle

The real value and processes of BLD are poorly understood at executive level

Confused and contradictory senior management thinking appeared throughout the survey. For example, even though the ability to develop strategic future oriented thinking in business leaders was largely unquestioned, 70 per cent of executives believed their organizational stock of future oriented leaders to be unsatisfactory, and 72 per cent perceived the organizational processes for developing future oriented thinking to be inadequate. Similarly, contradictions surfaced in the area of development methods. On the one hand, 41 per cent of executives expressed the view that the most effective way to develop future oriented leadership capabilities was by bringing together external and diverse views on the business to challenge conventional thinking. Yet when asked about the single most effective method for developing business leaders, nearly half of the executives believed direct personal experience or structured on-the-job development to be most important, even though these methods are more likely to replicate existing thinking than develop future perspective.

The lack of clarity at executive levels was also reflected in their observations about how best to evaluate the impact of BLD. Responses varied enormously, frequently confusing levels of analysis (the individual or the business) whilst failing to agree on which measures should be applied to specific BLD methods. This further reinforces the impression that executives are often uncertain about the relationship between the evaluation of BLD and its value.

Given that BLD is often attempted where either investment and/or organizational support are lacking, we also asked for views about what methods work best in such circumstances. Tellingly, few could even answer the question. In contrast, case studies of individual innovators in BLD indicated that creating the organizational capabilities required for the future in such circumstances required more challenging and politically astute approaches. In particular, the case studies demonstrated the importance of a number of personal capabilities characteristic of individuals successfully implementing BLD in difficult circumstances. They include the ability to manage relationships up, down and across the organization; being able to read competing agendas and design development initiatives with these interests in mind; being prepared to challenge the status quo; and having a personal confidence that they could make a difference.

Despite these tensions and contradictions, executives in the survey believed they were investing in BLD at or above the industry average. The conclusion is therefore difficult to avoid: BLD could be of much greater organizational value if senior executives had real clarity about its role and contribution.

Poorly discriminated BLD focus

We found that many organizations failed to make critical distinctions about two key elements of BLD strategy – the target population and the development content. Identifying target populations raises politically sensitive questions about whether BLD should be inclusive of all managers or targeted at individuals. The problem of BLD content raises difficult decisions about the balance of needs for individualized or corporately consistent subject matter. These differentiating factors reflected the poor quality thinking we found about BLD in many HR departments, and, not surprisingly, they significantly contribute to the confusion over different BLD strategies. For example, should a BLD strategy focus on developing a small cadre of high potential managers with an individualized curriculum, or on raising the quality of all managers using a consistent development content? Pursuing this in the executive survey, we found that lack of clarity was exacerbated by two factors – the distinctions between a short- or long-term BLD focus and the value attached to internal versus external knowledge in development activities. These help to explain some of the contradictory views identified above.

In essence, many organizations prioritized short-term development activities for business leaders at the expense of longer-term and wider strategic thinking. This was characterized by linking BLD to short/medium-term business goals and favouring internal business projects and on-the-job training as development activities. This bias is clearly evident when the perceived value and use of different development methodologies are compared, as detailed in Table 14.2.

Table 14.2 Value and use of BLD methodologies

Method	Respondents who rated the method of high value (%)	Respondents who rated the method as being frequently used (%)
Internal coaching/mentoring	69	45
External coaching/mentoring	71	25
Internal business projects	73	47
External business projects	46	13
Observation of business leaders	44	15
Business school development programme	57	27
In-company development programmes	53	45

Internal development programmes are used twice as often as external ones, internal coaching nearly twice as often as external, and internal projects over three times as often as external ones. A comparison of the perceived advantages of internally and externally focused development activities demonstrates their unique and differential value (see Table 14.3).

Internal development methodologies are valued for relevance, immediacy of implementation and their focus on building and using internal knowledge. In contrast, external experiences are valued for generating new ideas (see Zenger *et al.* 2000), a different perspective, and wider and more rigorous thinking – all considered by the survey participants to be key aspects of future oriented thinking. This may explain why, contrary to contemporary trends in best practice advice, external programmes were seen by executives in our initial survey to be nearly three times more likely than internal programmes to have business impact. External development experiences appear to encourage the breadth of perspective essential to future oriented business leadership. Whilst internal approaches undoubtedly deliver immediate business value, there is clearly a danger that overemphasis on internally focused development will divert attention away from activities that can promote more innovative strategic thinking. It also encourages business leaders to approach business strategy with a short-term mindset and perpetuates a short-term development focus.

Table 14.3 Comparison of the advantages of internal and external development experiences

Broad responses	External experiences — Specific responses	%	Internal experiences — Specific responses	%
Relating to the learning environment	e.g. 'objective view without company's influence', 'mistakes can be made without real-life costs'	11	e.g. 'to act in a known surrounding while trying new things', 'commonality of issues/goals'	11
Relating to the opportunities/ possibilities it offers	*Total:* *Networking:* e.g. 'to build an external network', 'the relationships which are established with other leaders' *Benchmarking:* e.g. 'comparing different styles', 'benchmarking, implementation and acceptance of world's best practices' *Shared strategic/leadership forum:* e.g. 'exchange with executives from other companies/industries', 'sharing of ideas, thus getting a better understanding of the "global" marketplace' *Gaining external/wider perspective:* e.g. 'variety of different approaches, experience and views', 'objectivity – getting a look at the business from the outside'	27	*Total:* *Relevance (to sector, business and individual needs):* e.g. 'tailored to meet specific goals', 'relates directly to the business' *Developing shared knowledge or culture:* e.g. 'common language developed', 'strengthening corporate values' *Specific business issue focus and application:* e.g. 'focus on company strategies/goals – internal support networks', 'more focus on the business' *Internal networking:* e.g. 'cultural knowledge/political networking', 'extending the mutual support network', 'teamwork' *Transferability/application:* e.g. 'ability to relate development to real-life business issues', 'can be transferred directly into own practice'	56
Relating to the input within these experiences	*Total:* *Academic perspectives (frameworks/expertise/ challenging/rigour):* e.g. 'specialists' expertise', 'wide view of concepts', 'unbiased perspectives' *New ideas:* e.g. 'different perspectives', 'input from other people with different mindsets' *Providing external view (benchmarking/ wider/different perspective):* e.g. 'exposure to intelligence outside usual sphere of operation', 'wide angle to business solutions'	40	*Total:* e.g. 'specific business knowledge', 'exposure to different aspects of leadership and management', 'a framework for building evaluating strategies'	9

Table 14.3 continued

Broad responses	External experiences			Internal experiences	
	Specific responses	*%*		*Specific responses*	*%*
Relating to personal capability outcomes (clarity, breadth and depth of thinking)	*Total:* e.g. 'independent thoughts, broader range of specific knowledge', 'skill development', 'different thinking in a wider context', 'creates objective judgement'	13		*Total:* e.g. 'building on internal leadership strength', 'improving performance', 'learn and grow from within the company and its goals and mission'	8
Other/don't know/missing data		9			16

Distinguishing between the value of internal and external knowledge, short-term and long-term development, between tailored or corporately consistent content, and targeted or inclusive populations offers the basis for creating greater clarity as to the real business value of BLD. These distinctions, whether made by HR/development professionals or well informed senior line management, enable greater alignment between development activity and business needs and provide the basis for a more thorough analysis of appropriate methodologies and evaluation criteria.

HR thinking is sometimes at odds with the business

We found that HR/development professionals significantly influence perceptions and practices of BLD, but that there was often a divergence of thinking between these professionals and senior executives, with their perspective on strategic relevance, as well as with line managers, with their perspective on operational relevance. The nature and potential impact of this divergence surfaced in the second phase findings. It was evident in the perceived link between BLD and business performance, where only 48 per cent of HR/development respondents saw a direct link, in contrast to 67 per cent of senior line managers. These groups also differed in how they valued specific BLD methodologies: 94 per cent of HR/development professionals rated internal business projects of high value, in comparison to only 67 per cent of executives, whilst only 42 per cent of HR/development professionals viewed business school programmes of value, in contrast to 64 per cent of senior managers. Without reliable evaluation, what explains the difference between the HR and the business view? Moreover, does this difference influence what happens in practice?

Given the perceived value of external experiences in developing new ideas and wider and more rigorous thinking, the evident preference of HR/development professionals for internally focused activity clearly has significant consequences for the design and execution of effective BLD. Our survey showed internal projects to be one of the most frequently used methodologies, and business school programmes to be one of the least used (see Table 14.2). Given the critical role of HR thinking in BLD strategy and implementation, if it is at odds with the business this would suggest that there is considerable scope for enhancing BLD relevance and impact by addressing this difference.

These findings have led us to develop a number of new ideas for reinforcing a virtuous circle in BLD, and in doing so to ensure alignment between business strategy, BLD strategy, methods and evaluation. We now explore these ideas in detail.

Achieving strategic alignment

The extent to which BLD is contested terrain was very evident in our four explanations for the disconnected and fragmented nature of BLD. For example, we found line management pursuing different leadership development approaches in order to retain local autonomy, and HR developing strategies guided by received HR best practice without sufficient consideration of business needs. In the executive survey and detailed case studies this political influence was again a substantive theme. Difference in perspectives continued to surface between line managers and HR/development professionals. Indeed, in the case studies an exploitation of such differences was central to the success of each manager's initiative.

Burgoyne and Jackson (1997) have postulated that the effectiveness of management learning in organizations has often been curtailed by a preoccupation with unitary values and processes. This unitary perspective oversimplifies the process of management learning by excluding many of the cognitive, symbolic and political aspects of management development activity. This has led to a situation where too many management development initiatives have failed to make an impact because they have focused on an idealized notion of what should be happening rather than factoring in the complexities of the people involved (*ibid.*). Rather than ignore the plurality of interests at work in the BLD arena, the following ideas deliberately embrace and expose some of these differences by forcing distinctions between different interests, needs and perspectives.

In particular, these differences in need and perspective highlight the importance of temporal distinctions in approaching BLD. As our research has highlighted, there is a tendency by senior management and HR/development professionals to give too much attention to the short-term twists and turns of business strategy as a key determinant of leadership development activity. Accordingly, the majority of the ideas we present here implicitly reflect the need to gain clarity about how best to achieve fit between the need for long- and short-term impact in the design and execution of BLD. We argue therefore that explicit recognition of different development populations, different sponsors, interest groups and strategic timeframes will form the basis for a more informed discussion about strategic alignment of BLD.

A discriminating approach to BLD strategy

There is of course no substitute for a close alignment between BLD activities and business strategy, but phase one demonstrated that this is difficult to achieve in practice. If BLD is not well understood as a process of improving business performance, many of the approaches used to create alignment will be crude and ineffective. In order for organizations to align BLD with business strategy, a much greater level of discrimination is required to differentiate between the use and value of different types of development. We suggest that executives can achieve this by forcing linkages between two sets of variables:

- the population to be developed – targeted or inclusive;
- the content of the development activities – tailored or corporately consistent.

Making these two distinctions creates four different strategic approaches to BLD (see Figure 14.3). The four distinguishable approaches and the form they take can be described as follows:

- *HiPo tailored*: highly targeted/individualized provision – a structured approach to BLD driven by the need for succession planning that targets high potential managers through talent spotting groups and nurtures individual development through very tailored activities;
- *HiPo programme*: highly targeted/corporately consistent provision – an approach in which groups of managers are identified and proceed through a series of planned and consistent HiPo activities driven by future corporate business needs;

Who? ⟍ What?	Targeted individuals	Inclusive
Individualized content	HiPo tailored	Self-motivated
Corporate consistency	HiPo programme	Generic programmes

Figure 14.3 BLD strategy framework

- *self-motivated*: inclusive/individualized provision – an approach with no prescribed methods or content, where the development opportunity is open to all but driven by individual motivation and skill in directing and managing their development for themselves;
- *generic programme:* – inclusive/corporately consistent provision of corporate-wide programmes – an approach driven by the widespread need to improve specific organization capabilities, often cascaded down through different levels of management and available to all.

These approaches represent different strategies that are not mutually exclusive. Indeed, in our case organizations we found evidence of all four in use in the same organization at different levels or in different divisions. But having clarity about the differences between these strategies and their appropriateness for different business circumstances can form the basis for challenging existing approaches and developing future BLD strategy. We would argue that, given the diversity and complexity of organizational forms today, those responsible for executive development should seek to establish a range of different BLD strategies so as to achieve alignment with differing business needs. The following questions are designed to facilitate this analysis:

- Is it clear where the business's current BLD development strategy sits in this framework?
- Is it clear which business needs and conditions support that position?
- Can a real payback to the business be demonstrated?
- Which set of factors (corporate consistency, individualization, targeting, inclusion) is most important for meeting current/future business needs?
- Do different business units/activities/levels/management populations require different approaches?
- How well are these approaches communicated to the different management populations so that they understand how their different needs are being managed?
- How will changes to the business influence the future positioning of its approach in this framework?

A discriminating approach to BLD methodologies

Having determined the most appropriate range of strategies for BLD in relation to an organization's business context, further alignment can be achieved by addressing the tension between current needs and future needs and between the valued but different benefits of acquiring internal and external ideas. This means differentiating between the following:

- the focus for the development – long-term versus short-term impact;
- the relative priority in acquiring internal and external organizational knowledge.

Forcing these two sets of distinctions enables those responsible for BLD to question the assumptions on which different BLD methodologies are selected. For example, if the business need is to develop a cadre of leaders capable of shaping future strategy and stimulating long-term, continuous innovation, executives would be advised to prioritize activities that equip their leaders with new ideas and the ability to challenge and take a broader/wider perspective. These requirements reflect a high degree of external organizational knowledge and are likely to be most effectively delivered through business school programmes, external coaching and external projects. Given the degree of personal development inherent in such change, this indicates the need for a HiPo tailored strategy that is based on individual needs. In contrast, if the business need is to align leadership behaviours to a consistent set of practices with a focus on strategic implementation, a priority toward a generic, corporately consistent approach with an emphasis on acquiring internal knowledge may be more appropriate. Within this strategy, in-company programmes, internal projects and mentors may be most appropriate.

Our research demonstrates, on the one hand, a preference for strategies and methodologies that reflect short-term impact and internally generated knowledge. On the other hand, it suggests that the most effective way of developing future oriented business leadership may well be through methods that emphasize the acquisition of external knowledge and personal capability to introduce counterculture ideas. The following questions can be used to evaluate the potential of different external activities to deliver the necessary relevance, diversity of view and personal development to facilitate future oriented thinking:

- Is it clear how the experience will meet the specific BLD requirement of a particular manager?
- How well does the person responsible for the external activity assess the suitability of the potential participant?
- If there are other external participants in the process, how diverse are they in terms of industry, role and culture? How is this diversity exploited in the experience?
- What processes are to be used to provide participants with relevance and applicability to themselves, their company and industry?
- What methods are used to ensure transfer and benefits of learning to the organization?
- How are participants supported in the workplace?
- What is the level of personal development involved? How does it challenge participants' existing mindsets and identify new ways of working?
- How is this personal development integrated with the new ideas?

A discriminating approach to evaluating outcomes

A differentiated approach to BLD strategy and methodology provides the basis for a more discerning evaluation of investment in BLD. Lack of clear objectives and the difficulty of establishing quantifiable results have been cited as significant reasons for the inadequate assessment of development activities. Evaluation methods routinely used in our survey reflected the whole range of individual and organizational criteria, immediate impact and long-term outcome measures. The BLD strategy framework can enable executives to make clearer connections between business need, development method and appropriate evaluation criteria (see Figure 14.4).

For example, in the HiPo tailored quadrant, succession planning is of key significance, and therefore evaluations that focus on talent flows, the retention of high performers, tracking the job moves of executives, etc. will be of particular value. Some form of individual performance assessment will also be useful, as the process of targeting implies a notion of differential contribution, and therefore that individual performance management assessment would be appropriate.

Who? / What?	Targeted individuals	Inclusive
Individualized content	HiPo Tailored *Talent management* *Personal business impact* *Individual performance assessment*	Self-motivated *Personal behaviour outcomes* *Personal business impact*
Corporate consistency	HiPo programme *Individual performance assessment* *Hard/soft business outcomes* *Personal business impact*	Generic programmes *Hard/soft business outcomes* *Broad company measures* *Personal business outcomes*

Figure 14.4 Evaluation of outcomes using the BLD strategy framework

In contrast, generic programmes appropriately employed to encourage widespread shifts in specific leadership capabilities would more effectively be assessed against hard and soft business outcomes such as culture change and bottom-line improvements. Measures such as attitude surveys and balanced scorecard methods would therefore be most appropriate.

A discriminating approach to career development

Best practice advice emphasizes the priority that should be given to developing home-grown talent for building and exploiting business knowledge and cultural and political know-how. Evidence from our case studies supports this. There is a danger, however, that following this advice alone may encourage talent to become focused on the short term and bound by immediate business issues. As we found that the internal processes for developing future oriented thinking are considered inadequate in most companies, these capabilities need to be developed through external exposure and challenge. It is also clear that if businesses are to benefit from importing challenging ideas from others there must be a capability among the home-grown talent to tolerate and work effectively with constructive provocation.

A prime emphasis on home-grown talent therefore is clearly over-simplistic. Whilst there is some evidence of differentiation in organizations in this regard – for example leaders receiving more tailored external development the more senior they become – it is naïve in current business conditions to limit the development of future oriented thinking to those at the top of the organization. In our view, a portfolio of BLD approaches needs to be developed that ensures the development of future oriented thinking throughout a managerial career. A home-grown BLD career path designed to introduce and integrate future oriented thinking should reflect the different approaches highlighted in the BLD strategy framework and could take the following route:

- *Generic*: at the early stages of a managerial career there is a need to focus on the development of internal organizational knowledge, such as business and cultural know-how. Given the operational focus of these junior roles, development is also likely to be focused on shorter-term internal projects. However, there is also the need for these managers to take risks, work in partnerships and to take a longer-term approach and so it's important that development at this stage does not become exclusively inwardly oriented.
- *HiPo programme*: as individuals are identified as high potential managers they are likely to require more targeted development in anticipation of corporate capabilities they will need in future roles. In particular, managers should be provided with a high degree of personal development in order that they acquire higher levels of personal awareness and an external business perspective, allowing them to enhance their visibility and credibility in the business.

- *HiPo tailored*: at senior levels development needs are likely to be more unique, and provision should be made for individuals to have access to a range of development methodologies. The focus here should be on long-term focused external provision and future oriented thinking.
- *Self-motivated*: at the most senior levels (but not exclusively so) executives control their own development. At this stage it is likely that all BLD would be focused on external knowledge and strategic leadership exclusively generated from external activities. So as to stimulate and support development capability, these should contain high degrees of personal challenge.

Using the strategy framework in this way leads to a greater level of alignment between long-term individual development and long-term development of strategic capability in the business.

A critical evaluation of the HR role

Our research identified many significant disconnections between the agenda and practices of HR/development professionals and line managers. Where strategic alignment is at issue these differences cannot be ignored. Those executives with a real commitment to creating a virtuous circle for BLD need to take a more critical stance on the approach of HR/development professionals to BLD. If these professionals are too entrenched in a mindset driven by 'best practice' conventions rather than specific business needs, executives will be better advised to take more direct responsibility for BLD.

If HR/development professionals are to avoid frequent criticism from line management of irrelevant BLD processes, much greater effort is required to gain clarity about business needs and their own role in meeting these. This will be even more important as organizations continue to fragment and business needs increasingly reflect different constituencies and stakeholders. Because of this, we consider that HR/development professionals need to invest much greater time and effort in critically reappraising their own values and approaches, and in communicating their role and the rationale for the diversity of BLD activity.

Developing a BLD capability despite the organization

The ideas explored above will enable senior management to create positive connections between different elements of the virtuous circle we have described and to facilitate a more discriminating approach to BLD strategy, methodology and evaluation. However, in the unfavourable circumstances created by political, financial and attitudinal barriers, executives and HR/development professionals need to consider approaches that are not dependent on top management support and organization-wide alignment if they are to add to the leadership capability of the business. Challenging current thinking will require political astuteness, networking and leadership in order to make a true difference, rather than relying on well accepted best practice models and safe in-company activities.

In those organizations where we found there is little gap between BLD and business strategy, business leaders appear to have initiated the development of those capabilities themselves. Thus if both HR/development professionals and line managers are to respond positively to this challenge they will need to take more risks and greater responsibility in overcoming frequent organizational inertia regarding BLD.

Conclusion

Our research deliberately focused on the role of business leadership in order to more readily identify the relationship between leadership development and business performance. Despite this distinction, implicit in this approach is a recognition of the value of leadership at all levels. As organizations become ever more fragmented and complex, there is increasing potential for managers to exert strategic influence in many different settings. To many commentators, leadership and strategy should no longer be the purview of senior management. Thus, several of the ideas we have explored here are applicable to leadership development activity in many different 'general' management development arenas, not just those of leadership at the top. They should help organizations choose their leadership development methods based on clear criteria that reflect issues of business strategy, target populations and differing development needs, rather than 'in vogue' or novel techniques. However, as our research has revealed, business leadership is characterized by particular political sensitivities and the consequences of poor strategic thinking at this level can have a significant organizational impact. For business leadership development in particular, then, they highlight the need for a more discriminating attitude, one that encourages the establishment of a virtuous circle of development, connecting business strategy with BLD strategy and processes for creating leadership for sustained business performance.

The requisite level of organizational and personal awareness needed for thinking about future strategy is hard to develop through short-term, inclusive and inwardly focused leadership development activities. In order to achieve this level of awareness, leaders' mindsets must be challenged, demanding a level of personal development inherent in highly tailored and targeted methodologies. Such methods as external coaching, projects and business school programmes are best suited to achieving this. Our research suggests that this focus requires a significant shift in current investment and thinking in BLD.

The tendency for HR/development professionals to favour an internally focused/best practice route indicates that it may be inadvisable to delegate to them this re-evaluation process. We have demonstrated that an overemphasis on internal processes of development may actively contribute to organizational disadvantage by encouraging an inward and introspective view that is not compatible with today's business environment. Senior management with a genuine commitment to BLD may therefore need to take a more questioning stance to their HR function's approach to this vital input to the business.

In turn, HR professionals need to be able to show that they are taking a business rather than HR view of their organization. Our data suggests that this will often mean being prepared to question traditional assumptions about HR best practice. This will include taking a critical view of the value and limitations of internal and external development activities in order that both may be deployed to strategic advantage. It will involve challenging uncritical inclusion at the expense of targeted impact and investment, and will require differentiated thinking about where organizational consistency is important, and, equally, where BLD diversity is important.

By far the most significant finding from the research reported here is that BLD is not recognized in any real or practical sense as a primary means of improving business performance. It is not well understood either by senior executives or HR/development professionals. It is conceptually confused, often disconnected from the business, and subject to professional HR dogma that can actively disadvantage future business competitiveness. Despite this situation the contribution of leadership to business success is widely assumed, and consequently considerable investment is made into BLD. The highest priority for senior executives must therefore be to consider this area of business activity with renewed vigour if damaging conventions of BLD are to be avoided and real strategic value is to be derived from business leader development.

References

Axel, H. (1999) 'Developing Leaders', *HR Executive Review*, Conference Board, 7(1).

Barker, R. (1997) 'How can we train leaders if we do not know what leadership is?', *Human Relations* 50(4): 343–62.

Burgoyne, M. and B. Jackson (1997) 'The arena thesis: management development as a pluralistic meeting point', in M. Burgoyne and M. Reynolds (eds) *Management Learning*, London: Sage.

Butcher, D., C. Bailey, M. Clarke and J. Burr (2002) *Business Leader and General Management Development, Creating Future Innovative Practice, Phase Two Report*, Research Report, Cranfield School of Management.

Cacioppe, R. (1998) 'An integrated model and approach for the design of effective leadership development programs', *Leadership and Organization Development Journal*, January–February, 19: 44–54.

Cairns, H. (1997) 'Study of current practice in assessing the impact of management development in international organizations', paper presented to the UNICON Conference, Creating the Future of International Executive Development Together: A Visioning Process, Lausanne, 2–5 April.

CEML (2001) *Meeting the Need*, a consultation paper, Piccadilly, London: Council for Excellence in Management and Leadership.

Crainer, S. and D. Dearlove (1999) *Gravy Training: Inside the Business of Business Schools*, San Francisco: Jossey-Bass.

Fiedler, F. (1996) 'Research on leadership selection and training: one view of the future', *Administrative Science Quarterly*, June, 41(2): 241–51.

Fulmer, R. (1997) 'The evolving paradigm of leadership development', *Organizational Dynamics*, spring, 25(4): 59–73.

Fulmer, R. and S. Wagner (1999) 'Leadership: lessons from the best', *Training and Development* 53(3): 28–33.

Fulmer, R., P. Gibbs and M. Goldsmith (2000) 'Developing leaders: how winning companies keep on winning', *Sloan Management Review* 2(1): 49–59.

Galunic, D. and K. Eisenhardt (2001) 'Architectural innovation and modular corporate forms', *Academy of Management Journal* 44(6): 1,229–49.

House, R. and R. Aditya (1997) 'The social scientific study of leadership: quo vadis?', *Journal of Management* 23(3): 409–73.

Lowe, K. and W. Gardner (2001) 'Ten years of the *Leadership Quarterly*: contributions and challenges for the future', *Leadership Quarterly* 11(4): 459–514.

Meldrum, M. and S. Atkinson (1998) 'Is management development fulfilling its organizational role?', *Management Decision* 36(8): 528–32.

Mole, G. (1996) 'The management training industry in the UK: a HRD director's critique', *Human Resources Management Journal* 6(1): 19–26.

Thomson, A., J. Storey, C. Mabey, C. Gray, E. Farmer and R. Thomson (1997) *A Portrait of Management Development*, London: Institute of Management.

Tichy, N. and E. Cohen (1997) *The Leadership Engine: How Winning Companies Build Leaders at Every Level*, New York: Harper Business.

Wall, S.J. and S.R. Wall (1995) *The New Strategists, Creating Leaders at All Levels*, New York: Free Press.

Zenger, J., D. Ulrich and N. Smallwood (2000) 'The new leadership development', *Training and Development* 54(3), March: 22.

15 Linking development with business

William Tate

Introduction

Leadership development activity has traditionally concentrated on the individual. It has shown less interest in the organization, either as customer or for building into the intervention design. Little consideration has therefore tended to be given to an express link with business purpose and outcomes. Because of this, leadership development interventions have often been ill equipped to make a significant impact on business performance.

A key issue for developers and learners is 'how' to transfer learning to the workplace. This question is well recognized, though far from easy to achieve in practice. Beyond this level there are more complex philosophical and strategic issues. These 'what' and 'why' questions are less well understood, and they directly involve business leaders.

Linking with business can make development both more effective and more relevant. Whether we define 'business' as the employing company or commercial activity in general, there are clear benefits to be gained by a variety of parties, including learners, bosses, the business and its many stakeholders.

While the benefits of stronger linkages will become apparent, paradoxically there are times when a loose connection can work best for the employer. There is also the important matter of what status development gives to the personal needs and aspirations of the individual manager. Where does it leave the case for developing human potential independently of the employer's goals? Indeed, the whole subject is actually quite a minefield. Finding technical design and support mechanisms to embed learning is just one aspect.

To focus development's purpose and conduct appropriately on business from these multiple perspectives requires a new mental framework. The chapter does the following:

- addresses the conceptual and strategic issues;
- challenges conventional assumptions about development's role and performance;
- explores a range of tactical devices and mechanisms;

- examines what some leading companies are doing and the motivation for their choices;
- offers suggestions about what more can be done.

It ends with an overview of the macro business scene and implications for organizations and leadership development.

The strategic challenge

Putting strategy ahead of training

Linking development with business can be approached both top down and bottom up. The former requires business leaders to take an informed view about how development activities can more directly serve business aims, address organization weaknesses, and help take advantages of opportunities and respond to threats. Bottom-up approaches consist of initiatives that developers themselves can take to make their current efforts have a greater impact on the business.

Together these make development a strategic activity before it is a training activity. Questions about purpose and stakeholders precede questions about methods. Development activities become a means to an end. The vital question for developers and business leaders alike becomes 'who and what is development in service of?'

The need to ask this question appears not to be self-evident. Development's unfulfilled potential to serve business needs has long been recognized. Rainbird's study concluded that neither 'the integration of the training function into other policy areas, nor the integration of employees through their involvement in training programmes, has occurred to any great extent' (1994: 87). Research by Ezzamel *et al.* showed that the 'integration of HRM [human resource management] and business strategy was the exception' (1996: 76). More recently, research undertaken by the Chartered Institute of Personnel and Development (CIPD) found that 'many organizations are putting their performance at risk because management development itself continues to be a victim of poor management practice, disconnected from the imperatives and challenges of the enterprise' (Court *et al.* 2002: ix).

Developing the organization and the business

Developers may see potential for linking their activities with the organization more than with the business. The latter consists of variables that are mainly outwardly focused, i.e. customers, markets, brands, prices, products, competition, etc. The organization, on the other hand, is the set of internal arrangements that enable a soundly conceived business to succeed in practice. Among the many organization variables are its structure, culture, systems, relationships, rules – and leadership (Tate 2003). This places the organization at the service of the business. Development can directly impact both sets of variables. In practice, it usually seeks to improve the way the organization works (via individual managers). Its impact on the business is usually indirect.

The terms 'the business' and 'the organization' are commonly used without such nice distinctions in mind. For the most part they are regarded as synonymous with *company*, *institution* and *enterprise*. Much of the time such loose usage doesn't matter. However, there are times when it is important to use the words distinctively.

One important lesson for developers is not to expect an *organization* intervention to rescue a company or an industry that is flawed in its fundamental *business*. The pensions mis-selling scandal of the 1990s was an industry-wide problem. It represented a collective failure of leadership to address political, competitive and ethical issues. Yet company leaders blamed their employees and poor training, and they launched wholesale retraining in the hope of winning round public opinion.

That is not to say that development should be constrained. Beyond helping a given employer achieve the organization's aims lies the role of business in society and the sustainable development agenda. In particular, there is a proactive role for leadership development to address these bigger issues about safeguarding tomorrow and promoting a more socially, ethically and environmentally aware agenda (Sadler 1999).

What or who is the target?

There are four possible levels for development interventions:

* individuals
* collective groups
* organization
* business.

For a variety of conceptual, political and practical reasons, developers traditionally spend most time on level 1. But it is at the other levels where development can have most impact on the employer's agenda. Some don't distinguish between collective development at level 2 and systemic development at level 3 (not helped by the possibility that the latter might, *inter alia*, entail the development of a group).

Individual-centred development is appropriate if, say, managers are not in employment or want to improve their marketability irrespective of who they work for. In such cases the individual, and not the business, is the legitimate concern of developers. But most development is sponsored by organizations, with the prime purpose of benefiting the employer. Even if the employer's motivation is to improve the individual's performance in order thereby to benefit the organization, this will only happen if the organization contributes context, concerns and content to the development process's planning and design.

If the development process is undertaken at arm's length from the organization's needs and realities, and concentrates on individuals' characteristics, qualities, capabilities and competences, there will be less impact on the organization. This typically happens when the organization is the sponsor but is willing to settle for individual-centred development, especially generic in design. The problem is exacerbated where there is no awareness of the possibility of the organization doing some work on itself; organizations too have their own shortcomings and development needs. Whatever the effectiveness of education and training in developing individual managers and leaders, in practice it will fall well short of improving the practice of effective leadership and management *in*, *of* and *by* organizations.

In terms of the inputs–outputs–outcomes continuum, conventional development primarily concentrates its expertise on the efficacy of the inputs. But if potential is to be realized, it requires two further ingredients: *will* and *opportunity*. 'Performance is potential minus interference' (Gallwey 2000: 17); this refers to personal psychological obstacles. But we can extend Gallwey's concept to the organizational level (see Figure 15.1). Most development activity enhances potential but does nothing about interference from above or below. There is a strong case for the management of obstacles being part of a new mindset.

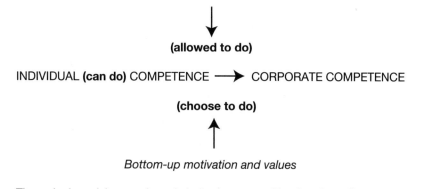

Top-down organization facilitation

Through a purposeful context and problems to solve, a supportive framework, an absence of needless restrictions and boundaries, a lack of obstacles to performance, appropriate checks and balances, etc.

↓

(allowed to do)

INDIVIDUAL **(can do)** COMPETENCE ⟶ CORPORATE COMPETENCE

(choose to do)

↑

Bottom-up motivation and values

Through clear vision, goals and challenges, a positive fear-free climate, constructive feedback, relevant job–person matches, fair recognition and rewards, etc.

Figure 15.1 Converting individual competence into corporate competence

The affected parties

Who is the challenge directed at? Whose behaviour needs to change? Who benefits? Linking development more strongly with business has implications for a range of human resource (HR) professionals and disciplines beyond those directly engaged in delivering leadership development and training. It affects the role of business leaders who have responsibility for overseeing development. It impacts upon the developers' customers and the company's customers. It holds implications for other potential beneficiaries beyond the traditional boundaries of the enterprise.

More controversially, the matters raised are arguably too important to be left to developers alone to supply the answers or to deliver improved development methods that better serve business ends. By definition the issues strike at the heart of how to make leadership *better in practice*. This goal reaches beyond how best to *develop* leaders' *capability*; it is also concerned with the avoidance of wasted potential. It is largely because developed ability frequently remains unrealized in practice that we need the discussion contained in this chapter.

Changing the mindset

Challenging assumptions

Development activity appears so self-evidently worth business investment that it can become immune from serious criticism. Yet development has traditionally been built on unquestioned and unproven assumptions that continue to constrain its relevance and effectiveness, for example the assumptions that:

* leadership is the sum of what individual leaders do;
* concerns about the quality of leadership are best addressed by developing individuals;
* development of the organization results from, and is best pursued via, personal development activities;
* development is synonymous with improvement;
* developers can be left to set their own agenda;
* development first means training;
* the training industry can provide most of the solutions;
* increased spending on development will result in better leadership.

The upshot is that the chief executive officer who is concerned about leadership typically assumes that the solution lies with development. But the connection between problem and solution is tenuous. The quality of leadership and management in companies and in Britain plc leaves much room for improvement (Storey and Tate 2000). Numerous enquiries by professional institutes and the government continue to reveal poor leadership and management skills in managers and companies. Despite increasing volumes of management training (Storey *et al.* 1997), under the present set of assumptions the quality of leadership and management in business is unlikely to improve significantly however much is spent on development (Clarke 1999).

The route to business improvement

The goal behind improving development's links with business is to obtain improvement for the employing organization, for the business world in general, and for the society that is impacted by business and upon which business depends. Achieving these goals requires strategies beyond those that focus on developing the individual in isolation:

> [Self-development methods] are now sometimes perceived as all very well for personal growth, but as less functional for moving forward the organization. The same point can be found embedded in the useful distinction between manager development and management development. The former can include all manner of educational and training experiences which enhance the individual. The latter more directly impacts on the functional capability of the managerial stock as a whole, and improves the collective management performance in a manner relevant to business needs.
>
> (Storey and Tate 2000: 198)

Weaknesses in the popular model have long been understood:

> individually oriented strategies of change, such as training, are not effective in bringing about organizational change. This is due to at least three basic problems. The first relates to the age-old issue in training – transfer of learning. The simple fact that most training occurs in a location other than the individual's work space produces the problem of re-creating the training milieu and learning back on the job. Critical mass is a second problem. How many people must one train to obtain the desired impact on the organization?...A third problem relates to the social psychological principle...that individual behaviour in a group context is considerably shaped and regulated by social norms. Individual training often requires individual deviance from accepted norms....Trainers...do not understand that groups are easier to change than individuals....Training should facilitate change, not attempt to provide it.
>
> (Burke 1972: 30–4)

Katz and Khan reinforced the argument for a systems perspective:

> Attempts to change organizations by changing individuals have a long history of theoretical inadequacy and practical failure. Both stem from a disregard of the systemic properties of organizations and from the confusion of individual changes with modification in organizational variables.
>
> (Katz and Khan 1978: 658)

Aside from social norms, organization forces of politics, bureaucracy and inertia conspire against the aspirations of even the most determined individual:

> Important though it is, individual excellence is only one component of business excellence. The most skilled, committed and enthused spirits can be dampened by a negative climate and inappropriate procedures. The desired outcomes will happen only when the whole system is subject to scrutiny.
>
> (McHale 2000: 54)

If we adopt a mindset that begins with the business's need for *leadership to be practised* (rather than how individuals' abilities are developed) and then ask how we can get that business need met, we are led down a different route. There are several consequences. One is that it engenders an *improvement* process rather than a *development* process. Another is that it brings organization development into close proximity with management development (the Confederation of British Industry uses the expression 'organizational management development').

The distinction between the individual and organizational ways of conceiving of development somewhat mirrors that of strategic HRM's growth over the last 20 years from the platform of traditional personnel management. The latter is focused on the needs and problems of individual employees, while strategic HRM takes the organization as its client. Whilst companies still need employees' everyday personnel needs to be administered, the HR profession has grown to embrace a more upstream, longer-term, business-driven role. In this more strategic model, the business itself provides the yardstick by which the function's success is measured.

Holistic thinking

In setting out its terms of reference, the UK government-sponsored Council for Excellence in Management and Leadership (CEML) began its life by equating management and leadership with managers. Ostensibly about the *activity* of 'management and leadership', its stated objective was 'to ensure that the UK has the managers and leaders of the future to match the best in the world'. The CIPD research *Developing Managers for Business Performance* (Court *et al.* 2002) did much the same. To a lesser extent, so did the UK government's Performance and Innovation Unit (PIU) research into *Effective Leadership in Delivering Public Services* (2000): its brief was 'to ensure that the public sector has the leaders it needs in the future'. The brief of the Institute of Management's *Leadership: The Challenge for All* (Horne and Stedman Jones 2001) was 'to address the question of how leadership potential is best developed, and the effectiveness of particular developmental tools'.

To their credit, each of these studies (some more than others) ultimately made proposals that extended into organization dimensions, most notably the PIU. But the core of work was initially shaped by a supply-side way of thinking, which equates improvement in leadership and management in organizations with individuals' development and training. This habitual way of thinking is, unsurprisingly, especially prevalent amongst providers. Lacking sufficient access to the dynamics inside organizations (both the factors that foster and those that thwart attempts at improving and practising leadership and management), they imply that all will be well with businesses if they are fed with a sufficient flow of qualified, talented and trained individuals.

We know this is not the full story, however. Consider the acute shortage of good school headteachers. Development processes such as the Heads, Teachers and Industry (HTI) initiative are imaginative and worthwhile, but they do nothing to address (any more than does high pay) deputy heads' perceptions of the job's lack of autonomy, unbearable workload, stiff accountability, excessive bureaucracy, inherent insecurity and risk of reorganization. This example simply makes the point that a multi-pronged approach to leadership is needed, one that combines demand- and supply-side strategies. CEML's research admitted to 'the propensity to seek supply-side solutions to demand problems' but muddied this by limiting the latter to the 'need to improve demand for management and leadership development' (CEML 2002: 12). Demand-side issues consist of more than this.

A balanced approach

The familiar approach (supply-side, detached, individual development, skills) takes no account of what organizations can and should do to make full use of talent, including that which they already have. Pouring more talent in at one end is only a partial solution if it leaks out further along the pipe. The answer lies in development activity that connects with the full reality of organizations, the business's unique agenda and the expectations of society. A business-led approach redresses the dominance of supply-side strategies. It reduces reliance on development 'providers' to make good the deficit. It takes account of the dynamics of organizations. And it admits to the work that organizations can and must do on themselves.

These lessons are now being learned in the public sector. The UK government's report on *Strengthening Leadership in the Public Sector* (PIU 2001), while focused primarily on leaders and leadership development, recommended taking into account such issues as:

* supporting leaders in post;
* the climate for effective leadership;
* arrangements for getting good leaders in place;
* the retention of good leaders;
* diversity in appointing leaders;
* incentivizing current and potential leaders;
* leaders' freedom to operate;
* space allowing leaders to lead, take risks and change course;
* decision-making and planning processes;

- public recognition;
- barriers to leadership (organizational, regulatory and cultural);
- the impact of systems and targets;
- accountability;
- the effect of organizational life-cycle on types of leaders needed;
- distinctive values of the organization;
- responsible followers (to act as a check on leaders).

The Institute of Management's research too found that

> people tend to mix their perceptions of the characteristics of leadership as displayed by individuals, with the concept of leadership as a specific role in an organization process. [The latter is] an *organizational* process: the types of systems and procedures that distribute responsibility, decision-making, knowledge and power within an organization.
>
> (Horne and Stedman Jones 2001: 15)

Disentangling development

Fresh thinking about leadership and how best to improve it requires a mental separation of leadership from leaders, and also from their development. This shifts the focus onto the *activity* of leadership more than its *personification*.

Leadership is to a stage performance what development programmes are to drama school. What we value most is the whole show. A successful stage performance depends on good relationships between the individual actors, and between them and the audience, good props, good front-of-house and back-of-house support, and – crucially – a compelling script or plot (Tate 1997). The same is true of an organization. Modern-day leaders need a sympathetic system and a relevant purpose if they are to succeed in the eyes of the organization and stakeholders. They also need critical followers:

> We might consider a failure of leadership and followership in the form of Rodney Ledward, the gynaecologist from William Harvey Hospital in Ashford, Kent, who was 'able to severely maim hundreds of women patients because of a hospital culture in which consultants were treated as "gods" and junior staff were afraid of telling tales'.
>
> (PIU 2001: 4, Annexe D; based on an article in the *Guardian*, 2 June 2000)

A key proposition behind this chapter is that it is possible to develop leadership by doing things other than by developing individual leaders. As the above example shows, changing the leadership culture is one such possibility. This is not to argue against development, just to make a case for opening minds to alternative organization-enhancing approaches to improving leadership *as practised*.

According to Ludwig Wittgenstein, the linguistic philosopher, if we want to think and act differently we need to speak differently. If we limit discussion to 'development' we instinctively think about a process that does things to individuals. 'Improvement', by contrast, is a more empowering word. Improvement is an outcome. Development becomes one of several ways of bringing about improvement.

> You can improve an organization's leadership by *recruiting* better leaders. You can *reward* the best leaders to help retain them. You can even make leadership better by *retiring* tired leaders. You can *rejuvenate* the leadership culture. You can *remove obstacles* in the path of those who wish to exercise leadership. You can *hang onto* talented leaders. You can plug the *gaps* in the relationships between leaders and between functions. Most of these valuable activities would not normally qualify as 'development' or receive the attention of developers.
>
> The remit of HR Development departments usually spans training, education, appraisal, career and succession issues. Responsibility for recruitment, reward and termination falls outside this definition. If we focus all improvement efforts on 'development', we may overlook other relevant HR activity, and we may exclude other HR specialists from improvement discussions and action.
>
> (Tate 2003)

Leadership as a system resource

The suggestion of mentally separating leadership from leaders implies that there are other relevant 'vehicles'. One approach is to think of leadership as a property of organizations *per se*. The Business Excellence Model by the European Foundation for Quality Management (EFQM 2002) and the Burke–Litwin Causal Model of Organizational Performance and Change (Burke and Litwin 1992) treat leadership as a component of the system, alongside other system components (e.g. culture, mission, competence, environment, etc.). This conception turns high-quality leadership into a resource, one of an organization's prime assets. A natural consequence of such thinking is that this asset has to be managed, paradoxical as that sounds. The Institute of Management hints at this resource concept when it advises that 'understanding leadership as an organizational process is essential to understanding how it might be improved and developed' (Horne and Stedman Jones 2001: 15).

If managing leadership seems a difficult concept to accept, consider what happens when leadership is not well managed. It languishes in backwaters, goes unrecognized, is misdirected, serves self-interested goals, lacks coordination with colleagues, escapes to competitors, damages the environment, and so on. In short, a poorly managed system allows leadership energy and potential to leech away or point at the wrong things.

Although making a slightly different point about the ease with which leadership talent can be wasted, focusing on the *systemic* nature of leadership sits comfortably with the notion that organizations need to learn as systems (Pedler *et al.* 1991). James supports this: 'the learning resides in the systems and processes of the organization not just in the individual minds of its members' (James 2002: 4–5).

Making practical connections

Managing leadership along the employment spectrum

Businesses may be described as being vertically or horizontally integrated; so too may development. Discussion thus far about linking development more closely with the business assumes vertical integration, i.e. linking the individual, through the organization, to business purpose and outcomes. But scope exists for horizontal linkages too.

James's review of best practice for CEML recognizes this: 'Leadership development must link to succession planning, which involves linking assessment, development, feedback, coaching and succession planning into one integrated system aligned with the strategy' (James 2002: 19). The PIU report recommends a 'more joined-up approach to recruitment, development and promotion' (PIU 2001: 1). An integrated model seeks to establish horizontal links between development and a range of other HR interventions that together increase the chance of obtaining the desired outputs for the business (see Figure 15.2).

By contrast, organizations that lack joined-up thinking across HR activities risk:

- developing leaders at considerable expense, then letting them languish in unimportant functions where their talents cannot be used fully;

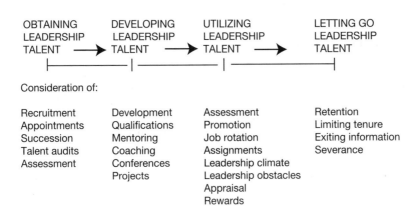

Figure 15.2 Managing leadership along the employment spectrum

- structuring the HR function in such a way that one department recruits talent while another selects people for redundancy on the cost criterion rather than ability;
- failing to act upon poor leaders when they become part of the problem rather than part of the solution;
- pouring leadership talent in at one end of the employment pipeline, and then carelessly letting it escape at the other.

An integrated approach calls for a structure, culture and licence for those with strategic HR responsibility to have access to relevant decisions affecting recruitment and selection, training and development, career and succession planning, manpower planning, reward and recognition, severance and so on. It also requires a spirit of cooperation rather than competition or a silo mentality between these specialisms.

Development-related issues arise at several places on the employment spectrum – phases in careers that call for optimal HR management. Besides having discrete development inputs at an appropriate career point, related considerations include the following:

- What leadership talent needs to enter the system?
- How can the most talented leaders be allocated to the most important jobs?
- Should newly developed leaders receive a change of job?
- What criteria are used to assess the effective practice of leadership?
- How is good leadership recognized and rewarded (and bad leadership 'punished')?
- What criteria are used to assess suitability for promotion to senior positions?
- What provision is made for successors?
- How is leadership talent escaping unplanned from, as well as formally exiting, the organization?

Line supervision of development

If developers are to link their activities more clearly to business purpose and outcomes they need to think strategically about what they do. They cannot do this in isolation. They need access to the organization's agenda – its direction, long-term plans, goals, business strategies, problems and opportunities.

One model consists of a dialogue process sponsored by the chief executive. Called *business, organization and management review*, this encourages managers to explore

> the connections between the business model(s) that will enable the enterprise to succeed in its competitive environment and the distinctive competencies that will support them. [Managers then explore] the gap between performance goals and actual performance and the required characteristics and capabilities of the organization.
>
> (Court *et al.* 2002: 20)

These authors advocate distinguishing between two agendas: sustaining the current business model and developing future business models, each holding distinctive implications for development activities.

Other than in large corporations, sophisticated planning processes like this seem quite rare. The amount of time business leaders spend with their developers may not be sufficient to build a relationship of trust and credibility from which true dialogue can emerge. Developers can find themselves pigeonholed or viewed negatively (Atkinson and Meldrum 1998). They may not be invited to business meetings, may not be expected to understand the business, to ask searching questions about it, or to know what to do with the information. Business leaders may or may not be enlightened about development's potential, and may or may not be skilled at opening up discussion and listening to developers' suggestions. Business leaders often display more *advocacy* than *enquiry* (Senge *et al.* 1994), when more of the latter is required.

In reality, both parties can be comfortable with the ringfencing that often surrounds developers' activity; this accords with many developers' self-image. For external providers this problem of isolation is exacerbated. The fashion for contracting out aspects of training and development risks widening the gap between organization problem and developer's solution.

An important context in which to foster mutual exploration is when the person with executive responsibility for the development function is appraised by the business leader to whom he or she reports. Some searching questions are shown below. They focus the mind of developers and help the business leader understand the contribution that development can make.

For business leaders who oversee development professionals

Questions to ask

- How do your strategies relate to where the company is currently, and to where it is going?
- What development are we doing which is markedly different from our competitors?
- What values and beliefs about development are driving the service you provide me with?
- What assumptions are you making about how easily off-the-job learning can be applied to the benefit of the business?
- What are you doing to migrate development activity towards actions which are most likely to realize a payoff, to the company and the individuals?

(extract from Tate 1995a)

Developing for the unknown

Whilst there is a danger that development activity is insufficiently related to the business, the opposite may also be true. There is a risk of development being too engaged with current issues and supportive of how the business is now, thereby maintaining the status quo and the current regime's interests (Hopfl and Dawes 1995). It may also rely on what is currently known about the likely future. If development activity is to realize its full contribution to the business, it needs to help learners to do the following:

*   see ways of doing things differently (which their bosses may not yet be in a position to recognize and value);
*   develop their potential as fully as possible in preparation for the unknown and unknowable (their own and the organization's).

Developers can find themselves walking a tightrope. On the one hand they risk accusation of colluding with their charges in subverting what they collectively perceive as dysfunctional behaviour and control processes in the organization (*ibid.*). On the other hand, if they accept things as they are they may insufficiently help the organization sustain itself at a higher level. Gosling and Ashton describe this dilemma:

> directors of courses find themselves in the midst of conflict…when, on the one hand, they assert a traditional professional dedication to the development of each student, but, on the other hand, reassure sponsors that their delegates will make continuing contributions to the corporation. In effect, such reassurances indicate that there will be no change in the dominant dependent relationship.
>
> (Gosling and Ashton 1994: 271)

An antidote to this lies in the relationship between developers and those to whom they are accountable. Dialogue based on a relationship of trust and embodied in a three-way learning contract (between sponsor, developer and learner) can bring out into the open and help resolve problems caused by conflicting roles, values and loyalties.

Learning contracts

Learning contracts can be helpful in achieving the goal of linking development with the business. They can clarify the balance in the developer's obligations and duty of care towards the learner *vis-à-vis* the boss. An example is shown below of the employer's side of the bargain (taken from an executive coaching-based development programme in corporate social responsibility).

Learning contract

The sponsoring organization will:

- be open to challenge from the executive, and will expect learning and change by both the executive and the organization as a result of the programme;
- expect challenges to concern the organization's present corporate social responsibility (CSR) values, goals, policies, strategies, processes and other activities;
- give the learning programme a high priority and allow the executive the necessary time off within his or her regular job to be able to engage fully with all aspects of the programme;
- allow the executive access to all persons, systems, information and concerns in the organization about CSR;
- make available all necessary resources to enable the executive fully to take part in the programme;
- convene appropriate discussions in-house, fully including the executive, to consider seriously the executive's advice and proposals arising from the programme;
- give honest feedback to the executive where proposals and ideas cannot be acted upon;
- give pre- and post-consideration to implications for the executive's career arising from the programme, and engage openly and honestly with the executive in discussion about this;
- discuss, agree and adhere to a confidentiality and privacy arrangement covering the interests of all three parties.

(from Conduct Becoming Ltd)

Some developers claim that they best serve the long-term interests of the business by being a catalyst for organizational (and social) change. This may call for 'a role in undermining the assumptions and values that create the rules of the game' (Clarke 1999: 47). An open and honest learning contract may be more problematical in this conception of the developer's role.

Transfer of learning

Linking development to business is assisted by using learning material that

- is clearly relevant to the business;
- directly impacts on learners' jobs.

These criteria are frequently unmet. Developers often choose the convenience and apparent cost- and time-effectiveness of generic materials (such as longstanding, well-researched case studies) rather than using material based on the current organizational and business context and the preoccupations and needs of their learners. They can place learning efficiency (a teaching/input considera-tion) ahead of learning effectiveness (an application/output consideration).

Alternatively, they may deliberately offer appealing experiences that are significantly different from work and psychologically 'safe'. These include personal growth and team development through outdoor challenges, building structures using Lego bricks to 'create metaphors and stories that add meaning to our identity, imbuing our descriptions of our workplace with emotion' (training psychologist), and exploring the leadership styles of Shakespearean characters. All such methods leave learners to find their own ways of transferring their learning back into their real work lives.

The consequence is that the further the materials and experiences are from the actuality, the greater is the gulf to be bridged. Mole argues forcibly that 'it is the issue of training transfer which gives the ultimate lie to genre training as an effec-tive method of management development and places it in its rightful domain, management entertainment' (1996: 13). He offers some tests. These include the question of the resemblance between the learning experience and the work, the familiarity of trainers with the work (job, organization and industry), and the nature of the involvement of the learner's management before and after training.

There is a further dimension to the 'reality' issue. Using company-specific material because of its direct relevance to real work issues assumes that all the learners may be from the same unit. This strengthens collegiate support for behaviour changes back at work. Yet the impact of learning with and from strangers, and even other sectors, with different goals, backgrounds, circum-stances and worldviews can be a powerful experience. In a southwest England-based, mixed-sector and mixed-size programme, managers from NatWest Investment Bank claimed to learn a lot about customer service from a local hairdresser (Centre for Tomorrow's Company 2000).

The case for greater proximity is not all one way. However, in respect of the favourable transfer of learning to work, the greater the face validity of the learning, the better the prospects. The options facing developers in choosing a learning experience are shown on the continuum set out in Figure 15.3.

Whilst the use of abstract learning material may be difficult for learners to relate to, as well as generating a transfer problem, the use of real learning mate-rial (i.e. the company's own current issues) is open to misuse. The British Bakeries example shows how 'reality' is a matter of degree.

British Bakeries

British Bakeries used to train its heads of departments in the skills of devel-oping strategies for their own functional areas. Learning as a team under the expert guidance of business educators, they had to produce a radical business strategy for the whole company. They were then required to present their new business strategy to their board of directors. The learning was a rich experience for the managers and the resulting strategy was of high quality. Having worked on and off for several months, the managers became very attached to their strategy and considered it superior to their board's. They were then shocked when the board politely listened but then did nothing with their strategy, correctly reminding the 'learners' that it was no more than a learning exercise (i.e. position 3, 'potentially real' on the continuum in Figure 15.3) because that was the deal they had struck with the developers.

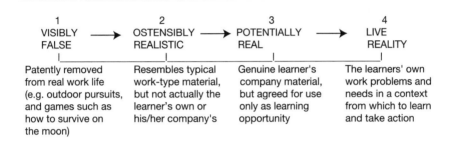

Figure 15.3 False–real learning material continuum
Source: Tate (1995a).

The problem with British Bakeries arose because the learners experienced the chosen material as 'live reality' (position 4 on the continuum). However, the sponsor and developers had decided that, despite its 'reality', the exercise was for learning purposes only (position 3). Reflect for a moment: how could the board directors realistically have been expected to admit that their subordinates' business strategy might be superior to their own? The contract between the parties was flawed and dangerously raised the learners' expectations. An example of how to overcome this kind of problem is offered by British Airways.

British Airways

The airline designed a management development programme aimed directly at the real business. It got its senior management, again learning off the job in teams and under expert tuition, to examine the changing nature of the competition. The managers learned the techniques and skills of competitor analysis by working on current material about Air France, Lufthansa, KLM, etc. They not only acquired new skills that they could use in the future, but took away with them completed up-to-date competitor analyses which they could immediately use back at work.

Brown draws on best practice cases in advising that

> Effective leadership development requires a systems approach combining formal training, on-the-job coaching, and developmental assignments in a mutually reinforcing way. This is achieved by closely linking leadership development to organizational culture and business goals....Individuals and organizations find that the line between work and learning is becoming blurred. Learning is part of getting work done; it is both an input and an output.
>
> (Brown 1999–2000: 13)

As a broad generalization, learning appears most likely to be effective in realizing changed action in the workplace if it does the following:

- takes place with colleagues rather than strangers;
- develops collective capability;
- focuses on the organization and business, not just the individual's skills;
- integrates with action to improve other system variables;
- employs real material rather than abstract/generic examples.

There are times when exceptions to the above are necessary and indeed desirable. The executive coaching model doesn't satisfy all the above criteria (the executive is not learning alongside colleagues) but is still able to bring learning and business into close proximity.

Whichever learning approach is used, it is important to have a clear understanding between all the parties about the nature of the learning experience and its relationship to workplace reality and the organization's needs.

Choosing the intervention: diversity

A potent factor affecting business success is the company's standing in society and the extent to which its mode of operating upholds and reflects society's values and composition. So when an organization stands accused of poor representation of minority groups, a lack of equal opportunities and racial prejudice, what should it do?

Some companies and public sector institutions resort to mandatory diversity training courses for everyone. However, this decision credits training with powers it doesn't possess. Moreover, it is an insult to many employees and risks wasting considerable sums of money. The root of the problem lies in the company's culture and its management policies and practices. Unless these change, newly trained individuals will make little impact. At best, training should be designed to work alongside other interventions, such as where the company advertises for recruits: 'Organization change should not be training led; training's role is to support change' (Tate 1995a: 74).

Companies often confuse two different drivers, one external and one internal. They either respond to external pressure (including legislation) aimed at making employment more equitable, or they value diversity for sound business reasons.

BT

BT regards 'the issue of diversification [*sic.*] as crucial because it reflects on the company's brand'. It therefore decides to fast-track its 25 most senior women to 'accelerate their progress onto its board'. The company's chosen vehicle is a course run by an external provider covering topics such as 'politicking, marketing oneself and learning how to influence senior colleagues, as well as life–work balance and career development'.

What should we make of BT's championing of women and its use of training courses to solve its diversity problem? Apart from a question mark over their power to change behaviour at an institutional level, what is the business rationale? How does this affect the ability of the business to cope with tomorrow's unknown and unknowable challenges? For an organization to survive in a complex environment (business, technological, political and social) calls for its internal resources to be equally diverse. This is known as Ashby's Law of Requisite Variety. Organizations can learn from nature: without such a multi-response capability an organism cannot compete and will die.

This principle is becoming increasingly important for organizations. Growing complexity means that opportunities and threats are becoming more diverse and rapid. Future challenges are becoming more difficult to predict: 'Old skills and responses may be insufficient to meet them' (James and Burgoyne 2002: 2).

Leaders are inclined to recruit in their own image (Chapman 1991). This may make them feel more comfortable but it can undermine the critical skills available to the organization. A crucial argument for diversity lies in the risk of complacency that may result from similarity and 'groupthink' (PIU 2001).

Digital Equipment

The computer manufacturer Digital was experiencing uncomfortable relationships in its management team in the UK. There was awkward dissent over business strategy from senior managers. So the leadership designed a management development programme that had as its express purpose 'to ensure the company's directors are supported'. Shortly thereafter the company hit trouble as it became clear that its business strategy for personal computers was badly flawed (its board thought that there was no market for PCs, believing that most individual managers would not want a

PC on their desk). What was needed here, in management development terms, was a 'fresh think' approach that would license managers to challenge the board, rather than a 'group think' approach that would generate compliance.

Some forms of diversity are more important than others. According to John *et al.* (1999), diverse *values* embody a primary inhibitor of organizational performance, while *social* diversity (ethnicity, class, gender and age) and *informational* diversity (knowledge, education and experience) generate higher levels of performance and satisfaction, especially when the task is non-routine. We might conclude from this that the contribution of development lies mainly in the informational domain and perhaps also in helping members to accept similar values to those espoused by the business.

Convergent versus divergent learning

Diversity in the workforce leads naturally to the issue of convergent versus divergent learning. Carefully tailored individual and organizational learning is part of that strategy. The effect of pure training is *convergence* of ability around an external view of best practice. It helps deliver performance against currently known and agreed business goals. By contrast, the effect of pure development and education is *divergence*. This capitalizes on the rich variety of views, ability and values found in humankind. Divergence is especially important for innovation since it generates both the freedom and the ability to challenge the status quo.

A careful balance between convergent and divergent learning approaches is needed to manage both today and tomorrow. The precise balance, and who needs which, depends on the business agenda, the form of organization and the operating environment.

Raising the developers' game

A recurring theme underpinning this chapter has been the need for developers to think strategically in order to serve the business. This final section offers a framework to do this, drawn from *Organisational Leadership* (www.organisational-leadership.com). It considers the business's environment, assesses the organization's current capability, identifies the leadership and management gap, and plans appropriate responses.

The changing environment

This embraces the leadership implications of the business as a consequence of the changing environment – political, social, legal, technological, ethical, ecological, etc. Stakeholders' expectations and pressures are examined for their impact and changing demands and expectations. In the context of governance, included in the mix are expectations of higher standards of probity in business leaders, and improved arrangements by company boards as they set direction, plan change, behave responsibly towards stakeholders, measure and report progress, and are held to account (Tate 2002).

Governance and sustainable development were among the themes identified by CEML's emergent business models research into the prerequisites for leadership in the 21st century. Others included learning to blend collaboration and competition, devolving power down and outwards, creating new metrics for valuing non-financial assets, understanding organization design and operations from a systems standpoint, and appreciating transnational dimensions of business models.

The business and organization context

This focus attempts to gain clarity over where the internal organization needs to be headed to serve the needs of the business. It captures the extent to which leadership resources are matched to the challenge of change. It asks: what is our map of the desired, possible and likely future? What organization is needed to serve that outcome? How will it need to differ from the present organization? What problems exist with the way it currently operates? What are the leaders unhappy with? What are the followers unhappy with? What interventions will get us to where we want to be? What consensus exists around any aim, need or desire to change the way the organization is run?

Leadership culture

This examines the existing leadership culture and where it is aligned with espoused behaviour or is in any respect dysfunctional in serving the organization's goals. Among the many issues explored are the criteria for becoming a member of the leadership cadre, how safe it is for people to challenge the leaders, the degree of openness and authenticity in the discourse between leaders, how widely leadership is distributed throughout the organization, and how power is manifested and exercised.

Leadership competence

This level of analysis is concerned with the specific and timely relevance of competences to the organization's current concerns and opportunities. It employs a four-way breakdown between:

- *emergent competences* that are of increasing importance to the organization (e.g. managing public–private partnerships);
- *legacy competences* that the organization will need less of in future (e.g. controlling a machine-like organization);

- *enduring competences* that the organization will always value (e.g. customer service);
- *transitional competences* that are relevant for the short term (e.g. privatizing nationalized industries).

The process also examines how the company distinguishes between leaders *doing things right* (competences) and *doing right things* (Tate 1996).

Summary

Not all development is undertaken with the employer as the explicit client and with organization-level improvement in mind, but that which is designed from this perspective is likely to be better served if a number of principles are observed. Key among these is regarding development as one improvement method with a clear business-related purpose in mind, undertaken in conjunction with other reinforcing activity.

Supporting this is the placing of the output of leadership practice ahead of the input of developing capability. That requires recognizing the organization as a system and managing leadership as one of its prime resources. That legitimizes interventions aimed at the system as well as the person. It means optimizing all talent and avoiding waste, as well as enhancing levels of talent through development processes. That, in turn, calls for cooperation and coordination between HR specialists involved at all points on the employment spectrum.

When it comes to designing learning, it requires political and practical judgements that focus on what will be relevant and can and will be supported and applied. It means tackling the thorny issue of an explicit or implicit contract between the parties as a way of managing expectations and building authentic relationships.

With the aim of making developers' activities more directly serve their business's needs and deliver business outcomes, the box below offers a framework of questions for developers to reflect on privately. It will help them challenge their own assumptions, and plan how to modify their relationships and practices with their various stakeholders.

Decision-making structure for strengthening development links with business: questions for developers to ask themselves

1 Stakeholders
- Who are my stakeholders? Which are key? Who impacts on my work? Who is impacted by my work?
- How am I held to account? By whom?

- What duty do I owe to my organization sponsor?
- What duty do I owe to learners in my charge?
- How clear is my contract with the various parties?

2   Business know-how
- What more should I know about the current and future business?
- What is changing about what managers should learn?
- How can I find out more about the chief executive's preoccupations?
- How can I build a better relationship between development and business leaders?

3   Horizontal integration
- How can development professionals work more closely with other HR specialists?
- How can development activity reinforce, and be reinforced by, other employment levers?

4   Organization development
- How can the leadership and management culture be improved?
- How can the management hierarchy work more effectively?
- How can I help remove obstacles in the path of learners?

5   Needs analysis
- What are the organization's general needs for improved leadership and management?
- Which of these needs are best met by development activity? And which by other forms of improvement?
- Where is leadership and management talent leaking away? How can the loss be minimized?
- What are the main gaps in the organization that development activity can help plug?
- If leadership and management were to be regarded as resources not to be squandered, how well are they being managed?
- How can I surround managers and leaders with all ingredients necessary to get 'the painting, not the artist'?

6   Balance
- What balance do I seek between training to solve short-term known needs and sustain the current business, and developing talent for future unspecified needs and tomorrow's business model?
- How much time relatively do I spend developing individuals, groups, the organization?

7   The role of business in society
- What role should I play in developing managers and leaders attuned to society's expectations of business?

8   Transfer of learning
- How wide is the gap between learning and action?
- How can my design of learning interventions minimize that gap?
- How can I and others help learners bridge that gap?

9   Evaluation model
- How can I focus more on 'Are learners doing anything different?' and 'Is the business benefiting?', than 'Did they enjoy it?' and 'Did they learn anything?'

10   Private conscience
- How much do I really care about the business as long as I help individual managers learn?
- How much do I want managers to be developed to undermine or to support their own management?
- What risks do I fear in attempting to more closely meet the business's needs?
- How much do I want to be left with a free hand even though it might not be healthy for the organization?

References

Atkinson, S. and M. Meldrum (1998) 'Don't waste money on management development', *Organisations & People*, November: 4–10.

Brown, P. (1999–2000) 'New directions in leadership development: a review of trends and best practices', *Public Manager*, Winter: 37–41.

Burke, W.W. (1972) 'The role of training in organization development', *Training and Development*, American Society for Training and Development, 26(9): 30–4.

Burke, W.W. and Litwin, G.H. (1992) 'A causal model of organizational performance and change', *Journal of Management* 18(3): 523–45.

CEML (2002) *Managers and Leaders: Raising our Game*, London: Council for Excellence in Management and Leadership.

Centre for Tomorrow's Company (2000) *Pathfinder Programme*, London: Centre for Tomorrow's Company.

Chapman, J.A. (1991) 'Matching people and organizations', *Administrative Science Quarterly* 36: 459–84.

Clarke, M. (1999) 'Management development as a game of meaningless outcomes', *Human Resource Management Journal* 9(2): 38–49.

Court, S., D. Young and C. Chambers (2002) *Developing Managers for Business Performance*, London: Chartered Institute of Personnel and Development.

EFQM (2002) *Business Excellence Model*, London: European Foundation for Quality Management.

Ezzamel, M., S. Lilley, A. Wilkinson and H. Wilmott (1996) 'Practices and practicalities in human resource management', *Human Resource Management Journal* 6(1): 63–80.

Gallwey, T. (2002) *The Inner Game of Work*, London: Texere Publishing.

Gosling, J. and D. Ashton (1994) 'Action learning and academic qualifications', *Management Learning* 25(2): 263–74.

Hopfl, H. and F. Dawes (1995) 'A whole can of worms! The contested frontiers of management development and learning', *Personnel Review* 24(6): 19–28.

Horne, M. and D. Stedman Jones (2001) *Leadership: The Challenge for All*, London: Institute of Management.

James, K. (2002) *Leadership and Management Excellence: Corporate Development Strategies*, London: Council for Excellence in Management and Leadership.

James, K. and J. Burgoyne (2002) *Leadership Development: Best Practice Guide for Organizations*, London: Council for Excellence in Management and Leadership.

John, K.A., G.B. Northcraft and M.A. Neale (1999) 'Why differences make a difference', *Administrative Science Quarterly* 44: 741–63.

Katz, D. and R.L. Khan (1978) *The Social Psychology of Organisations*, New York: Wiley.

McHale, J. (2000) 'Thought for tomorrow', *People Management*, 20 January: 54.

Mole, G. (1996) 'The management training industry in the UK: an HRD director's critique', *Human Resource Management Journal* 6(1): 19–26.

Pedler, M., J. Burgoyne and T. Boydell (1991) *The Learning Company: A Strategy for Sustainable Development*, Maidenhead: McGraw-Hill.

Performance and Innovation Unit (2000) *Effective Leadership in Delivering Public Services* (study), London: HM Government Cabinet Office.

—— (2001) *Strengthening Leadership in the Public Sector* (report), London: HM Government Cabinet Office.

Rainbird, H. (1994) 'The changing role of the training function: a test for the integration of human resource and business strategy', *Human Resource Management Journal* 5(1): 72–90.

Sadler, P. (1999) *Leadership in Tomorrow's Company*, London: Centre for Tomorrow's Company.

Senge, P.M., C. Roberts, Richard B. Ross, B.J. Smith and A. Kleiner (1994) *The Fifth Discipline Fieldbook: Strategies and Tools for Building Learning Organizations*, London: Nicholas Brealey.

Storey, J. and W. Tate (2000) 'Management development', in S. Bach and K. Sisson (eds) *Personnel Management*, 3rd edition, Oxford: Blackwell.

Storey, J., C. Mabey and A. Thomson (1997) 'What a difference a decade makes', *People Management*, 12 June: 28–30.

Tate, W. (1995a) *Developing Corporate Competence: A High-Performance Agenda for Managing Organizations*, Aldershot: Gower.

—— (1995b) *Developing Managerial Competence: A Critical Guide to Methods and Materials*, Aldershot: Gower.

—— (1996) 'Development – on or off the rails?', *Organisations & People* 3(4): 22–6.

—— (1997) 'Developing an integrative framework for corporate competence', paper presented at 'Competence – a Source of Competitive Advantage', the annual conference of the Centre for Labour Market Studies, Leicester University, 10 September.

—— (2000a) *Implications of Futures Studies for Business, Organisation, Management and Leadership*, London: Council for Excellence in Management and Leadership.

—— (2000b) *Emergent Business Models*, London: Council for Excellence in Management and Leadership.

—— (2000c) *The Business of Innovation*, Woking: Prometheus Consulting.

—— (2002) 'Governance and leadership', in *Corporate Social Responsibility Manual*, London: Spiro Press.

—— (2003) *The Organisational Leadership Audit*, Cambridge: Cambridge Strategy Publications.

16 A new look at dispersed leadership: power, knowledge and context

Tim Ray, Stewart Clegg and Ray Gordon

Introduction

By comparing Anglo-Saxon approaches to *individual leaders* with business practice in Japan's group-oriented society, we shed new light on a number of the underlying issues addressed in this book. In particular, we critically assess the now popular idea of 'dispersed' or 'distributed' leadership. If this is to have any real meaning, we see the need to understand it alongside issues of power, knowledge and context.

Japan's distinct history has given rise to power and knowledge relations that represent an interesting point of comparison – or counterfactual – to Anglo-Saxon ideals of liberal individualism, market-rational entrepreneurship, explicit reasoning and formal rules. Whereas much of the Anglo-Saxon literature on leadership focuses on the processes by which individual leaders control strong hierarchies by stretching and subverting – if not indeed actually breaking – the rules to achieve change, Japanese society is dominated by implicit rules that privilege obligations to the group over ostentatious displays of individualism. This basic point of contrast presents us with significant challenges when thinking about 'leadership' and its development.

Close community relationships within Japanese groups lower the marginal costs of information transfer and allow members to act in a highly coordinated way: basically, they will ostracize and retaliate against those who break their code. The leader is subject to the disciplinary authority of followers, and displays of excessive individualism go against the rules. Because power is enabled and constrained by rules, it is deeply embedded within knowledge; thus, we revisit the knowledge debate to consider Polanyi's (1967) original interpretation of the tacit dimension as the inexplicable mental processes that guide the ability to act and think in the active process of 'doing things'. Discussion of leadership can thus be connected with the appreciation of context in which it is applied, as well as rules and power that shape that context. Different power actors in different contexts will operate in and through different rationalities, according to interpretative rules for producing sense. Ultimately, sense and truth cannot be separated from the context in which they are generated and used in reflexively automatic practice. The meanings of information signals – speech, tone of voice, body language, significant silences or any sign that can be 'read' as meaningful – are shaped by the accumulated learning of individuals and groups who are meaningfully connected; contexts are bounded in terms of who is inside and outside. Rationality is guided by what insiders are able to interpret as meaningful; outsiders might read the same signs differently.

Consider the context of collective learning in self-organizing communities of practice that generates knowledge held in common by insiders. Such knowledge generation is 'self-policing' – participants have to demonstrate themselves to be competent and trusted to contribute, according to the insider's implicit code of practice; those who fall short of the mark risk being marginalized or ignored. Self-sustaining communities can emerge as significant social 'containers' (Wenger 2000: 229) for competences that underpin the wider knowledge-generating 'ecology'. While these communities embrace those who, by common consent, are leading figures, the balance of disciplinary authority that confers this status is community-based. Tacit knowledge, held in common by members, is fundamental to the reflexively automatic interpretation of the insider's implicit code and judgements on the authority of leaders. Communities of practice represent a learning context in which membership is shaped by collective judgements about competence and compliance with insider norms.

What happens when we inspect a radically different context of, and for, sense-making to see what happens to certain central ideas of leadership and power? Japan provides an interesting counterfactual for such an exercise. It is the only G-7 economy whose traditional social values owe virtually nothing to Mediterranean origins; the others share Judaeo-Graeco-Roman traditions to an extent that the differences amongst them appear less pronounced when they are compared to Japan (Dore 1973: 419). These differences are especially dramatic when Japan's institutional 'rules of the game' (North 1990) are compared with common Anglo-Saxon presuppositions about individualism. As we will argue, power relations mediated by Japan's rules of play deny legitimacy to self-organizing boundaries spanning communities of practice. Different contexts are defined by different rules; different rules produce different power plays.

The importance of context

Because rationality is bounded it can never account for itself: hence, reflexivity is inherent to its practice. Human rationality is always context dependent because, as Wittgenstein (2001) demonstrated unequivocally, no rule could ever account for its own interpretation – thus, context cannot be reduced to rules. All science occurs in the context of what realist philosophers of science refer to as 'standing conditions'. These standing conditions provide for the prevalence of the sense that the science makes of the world of object relations, against naturally occurring conditions. Standing conditions are definite sets of contextual experimental conditions, such as ensuring a sterile laboratory environment, maintaining a vacuum or a stable temperature. Without these conditions being maintained by the experimentalist the predicted relations that the research setting seeks to display would not occur. Thus, a context for stable object relations has to be artfully contrived so that the context has no effect other than that sought experimentally. A science of objects needs to appear to be context free; otherwise, it cannot provide a general theory. Put simply, iron filings should always display the same dispositional behaviour when introduced to the poles of a magnet, irrespective of whether the experiment occurs in Japan or the United States or of who is the experimentalist. These variables simply are not important to the 'sense' that the filings make of their patterning around the magnetic poles. Nor are they relevant to the sense that the experimentalist makes.

Had we been thinking about how managers might respond to the twin poles of a strategic threat, rather than iron filings responding to a magnet, the situation would be very different. The patterns that emerge are not the result of laws that inexorably create a certain pattern. There is far more indeterminateness. Patterns are established by rules that are applied locally, *in situ*, by the actors themselves. These rules are not external – although they may generate tangible traces, revealed in manuals or procedures. They are, instead, the result of a complex mastery of skills that enables the actors to cope with new situations according to some categories for making sense that involve the application of members' implicit rules. The use of these skills to 'do things' in practice is always reflexively automatic; that is, they cannot be analysed simply in terms of those rules that might be thought to constitute them. Such rules become themselves the instinctive grounds of any action, action that is capable of improvising in unpredictable ways around and between any sense that the rules might make. Rules cannot account for their own interpretation *in situ* by actors. Social science has to interpret its own context. And studies that take these interpretations as their frame of reference are only ever as ontologically secure as these intersubjective interpretations are stable. If sensemaking changes, reality changes.

Context is a matter of stable sensemaking conditions. However, there are no guarantees of, or for, such conditions. No context stands outside power. If that were the case, context would exist nowhere: outside understanding, outside possibility, outside sensemaking. As Foucault says, 'power produces knowledge...power and knowledge directly imply one another...there is no power relation without the creative constitution of a field of knowledge, nor any knowledge that does not presuppose and constitute at the same time power relations' (1977: 27). In such a view, rationalities and powers are fused. Different power actors will operate in and through different rationalities. The different rationalities will have their different rules for producing sense – at the more formal outer limits – for producing truth. In fact, sense and truth cannot be separated from the ensemble of rules that constitute them – and their obverse – as such. To adopt a discursive analysis of rationality is to see what people say as the means whereby rationality and power become interwoven. People may be in a position to say anything, given the infinity of discourse, but they rarely surprise the well-grounded analyst with their discursive moves. Which is not to say that language games are predictable – although sometimes they are – but to suggest that they are explicable. We can understand and constitute the senses that are

being made as well as the conditions of existence and underlying tacitly interpreted assumptions that make such sense possible. And in this way we can begin
to understand the different forms of agency that find expression in organizational contexts, where the players make sense of rules that they actively construct
and deconstruct in the context of their action.

Contextualism implies that whatever regularities occur empirically will always
be situational. To the extent that researchers address the rules, values and related
power/knowledge processes that generate order and reduce uncertainty in
exchange, they will have a sound grasp of the socially and historically conditioned
context within which sense is made. With these understandings, researchers can
avoid the relativism that they are sometimes charged with: their understandings
will be framed within deeply embedded foundations that the actors find normal
and acceptable to use. And these vary from context to context, especially when we
consider differences between contexts such as those of Japan and the US. Let us
consider the conventional US leadership literature first.

Power and the context of leadership

The mainstream leadership literature offers four 'traditional' approaches – trait,
style, contingency and new leadership – in each of which there is a seemingly
unproblematic distinction between leaders and followers. But there is also
dispersed leadership, in which the question of who has the capacity to achieve a
difference – power – is more awkward. Dispersed leadership raises questions
about how the 'rules of the game' enable and constrain the process of leadership
in a particular context.

The trait theories focused their attention on determining what attributes and
qualities differentiated leaders from followers. Theorists such as Bingham (1927),
Bowden (1927) and Schenk (1928) concentrated on the personal attributes and
characteristics of 'good' leaders – extraordinary individuals who were revered by
their followers. Subsequently, style theorists explored the idea that the leadership
qualities could be explained in terms of how leaders behaved. For instance,
McGregor (1960) suggested that the behaviour of leaders could be grouped into
two distinct styles. What he termed theory X was a directive style and theory Y
was a supportive style; both styles achieve success in different circumstances.
Contingency theories considered the possibility that there was no one best solution to every problem; extraordinary individuals have to lead by making the
choice that is most appropriate to prevailing circumstances.

A variation on the genre of traditional leadership theories is evident in the so-
called 'new paradigm', which depicts leaders as 'managers of meaning' rather
than influence mandators (Bryman 1996: 280). This management of meaning
embraces transactional, transformational and culture-based approaches. In the
transaction model, leadership is a form of negotiated exchange between leaders
and followers. For transformational theorists, leadership is organized according
to a number of charismatic and situationally correlated dimensions; good leadership depends on more than tangible inducements. Culture-based approaches

relate successful leadership to an ability to synchronize style with the organization's culture.

Notwithstanding their diversity, each of the traditional approaches (trait, style, contingency and new leadership) presents the relationship between leaders and followers as a dualism, the nature of which is central to their conceptualization of leadership. Leaders are given a position of privilege because they are considered to be superior to their followers, either through natural ability or through the possession of appropriate attributes: if leaders were not superior, people would not follow them. Even the literature that engages with followers retains the enabling assumption that leaders are extraordinary individuals who are superior to 'their' followers. Thus the voice of leaders typically contrasts with implicit assumptions about the silence of their followers.

Although leadership involves the practice of power to achieve a difference, much of the leadership literature is devoid of a critical discussion of power. Nowhere is the connection between power and leadership less evident and more needed than in the area of work that Bryman (1996) categorizes as *dispersed leadership*, which embraces work on themes such as 'superleadership' (Manz and Sims 1991; Sims and Lorenzi 1992), 'real teams' (Katzenbach and Smith 1993), 'self-leadership' (Kirkman and Rosen 1999; Kouzes and Posner 1993; Uhl-Bien and Graen 1998); 'leadership as a process' (Hosking 1991; Knights and Willmott 1992); and 'distributed leadership' (Senge 1999). In a generic sense, these theories represent growing interest in the decentralization of leadership skills and responsibilities in an organization. There is a new focus on the sharing of power between leaders and followers – leadership is not an abstract quality but a process. With the espoused sharing of power in mind, it seems reasonable to expect that critical analysis of power would be pivotal to meaningful interpretations of the processes by which 'dispersion' is achieved.

Some management theorists have attempted to address the link between leadership and power critically. In the field of education, Dunlop and Goldman (1991) and Kreisberg (1992) have developed the theme of 'power through' and 'power with' instead of 'power over'. The terms 'power through' and 'power with' reflect emancipative approaches to leadership that advocate the empowerment of followers and allow flatter organizational structures. Notwithstanding their merits, these contributions do not engage with the processes by which power becomes constituted in the meaning of an organization's practices. Consequently, there is a need to be clear about the processes by which the 'power with' and 'power through' appellations differ from historically embedded organizational practice of 'power over'.

Haugaard (1997) argues that the effects of deep-seated antecedents related to power are unobtrusive. That is to say, they go largely unnoticed, because, over time, the continual reinforcement of differential power relationships results in the roles that constitute these relationships, particularly leadership roles, acquiring a form of social capital that becomes a taken-for-granted reality: a position of privilege and political leverage over others that these others do not question. Rather, these roles become a reified 'truth' that is a natural part of the order of things (*ibid.*: 213). And from the point of view of establishing the role of leadership in the collective psyche, historical reinforcement of the natural superiority of the leader and the need for effective leadership have become an indisputable 'reality' (Sievers 1994).

If leaders do not act with respect to the organization's historical antecedents, codes of order and disciplined practices, they risk losing the support of their followers. With the reification of leadership in mind, historical antecedents, codes of order and disciplined practices related to leadership and power for most organizations, in a practical sense, have problematic implications for dispersed leadership. For instance, if, in an attempt to disperse leadership, traditional leaders de-differentiate their relationship with their followers, these followers may well see them as behaving inappropriately. In such a case, followers may react by seeking to replace the leader with a more traditionally oriented alternative. Thus, if leaders wish to lead they will need to maintain their 'differential status'. To do this they will need to be perceived by their followers as behaving as a leader 'should', as behaving with respect to the disciplined practice that reflects 'good' leadership for their organization (Haugaard 1997).

In addition, Weber's structures of dominancy and Foucault's disciplined practices illustrate that organizations are not equitable social systems (Clegg 1989). Those people in positions of dominance, those with a strong voice, are more likely to shape the nature of change in social settings. Organizational leaders in particular, as per the leader/follower dualism, have traditionally held positions of dominance. As Haugaard (1997) notes, people who hold positions of dominance, by virtue of the acceptance by others of their superiority, become legitimate 'carriers of meaning' and 'producers of truth'. Not surprisingly, then, people have come to rely on leaders to make decisions, or, as Foucault would say, 'construct new truths': a phenomenon that is central to the transformational leadership thesis. In consequence, however, the privileged position held by traditional leaders has allowed them to control agendas and thus 'produce a corpus of statements which not only create new "truths", but also recreate the justification for their own existence' (Haugaard 1997: 208). In short, this privileged position has allowed traditional leaders to consolidate their need to exist and embed their right to power within the historical antecedents and meaning systems of organizations.

An embedded right to power would render the notion of dispersed leadership problematic. When introducing dispersed leadership, one is left pondering questions such as 'what happens to the reality of leadership when power is shared between the leader and the follower?' If the identity of leaders and followers is no longer differentiated, who leads and who follows? Is the sharing of power between leaders and followers not unlike the shifting limits to power in organizations, rendering leadership an untruth?

The deconstruction of the mainstream management literature on leadership shows that, in general, theorists in the field have tended to treat the relationship between leadership and power as being unproblematic. Contributors to this literature regard the superiority of leaders as an unremarkable phenomenon and therefore offer little, if any, critical evaluation of the implications associated with this superiority. Even the dispersed leadership theorists, who, although perhaps somewhat perfunctorily, argue for the sharing of power between leaders and followers, continue with the apolitical approach adopted by the vast majority of traditional leadership theorists. They position leadership within unquestioned and unmentioned assumptions about the nature of hierarchy and domination. While these assumptions may work for the context of Western – especially US – leadership, they barely work at all for contexts where leadership is both far less individualistic and far less dependent on an authority derived from hierarchy, despite whatever groups subject to it might think. Japan offers such a counterfactual.

The history and the practice of power in Japanese organizations

It should hardly be surprising, given our contextualist position, that we regard the practice of leadership in Japan as different from that represented in the predominantly North American literature. Although it is easy to be bamboozled by cultural views in which any country is understood simply in terms of a legacy from the past, Japan's 'rules of the game' afford a degree of power to collective tacit knowledge that achieves a subtle, but pervasive and persistent, influence on the consistency with which inherited 'scripts' are read by successive generations. In the modern era such scripts have easily accommodated Western passages, but the meanings that are read by Japanese insiders are not necessarily congruent with outsider expectations. Japan's 'interpretation code' (Itami 1992) is predicated on power and knowledge relations in which the 'common instinct' that is generated by long-term interaction amongst insiders guides practice with an elegant simplicity (*wabi-sabi*) that is not commensurate with precious displays of individualism and Anglo-Saxon models of leadership.

For more than two centuries, Japan's pre-industrial international isolation provided a sheltered environment. Instead of the painful, slow and contested emergence of market-rationality that propelled the West into the industrial era, with its concomitant individualism, stable government over a homogenous population of insiders fostered much more collectivist power/knowledge relations. In these contexts, reflexively automatic power embodied in tacit knowledge, held in common by members of tightly bounded and stable community groups, achieved binding disciplinary authority over members. The disciplinary authority of 'here and now' common instinct became an embedded and largely unchallenged part of the order of things. Whereas Western notions of leadership centre on the heroic achievements of extraordinary individuals, Japan's 'rules of the game' are oriented towards team activities. The champion high-jumper is not necessarily the best football or rugby player; and trying to play a team sport according to the rules for a competition amongst individuals would be a recipe for confusion.

Over the last 150 years, Japan's gatekeeper organizations have learned the international rules of play. While the misreading of Western intention and meaning might cause friction, confusion or disappointment, Japan's ability to read the line of play and compete effectively has enabled it to rank with the United States as an economically significant nation. Relatively few Westerners have made an effort to learn Japan's rules of play, and many of those who were once eager to replicate Japan's rapid economic growth can do no more than imagine what might lie behind the façade, which, now that growth rates have stalled, they imagine as irretrievably faded. Suddenly the desire to imitate Japan has given way to a wave of triumphalism: Japan's recovery would depend on becoming more like the West. But Japan's history of power/knowledge relations runs counter to the convergence thesis.

For at least three centuries, Western cultures have tended to privilege objective knowledge and the scientific method, with the growing interest in 'useful knowledge' according to business and other 'needs' being a comparatively recent phenomenon (Langrish *et al.* 1972; Gibbons *et al.* 1994; Nowotny *et al.* 2001). In contrast, Japan's imprinting conditions for industrialization were forged in substantial isolation, hermetically separated from the citadels of academic science and economic growth impelled by market-rational capitalism's 'perennial gale of creative destruction' (Schumpeter 1976: 84). In 1603 the Tokugawa Shogunate established a government that ruled without serious opposition for 250 years. From 1639 Japanese could not travel abroad and Japan's contact with the outside world was limited to trade relations with China and the Netherlands, conducted through the port of Nagasaki. The Shogunate's centralized authority flowed to local communities through vertical chains, with the samurai class acting as the Shogunate's local agents. These samurai were paid a salary (in rice) but were neither landed gentry nor merchants. Rather, they were enrolled in the activities and fortunes of their local community and expected to broker their authority according to the insider's standards of welfare and human dignity.

When Commodore Matthew Perry delivered US demands to open trade relations in 1853, fear of colonization undermined the Shogunate's authority. But the Meiji Restoration in 1868 – which many take to mark the birth of modern Japan – was an adjustment to the established authority structure; it was neither a Norman Conquest nor a French Revolution (Mason and Caiger 1972: 217). Under the slogan 'rich nation, strong army' (*fukoku kyôhei*), the Meiji government sought to establish a prosperous nation that remained free from Western colonization. From the outset, Japan's industrialization was 'plan-rational' (Johnson 1992: 19); instead of simply setting the formal rules of play, as in market-rational Anglo-Saxon economies, the Japanese government became intimately involved with shaping the structure of industry and setting goals for innovation.

Many aspects of Japan's outward appearances acquired a Western hue. The foundation of the University of Tokyo in 1876 paved the way towards today's comprehensive provision of higher education. But, in reality, Japan's early universities were not properly equipped for research and were essentially agencies for training bureaucrats (Itakura and Yagi 1974: 166). In contemporary Japan the vertical ranking position of universities selects the country's elite – the higher-ranking universities have harder entrance exams. Graduation is almost assured to those who are able to enter; and the university's ranking position (as opposed to variations in teaching and research standards) fixes the status that accrues to its graduates. Expectations of career-long employment for male employees – recruited on a one-off basis from an entry-level-only labour market – enable them to be disciplined according to the workplace organization's internal code (Ray 2002).

Although there was a high rate of labour mobility amongst factory workers at the beginning of Japan's industrialization, employers started to strengthen links with their employees through payments in kind. By the end of the First World War, Japanese manufacturers had established a practice whereby each spring large companies hired boys who were leaving school and indentured them as firm members. Such recruits exhibited a sense of loyalty and a willingness to accept insider workplace rules in ways that resonated with Japan's pre-industrial traditions. In the 1920s and 1930s uniforms for workers appeared, along with badges and insignia denoting rank. The military-industrial complex responsible for fuelling imperialist expansionism accentuated the trend. It also pushed small and medium-sized enterprises towards particular *zaibatsu* (groups of companies owned by a single family), thereby curtailing much of their freedom to negotiate business arrangements (Miyashita and Russell 1996: 17) as they became locked into fixed supply chains, in which each firm was dependent on the one above for orders. These *zaibatsu* became interleaved with the governmental bureaucracy and were instrumental in the implementation of centralized 'plan-rational' authority through their vertically segmented chains.

At one level the establishment of Japan's parliamentary democracy in 1890 served as a demonstration of modernity to the West while also reflecting a polit-ical struggle amongst Meiji oligarchs who sought to create a weak parliament staffed by their own supporters, although it was the bureaucrats – both military and civilian – who arrogated power to themselves (Johnson 1992: 37). For Johnson (1995: 29), the removal of Japan's military interests in 1945 freed the civilian bureaucracy from its greatest rival. When the Allied Occupation ended in 1952, the Ministry of International Trade and Industry (MITI) was able to engineer the reformation of military-era *zaibatsu* groups of companies into 'headless' bank-based *keiretsu*. Although the extent of MITI's role as the prin-cipal architect of subsequent miracle growth has been the subject of debate (Porter *et al.* 2000: 20), *keiretsu* embody remarkably stable arrangements of trading relations.

Within Japan's macro-level structural stability, post-war recovery was supported by life-long employment for male employees which emerged as an established part of business practice, in part as a response to the new union pres-sures of the democratic era. Although popular images of changing Japan are apt to dismiss so-called lifetime employment as a luxury for ineffective workers or a threat to managerial efficiency, this misrepresents the implicit but nevertheless mutually binding social contract between upper-level employers and their permanent male members of staff. To be sure, not everybody in Japan *works for life*. Most of Japan's female employees remain peripheral to organizational career structure and there are various categories of non-permanent staff working with permanent colleagues on a long-term de facto regular basis (albeit for less money and security). But permanent male employees who are engaged on a career-long basis are linked to their employers through an implicit but mutually binding social contract. While it might be possible for these core insiders to leave in the early stages of a career to 'start again' elsewhere (salary is normally dependent upon the number of years served), job hopping retains a stigma and employees soon become too old to win the trust of a new employer. While labour mobility is increasing as employers and employees broker new arrangements, these do not equate to Anglo-Saxon career building by moving between organizations. Japan has yet to reveal signs of developing a significant labour market for specialists (Gilson and Roe 1999).

In the now classic text *Japanese Society*, Nakane developed the idea that *ba* 'sets a boundary and gives a common basis to a set of individuals who are located or involved in it' (1970: 1). Within Japan's company-as-family workplace *ba*, a nuanced understanding of age-related seniority embodies implicit rules about who should be treated with what degree of respect, shaping knowledge and power relations between senior managers and their subordinates. Inasmuch as everyone has a hand in the planning process, they appreciate the intended direction of progress. Insiders empathize with their colleagues' aspirations and have a common instinct that affords them a sense of how they will act in any given set of circumstances; surprises are rare and there is a high degree of 'automatic coordination'. Working, learning and innovation, which are often assumed to be conflicting activities in Anglo-Saxon contexts (Brown and Duguid 1991), comprise intermingled aspects of daily practice. Whereas Weick and Westley have argued that the phrase 'learning organization' qualifies as an oxymoron – 'to learn is to disorganize and increase variety. To organize is to forget and reduce variety' (1996: 440) – the learning organization is an embedded part of the Japanese order of things. Formal hierarchy is often overlain by 'notional equality' in fixed-term project teams (embracing members from all levels) to achieve specific objectives – senior staff think and typically drink with the team but nonetheless remain senior staff (see Kono and Clegg 1998, 2001; Ray and Little 2001).

But Japanese notions of 'our company' – an organization in which insiders (us) deal with outsiders (them) – does not make much sense without reference to Japan's 'rules of the game'. And this is where the essential aspects of its role as a counterfactual to Anglo-Saxon individualism might be overlooked or misunderstood by those who seek to translate Japan's specificity into the currency of North American leadership literature. Formal laws and rules represent symbols of authority, not something that the possessor of authority should actually have to use; group affiliation – and principally workplace affiliation – is essential to social standing, and the disciplinary authority of the relevant collective is instinctively automatic.

Of course, the implicit rules that enable and constrain practice in Japan can be represented explicitly (as illustrated by the myriad etiquette guides for visitors), but these cannot account for the reflexively automatic interpretation of these rules by insiders. Indeed, many outsiders might find it difficult to credit the significance of practices that appear merely quaint or exotic, but, unlike insiders, they are largely immune to the unthinkable social consequences of ostracism (see Miyamoto 1995). Yet, for insiders, the collective instinct is compelling and continual participation is essential to maintain the 'here and now' spirit of sustained membership (as is, for example, illustrated by concern about taking too much of the allocated holiday entitlement – some display of sacrifice is essential to demonstrating appropriate commitment to the group). Japanese children who accompany their parents on overseas postings are prone to lose the necessary emotional nuance and can find themselves severely disadvantaged when they return to Japan – as the famous saying warns, 'the nail that sticks out is hammered down'.

By their very nature, Japan's implicit rules are not readily apparent to outsiders. While Japan's spectacular economic development has been under-pinned by an ability to learn from across the world, formal rules and labour mobility of a society of atomized individuals lack legitimacy in the local context. To be sure, the benefits of positivist science can be exploited with dramatic effect in Japanese technology: continuous incremental improvement has led the world to a new era of high technology, high reliability products – but in Japan science has only ever been one way (amongst many ways) of resolving uncertainty and improving practice.

For Polanyi (1967: 22), the tacit dimension[1] represented a way out of Plato's concern with a paradox: to search for a solution to a problem is absurd, because if you know what you are looking for you have not got a problem; conversely, if you not know what you are looking for you cannot expect to find anything. Yet hunch and intuition abound. The ability to act and think is guided by an instinc-tive, reflexively automatic knowledge that (according to Polanyi's definition) cannot be objectified in any scientific sense. Although knowledge managers find it convenient to talk about 'capturing' tact knowledge, they are typically concerned with developing inchoate explicit knowledge into more refined concepts. Of course, they are using tacit knowledge in the process of improving that explicit knowledge; but the tacit knowledge in question is neither consumed nor diminished by its use – it is not 'converted' – on the contrary, people normally learn (i.e. generate new knowledge) from experience.

While the ontological status of groups remains controversial, Cook and Brown (1999) argue that not every human action undertaken by a group can be usefully or meaningfully reduced to an account of actions of individual members. And, amid Japan's group-oriented society, this provides an essential element in meaningful interpretations of the insider–outsider divide. Although collective explicit knowledge is achieving considerable currency in the Western management literature – for example through storytelling (Denning 2001) – there is often a failure to grasp the sense in which the knowledge held in common has value that arises precisely because it is held in common. Collective knowledge is a 'free resource' (Penrose 1995: 78) for insiders that can be reused without incurring additional cost. And the role of reflexively automatic collective tacit knowledge in shaping the interpretation of 'rules of the game' and the practice of power is often misrepresented or overlooked (Clegg and Ray 2003).

Learning from Japan?

By the 1980s the cultural and organizational characteristics of Japanese management had become fashionable in management consulting and theory circles. Books published in praise of Japanese management commanded attention – and titles typical of the era included *Japan as Number One* (Vogel 1979), *Theory Z* (Ouchi 1981) and *Made in America* (Dertouzous *et al.* 1989). But, arguably, the most important contribution to the genre was not actually on Japanese management at all – *In Search of Excellence*, by Peters and Waterman (1982). Although this book dealt with cultures of excellence in US corporations, it did so in response to the 'Japanese threat'. The authors sought authentically American sources of cultural advantage in US corporations to rival the advantages of Japanese corporate cultures. The book's heyday in the West coincided with a moment in the early 1980s when US confidence – both political and economic – seemed to be at its lowest ebb, after the debacles of Vietnam, the Iranian hostages saga and the lacklustre Carter administration. Smokestack industries were dying, the agricultural heartlands appeared to be in great distress, and everywhere US industry seemed to be under threat. And the number one threat was clearly Japan. In VCRs, automobiles, cameras, entertainment systems, televisions and many other high quality, high reliability products, the spectre of unstoppable Japanese competition loomed; US manufacturers were rapidly losing ground to Japanese manufacturers, and in some cases, such as VCRs and colour televisions, vacating the field entirely. Not surprisingly, students and professors in the business schools wanted to know how it was possible, how Japan had managed to become predominant. That was in the 1980s, when Tom Peters made America – and the world – discover 'excellence'.

Now the West has rediscovered leadership. A decade after Japan's miracle growth faltered in the early 1990s, just as the United States began its long boom, there is a new mood of Anglo-Saxon triumphalism. Books such as *Can Japan Compete?* reasserted a faith in universal solutions because, despite earlier concerns to the contrary, 'Japan is not a special case after all'[2] (Porter *ibid.* 2000: 100). Suddenly advances in information communication technology fuelled images of global convergence and the New Economy. In the era of empowerment, knowledge management afforded leaders more control and (in what some might view as a final act of contrition) a Japanese model of knowledge creation came to be seen to underpin the quest for universalism. Nonaka and Takeuchi offered the world tacit–explicit 'knowledge conversion' – by converting tacit knowledge into 'words or numbers that anyone could understand' (1995: 9) it appeared as if contextual boundaries should not be a barrier to getting the right information to the right place. The enigma of Japanese knowledge creation was no longer endemic to Japanese companies but 'universal' (*ibid.*: 246); indeed, their account even resonates with faint echoes of Taylor's notion of 'scientific management'.

F.W. Taylor's conception of leadership was one of command and control: the type of leadership that one might expect from a scion of a wealthy Yankee family in the aftermath of the Civil War. His views were allied with an ineffable belief in the superiority of rational engineering knowledge over any dilettante claims to be born to rule or local knowledge embedded in workshop ways of doing things. For Nonaka and Takeuchi, Taylor was too top down; scientific management, 'failed to perceive the experiences and judgements of the workers as a source of new knowledge' (*ibid.*: 36). In contrast, Nonaka and Takeuchi advocate 'middle-up-down' management, in which new ideas churn forth from every part of the organization, not only those who are charged with leading. Perhaps this might be seen as 'scientific management for all' – a version of Taylorism in which everyone is 'empowered' to lead, albeit with implications for direction.

In developing their knowledge-creating spiral, Nonaka and Takeuchi argue that tacit–explicit knowledge conversion carries the message about new knowledge to an expanding community of individuals. The insider–outsider distinction that is fundamental to group-oriented practice in Nakane's concept of *ba* (which depends on boundaries for its meaning) is avoided because 'knowledge is created only by individuals' (*ibid.*: 239). This assumption makes things more simple: a group is derived from the sum of individuals and there is an ontological continuum that moves from the individual, through sectional, departmental, divisional and organizational boundaries (*ibid.*: 72). Although the Japanese concept of *ba* as a 'bounded interaction field' (with an explicit emphasis on the importance of 'boundaries') has achieved currency amongst Japanese writers on management (Itami 1992), Nonaka's recent adoption of *ba* involves a more ambiguous approach to the insider–outsider issue: '*Ba* sets a boundary for interaction amongst individuals, and yet its boundary is open' (Nonaka *et al.* 2000: 15). Thus, context is denied: knowledge is separated from power and information from meaning – leadership is dispersed to the point where it disappears.

Adopting Nonaka and Takeuchi's assumption that knowledge is ultimately 'all of one type' and can be moved, in an problematic manner, from one context to another (as if power relations were suspended) implies that Japan is in essence the same as the United States or, for that matter, any other context that is approaching the Anglo-Saxon normative ideal of market-rational individualism and formal rules. Learning from Japan and appreciating its contribution as a counterfactual depends on understanding why its power/knowledge nexus is incommensurate with Anglo-Saxon 'rules of the game'. Tacit knowledge is different from explicit knowledge, and individual knowledge is different from collective knowledge. The power that Japan's 'rules of the game' afford to collective tacit knowledge is not commensurate with the individual leadership of an American president or a British prime minister. To assume otherwise (for example through 'knowledge conversion' and universalism) is not a good basis for analysis: to assume necessary convergence is not a useful way of interpreting diversity.

Conclusion: rules of the game and their interpretation

For North (1990), historical evolution involves both informal constraints (sanctions, customs, traditions and codes of conduct) and formal rules (constitutions, laws and property rights). His thesis is that progress from a less complex society towards a more complex society (as illustrated by the evolution of the United States) involves a unidirectional move – albeit lengthy and uneven – from informal constraints to formal rules that facilitate increased specialization and greater division of labour (*ibid.*: 46). The story might ring true for the US; it might even be an inspirational account for other jurisdictions that share a common Anglo-Saxon heritage, but the implication that progress is a normative teleological march towards formal rules – and the discipline of market-rational 'atomized' individual actors acting according to causal power relations – does not fit well with Japan's 150-year transition from late feudalism into technological and economic superpower status. Extrapolating a specific economic history from its institutional context and then assuming that it provides an acontextual scientific account of all histories, wherever, is to make one fundamental scientific error, one which the philosopher Wittgenstein (2001) demonstrated when he argued that no rule – whether implicit or explicit – could ever account for its own interpretation in practice, and thus that context cannot be reduced to rules. In fact, rules will always be contextual, and thus what is important for economic and social analysis is an appreciation of the context of enquiry.

There is one evident reason for the importance of context: it provides the subtle, implicit, tacitly interpreted cues for enacting everyday actions that become the data for social scientists to interpret – drawing reflexively on their subtle, implicit and tacitly interpreted cues, organized into theories, models and assumptions while doing so. The active process of 'doing things' in practice is always shaped by the reflexively automatic use of 'here and now' tacit knowledge that is deployed locally, *in situ*, by the actors themselves. And this is as true of theorists doing the accounting as it is for the everyday actors whose action is being accounted for. According to Polanyi's (1967) conception of the tacit dimension as a representation of the inexplicable mental processes that shape the ability to act and think, tacit knowledge is essential to reflexive activity. And, amid the stretch from the macro-level environment to micro-level practice, the processes by which the 'rules of the game' afford power to tacit knowledge have a profound influence on the nature and significance of practices that are enabled and constrained in any specific context of either practice or theoretical interpretation of such practice. Although North (1990: 81) recognizes tacit knowledge, he appears to be oblivious to its consequences for the practice of power. Reflexively automatic activity is never innocent of context – it situates itself on the boundaries between the seemingly possible and imagination about what might be possible. Hunch and intuition are amongst the ever-present servants of imagination that guide the voyage into novelty – they emerge from practice and shape the interpretation of 'the rules' in the active process of practice.

North's influential account demonstrates what happens when ratiocination overwhelms context. The unspoken, the subtle and the specific lose their distinction in the way that the general, the acontextual and the abstract frame them. Theory, by definition, is an abstraction. As long as such theory is an abstraction from and within a specific context, it may be scientifically valid and reliable – even anthropologically thick in its description – but when it is applied to another context, a different form of life, a strange anthropology and practices whose generative structure is constituted from different frames, guided by different accumulations of tacit knowledge and taken-for-granted expectations, then misunderstanding – or rather not-understanding – can occur, as a generation of sociologists, influenced by Bendix (1956), were well aware. Interpreting Japan through the history and institutions of the US may be a case in point.

Reflecting on Foucault's power/knowledge nexus, our understanding of leadership needs to be changed or, more accurately, reconstituted. Japan as counterfactual suggests that conceptions of leadership – whether conceived as an acontextual, largely psychologically stable matter of (culturally) specific personality traits, or thought of merely as a range of (culturally specific) contingent phenomena, or regarded as charismatic new leadership that boldly goes where others would not – do not work well in the Japanese power/knowledge context. At this time, it seems safe to assert that in Western societies, not to mention most other societies, our understanding of leadership has not been reconstituted. Of course, if we were able to find a counterfactual to these practices we would have the basis for thinking about a different conceptualization of power. Our argument has been that Japan offers such a case.

Notes

1   Polanyi's conception of the tacit dimension stemmed from his famous observation that '*we can know more than we can tell*' (1967: 4). In speculating about what this meant, Polanyi discussed the police's introduction of photo-fit identification as a way of revealing the tacit dimension of face recognition, but cautions that we cannot tell how we do this. He also considers the use of practical classes in university education to teach ideas that cannot be told, arguing that this is only possible 'by relying on the pupil's intelligent cooperation for catching the meaning of the demonstration' (*ibid.*: 5).

2   There are, however, cracks in this veneer of uncritical realism; as one might expect with two such distinguished Japanese co-authors, Japan's specificity is not ignored completely. In the book's conclusion, the authors argue that Japan's stability-based system has already given way to a competition-based system in those parts of the economy that are productive and successful; the challenge is to spread this competition-based system throughout the economy. Accordingly,

> Japan will need to embrace some elements of the Western approach, much as it has done in the past. The result, however, will not be a clone of American capitalism but a new and distinctly Japanese conception of competition. Where will the uniqueness lie?
>
> (Porter *et al.* 2000: 188)

References

Bendix, R. (1956) *Work and Authority in Industry*, Berkeley, CA: University of California Press.

Bingham, W.V. (1927) 'Leadership', in H.C. Metcalf (ed.) *The Psychological Foundations of Management*, New York: Shaw.

Bowden, A.O. (1927) 'A study on the personality of student leadership in the United States', *Journal of Abnormal Social Psychology* 21: 149–60.

Brown, J.S. and P. Duguid (1991) 'Organizational learning and communities-of-practice: towards a unified view of working, learning and innovating', *Organization Science* 2(1): 40–57.

Bryman, A. (1996) 'Leadership in organizations', in S.R. Clegg, C. Hardy, C. and W.R. Nord, *Handbook of Organization Studies*, London: Sage.

Clegg, S. (1989) *Frameworks of Power*, London: Sage.

Clegg, S. and T. Ray (2003) 'Power. Rules of the game and the limits to knowledge management: lessons from Japan and Anglo-Saxon alarms', *Prometheus* 21(1): 23–40.

Cook, S. and J.S. Brown (1999) 'Bridging epistemologies: the generative dance between organizational knowledge and organizational knowing', *Organization Science* 10(4): 381–400.

Denning, S. (2001) *The Springboard: How Storytelling Ignites Action in Knowledge-era Organizations*, London: Butterworth-Heinemann.

Dertouzous, M.L., R.K. Lester and R.M. Solow (1989) *Made in America*, Boston, MA: MIT Press.

Dore, R. (1973) *British Factory – Japanese Factory: The Origins of National Diversity in Industrial Relations*, London: George Allen & Unwin.

Dunlop, D.M. and P. Goldman (1991) 'Rethinking power in schools', *Education Administration Quarterly* 27(1): 5–29.

Eden, D. (1984) 'Self-fulfilling prophecy as a management tool: harnessing Pygmalion', *Academy of Management Review* 9: 64–73.

Foucault, M. (1977) *Discipline and Punish: The Birth of the Prison*, London: Penguin Books.

Gibbons, M., C. Limoges, H. Nowotny, S. Schwartzman, P. Scott and M. Trow (1994) *The New Production of Knowledge: The Dynamics of Science and Research in Contemporary Societies*, London: Sage.

Gilson, R. and M. Roe (1999) 'Lifetime employment: labor peace and the evolution of Japanese corporate governance', *Columbia Law Review* 1(2): 508–40.

Haugaard, M. (1997) *The Constitution of Power: A Theoretical Analysis of Power, Knowledge and Structure*, Manchester: Manchester University Press.

Hosking, D.M. (1991) 'Chief executives, organizing processes and skill', *European Journal of Applied Psychology* 41: 95–103.

Itakura, K. and E. Yagi (1974) 'The Japanese research system and the establishment of the Institute of Physical and Chemical Research', in S. Nakayama, D. Swain and E. Yagi (eds) *Science and Society in Modern Japan*, Cambridge, MA: MIT Press.

Itami, H. (1992) 'Firm as an informational "*ba*" (interactive field)', in Y. Ijiri (ed.) *Information and Internationalization*, Pittsburgh: Carnegie–Mellon University Press.

Johnson, C. (1992) *MITI and the Japanese Miracle: The Growth of Industrial Policy, 1925–1975*, Tokyo: Charles E. Tuttle Co.

—— (1995) *Japan: Who Governs? The Rise of the Developmental State*, New York: W.W. Norton.

Katzenbach, J.R. and D.K. Smith (1993) *The Wisdom of Teams: Creating the High Performance Organization*, Boston, MA: Harvard Business School Press.

Kirkman, B.L. and B. Rosen (1999) 'Beyond self-management: antecedents and consequences of team empowerment', *Academy of Management Journal* 42(1): 58–74.

Knights, D. and H. Willmott (1992) 'Conceptualizing leadership processes: a study of senior managers in a financial services company', *Journal of Management Studies* 29: 761–82.

Kono, T. and S. Clegg (1998) *Transformation of Corporate Culture*, Berlin: Walter de Gruyter.

—— (2001) *Trends in Japanese Management*, London: Palgrave.

Kouzes, J.M. and B.Z. Posner (1993) *Credibility: How Leaders Gain and Lose It, Why People Demand It*, San Francisco: Jossey-Bass.

Kreisberg, S. (1992) *Transforming Power: Domination, Empowerment and Education*, Albany, NY: State University of New York Press.

Langrish, J., M. Gibbons, W.G. Evans and F.R. Jevons (1972) *Wealth from Knowledge: A Study of Innovation in Industry*, Basingstoke: Macmillan.

McGregor, D. (1960) *The Human Side of Enterprise*, New York: McGraw-Hill.

Manz, C.C. and H.P. Sims (1991) 'Superleadership: beyond the myth of heroic leadership', *Organizational Dynamics* 19: 18–35.

Mason, R.H.P. and J.G. Caiger (1972) *A History of Japan*, Rutland, VT, and Tokyo: Charles E. Tuttle Company.

Miyamoto, M. (1995) *Straightjacket Society*, Tokyo: Kodansha International.

Miyashita, K. and D. Russell (1996) *Keiretsu: Inside the Hidden Japanese Conglomerates*, New York: McGraw-Hill.

Nakane, C. (1970) *Japanese Society*, Berkeley, CA: University of California Press.

Nonaka, I. and H. Takeuchi (1995) *The Knowledge-Creating Company*, Oxford: Oxford University Press.

Nonaka, I., R. Toyama and N. Konno (2000) 'SECI, ba and leadership: a unified model of dynamic knowledge creation', *Long Range Planning* 33(4): 5–34.

North, D. (1990) *Institutions, Institutional Change and Economic Performance*, Cambridge: Cambridge University Press.

Nowotny, H., P. Scott and M. Gibbons (2001) *Re-Thinking Science: Knowledge and the Public in an Age of Uncertainty*, Cambridge: Polity Press.

Ouchi, W. (1981) *Theory Z*, Redding, MA: Addison-Wesley.

Penrose, E. (1995) *The Theory of the Growth of the Firm*, Oxford: Oxford University Press.

Peters, T. and R. Waterman (1982) *In Search of Excellence*, New York: Harper & Row.

Polanyi, M. (1967) *The Tacit Dimension*, London: Routledge & Kegan Paul Ltd.

Porter, M., H. Takeuchi and M. Sakakibara (2000) *Can Japan Compete?*, Basingstoke: Macmillan.

Ray, T. (2002) 'Managing Japanese organizational knowledge creation: the difference', in S. Little, P. Quintas and T. Ray (eds) *Managing Knowledge: An Essential Reader*, London: Sage.

Ray, T. and S. Little (2001) 'Collective tacit knowledge and practice in Japan's workplace ba', *Creativity and Innovation Management* 10(3): 153–64.

Schenk, C. (1928) 'Leadership', *Infantry Journal* 33: 111–22.

Schumpeter, J. (1976) *Capitalism, Socialism and Democracy*, London: George Allen & Unwin.

Senge, P.M. (1999) 'Towards an ecology of leadership: developmental journeys of three leaders', *Change and Development Journeys into a Pluralistic World*, Annual Meeting of the Academy of Management, Chicago, 6–11 August.

Sievers, B. (1994) *Work, Death and Life Itself: Essays on Management and Organization*, New York: Walter de Gruyter.

Sims, H.P. and P. Lorenzi (1992) *The New Leadership Paradigm*, Newbury Park, CA: Sage.

Uhl-Bien, M. and G.B. Graen (1998) 'Individual self management: analysis of professionals' self-managing activities in functional and cross-functional work teams', *Academy of Management Journal* 41(3): 340–50.

Vogel, E.F. (1979) *Japan as Number One: Lessons for America*, Cambridge, MA: Harvard University Press.

Weick, K. and F. Westley (1996) 'Organizational learning: affirming an oxymoron', in S. Clegg, C. Hardy and W. Nord (eds) *Handbook of Organization Studies*, London: Sage.

Wenger, E. (2000) 'Communities of practice and social learning systems', *Organization* 7(2): 225–46.

Wittgenstein, L. (2001) *Philosophical Investigations*, Oxford: Blackwell Publishers.

Part VII

Conclusions

17 Bringing the strands together

John Storey and Iain Mangham

It was noted in the Introduction that interest and activity in the subject of 'leadership' are both running at extraordinarily high levels. In addition, it was also observed that an emergent set of contemporary critical themes could be identified. It was then demonstrated, through a literature review in Chapter 2, that the sheer volume of studies to date had not in themselves helped to clarify the picture. Vast numbers of empirical studies were inconsequential in outcome and often trivial in design. The 'theories' of leadership were lacking in breadth and were often addressing different phenomena. Hence the central rationale and the intended contribution of this volume has been to help cut a way through the noise by focusing attention on the identified critical issues and the emergent key trends.

The key themes identified in Chapter 1 as deserving close attention can be summarized and synthesized as follows. First, that there are changing interpretations, understandings and assumptions about what constitutes 'leadership' – and more specifically 'effective leadership'. This latter point is related of course to the question of the link between leadership and performance outcomes. Various chapters in the book have suggested that interpretations of desired models of leadership are culturally shaped and that currently there is evidence of a further shift, with growing doubts about the acceptability, viability and sustainability of the charismatic/transformational model. Second, and consequent to the first point, the attempts to delineate the 'competences' of leadership were picked out as another current issue. Third, we identified the study of leadership development initiatives, interventions and methods as an issue of pressing current concern. Various chapters were critical of conventional methods of leadership development and a number of alternative approaches were sketched.

So, as we approach the end, what have we found? Our findings can be summarized under two main headings: conceptions of leadership, and an integrative framework of leadership as a process and a constituted social phenomenon.

Conceptions of leadership

The object of inquiry – leadership – is formed and constituted by the theories and conceptualizations of it. These understandings and interpretations reflect the concerns and agendas of the observers and the other players who are interested in, and usually, if not invariably, have a stake in, the phenomenon. For example, a number of stakeholders have interests to protect and advance. As we noted in Chapter 2, people occupying privileged positions usually want to account for their occupancy in terms of expertise and other forms of legitimate and rational explanation. Hence they often welcome (controlled and negotiated) explorations of the nature and source of this alleged exceptionality.

These efforts are bolstered by other stakeholders. For example, major business schools have an interest in fostering the notion that 'leaders' are the key to organizational success. It follows that preparation for the priesthood is crucial and worth spending (or rather investing) large sums of money on. This is illustrated by the advertising for the London Business School's Senior Executive Programme.[1] Headlined with the confident and uncompromising assertion that 'Inspiring Leaders Create the Future', the course notice goes on to assert that '[t]he best leaders galvanize their organization into action, move boundaries and transform industries'. With this prior emphatic statement, the agenda and the problematic are allowed to move rapidly to addressing the classic twofold questions of nearly all existing leadership research, namely:

- What are the attributes or competences, if any, that demarcate the best leaders from the rest?
- If such attributes and competences can be identified how can they be accrued and learned?

However, as we have seen, it is patently evident that there are no clear answers to these two frequently asked questions. The many attempts to provide answers reveal contradictory outcomes. They may not in fact be the best questions with which to commence; they are certainly not the only worthwhile questions to pose. As we have argued from the outset of this book, interpretations of leadership are shaped and influenced by the ideational and indeed ideological context. The *belief* (for ultimately that is what it is) in the capability of those in senior positions to 'galvanize organizations' or to 'move boundaries and transform industries' is highly tendentious. (This term is used here in tune with the dictionary definition of 'having a purposed tendency; composed or written with such a tendency'.) Studies which have attempted to reveal the difference made by executive succession have been inconclusive – often because they have been limited and poorly designed. Pfeffer (1977) argues that even chief executive officers (CEOs) are in reality normally severely constrained by market conditions, organizational political constraints and other factors, and that in consequence their true impact on organizational effectiveness is usually very limited. Yukl concurs but is more circumspect, arguing that CEOs have only 'moderate influence' (1989: 276). The implication is that future research should explore leadership in the context of the wider array of factors and processes in organizations.

This brings us to the second of our headings.

An integrating framework

In Chapter 2 we presented and discussed 'the leadership constellation' – the interlocking factors of context, perceived need, behavioural requirements and development methods. Bearing in mind the points discussed above, it is possible to widen this in order to outline a more integrative framework for interpreting leadership. This is illustrated in Figure 17.1.

This framework takes account of the wider ideological and ideational context (first box on the far left). This sets the scene for the kind of priority which is accorded to the idea of leadership in the first place, and also shapes the understanding of its nature. For example, as was discussed in Chapter 2, the extraordinarily high value given to charismatic and transformational leadership in the 1980s and 1990s was associated with the wider priority at that time to undertake a radical restructuring of industry and the public services. We noted that the messages of Tom Peters[2] (which received enthusiastic responses from industrialists) concerning new forms of competition, new approaches to organizational design and new interpretations about the meaning of work (e.g. empowered, fulfilling, engaging, customer-focused, etc.) also contained messages about new forms of leadership. In other words, the new orthodoxy about appropriate leadership was inextricably embroiled in the material and ideological context of the time. As we also noted in that chapter, a new mood is evident (signalled for example, in the works of de Vries, Khurana, Maccoby and Fullan). The new ideological context of the 21st century requires a form, or rather forms, of leadership which display more evident signs of integrity, intelligence and thoughtfulness. There are also some signs (though as yet less uniform than

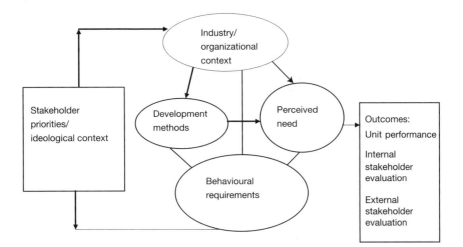

Figure 17.1 An integrating framework

the others) that the expectation that leaders in the future should have and display in-depth knowledge of their industry may also be part of the emergent context.

Figure 17.1 makes clear that there are two types or levels of context, because in the next box (top centre) the industry and organizational level of context is of a different order than the wider ideological one identified in the first. If the tendency detected in the previous paragraph develops – i.e. that industry knowledge and experience become an expected requisite – then the saliency of the governing factors in this box will increase.

The perceived need for leadership and for a particular kind of leadership is a further key aspect. This, as explained in Chapter 2, goes beyond the mechanistic notion of 'fit' sometimes found in the contingency approach to leadership. Even at this level, perceptions of need can be very much influenced by 'non- (economically) rational' considerations such as emulation and crowd following. The perceived need in recent years has often been of the kind which seeks to defend and promote the reputational capital of organizations by having a high profile leader at the helm (if only mainly for symbolic reasons).

Behavioural requirements and competences will nevertheless seemingly always be part of any theory of leadership. They express what capabilities and behaviours are expected or required of persons held to be leaders or in leadership positions. As we have seen, these can either be approached in universalist and essentialist terms (that is, based on the assumption that leaders are special people who will exhibit these behaviours, which can be uncovered and even predicted through well-honed instruments) or in contingent terms (that is, certain patterns of behaviours are deemed to be suitable for different challenges). We saw in Chapter 2 that research can be circular insofar as followers are surveyed for their understandings of what makes for a competent leader. The quantitative 'findings', although persuasive, are often merely echoes of the orthodoxy and received opinion of that time and place. Nonetheless, despite these dangers it seems inconceivable that future research and discussions about leadership will be able to escape paying attention to the behavioural attributes of leaders.

This brings us to leadership development methods – the range of ways in which leaders and potential leaders might be trained and developed. Chapters 5–11 all attended to this problematic. Developing trends in modes of leadership interventions were identified in some detail. The issue here is complicated by multiple considerations: what 'works', at what cost, and what is socially acceptable to the target audience. We have seen evidence that occupants of top (leadership) positions are on the whole reluctant to participate in leadership development activities – for a host of reasons. As we have seen in the discussion above, and as is shown in Figure 17.1, there is a close relationship between identified behavioural requirements/expectations at any one time and the wider ideological context. Moreover, wanted behaviour is usually very dependent on what has gone before. If organizations have stagnated there may be a desire for a change-oriented leader. If conversely the organization has experienced a prolonged or intensive period of change management there may be a desire for a leader who promises to consolidate and stabilize.

In the framework shown in Figure 17.1, outcomes are seen as multifaceted. They are expressed here in three categories: unit performance, internal stakeholder evaluation and external stakeholder evaluation. The first indicates the possibility for some objective measures of unit performance (e.g. company performance indicators such as growth, market share, sales, profits and so on). The other categories, internal and external stakeholder evaluations, allow for the subjective judgements of those with specific sets of expectations from the leader or leaders. For example, in the UK the Learning and Skills Council was recently prompted by Sir Bryan Sanderson (former chairman of BP) to conduct a survey of the satisfaction levels of learners in further education colleges and similar training arenas. He expressed surprise at the lack of attention to consumer attitudes and responses in this sphere of educational services. This is just one indication of the potential for a broader perspective concerning leadership outcomes.

We are suggesting that future research should take a more holistic approach when undertaking studies of 'leadership', by paying attention to each and all of these interacting variables.

Looking to the future

It has been suggested in this volume that we have been through a couple of decades which have been characterized by an intense promotion of the idea of charismatic/transformational leadership. If, as has also been suggested, there is now a growing disenchantment with this model, then the question naturally arises as to what will take its place. If leadership is viewed as mainly an attributional phenomenon, the search for the answer to this question would be directed to the social and economic climate. If it is viewed, conversely, in more functional terms, the search would focus on an analysis of the kinds of economic and social problems to be faced and the kinds of solutions deemed likely to be required.

In practice the two forms of analysis seem to proceed curiously in tandem. It is usually very difficult to disentangle a purely functional analysis from an ideologically influenced analysis. For example, the tide at the moment seems to be moving in the direction of collective or distributed leadership as the favoured mode (see, for example, Denis *et al.* 2001). This appeals, in part, because it represents the kind of reaction to the excesses of the individual hero leader discussed above. In part it is also 'found' to be in tune with the preferred cultures and structures of organizations which lean towards empowered teams, distributed responsibility, network forms, and which extol the value of knowledge workers. The professional services firms, with their player-managers and distributed knowledge networks, represent one significant contemporary model with wide appeal. What this point clearly indicates is that preferred models of leadership cannot be understood in isolation from wider tendencies, theories and patterns in social organization. The implication for us is that the study of leadership in the future would be improved if it was to be considered as simply one part of a bigger organizational picture. Collective, distributed or highly concentrated leadership represents the outcomes of a negotiated order. Power, perceived interests and social interpretations are the driving factors.

One final observation is worth making. It used to be common to ask what would be the next big idea after 'knowledge management'. Judging by new job titles and new business initiatives in the USA, one contender must be the notion of 'thought leadership'. Such a development, with its Orwellian connotations, might also suggest a trend beyond transformational leadership.

Notes

1   *Financial Times*, 31 March 2003.
2   See, for example, Peters and Waterman (1982).

References

Denis, J.L., L. Lamothe and A. Langley (2001) 'The dynamics of collective leadership and strategic change in pluralistic organizations', *Academy of Management Journal* 44(4): 809–37.

Peters, T. and R. Waterman (1982) *In Search of Excellence*, New York: Harper & Row.

Pfeffer, J. (1977) 'The ambiguity of leadership', *Academy of Management Review* 2: 104–12.

Yukl, G. (1989) 'Managerial leadership: a review of theory and research', *Journal of Management* 15(2): 251–89.

Index